THE ARMCHAIR
BOOK OF BASEBALL

THE ARMCHAIR
BOOK OF BASEBALL

Edited by John Thorn
Illustrations by James Stevenson

COLLIER BOOKS
Macmillan Publishing Company
New York

Maxwell Macmillan Canada
Toronto

Maxwell Macmillan International
New York   Oxford   Singapore   Sydney

Copyright © 1985 by John Thorn and David Reuther

Illustrations © 1985 by James Stevenson

Collier Books   Maxwell Macmillan Canada, Inc.
Macmillan Publishing Company   1200 Eglinton Avenue East
866 Third Avenue   Suite 200
New York, NY 10022   Don Mills, Ontario M3C 3N1

Macmillan Publishing Company is part of the Maxwell
Communication Group of Companies.

Library of Congress Cataloging-in-Publication Data
The Armchair book of baseball / edited by John Thorn; illustrations
   by James Stevenson—1st Collier Books ed.
      p.   cm.
   Reprint. Previously published: New York: Scribner's, c1985.
   Includes bibliographical references.
   ISBN 0-02-054721-8
   1. Baseball.   I. Thorn, John, 1947–   .
[GV867.A75   1992]   91-32760   CIP
796.357—dc20

Macmillan books are available at special discounts for bulk purchases
for sales promotions, premiums, fund-raising, or educational use.
For details, contact:

Special Sales Director
Macmillan Publishing Company
866 Third Avenue
New York, NY 10022

First Collier Books Edition 1992

10 9 8 7 6 5 4 3 2 1

Printed in the United States of America

CONTENTS

Introduction

Baseball is the writer's game. From the Elysian Fields of Hoboken to the green fields of the mind, the grand old game and the printed word were made for each other. The game's primal team, the 1842 Knickerbockers, were named in tribute to Washington Irving, who as Diedrich Knickerbocker borrowed a folk tale from Europe and molded it into "Rip Van Winkle"—much as America took the English game of rounders and made it over as baseball. (Irving's 1820 story opens with some lines by a fellow named Cartwright; occultists may make of that what they will.) No other sport plays upon the heart and mind so subtly, with so delightful a blend of the simple and the complex—like a magician's stunt or a phrase well-turned. It is a classically beautiful game, its appeal more form than color; yet the color deepens in retrospect, both in the memory and in print, so that thinking about baseball provides a pleasure quite different from that had by watching it.

The way we think about baseball, and the way writers depict it, has changed in the past twenty years or so. Fans are not as fanatic nor writers as florid: the "gee whiz" style pretty much went out with Kilroy, and the hard-boiled, sardonic stance that followed seems now a self-caricature. Rice, Runyon, Gallico, Cannon—these were giants in their day, but in some measure because the general level of baseball writing was so poor: the styles they pioneered were risky, and lesser scriveners trying their hands at it were guilty of some truly wretched excesses. The terrain of recent baseball literature may not display the lofty peaks of the Golden Age, but the overall level is assuredly higher. This phenomenon happens to parallel one that has been observed in baseball (see the discussion in this volume by Stephen Jay Gould).

The Armchair Book of Baseball celebrates the writer's game, principally of the past two decades, a period that began with pundits anointing professional football as the new national pastime and closed with baseball at unprecedented heights of popularity. These years brought significant new events—divisional play, artificial turf, the designated hitter, free agency; new luminaries—Rose, Seaver, Jackson, Schmidt, Steinbrenner; and new trends—statistical analysis, revisionist history, tell-all memoirs. And best of all for the reader, the past two decades have brought an outpouring of good, fresh baseball writing—so much, in fact, that I could more easily have gathered a book three times this size with no diminution of quality.

The general principles of selection were two: to bring together the best writing that, when collected, would present a panoramic view of today's game and how it got to be that way and to include no more than one piece by any writer (otherwise, what reason could there be not to reprint the complete opus of Lee Allen?). An additional consideration was to avoid pieces that had been anthologized elsewhere, notably in Charles Einstein's splendid *Fireside Book of Baseball*, a three-volume series begun in 1956.

I wish to thank artist James Stevenson; Maron Waxman and Marta Goldstein of Scribners; designer Alan Benjamin; and as usual, friend and collaborator David Reuther. For bibliographic help and courtesy beyond the call, I am grateful to Tom Heitz of the National Baseball Library in Cooperstown; a special tip of the cap as well to Myron Smith, whose outstanding bibliography of baseball I was fortunate to examine in manuscript. And for leads to offbeat baseball pieces, my colleagues in the Society for American Baseball Research—principally, Dan Hotaling, Fred Ivor-Campbell, Charlie Owen, and Lyle Spatz; also, Marty Appel, Bob Barnett, Merritt Clifton, Frederick C. Collingnon, Jr., Steven G. Cotton, Bill Felber, Barry Gifford, Tom Granahan, John R. Husman, Jack Kavanagh, Bob Koltermann, Dan Schlossberg, James K. Skipper, Jr., Jim Smith, Ray Welsh.

JOHN THORN
Saugerties, New York

THE ARMCHAIR
BOOK OF BASEBALL

The alliterative title of this first piece plays upon that of a Conan Doyle story, *A Study in Scarlet*, which introduced a certain detective with extraordinary powers of deduction. Appropriate, in that Lee Allen was the Sherlock Holmes of baseball—the finder of lost players, connoisseur of curious facts, debunker of well-entrenched myths, and until his death in 1969 the Historian of the Baseball Hall of Fame. His demographic files and unparalleled knowledge of the game were essential resources in the creation of *The Baseball Encyclopedia*. Besides, he was a writer of warmth and charm, as this chapter from *The Hot Stove League* (1955) attests.

LEE ALLEN

A Study in Suet

During the nation's great depression, when attendance dwindled and even major-league teams faced an uncertain future, life was particularly burdensome for the two clubs in Philadelphia. Shibe Park, the home of the Athletics, and Baker Bowl, the shabby nesting place of the Phillies, were seldom filled to capacity. One dreary afternoon, Dave Driscoll, business manager of the Dodgers, was walking in Philadelphia and chanced to pass Baker Bowl. The Phillies were on the road, but in spite of that a pathetic vendor of peanuts was hawking his wares before an imaginary crowd near the entrance to the bleachers.

"There won't be a crowd here today," Driscoll told him. "Why don't you go to Shibe Park?"

"I've been to Shibe Park," the vendor replied. "There's nobody there either."

It was this situation that helped explain a remark made at the time by Joe McCarthy, the great manager of the Yankees. McCarthy had a pitcher at New York by the name of Walter Brown, a mammoth right-hander. Although possessed of a great number of physical assets, Brown was used sparingly. When he did work, it was usually in Philadelphia against the Athletics.

"Why is it you pitch Brown only in Philadelphia?" McCarthy was asked one day.

"It's the only way I know to fill Shibe Park," Joe quipped.

McCarthy's reasoning was impeccable, for Walter, at 265 pounds, was the heaviest player who had ever appeared on the major-league scene. Strangely, he owed his start to one of the lightest men the game has ever known, Rabbit Maranville. During the season of 1925, Maranville managed the Cubs for about a month, and it was at that time that Brown, a sandlotter who had been pitching around Brockton, Massachusetts, reported to him. Walter was so heavy that he found traveling uncomfortable, but he was to do plenty of it during his career. The trail that began in Chicago led to Sarasota, New Orleans, Cleveland, Omaha, Oklahoma City, New York, Jersey City, Newark, Cincinnati, and New York again before he wound up his career in 1941. He is now the proprietor of a sporting goods store at Freeport, Long Island.

The peculiar thing about Brown's weight was that he put on 68 of his 265 pounds during a single winter. He belonged to Cleveland at the time and weighed only 197 at the close of the 1927 season. But after an operation for the removal of his tonsils, he shot up to 265, and despite working out five hours a day at the YMCA gymnasium, he was never able to shed the excess suet.

But Brown was no clown. He pitched big-league ball for twelve years and won more games than he lost. He was also a particular favorite at Newark, where he won twenty and lost six in 1934 and led the International League in earned-run percentage. Hy Goldberg of the Newark *Evening News* was asked one day what sort of stuff Brown threw. "He throws a fastball, curve, and the biggest shadow in baseball," Goldberg sallied.

Players as fat as Brown usually delight the galleries. When a player can overcome the handicap of excess weight, it is usually because he has other assets that more than make up for his bulk. Cy Young, winner of more games than any pitcher in major-league history, reached his greatest peak of popularity toward the end of his career, when a bulging paunch made it almost impossible for him to field bunts. Ernie Lombardi, who sometimes weighed close to 240, was the most popular performer that Cincinnati ever had.

Bob Fothergill was another of the game's famed fatties who attained a tremendous degree of popularity. A stroke cut him down at the age of thirty-nine in 1938, but he is still recalled with sweet nostalgia in Detroit, where the fans worshipped him and where he simply pulverized the ball from 1922 through 1929.

Waite Hoyt, one of the finest of Yankee pitchers and now a Cincinnati broadcaster, still shudders whenever he thinks about pitching to Fothergill and his mates. "It was awful," Hoyt has frequently said. "The Yankees would go into Detroit for a series in August and find that the entire Tiger outfield would be hitting nearly .400. Ty Cobb and Harry Heilmann were bad enough, but in some ways Fothergill was the most frightening of all. He was murder!"

Fothergill weighed about 235 pounds when he was in shape, but he was surprisingly light on his feet. Once, thinking he had been thrown at by George Earnshaw of the Athletics, he smashed a majestic home run and then climaxed his tour of the bases with a somersault that saw him land on home plate with both feet.

His full name was Robert Roy Fothergill, and he carried a handsome suitcase around the American League that had his initials, R.R.F., in big letters. When asked what they stood for, he would always reply, "For Runs Responsible For."

Fothergill really belonged in a previous age. He was one of the last of those rare spirits who appeared to play for the fun of it, and he seemed able to extract the fullest amount of pleasure from life. After the game, you could find him with a thick porterhouse steak and a seidel of beer, and he would chuckle to himself and mumble out of the side of his mouth, "Imagine getting paid for a life like this!"

Finally, Detroit sold him to the White Sox, but before leaving the team he made fifty-one separate bets with friends that he would get a safe hit the first time up in his new uniform. Several days later all fifty-one received identical telegrams: "Pay up. I singled to left."

Frank (Shanty) Hogan was a catcher whose dietary requirements startled John McGraw, led to frequent finings, and were responsible for some of the game's most repeated stories. Hogan weighed about 240 when in his best form, and it is probable that at certain times he weighed almost as much as Walter Brown. This would be difficult to prove for, unlike Brown and Fothergill, Hogan was reluctant to get on the scales. Chief Bender, the veteran scout of the Athletics, recalls that when he was a coach for the Giants in 1931, Hogan bet four or five players five dollars each that he would weigh 230 or less when the season began, but that when the campaign did start, they could not induce him to settle the argument.

Hogan may have been fat, but he had plenty of courage. One day, after being hit on the jawbone by a fastball from the hand of Guy Bush of the Cubs, he trotted to first base without even rubbing his chin.

Still another leading heavyweight was Garland Buckeye, a big bird from Heron Lake, Minnesota, who had trials with the Senators, Indians, and Giants for a decade starting in 1918. Buckeye was a southpaw pitcher, and his weight was officially listed at 238. He was also a good batter, but was far too portly to be used at any other position. His weight put him on the defensive, and he used to say, "I'm not fat really. Now just feel that leg. You can see I'm just big-boned." Buckeye did his last professional pitching at Milwaukee. One day he attempted to field a bunt, fell on his stomach, and was helped to his feet by two infielders. That was enough to teach him it was time to quit the game. . . .

The first player to quit the game because of being overweight was Ned

Williamson of the Chicago White Stockings, considered the greatest third baseman who ever lived, and a fine shortstop as well, at the time of his death. Williamson was a member of a band of players that toured the world following the season of 1888, and in a game at Paris, France, he was injured in a strange manner, cutting his knee on a rock that lay on the field while sliding into third. The enforced idleness following his injury caused him to gain an enormous amount of weight, and he was never able to regain his old form, abandoning the game after the season of 1890. He then became a victim of dropsy and died at Hot Springs, Arkansas, where he had gone for treatment, March 3, 1894.

When Babe Ruth started spraying home runs around American League lawns in 1919 and finished with twenty-nine for the season, writers were hard put to discover whose record he had surpassed. At first it was believed that John (Buck) Freeman of Washington had set the mark at twenty-five in 1899, but then Ernest J. Lanigan, one of the game's foremost authorities, made it known that Williamson had hit twenty-seven for the White Stockings in 1884.

Actually, Williamson's home run record is somewhat tainted. Prior to 1884, all fair balls hit over the short fences at Chicago were ruled two-base hits. The rule was changed that winter, and the result was something of a joke. The 1884 National League schedule called for only fifty-six contests in each park, and the White Stockings connected for 131 home runs in their home games and their opponents for sixty-one more. When Williamson socked three over the beckoning barrier in right in the second game on Decoration Day, he became the first major leaguer to account for that many in the same game. Of his twenty-seven homers, only two were smashed out on the road, both at Buffalo.

Williamson and Ruth were alike in many ways. Ned was childless but, like Ruth, genuinely devoted to children. He always carried candy and pennies for them, and when his funeral was held at his home in Chicago, the house was jammed with hundreds of urchins who looked as if their hearts would break.

Players who have attracted attention because they were underweight have been much more rare than those who had to struggle to get the pounds off. One of the first was Frederick (Bones) Ely, a shortstop who lasted from 1884 to 1902. Ely's nickname is self-explanatory, and when he batted he presented such a delicate picture that fans were afraid a pitched ball might splinter him.

Most of the extremely light players attained prominence in the nineteenth century. William (Candy) Cummings, now immortalized at Cooperstown because he is believed to have discovered the curveball, actually weighed only 120 in his prime. Dave Birdsall, with Boston of the old National Association, was the lightest catcher at 126 pounds. Bobby Mitchell, who became the major leagues' first southpaw when he joined Cincinnati in 1877, weighed in at 135.

Mitchell's catcher, George Miller, weighed only 150, and when they joined the Reds from a team at Springfield, Ohio, that year, they were known as the Pony Battery.

Bill Veeck's midget, Eddie Gaedel, of course, was the lightest player of all time. It seems unlikely that any professional of the future will weigh less than his 65 pounds.

There are other physical characteristics, aside from weight, that have made certain players stand out. Slowness of foot, small feet, bowleggedness, baldness, and the wearing of glasses or mustache have often marked players for ridicule.

The smallest feet in major-league history were the property of Art Herring, a pitcher who spent most of his career with the Tigers and Dodgers. He wore a size three shoe. Myril Hoag, an outfielder with the Yankees, also had a peculiar pair of feet, wearing a size four shoe on one tootsy and a four and one-half on the other.

Lave Cross, a catcher and third baseman who played in the majors for twenty-one years, mostly with the Philadelphia teams, was the most bowlegged player of all time, although, in this department Honus Wagner was not far behind.

Most players of today do not affect mustaches, and when they do, they wear trim, businesslike ones. The last mustache of the handlebar variety adorned the lip of Silent John Titus, outfielder of the Phillies from 1903 to 1912. After returning to his home at St. Clair, Pennsylvania, as a young man following the Spanish–American War, Titus grew his mustache, along with friends who were members of the St. Clair Athletic Club, as a group project. When he joined the Phillies, he retained it, and it made him recognizable on the field in the days when players were not numbered.

Titus also invariably draped a toothpick in his mouth, both at bat and in the field, claiming it kept chewing tobacco off his teeth. Rival pitchers always tried to knock it out of his mouth, but none succeeded, although Albert (Lefty) Leifield of the Pirates came closest, knocking off his cap one day. Titus always kept the toothpick at the side of his mouth until he decided to take a swing at the ball, and then he moved it in toward the center. Pitchers eventually discovered this mannerism and forced him to hit at bad pitches whenever they saw the toothpick change position, and began to whittle down his batting average.

Full beards, of course, have disappeared from American faces, and except on the chins of eccentrics have not been seen for years. In his excellent book, *Lost Men of American History*, Stewart Holbrook has traced the history of beards and mustaches in the United States, pointing out that not a single signer of the Declaration of Independence wore one, but that they came into favor about 1860. In baseball, there was an old belief that hair on the face was an aid to eyesight, and though players were ashamed to wear glasses, they raised mustaches instead. The last player in the majors to wear a full beard on the field was Jack Remsen, an outfielder with Brooklyn who last played in 1884. Clark Griffith, owner of the Washington Senators, signed a bearded pitcher, Allen Benson, in 1934, but that was mostly a stunt, and Benson, a House of David alumnus, disappeared after working in only two games.

Bald players have long been grateful for the custom of wearing caps. Tony Rensa, a catcher with the Tigers and Phillies in 1930, was so sensitive about his bald pate that he fastened his cap to his head with great wads of chewing gum. Every time he threw off his mask to chase a high foul, his cap remained on his head, and he was spared the indignity of titters from the crowd.

Jimmy Ring, who pitched for the Phillies when Art Fletcher managed the team, always refused to work in the opening game of the season, and Fletcher believed it was because he would have to bare his head when "The Star-Spangled Banner" was played. It seems that early in his career Ring was warming up to pitch an opener when the band began to blare, and there was nothing for him to do but expose his head of skin. Fletcher claimed that he found the remarks from the stands so embarrassing that he vowed never again to pitch an opening game. Fortunately for Jimmy, he did his pitching in the days before World War II. Since that time, the national anthem has been standard procedure at most parks, not only for the opener but every day.

By general consent the *New Yorker* essayist is in a league all his own, having retired the trophy with his third winning collection of writings on baseball: *Late Innings*, in which this splendid piece appears. The time is May 1981, the battleground is Yale Field, and the antagonist lancers are Ron Darling of the Elis and Frank Viola of St. John's; the chorus features the author and Joe Wood, ninety-one years old. In 1912, known as Smokey Joe, Wood had gone 34–5 for the Red Sox, with three more wins in the World Series—including the finale, over Christy Mathewson in extra innings. History may be a seamless web, in Bruce Catton's phrase, but on this day the juncture of past, present, and future was inspiringly clear.

ROGER ANGELL

The Web of the Game

JUNE 1981

An afternoon in mid-May, and we are waiting for the game to begin. We are in shadow, and the sunlit field before us is a thick, springy green—an old diamond, beautifully kept up. The grass continues beyond the low chain-link fence that encloses the outfield, extending itself on the right-field side into a rougher, featureless sward that terminates in a low line of distant trees, still showing a pale, early-summer green. We are almost in the country. Our seats are in the seventh row of the grandstand, on the home side of the diamond, about halfway between third base and home plate. The seats themselves are more comforting to spirit than to body, being a surviving variant example of the pure late-Doric Polo Grounds mode: the backs made of a continuous running row of wood slats, divided off by pairs of narrow cast-iron arms, within which are slatted let-down seats, grown arthritic with rust and countless layers of gray paint. The rows are stacked so closely upon each other (one discovers) that a happening on the field of sufficient interest to warrant a rise or half-rise to one's feet is often made more memorable by a sharp crack to the kneecaps delivered by the backs of the seats just forward; in time, one finds that a dandruff of gray paint flakes from the same source has fallen on one's lap and scorecard. None of this matters, for this view and these stands and this park—it is Yale Field, in New Haven—are renowned for their felicity. The grandstand is a low, penumbrous steel-post shed that holds the infield in a pleasant horseshoe-curved embrace. The back wall of the grandstand, behind the uppermost row of seats, is broken by an arcade of open arches, admitting a soft back light that silhouettes the upper audience and also discloses an overhead bonework of struts and beams supporting the roof—the pigeonland of all the ballparks of our youth. The game we are waiting for—Yale vs. St. John's University—is a considerable event, for it is part of the National Collegiate Athletic Association's Northeast regional tournament, the winner of which will qualify for a berth at the national collegiate championships in Omaha in June, the World Series of college baseball. Another pair of teams, Maine and Central Michigan—the Black Bears and the Chippewas—have just finished their game here, the first of a doubleheader. Maine won it, 10–2, but the ultimate winner will not be picked here for three more days, when the four teams will have completed a difficult double-elimination tournament. Good, hard competition, but the stands at Yale Field are half empty today. Call them half full, because everyone on hand—some twenty-five hundred fans—must know something about the quality of the teams here, or at least enough to qualify either as a partisan or as an expert, which would explain the hum of talk and expectation that runs through the grandstand even while the Yale team, in pinstriped home whites, is still taking infield practice.

I am seated in a little sector of senior New Haven men—Townies rather than Old Elis. One of them a couple of rows in front of me says, "They used to fill this place in the old days, before there was all the baseball on TV."

His neighbor, a small man in a tweed cap, says, "The biggest crowd I ever saw in here—the biggest ever, I bet—was for a high-school game. Shelton and Naugatuck, about twenty years ago."

An old gent with a cane, seated just to my left, says, "They filled it up that day the Yankees came here, with Ruth and Gehrig and the rest of them. An exhibition game."

A fan just beyond the old gentleman—a good-looking man in his sixties, with an open, friendly face, a large smile, and a thick stand of gray hair—leans toward my neighbor and says, "When *was* that game, Joe? 1930? 1932?"

"Oh, I can't remember," the old man says. "Somewhere in there. My youngest son was mascot for the Yankees that day, so I could figure it out, I suppose." He is not much interested. His eyes are on the field. "Say, look at these fellows throw!" he says. "Did you see that outfielder peg in the ball?"

"That was the day Babe Ruth said this was about the best-looking ballpark he'd ever ever seen," the man beyond says. "You remember that."

"I can remember long before this park was built," the old man says. "It was already the Yale ballfield when I got here, but they put in these stands later—Who is this shortstop? He's a hefty-looking bird."

"How many Yale games do you think you've seen, Joe?" the smiling man asks.

"Oh, I couldn't begin to count them. But I haven't seen a Yale team play in—I don't know how long. Not for years. These fellows today, they play in the Cape Cod League in the summers. They let the freshmen play here now, too. They recruit them more, I suppose. They're athletes—you can see that."

The Yale team finishes its warm-up ritual, and St. John's—light-gray uniforms with scarlet cap bills and scarlet socks—replaces it on the field.

"St. John's has always had a good club," the old man tells me. "Even back when my sons were playing ball, it was a good ball team. But not as good as this one. Oh, my! Did you see this catcher throw down to second? Did you see that! I bet you in all the years I was here I didn't have twenty fellows who could throw."

"Your sons played here?" I ask him. "For Yale?"

"My son Joe was captain in '41," he says. "He was a pitcher. He pitched against my son Steve here one day. Steve was pitching for Colgate, and my other son, Bob—my youngest—was on the same Colgate team. A good little left-handed first baseman."

I am about to ask how that game turned out, but the old man has taken out a small gold pocket watch, with a hunting case, which he snaps open. Three-fourteen. "Can't they get this *started*?" he says impatiently.

I say something admiring about the watch, and he hands it to me carefully. "I've had that watch for sixty-eight years," he says. "I always carried it in my vest pocket, back when we wore vests."

The little watch has a considerable heft to it: a weight of authority. I turn it over and find an inscription on the back. It is in script and a bit worn, but I can still make it out:

PRESENTED TO JOE WOOD
BY HIS FRIEND A. E. SMITH
IN APPRECIATION OF HIS SPLENDID
PITCHING WHICH BROUGHT THE
WORLD'S CHAMPIONSHIP
TO BOSTON IN 1912.

"Who was A. E. Smith, Mr. Wood?" I ask.

"He was a manufacturer."

I know the rest. Joe Wood, the old gentleman on my left, was the baseball coach at Yale for twenty years—from 1923 to 1942. Before that, he was a sometime outfielder for the Cleveland Indians, who batted .366 in 1921. Before *that*, he was a celebrated right-handed pitcher for the Boston Red Sox—Smokey Joe Wood, who won thirty-four games for the Bosox in 1912, when he finished up with a record of 34–5, pitching ten shutouts and sixteen consecutive victories along the way. In the World Series that fall—one of the two or three finest ever played—he won three of the four games he pitched, including the famous finale: the game of Hooper's catch and Snodgrass's muff and Tris Speaker's killing tenth-inning single. Next to Walter Johnson, Smokey Joe Wood was the most famous fastballer of his era. Still is, no doubt, in the minds of the few surviving fans who saw him at his best. He is ninety-one years old.

None of this, I should explain—neither my presence at the game nor my companions in the stands—was an accident. I had been a fervent admirer of Smokey Joe Wood ever since I read his account of his baseball beginnings and his subsequent career in Lawrence Ritter's *The Glory of Their Times*, a cherished, classic volume of oral history of the early days of the pastime. Mr. Wood was in his seventies when that book was published, in 1966, and I was startled and pleased a few weeks ago when I ran across an article by Joan Whaley, in *Baseball Digest*, which informed me that he was still hale and still talking baseball in stimulating fashion. He was living with a married daughter in New Haven, and my first impulse was to jump in my car and drive up to press a call. But something held me back; it did not seem quite right to present myself uninvited at his door, even as a pilgrim. Then Ron Darling and Frank Viola gave me my chance. Darling, who was a junior at Yale this past year, is the best pitcher ever to take the mound for the Blue. He is better than Johnny Broaca, who went on to pitch for the Yankees and the Indians for five seasons in the mid-1930s; he is better than Frank Quinn, who compiled a 1.57 career earned-run average at Yale in 1946, '47, and '48. (He is also a better all-around ballplayer than George Bush, who played first base and captained the Elis in 1948, and then somehow drifted off into politics instead of baseball.) Darling, a right-handed fastball thrower, won eleven games and lost two as a sophomore, with an earned-run average of 1.31, and this year he was 9–3 and 2.42, with eighty-nine strikeouts in his ninety-three innings of work—the finest college pitcher in the Northeast, according to major-league scouts, with the possible exception of Frank Viola, a junior left-handed curveball ace at St. John's, who was undefeated this year, 9–0, and had a neat earned-run average of 1.00. St. John's, a Catholic university in Queens, is almost a baseball powerhouse—not quite in the same class, perhaps, as such perennial national champions or challengers as Arizona, Arizona State, Texas, and Southern California, whose teams play Sun Belt schedules of close to sixty games, but good enough to have gone as the Northeast's representative to the national tournament in

Omaha in 1980, where Viola defeated the eventual winner, Arizona, in the first round. St. John's, by the way, does not recruit high-school stars from faraway states, as do most of these rival college powers; all but one player on this year's thirty-three-man Redmen squad grew up and went to school in New York City or in nearby suburbs. This 1981 St. John's team ran off an awesome 31–2 record, capturing the Eastern College Metro (Greater New York, that is) elimination, while Yale, winning its last nine games in a row, concluded its regular season with a record of 24–12–1, which was good enough to win its first Eastern Intercollegiate League championship since 1956. (That tie in Yale's record was a game against the University of Central Florida, played during the Elis' spring-training tour in March, and was called because of darkness after seven innings, with the score tied at 21–21. Darling did not pitch that day.) The two teams, along with Central Michigan (Mid-America Conference) and Maine (New England Conference), qualified for the tournament at New Haven, and the luck of the draw pitted Yale (and Darling) against St. John's (and Viola) in the second game of the opening doubleheader. Perfect. Darling, by the way, had indicated that he might be willing to turn professional this summer if he were to be picked in an early round of the annual amateur draft conducted by the major leagues in mid-June, and Viola had been talked about as a potential big-leaguer ever since his freshman year, so their matchup suddenly became an obligatory reunion for every front-rank baseball scout east of the Ohio River. (About fifty of them turned up, with their speed-guns and clipboards, and their glowing reports of the game, I learned later, altered the draft priorities of several clubs.)

Perfect, but who would get in touch with Mr. Wood and persuade him to come out to Yale Field with me for the game? Why, Dick Lee would—Dick Lee, *of course*. Richard C. Lee (he was the smiling man sitting just beyond Smokey Joe in our row) is a former Democratic mayor of New Haven, an extremely popular (eight consecutive terms, sixteen years in office), innovative officeholder who, among other things, presided over the widely admired urban renewal of his city during the 1960s and, before that, thought up and pushed through the first Operation Head Start program (for minority-group preschoolers) in the country. Dick Lee knows everybody in New Haven, including Smokey Joe Wood and several friends of mine there, one of whom provided me with his telephone number. I called Lee at his office (he is assistant to the chairman of the Union Trust Company, in New Haven) and proposed our party. "Wonderful!" he cried at once. "You have come to the right man. I'll bring Joe. Count on me!" Even over the telephone, I could see him smiling.

Dick Lee did not play baseball for Yale, but the nature of his partisanship became clear in the very early moments of the Yale–St. John's game. "Yay!" he shouted in a stentorian baritone as Ron Darling set down three St. John's batters in order in the first. "Yay, Ron *baby*!" he boomed out as Darling dismissed three more batters in the second, fanning the last two. "Now *c'mon*, Yale! Let's get something started, gang! Yay!" Lee had told me that he pitched for some lesser-known New Haven teams—the Dixwell Community House sandlot team and the Jewish Home for Children nine (the Utopians), among others—while he was growing up in the ivyless Newhallville neighborhood. Some years later, having passed up college altogether, he went to work for Yale as its public-relations officer. By the time he became mayor, in 1953, the university was his own—another precinct to be worried about and looked after. A born politician, he appears to draw on some inner deep-water reservoir of concern that enables him to preside effortlessly and affectionately over each encounter of his day; he was the host at our game, and at intervals he primed Joe Wood with questions about his baseball past, which he seemed to know almost by heart.

"Yes, that's right, I did play for the Bloomer Girls a few games," Mr. Wood said in response to one such cue. "I was about sixteen, and I was pitching for our town team in Ness City, Kansas. The Bloomer Girls were a barnstorming team, but they used to pick up a few young local fellows on the sly to play along with them if they needed to fill out their lineup. I was one of those. I never wore a wig, though—I wouldn't have done that. I guess I looked young enough to pass for a girl anyway. Bill Stern, the old radio broadcaster, must have used that story about forty times, but he always got it wrong about the wig."

There was a yell around us, and an instantly ensuing groan, as Yale's big freshman catcher, Tony Paterno, leading off the bottom of the second, lined sharply to the St. John's shortstop, who made a fine play on the ball. Joe Wood peered intently out at the field through his thickish horn-rimmed spectacles. He shook his head a little. "You know, I can't hardly follow the damned ball now," he said. "It's better for me if I'm someplace where I can get up high behind the plate. I was up to Fenway Park for two games last year, and they let me sit in the press box there at that beautiful park. I could see it all from there. The grounds keeper has got that field just like a living room."

I asked him if he still rooted for the Red Sox.

"Oh, yes," he said. "All my life. A couple of years ago, when they had that big lead in the middle of the summer, they asked me if I'd come up and throw out the first ball at one of their World Series games or playoff games. But then they dropped out of it, of course. Now it looks like it'll never happen."

He spoke in a quiet, almost measured tone, but there was no tinge of disappointment or self-pity in it. It was the voice of age. He was wearing a blue windbreaker over a buttoned-up plaid shirt, made formal with a small dark-red bow tie. There was a brown straw hat on his bald head. The years had imparted a delicate thinness to the skin on his cheeks and neck, but his face had a determined look to it, with a strong chin and a broad, unsmiling mouth. Watching him, I recalled one of the pictures in *The Glory of Their Times*—a team photograph taken in 1906, in which he is sitting cross-legged down in front of a row of men in baggy baseball pants and lace-up, collared baseball shirts with "NESS CITY" across the front in block letters. The men are standing in attitudes of cheerful assurance with their arms folded, and their mushy little baseball gloves are hanging from their belts. Joe Wood, the smallest player in the picture, is wearing a dark warm-up shirt, with the sleeves rolled halfway up his forearms, and his striped baseball cap is pushed back a little, revealing a part in the middle of his hair. There is an intent, unsmiling look on his boyish face—the same grave demeanor you can spot in a subsequent photograph, taken in 1912, in which he is standing beside his Red Sox manager, Jake Stahl, and wearing a heavy woollen three-button suit, a stiff collar, a narrow necktie with a stickpin, and a stylish black porkpie hat pulled low over his handsome, famous face: Smokey Joe Wood at twenty-two. (The moniker, by the way, was given him by Paul Shannon, a sportswriter for the Boston *Post*; before that, he was sometimes called Ozone Wood—"ozone" for the air cleaved by the hapless batters who faced him.) The young man in the photographs and the old man beside me at the ballpark had the same broad, sloping shoulders, but there was nothing burly or physically imposing about him then or now.

"What kind of a pitcher were you, Mr. Wood?" I asked him.

"I had a curve and a fastball," he said. "That's all. I didn't even have brains enough to slow up on the batters. The fastball had a hop on it. You had to be *fast* to have that happen to the ball."

I said that I vividly recalled Sandy Koufax's fastball, which sometimes seemed to jump so violently as it crossed the plate that his catcher had to shoot up his mitt to intercept it.

"Mine didn't go up that far. Just enough for them to miss it." He half turned to me as he said this, and gave me a little glance and an infinitesimal smile. A twinkle. "I don't know where my speed came from," he went on. "I wasn't any bigger or stronger-looking then than I am now. I always could throw hard, and once I saw I was able to get batters out, I figured I was crazy enough to play ball for a living. My father was a criminal lawyer in Kansas, and before that out in Ouray, Colorado, where I first played ball, and my brother went to law school and got a degree, but I didn't even graduate from high school. I ate and slept baseball all my life."

The flow of recollection from Joe Wood was perhaps not as smooth and rivery as I have suggested here. For one thing, he spoke slowly and with care—not unlike the way he walked to the grandstand at Yale Field from the parking lot beyond left field, making his way along the grass firmly enough but looking where he was going, too, and helping himself a bit with his cane. Nothing infirm about him, but nothing hurrying or sprightly, either. For another, the game was well in progress by now, and its principals and sudden events kept interrupting our colloquy. Ron Darling, a poised, impressive figure on the mound, alternated his popping fastballs with just enough down-breaking sliders and an occasional curveball to keep the St. John's batters unhappy. Everything was thrown with heat—his strikeout pitch is a Seaver-high fastball, but his slider, which slides at the last possible instant, is an even deadlier weapon—but without any signs of strain or anxiety. He threw over the top, smoothly driving his front (left) shoulder at the batter in picture-book style, and by the third or fourth inning he had imposed his will and his pace on the game. He was rolling. He is a dark-haired, olive-skinned young man (he lives in Millbury, Massachusetts, near Worcester, but he was born in Hawaii; his mother is Chinese–Hawaiian by birth) with long, powerful legs, but his pitcherlike proportions tend to conceal, rather than emphasize, his 6 feet 2 inches and 195 pounds. He also swings the bat well enough (.331 this year) to play right field for Yale when he isn't pitching; in our game he was the designated hitter as well as the pitcher for the Elis.

"That's a nice build for a pitcher, isn't it?" Joe Wood murmured during the St. John's fifth. Almost as he spoke, Darling executed a twisting dive to his right to snaffle a hard-hit grounder up the middle by Brian Miller, the St. John's shortstop, and threw him out at first. (Hey-*hey!*" Dick Lee cried. "Yay, Ronnie!") "*And* he's an athlete out there," Wood added. "The scouts like that, you know. Oh, this fellow's a lot better than Broaca ever was."

Frank Viola, for his part, was as imperturbable as Darling on the mound, if not quite as awesome. A lanky, sharp-shouldered lefty, he threw an assortment of speeds and spins, mostly sinkers and down-darting sliders, that had the Yale batters swinging from their shoe tops and, for the most part, hammering the ball into the dirt. He had the stuff and poise of a veteran relief pitcher, and the St. John's infield—especially Brian Miller and a stubby, ebullient second baseman named Steve Scafa—performed behind him with the swift, almost haughty confidence that imparts an elegance and calm and sense of ease to baseball at its best. It was a scoreless game after five, and a beauty.

"What was the score of that game you beat Walter Johnson in, in your big year?" Dick Lee asked our guest between innings.

We all knew the answer, I think. In September of 1912, Walter Johnson came to Fenway Park (it was brand-new that year) with the Senators and pitched against young Joe Wood, who then had a string of thirteen consecutive victories to his credit. That summer, Johnson had established a league record of sixteen straight wins, so the matchup was not merely an overflow, sellout affair but perhaps the most anticipated, most discussed nonchampionship game in the American League up to that time.

"We won it, 1–0," Joe Wood said quietly, "but it wasn't his fault I beat him that day. If he'd had the team behind him that I did, he'd have set every kind of record in baseball. You have to remember that Walter Johnson played for a second-division team almost all through his career. All those years, and he had to work from the bottom every time he pitched."

"Were you faster than he was?" I asked.

"Oh, I don't think there was ever anybody faster than Walter," he murmured.

"But Johnson said just the opposite!" Dick Lee cried. "He said no one was faster than *you*."

"He was just that kind of fellow, to say something like that," Wood said. "That was just like the man. Walter Johnson was a great big sort of a pitcher, with hands that came clear down to his knees. Why, the way he threw the ball, the only reason anybody ever got even a foul off him was because everybody in the league knew he'd never come inside to a batter. Walter Johnson was a prince of men—a gentleman first, last, and always."

It came to me that this was the first time I had ever heard anybody use the phrase "a prince of men" in a nonsatiric fashion. In any case, the Johnson–Wood argument did not really need settling, then or now. Smokey Joe went on to tie Johnson with sixteen straight victories that season—an American League record, subsequently tied by Lefty Grove and Schoolboy Rowe. (Over in the National League that year, Rube Marquard won *nineteen* straight for the Giants—a single-season mark first set by Tim Keefe of the Giants in 1888 and untouched as yet by anyone else.) Johnson and Wood pretty well divided up the A.L. mound honors that summer, when Johnson won thirty-two games and lost twelve, posting the best earned-run average (1.39) and the most strike-outs (303), while Wood won the most games and established the best winning percentage with his 34–5 mark (not including his three World Series wins, of course).

These last figures are firmly emplaced in the baseball crannies of my mind, and in the minds of most students of the game, because, it turned out, they represent the autumn of Joe Wood's pitching career as well as its first full flowering. Early in the spring of 1913, he was injured in a fielding play, and he was never near to being the same pitcher again. One of the game's sad speculations over the years has been what Joe Wood's status in the pantheon of great pitchers would be if he had remained sound. I did not need any reminder of his accident, but I had been given one just the same when Dick Lee introduced me to him, shortly before the game. We had stopped to pick up Mr. Wood at his small, red-shuttered white house on Marvel Road, and when he came down the concrete path to join us I got out of Lee's Cadillac to shake the hand that once shook the baseball world.

"Mr. Wood," I said, "this is a great honor."

"Ow—ow!" he cried, cringing before me and attempting to extricate his paw.

"Oh, oh . . . I'm *terribly* sorry," I said, appalled. "Is it—is this because of your fall off the roof?" Three years ago, at the age of eighty-eight, he had fallen off a ladder while investigating a leak, and had cracked several ribs.

"Hell, no!" he said indignantly. "This is the arm I threw out in 1913!"

I felt awful. I had touched history—and almost brought it to its knees.

Now, at the game, he told me how it all happened. "I can't remember now if it was on the road or at Fenway Park," he said. "Anyway, it was against Detroit. There was a swinging bunt down the line, and I went to field it and slipped on the wet grass and went down and landed on my hand. I broke it right here." He pointed to a spot just below his wrist, on the back of his freckled, slightly gnarled right hand. "It's what they call a subperiosteal fracture. They put it in a cast, and I had to sit out a while. Well, this was in 1913, right after we'd won the championship, and every team was out to get us, of course. So as soon as the cast came off, the manager would come up to me every now and then and want to know how soon I was going to get back to pitching. Well, maybe I got back to it too soon and maybe I didn't, but the arm never felt right again. The shoulder went bad. I still went on pitching, but the fastball had lost that hop. I never threw a day after that when I wasn't in pain. Most of the time, I'd pitch and then it would hurt so bad that I wasn't able to raise my hand again for days afterward. So I was about a halftime pitcher after that. You have to understand that in those days if you didn't work you didn't get paid. Now they lay out as long as they need to and get a shot of that cortisone. But we had to play, ready or not. I was a married man, just starting a family, and in order to get my check I had to be in there. So I pitched."

He pitched less, but not much less well. In 1915, he was 15–5 for the Red Sox, with an earned-run average of 1.49, which was the best in the league. But the pain was so persistent that he sat out the entire 1916 season, on his farm, near Shohola, Pennsylvania, hoping that the rest would restore his arm. It did not. He pitched in eight more games after that—all of them for the Cleveland Indians, to whom he was sold in 1917—but he never won again.

"Did you become a different kind of pitcher after you hurt your arm?" I asked. "More off-speed stuff, I mean?"

"No, I still pitched the fastball."

"But all that pain—"

"I tried not to think about that." He gave me the same small smile and bright glance. "I just loved to be out there," he said. "It was as simple as that."

Our afternoon slid by in a distraction of baseball and memory, and I almost felt myself at some dreamlike doubleheader involving the then and the now—the semi-anonymous strong young men waging their close, marvelous game on the sunlit green field before us while bygone players and heroes of baseball history—long gone now, most of them—replayed their vivid, famous innings for me in the words and recollections of my companion. Yale kept putting men aboard against Viola and failing to move them along; Rich Diana, the husky center fielder (he is also an All-Ivy League halfback), whacked a long double to left but then died on second—the sixth stranded Eli base runner in five innings. Darling appeared to be struggling a little, walking two successive batters in the sixth, but he saved himself with a whirling pickoff to second base—a timed play brilliantly completed by his shortstop, Bob Brooke—and then struck out St. John's big first baseman, Karl Komyathy, for the last out. St. John's had yet to manage a hit against him.

In the home half of the sixth, Yale put its leadoff batter aboard with a single but could not bunt him along. Joe Wood was distressed. "I could teach these fellows to bunt in one minute," he said. "Nobody can't hardly bunt anymore. You've got to get your weight more forward than he did, so you're not reaching for the ball. And he should have his right hand higher up on the bat."

The inning ended, and we reversed directions once again. "Ty Cobb was the greatest bat-handler you ever saw," Wood said. "He used to go out to the ballpark early in the morning with a pitcher and work on hitting the ball to all fields, over and over. He batted that strange way, with his fists apart, you know, but he could have hit just as well no matter how he held it. He just knew what to do with a bat in hand. And base running—why, I saw him get on base and steal second, steal third, and then steal home. *The* best. A lot of fellows in my time shortened up on the bat when they had to—that's what the St. John's boys should try against this good pitcher. Next to Cobb, Shoeless Joe Jackson was the best left-handed hitter I ever saw, and he was always down at the end of the bat until there were two strikes on him. Then he'd shorten up a little, to give himself a better chance."

Dick Lee said, "That's what you've been telling Charlie Polka, isn't it, Joe?"

"Yes, sir, and it's helped him," Wood said. "He's tried it, and now he knows that all you have to do is make contact and the ball will fly a long way."

Both men saw my look of bewilderment, and they laughed together.

"Charlie Polka is a Litte League player," Dick Lee explained. "He's about eleven years old."

"He lives right across the street from me," Wood said. "He plays for the 500 Blake team—that's named for a restaurant here in town. I've got him shortened up on the bat, and now he's a hitter. Charlie Polka is a natural."

"Is that how you batted?" I asked.

"Not at first," he said. "But after I went over to Cleveland in 1917 to join my old roommate, Tris Speaker, I started to play the outfield, and I began to take up on the bat, because I knew I'd have to hit a little better if I was going to make the team. I never was any wonder at the plate, but I was good enough to last six more years, playing with Spoke."

Tris Speaker (Wood had called him by his old nickname, Spoke) was the Joe DiMaggio or Willie Mays of the first two decades of this century—the nonpareil center fielder of his day. "He had a beautiful left-handed arm," Joe Wood said. "He always played very shallow in center—you could do that in those days, because of the dead ball. I saw him make a lot of plays to second base from there—pick up what looked like a clean single and fire the ball to second in time to force the base runner coming down from first. Or he could throw the ball behind a runner and pick him off that way. And just as fine a man as he was a ballplayer. He was a Southern gentleman—well, he was from Hubbard, Texas. Back in the early days, when we were living together on the beach at Winthrop during the season, out beyond Revere, Spoke would sometimes cook up a mess of fried chicken in the evening. He'd cook, and then I'd do the dishes."

Listening to this, I sensed the web of baseball about me. Tris Speaker had driven in the tying run in the tenth inning of the last game of the 1912 World Series, at Fenway Park, after Fred Merkle and Chief Meyers, of the Giants, had let his easy foul pop fall untouched between them. A moment or two later, Joe Wood had won his third game of the Series and the Red Sox were champions. My father saw that game—he was at Harvard Law School at the time, and got a ticket somehow—and he told me about it many times. He was terrifically excited to be there, but I think my mother must have relished the famous victory even more. She grew up in Boston and was a true Red Sox fan, even though young women didn't go to many games then. My father grew up in Cleveland, so he was an Indians rooter, of course. In 1915, my parents got married and went to live in Cleveland, where my father began to practice law. Tris Speaker was traded to the Indians in 1916—a terrible shock to Red Sox fans—and Joe Wood came out of his brief retirement to join him on the club a year later. My parents' first child, my older sister, was born in Cleveland late in 1916, and the next year my father went off to Europe—off to the war. My mother once told me that in the summer afternoons of 1917 she would often push a baby carriage past League Park, the Indians' home field, out on Linwood Avenue, which was a block or two away from my parents' house. Sometimes there was a game going on, and if she heard a roar of pleasure from the fans inside she would tell herself that probably Tris Speaker had just done something special. She was lonely in Cleveland, she told me, and it made her feel good to know that Tris Speaker was there in the same town with her. "Tris Speaker and I were traded to Cleveland in the same year," she said.

A yell and an explosion of cheering brought me back to Yale Field. We were in the top of the seventh, and the Yale second baseman and captain, Gerry Harrington, had just leaped high to snatch down a burning line drive—the force of it almost knocked him over backward in midair. Then he flipped the ball to second to double off a St. John's base runner and end the inning. "These fellows came to *play!*" Dick Lee said.

Most no-hitters produce at least one such heaven-sent gift somewhere along the line, and I began to believe that Ron Darling, who was still untouched on the mound, might be pitching the game of his young life. I turned to ask Mr. Wood how many no-hitters he recalled—he had seen Mathewson and Marquard and Babe Ruth (Ruth, the pitcher, that is) and Coveleski and the rest of them, after all—but he seemed transfixed by something on the field. "Look at *that!*" he said, in a harsh, disbelieving way. "This Yale coach has his own coaches out there on the lines, by God! They're professionals—not just players, the way I always had it when I was here. The coach has his own coaches . . . I never knew that."

"Did you have special coaches when you were coming up with the Red Sox?" I said, hoping to change his mood. "A pitching coach, I mean, or a batting coach?"

He didn't catch the question, and I repeated it.

"No, no," he said, a little impatiently. "We talked about the other players and the pitchers among ourselves in those days. We players. We didn't need anybody to help us."

He was staring straight ahead at the field. I thought he looked a bit chilly. It was well past five o'clock now, and a skim of clouds had covered the sun.

Dick Lee stole a glance at him, too. "Hey, Joe, doesn't this Darling remind you a little of Carl Hubbell on the mound?" he said in a cheerful, distracting sort of voice. "The way he picks up his front leg, I mean. You remember how Hubbell would go way up on the stretch and then drop his hands down by his ankles before he threw the ball?"

"Hubbell?" Joe Wood said. He shook his head, making an effort. "Well, to me this pitcher's a little like that fellow Eckersley," he said slowly. "The way he moves forward there."

He was right. Ron Darling had exactly the same float and glide that the Red Sox' Dennis Eckersley conveys when he is pitching well.

"How do today's players compare with the men you played with, Mr. Wood?" I asked.

"I'd rather not answer that question," he said. He had taken out his watch again. He studied it and then tucked it away carefully, and then he glanced over at me, perhaps wondering if he had been impolite. "That Pete Rose plays hard," he added. "Him and a few more. I don't *like* Pete Rose, exactly, but he looks like he plays the game the way we did. He'd play for the fun of it if he had to."

He resumed his study of the field, and now and then I saw him stare again at the heavyset Yale third-base coach on our side of the diamond. Scoreless games make for a long day at the ballpark, and Joe Wood's day had probably been longer than ours. More than once, I had seen him struggle to his feet to catch some exciting play or moment on the field, only to have it end before he was quite up. Then he would sit down again, leaning on his cane while he lowered himself. I had more questions for Mr. Wood, but now I tried to put them out of my mind. Earlier in the afternoon, he had remarked that several old Yale players had dropped in at his house before the game to say hello and to talk about the old days. "People come by and see me all the time," he had said. "People I don't even know, from as far away as Colorado. Why, I had a fellow come in all the way from Canada the other day, who just wanted to talk about the old days. They all want that, somehow. It's gone on too long."

It had gone on for him, I realized, for as long as most lifetimes. He had played ball for fourteen years, all told, and people had been asking him to talk about it for nearly sixty years. For him, the last juice and sweetness must have been squeezed out of these ancient games years ago, but he was still expected to respond to our amateur expertise, our insatiable vicariousness. Old men are patronized in much the same fashion as athletes; because we take pride in them, we expect their intimacy in return. I had intruded after all.

We were in the eighth now . . . and then in the ninth. Still no score, and each new batter, each pitch was greeted with clappings and deepening cries of encouragement and anxiety from the stands and the players alike. The close-packed rows hummed with ceaseless, nervous sounds of conversation and speculation—and impatience for the dénouement, and a fear of it, too. All around me in our section I could see the same look of resignation and boredom and pleasure that now showed on my own face, I knew—the look of longtime fans who understand that one can never leave a very long close game, no matter how much inconvenience and exasperation it imposes on us. The difficulty of baseball is imperious.

"Yay! Yay!" Dick Lee cried when Yale left fielder Joe Dufek led off the eighth with a single. "Now come *on*, you guys! I gotta get home for dinner." But the next Yale batter bunted into a force play at second, and the chance was gone. "Well, all right—for *breakfast*!" Lee said, slumping back in his seat.

The two pitchers held us—each as intent and calm and purposeful as the other. Ron Darling, never deviating from the purity of his stylish body-lean and leg-crook and his riding, down-thrusting delivery, poured fastballs through the diminishing daylight. He looked as fast as ever now, or faster, and in both the ninth and the tenth he dismissed the side in order and with four more strikeouts. Viola was dominant in his own fashion, also setting down the Yale hitters one, two, three in the ninth and tenth, with a handful of pitches. His rhythm—the constant variety of speeds and location on his pitches—had the enemy batters leaning and swaying with his motion, and, as antistrophe, was almost as exciting to watch as Darling's flair and flame. With two out in the top of the eleventh, a St. John's batter nudged a soft little roller up the first-base line—such an easy, waiting, schoolboy sort of chance that the Yale first baseman, O'Connor, allowed the ball to carom off his mitt: a miserable little butchery, except that the second baseman, seeing his pitcher sprinting for the bag, now snatched up the ball and flipped it toward him almost despairingly. Darling took the toss while diving full-length at the bag and, rolling in the dirt, beat the runner by a hair.

"Oh, my!" said Joe Wood. "Oh, my, oh, my!"

Then in the bottom of the inning Yale suddenly loaded the bases—a hit, a walk, another walk (Viola was just missing the corners now)—and we all came to our feet, yelling and pleading. The tilted stands and the low roof deepened the cheers and sent them rolling across the field. There were two out, and the Yale batter, Dan Costello, swung at the first pitch and bounced it gently to short, for a force that ended the rally. Somehow, I think, we knew that we had seen Yale's last chance.

"I would have taken that pitch," I said, entering the out in my scorecard. "To keep the pressure on him."

"I don't know," Joe Wood said at once. "He's just walked two. You might get the cripple on the first pitch and then see nothing but hooks. Hit away."

He was back in the game.

Steve Scafa, leading off the twelfth, got a little piece of Darling's first pitch on the handle of his bat, and the ball looped softly over the shortstop's head and into left: a hit. The loudspeakers told us that Ron Darling's eleven innings of no-hit pitching had set a new N.C.A.A. tournament record. Everyone at Yale Field stood up—the St. John's players, too, coming off their bench and out onto the field—and applauded Darling's masterpiece. We were scarcely seated again before Scafa stole second as the Yale catcher, Paterno, bobbled

the pitch. Scafa, who is blurrily quick, had stolen thirty-five bases during the season. Now he stole third as well. With one out and runners at the corners (the other St. John's man had reached first on an error), Darling ran the count to three-and-two and fanned the next batter—his fifteenth strikeout of the game. Two out. Darling sighed and stared in, and then stepped off the mound while the St. John's coach put in a pinch-runner at first—who took off for second on the very next pitch. Paterno fired the ball quickly this time, and Darling, staggering off the mound with his follow-through, did not cut it off. Scafa came 10 feet down the third-base line and stopped there, while the pinch-runner suddenly jammed on the brakes, stranding himself between first and second: a play, clearly—an inserted crisis. The Yale second baseman glanced twice at Scafa, freezing him, and then made a little run at the hung-up base runner to his left and threw to first. With that, Scafa instantly broke for the plate. Lured by the vision of the third out just a few feet away from him on the base path, the Yale first baseman hesitated, fractionally and fatally, before he spun and threw home, where Scafa slid past the tag and came up, leaping and clapping, into the arms of his teammates. That was the game. Darling struck out his last man, but a new St. John's pitcher, a right-handed fireballer named Eric Stampfl, walked on and blew the Elis away in their half.

"Well, that's a shame," Joe Wood said, getting up for the last time. It was close to six-thirty, but he looked fine now. "If that man scores before the third out, it counts, you know," he said. "That's why it worked. I never saw a better-played game anyplace—college or big-league. That's a swell ballgame."

Several things happened afterward. Neither Yale nor St. John's qualified for the college World Series, it turned out; the University of Maine defeated St. John's in the final game of the playoffs at New Haven (neither Viola nor Darling was sufficiently recovered from his ordeal to pitch again) and made the trip to Omaha, where it, too, was eliminated. Arizona State won the national title. On June 9th, Ron Darling was selected by the Texas Rangers at the major-league amateur-player draft in New York. He was the ninth player in the country to be chosen. Frank Viola, the thirty-seventh pick, went to the Minnesota Twins. (The Seattle Mariners, who had the first pick this year, had been ready to take Darling, which would have made him the coveted No. 1 selection in the draft, but the club backed off at the last moment because of Darling's considerable salary demands. As it was, he signed with the Rangers for a hundred-thousand-dollar bonus.) On June 12th, the major-league players unanimously struck the twenty-six big-league teams. The strike has brought major-league ball to a halt, and no one can predict when play will resume. Because of this sudden silence, the St. John's–Yale struggle has become the best and most vivid game of the year for me, so far. It may stay that way even after the strike ends. "I think that game will always be on my mind," Ron Darling said after it was over. I feel the same way. I think I will remember it all my life. So will Joe Wood. Somebody will probably tell Ron Darling that Smokey Joe Wood was at the game that afternoon and saw him pitch eleven scoreless no-hit innings against St. John's, and someday—perhaps years from now, when he, too, may possibly be a celebrated major-league strikeout artist—it may occur to him that his heartbreaking 0–1 loss in May 1981 and Walter Johnson's 0–1 loss at Fenway Park in September 1912 are now woven together into the fabric of baseball. Pitch by pitch, inning by inning, Ron Darling had made that happen. He stitched us together.

Kafka would laugh out loud. This classic assault on sense and syntax is generally associated with Abbott and Costello, who, having performed it in the 1945 film *Naughty Nineties*, are presumed to have written it. They didn't. Who did? Naturally. When Bud and Lou first formed a team in 1937, each was an experienced vaudeville comic. A key ingredient of their enormous success in the 1940s and 1950s was a file of some 2,000 stock routines from the burlesque stage, including "Who's on First?" The version transcribed below was presented to the Baseball Hall of Fame in 1956.

ANONYMOUS

Who's on First?

ABBOTT: You know, strange as it may seem, they give ball players nowadays very peculiar names. . . . Now, on the Cooperstown team we have Who's on first, What's on second, I Don't Know is on third—

COSTELLO: That's what I want to find out. I want you to tell me the names of the fellows on the Cooperstown team.

ABBOTT: I'm telling you. Who's on first, What's on second, I Don't Know is on third.

COSTELLO: You know the fellows' names?

ABBOTT: Yes.

COSTELLO: Well, then, who's playin' first?

ABBOTT: Yes.

COSTELLO: I mean the fellow's name on first base.

ABBOTT: Who.

COSTELLO: The fellow's name on first base for Cooperstown.

ABBOTT: Who.

COSTELLO: The guy on first base.

ABBOTT: Who is on first base.
COSTELLO: Well, what are you asking me for?
ABBOTT: I'm not asking you—I'm telling you. Who is on first.
COSTELLO: I'm asking you—who's on first?
ABBOTT: That's the man's name.
COSTELLO: That's who's name?
ABBOTT: Yes.
COSTELLO: Well, go ahead, tell me!
ABBOTT: Who.
COSTELLO: The guy on first.
ABBOTT: Who.
COSTELLO: The first baseman.
ABBOTT: Who is on first.
COSTELLO: Have you got a first baseman on first?
ABBOTT: Certainly.
COSTELLO: Well, all I'm trying to find out is what's the guy's name on first base.
ABBOTT: Oh, no, no, What is on second base.
COSTELLO: I'm not asking you who's on second.
ABBOTT: Who's on first.
COSTELLO: That's what I'm trying to find out.
ABBOTT: Well, don't change the players around.
COSTELLO: I'm not changing anybody.
ABBOTT: Now, take it easy.
COSTELLO: What's the guy's name on first base?
ABBOTT: What's the guy's name on second base.
COSTELLO: I'm not askin' ya who's on second.
ABBOTT: Who's on first.
COSTELLO: I don't know.
ABBOTT: He's on third. We're not talking about him.
COSTELLO: How could I get on third base?
ABBOTT: You mentioned his name.
COSTELLO: If I mentioned the third baseman's name, who did I say is playing third?
ABBOTT: No, Who's playing first.
COSTELLO: Stay offa first, will you?
ABBOTT: Please. Now what is it you want to know?
COSTELLO: What is the fellow's name on third base?
ABBOTT: What is the fellow's name on second base.
COSTELLO: I'm not askin' ya who's on second.
ABBOTT: Who's on first.

COSTELLO: I don't know.
ABBOTT & COSTELLO: Third base.

COSTELLO: (*Makes noises*) You got an outfield?
ABBOTT: Oh, sure.
COSTELLO: Cooperstown has got a good outfield?
ABBOTT: Oh, absolutely.
COSTELLO: The left fielder's name?
ABBOTT: Why.
COSTELLO: I don't know, I just thought I'd ask.
ABBOTT: Well, I just thought I'd tell you.
COSTELLO: Then tell me who's playing left field.
ABBOTT: Who's playing first.
COSTELLO: Stay out of the infield.
ABBOTT: Don't mention any names out here.
COSTELLO: I want to know what's the fellow's name in left field.
ABBOTT: What is on second.
COSTELLO: I'm not asking you who's on second.
ABBOTT: Who is on first.
COSTELLO: I don't know.
ABBOTT & COSTELLO: Third base.
COSTELLO: (*Makes noises*)
ABBOTT: Now take it easy, man.
COSTELLO: And the left fielder's name?
ABBOTT: Why.
COSTELLO: Because.
ABBOTT.: Oh, he's center field.
COSTELLO: Wait a minute. You got a pitcher on the team?
ABBOTT: Wouldn't this be a fine team without a pitcher.
COSTELLO: I don't know. Tell me the pitcher's name.
ABBOTT: Tomorrow.
COSTELLO: You don't want to tell me today?
ABBOTT: I'm telling you, man.
COSTELLO: Then go ahead.
ABBOTT: Tomorrow.
COSTELLO: What time?
ABBOTT: What time what?
COSTELLO: What time tomorrow are you gonna tell me who's pitching?
ABBOTT: Now listen, Who is not pitching. Who is on—
COSTELLO: I'll break your arm if you say who's on first.
ABBOTT: Then why come up here and ask?

COSTELLO: I want to know what's the pitcher's name.

ABBOTT: What's on second.

COSTELLO: I don't know.

ABBOTT & COSTELLO: Third base.

COSTELLO: Ya gotta catcher?

ABBOTT: Yes.

COSTELLO: The catcher's name.

ABBOTT: Today.

COSTELLO: Today. And Tomorrow's pitching.

ABBOTT: Now you've got it.

COSTELLO: That's all. Cooperstown got a couple of days on their team. That's all.

ABBOTT: Well, I can't help that.

COSTELLO: (Makes noises)

ABBOTT: All right. What do you want me to do?

COSTELLO: Gotta catcher?

ABBOTT: Yes.

COSTELLO: I'm a good catcher too, you know.

ABBOTT: I know that.

COSTELLO: I would like to play for the Cooperstown team.

ABBOTT: Well, I might arrange that.

COSTELLO: I would like to catch. Now, I'm being a good catcher, Tomorrow's pitching on the team and I'm catching.

ABBOTT: Yes.

COSTELLO: Tomorrow throws the ball and the guy up bunts the ball.

ABBOTT: Yes.

COSTELLO: Now, when he bunts the ball—me being a good catcher—I want to throw the guy out at first base, so I pick up the ball and throw it to who?

ABBOTT: Now, that's the first thing you've said right.

COSTELLO: (shouts) I don't even know what I'm talking about.

ABBOTT: Well, that's all you have to do.

COSTELLO: Is throw it to first base.

ABBOTT: Yes.

COSTELLO: Now, who's got it?

ABBOTT: Naturally.

COSTELLO: Who has it?

ABBOTT: Naturally.

COSTELLO: Naturally.

ABBOTT: Naturally.

COSTELLO: I throw the ball to Naturally.

ABBOTT: You throw it to Who.

COSTELLO: Naturally.

ABBOTT: Naturally. Well, say it that way.

COSTELLO: That's what I'm saying.

ABBOTT: Now don't get excited. Now don't get excited.

COSTELLO: I throw the ball to first base.

ABBOTT: Then Who gets it.

COSTELLO: He better get it.

ABBOTT: That's it. All right now, don't get excited. Take it easy.

COSTELLO: Hmmmmmph.

ABBOTT: Hmmmmmph.

COSTELLO: Now, I throw the ball to first base, whoever it is grabs the ball, so the guy runs to second.

ABBOTT: Uh-huh.

COSTELLO: Who picks up the ball and throws it to What. What throws it to I Don't Know. I Don't Know throws it back to Tomorrow—a triple play.

ABBOTT: Yeah. It could be.

COSTELLO: Another guy gets up and it's a long fly ball to center. Why? I don't know. And I don't care.

ABBOTT: What was that?

COSTELLO: I said, 'I don't care.'

ABBOTT: Oh, that's our shortstop.

Old Anon, that most prolific and versatile of authors, is the only one to appear twice in this volume. Before composing "Who's on First?" he was a staffer for *The New York Times*, wherein this grand description of a rather ordinary game appeared on April 26, 1912. They don't write 'em like this any more—mixing the rhythms of Broadway and ancient Greece—and more's the pity. "Here's one that will bring the weeps," indeed: not for a ballgame lost but for a style of baseball writing that, because of its excesses in the 1920s, was not mourned upon its passing. Today's reporter views his efforts as secondary to the game and its players, an attitude that is commendably modest but tends to produce bland, "just-the-facts-ma'am" coverage of the incidents of the game, embellished only by banal quotes about hanging curveballs and "seeing the ball good." The nameless scribe who gladdened the hearts of *Times* readers back in 1912 reminds one of Rice and Runyon and, in spots, of another nameless scribe to whom history has given the name Homer.

ANONYMOUS

Yankees Toss Game Away in Thirteenth

Here's one that will bring the weeps.

The Yankees and the Athletics were tied in the thirteenth inning at 4–4. Rube Oldring jarred Ford's damp hurl to the center lawn for a single. Ford's next moist fling slipped and went wild, Oldring racing to second, and then to third. Gabby Street recovered the unruly ball, made a desperate heave to Coleman at third base, and the ball traveled on to left field, Oldring coming home with the run which won the game. Score, 5–4.

Play on, professor—a little more of that funeral march.

Some 3,500 persons, mostly men, sat through to the bitter end, and everyone got cold smoked beef when he walked into the Missus for dinner at 7:30 last evening. That wasn't all they got.

This is the conversation, husband speaking: "Say, Mrs. Wife, you ought to have seen that pitching duel between Bender and Ford. The Yanks tied it up in the sixth, and after that both flingers were airtight."

Mrs. Wife now talking: "Say, you, what do you think this is—an all-night lunch? Why don't you board up at the ballpark? You'll find something to eat at the 'Ham-And' place around the corner."

It was a ball game worth missing your dinner for. The Yankees showed more fight and vim than in any game this season. For a long time they refused to be whipped, and their chances were just as good as the world's champions until they cracked in the thirteenth inning and began to toss the ball all over the lot. Wolverton's men had several excellent chances to win the game, but they lacked the final punch.

The Yankees are in pretty bad shape, and had to rely on green recruits to fill the gaps made by the hospital patients. The whole outfield is now disabled, Hartzell being yesterday's victim, while Cree and Walter are still recuperating.

In the second inning, Daniels in center and Hartzell in right both chased after Bender's high fly. The players came together with an awful bump, and Hartzell stretched out on the grass, unconscious. A gash was cut in his chin, and he was carried to the clubhouse. Benny Kauff took his place, and was all hot sand and ginger in the game. Kauff made two fine hits and ran the bases fast, scoring two of the Yankee runs.

It was a toss-up between Bender and Ford. Both pitched great after the sixth inning, getting stronger as they went along. It was the first big game the big Chippewa Indian has pitched since the World Series last fall, and he looks as if he were good for a couple more World Series. Ford was back to his best form and, with men on the bases, was very effective. Ragged support behind him aided the Athletics in their run harvest.

Philadelphia activity started in the second. Murphy was safe when Martin threw wild to Chase at first. McInnis beat out a bunt to Ford, and Barry sacrificed the pair up a notch. Then, who comes along but Ira Thomas, who wallops a "pippin" to deep center for a zwei hassocks, scoring Murphy and McInnis. The Yanks got one in that stanza, when Kauff ripped a single to center, went down to second on Zinn's out, and scored on Gardner's hit to the middle patch.

In the fourth, Barry did a brazen piece of business. Murphy singled, went to second on McInnis's out and to third on a passed ball. Barry's roller went to Coleman, and Murphy was nailed while skipping up and down the third-base line, Barry racing around to third, while half a dozen Yankees riveted their attention on Murphy. As Ford was pitching to Thomas, Barry started down the third-base line like a runaway colt.

The mammoth nerve of him! The grand larceny was committed with all the Yankees looking on with their baby-blue eyes wide open. Barry slid in safe, while the Yankees continued the nap. Get out the alarm clock.

In the fifth, Oldring was safe on a rap which skinned Gardner's shins, and he scored on Collins's double to right. In the same inning, the Yankees began to rush up from behind. Gardner singled and Street strolled. Ford sacrificed them along a base, and they both tore home on Daniels's safe smash to center.

Sixth inning—Yanks at bat, two out. Benny Kauff banged out a safety to right and went to second when Murphy juggled the ball. Kauff scored on Zinn's single to center. The score is tied. Nifty, what?

Ford and Bender both closed up like morning glories in the sun. At nine innings, not a run in sight. Tenth inning, the same thing. In the eleventh inning, Collins walked on Ford's only pass of the day, and got to third on two outs. He stuck there as if planted in glue.

The Yankees should have won in the twelfth inning. Young Martin, the new shortstopper whom Wolverton has just recalled from Rochester, poled a high-powered three-bagger to the darkest corner of right field. He had plenty of time to make the circuit, but was held at third base because of poor coaching. It was a burning shame that such a healthy smash could go to seed, but Martin was tagged coming in on Zinn's grounder.

Then followed the fitful thirteenth, when the strong-armed pegs of Ford and Street permitted Oldring to breeze home with the hurrah tally.

Employees of the New York Yankees know that the boss's door is always open: it revolves. Managers, coaches, p.r. men, secretaries, and of course players—all are advised to keep their bags packed. Yet George M. Steinbrenner III—the man Red Smith referred to simply as "George III"—is not hard of heart, only of head, as were his various spiritual ancestors and contemporary peers. The impetuous/domineering style of ownership was patented by Chris Von Der Ahe, owner of the champion St. Louis Browns of the 1880s, and refined by such men as the Giants' Andrew Freedman and the Indians' Bill Veeck. And if Yankee fans think George is overinvolved with the on-field operations of the team, let them recall that Braves' owner Ted Turner once managed the team from the dugout—in uniform!—and Oakland's Charlie Finley once tried to bribe Vida Blue to change his given name to "True."

RUSSELL BAKER

Love Me, Love My Bear

I have never been able to fire anybody and, as a result, promotions have always passed me by. This is why I sought out George Steinbrenner, the owner of the New York Yankees and probably the most successful firer in the annals of unemployment.

Naturally, I had expected to meet an ogre, and, so, was delighted by the charm with which he received my proposal. I began by confessing that it was unusual. "Mr. Steinbrenner," I explained, "I want to study firing and I want to study under the best man in the field. Will you help me learn?"

Instead of the tirade I anticipated, these words produced a strange silence during which his eyes moistened and he struggled to hold back emotion. At length he said, "The best. . . . Nobody's ever said anything like that about me before."

"Oh, you have a good heart, Mr. Steinbrenner. I can see that. I know you'll help me, sir." He dabbed at his eyes with a handkerchief.

"I haven't been all torn up inside like this since the time they took away my teddy bear," he said, picking up the phone and asking his receptionist to step in.

"Yes, Mr. Steinbrenner?" said the receptionist.

"You're fired," he said.

"May I ask why?"

"For letting in people who remind me of the time they took my teddy bear away. I can't run a baseball team while I'm wondering whatever happened to that dear old teddy bear of mine."

When the receptionist had gone, I expressed admiration for the ease and rapidity with which he had conducted the firing. "Why, the receptionist didn't even call you a brute or an ingrate," I said.

"She didn't dare," said Mr. Steinbrenner. "If she had, she would have blown her chances of managing the Yankees."

I couldn't believe that, after firing her from a receptionist's job, he would hire her back to manage the team.

"Why not?" he asked. "At the rate I fire managers, I can't afford to be picky. Which reminds me—"

He dialed the phone. "I'm calling a sportswriter pal," he whispered. Then: "This is George, Sol. . . . Yeah, terrible about that last road trip. I've got it from the horse's mouth the Yankees are looking for a new manager. . . . Don't quote me."

He hung up. I felt radiant with hero worship. Mr. Steinbrenner was not only going to fire the manager; he was letting me know how he did it. "That will be headlines in the paper tomorrow," I said.

"You bet your sweet patootie," he said. "It'll put the Yankees back on page one, stir up the fans, get the old turnstiles clicking faster. When you fire somebody, son, fire with a purpose. It's good for the box office."

"You're the greatest, Mr. Steinbrenner."

"Now don't go getting me all choked up again," he said.

I saw this was the moment to push my case. "If it's not asking too much," I said, "could I come in some day and fire somebody for you while you watched me to make sure I'm doing it right?"

He rose from his desk and embraced me. "I like you, kid. You could be good, really good," he said. "I'm putting you on the payroll as junior assistant in charge of minor firings. Be in here tomorrow morning early and I'll let you fire a couple of peanut vendors."

I was too overcome to trust my voice, so I merely nodded, sniffled, and moved to the door.

"Before you go," he said.

"Yes."

"About this manager I've got to fire—do you know who's managing the Yankees this week?"

Not wanting to blow my big chance by revealing that I didn't follow baseball, I gave him the name of the only baseball manager I could remember. "It's Earl Weaver," I said.

As I left, he had Weaver on the telephone. "Earl, baby," he was saying, "you're through. Drop by the cashier's window and pick up your paycheck. . . ."

I reported early next morning to fire peanut vendors. Mr. Steinbrenner led in the first, then stood behind me to observe my technique. The peanut vendor was a small, cuddly fellow with plump, round cheeks and a great deal of hair.

"Vendor," I snarled, and then paused.

"Yes sir. Bag of peanuts, sir?"

"What are you waiting for?" asked Mr. Steinbrenner. "Give him the ax."

"I can't," I said.

"Can't! Why not?"

"He reminds me of my dear old teddy bear," I said.

I heard Mr. Steinbrenner snuffle and suppress a sob behind me. Then: "Nobody can talk about teddy bears around me and get away with it," he said in a voice hoarse with sorrow. "You're fired."

I was leaving the Stadium when a guard said Mr. Steinbrenner wanted me on the phone. "Give me your phone number, kid," he said. "I'm going to need some new managers next spring."

This article by the fifteen-year major-league veteran appeared not in *The Sporting News* or the Sunday sports section, but in the September 1941 issue of the *Atlantic Monthly*. Then again, the writer was not your ordinary ballplayer: He was a *summa cum laude* graduate of Princeton, master of a dozen languages (in none of which, it was observed, could he hit), and, it was revealed after his death in 1972, a master spy in both Japan and Occupied Europe. Ironically, the intellectual who could describe the catcher as "the Cerberus of baseball" himself wielded the tools of ignorance, and in 1924 he was the object of that famous scouting-report barbarism, "Good field, no hit."

MOE BERG

Pitchers and Catchers

I

Baseball men agree with the philosopher that perfection—which means a pennant to them—is attainable only through a proper combination of opposites. A team equally strong in attack and in defense, well-proportioned as a unit, with, of course, those intangibles, morale, enthusiasm, and direction—that is the story of success in baseball. Good fielding and pitching, without hitting, or vice versa, is like Ben Franklin's half a pair of scissors—ineffectual. Lopsided pennant failures are strewn throughout the record books. Twenty-game winners or .400 hitters do not ensure victory. *Ne quid nimis.* Ty Cobb, baseball genius, helped win pennants early in his career, but from 1909 through 1926, his last year at Detroit, he and his formidable array of hitters failed—they never found the right combination. Ed Walsh, the great White Sox spitball pitcher, in 1908 won forty or practically half of his club's games, to this day an individual pitching record, but alone he couldn't offset his own "hitless wonders." Walter Johnson the swift, with over 400 victories, waited almost twenty years before his clubmates at Washington helped him to a championship. Every pennant winner must be endowed both at the plate and in the field. Even Babe

Ruth's bat, when it loomed largest, couldn't obscure the Yankees' high-caliber pitching and their tight defense in key spots.

With all the importance that hitting has assumed since the Babe and home runs became synonymous, I note that Connie Mack, major-league manager for almost half a century, household name for strategy wherever the game is played, still gives pitching top rating in baseball.

A Walter Johnson, a Lefty Grove, a Bob Feller, cannon-ball pitchers, come along once in a generation. By sheer, blinding speed they overpower the hitter. Johnson shut out the opposition in 113 games, more than the average pitcher wins in his major-league lifetime. Bob Feller continues this speed-ball tradition. We accept these men as pitching geniuses, with the mere explanation that, thanks to their strong arms, their pitches are comparatively untouchable. When Walter Johnson pitched, the hitter looked for a fastball and got it; he looked— but it didn't do him much good. Clark Griffith, then manager of the Washington Club, jestingly threatened Walter with a fine any time he threw a curve. "Griff" knew that no variation in the speed king's type of pitch was necessary. But what of the other pitchers who are not so talented?

Many times a pitcher without apparent stuff wins, whereas his opponent, with what seems to be a great assortment, is knocked out of the box in an early inning. The answer, I believe, lies in the bare statement, "Bat meets ball"; any other inference may lead us into the danger of overcomplication. The player himself takes his ability for granted and passes off his success or lack of it with "You do or you don't." Call it the law of averages.

Luck, as well as skill, decides a game. The pitcher tries to minimize the element of luck. Between the knees and shoulders of the hitter, over a plate just 17 inches wide, lies the target of the pitcher, who throws from a rectangular rubber slab on a mound 60 feet, 6 inches distant. The pitcher has to throw into this area with enough on the ball to get the hitter out—that is his intention. Control, natural or acquired, is a prerequisite of any successful pitcher: he must have direction, not only to be effective, but to exist.

Because of this enforced concentration of pitches, perhaps the game's most interesting drama unfolds within the limited space of the ball-and-strike zone. The pitcher toes the mound; action comes with the motion, delivery, and split-second flight of the ball to the catcher. With every move the pitcher is trying to fool the hitter, using his stuff, his skill and wiles, his tricks and cunning, all his art to win.

Well-known to ballplayers is the two-o'clock hitter who breaks down fences in batting practice. There is no pressure; the practice pitcher throws ball after ball with the same motion, the same delivery and speed. If the practice pitcher varies his windup or delivery, the hitters don't like it—not in batting practice— and they show their dislike by sarcastically conceding victory by a big score to the batting practice pitcher and demanding another. This is an interesting phenomenon. The hitter, in practice, is adjusting himself to clocklike regularity of speed, constant and consistent. He is concentrating on his timing. He has to coordinate his vision and his swing. This coordination the opposing pitcher wants to upset from the moment he steps on the rubber and the game begins. The very duration of the stance itself, the windup and motion, and the form of delivery are all calculated to break the hitter's equilibrium. Before winding up, the pitcher may hesitate, outstaring the notoriously anxious hitter in order to disturb him. Ted Lyons, of the Chicago White Sox, master student of a hitter's habits, brings his arms over his head now once, now twice, three or more times, his eyes intent on every move of the hitter, slowing up or quickening the pace of his windup and motion in varying degrees before he delivers the pitch. Cy Young, winner of most games in baseball history—he won 511—had four different pitching motions, turning his back on the hitter to hide the ball before he pitched. Fred Marberry, the great Washington relief pitcher, increased his effectiveness by throwing his free, nonpivot foot as well as the ball at the hitter to distract him.

In 1884, when Connie Mack broke in as a catcher for Meriden, Charlie Radbourn—who won sixty games for Providence—could have cuffed, scraped, scratched, fingernailed, applied resin, emery, or any other foreign substance to, or spit on the two balls the teams started and finished the game with. "Home-Run" Baker, who hit two balls out of the park in the 1911 World Series to win his nickname—and never more than twelve in a full season—characterizes a defensive era in the game. During the last war, it was impossible to get some of the nine foreign ingredients that enter into the manufacture of our baseball. To make up for the lack of the superior foreign yarn, our machines were adjusted to wind the domestic product tighter. In 1919, when the war was over, the foreign yarn was again available, but the same machines were used. The improved technique, the foreign ingredients, Babe Ruth and bat, conspired to revolutionize baseball. It seems prophetic, with due respect to the Babe, that our great American national game, so native and representative, could have been so completely refashioned by happenings on the other side of the world.

II

The importance of the bat has been stressed to such an extent that, since 1920, foreign substances have been barred to the pitcher, and the spitball outlawed. The resin bag, the sole concession, is used on the hands only to counteract perspiration. The cover of the ball, in two sections, is sewed together with stitches, slightly raised, in one long seam; today's pitcher, after experimentation and experience, takes whatever advantage he can of its surface to make his various pitches more effective by gripping the ball across or along two rows of stitches, or along one row or on the smooth surface. The pitcher is always working with a shiny new ball. A game today will consume as many as eight dozen balls instead of the two roughed and battered ones which were the limit in 1884.

With the freak pitch outlawed and the accent put on hitting in the modern game, the pitcher has to be resourceful to win. He throws fast-, slow-, and breaking balls, all with variations. He is fortunate if his fastball hops or sinks, slides or sails, because, if straight as a string or too true, it is ineffective. The ball has to do something at the last moment. The curve must break sharply and not hang. To add to his repertory of balls that break, the pitcher may develop a knuckle ball (fingers applied to the seam, knuckled against, instead of gripping the ball), a forkball (the first two fingers forking the ball), or a screwball (held approximately the same as an orthodox fastball or curveball but released with a twist of the wrist the reverse of a curve). The knuckle and forkballs flutter through the air, wavering, veering, or taking a sudden lurch, without revolving like the other pitches; they are the modern counterpart of the spitball, a dry spitter.

The pitcher studies the hitter's stance, position at the plate, and swing, to establish the level of his natural batting stroke and to detect any possible weakness. Each hitter has his own individual style. The pitcher scouts his form and notes whether he holds the bat on the end or chokes it, is a free swinger or a chop hitter. He bears in mind whether the hitter crowds, or stands away from, the plate, in front of or behind it, erect or crouched over it. Whether he straddles his legs or strides forward to hit, whether he lunges with his body or takes a quick cut with wrist and arm only, whether he pulls a ball, hits late or through the box—all these things are telltale and reveal a hitter's liking for a certain pitch, high or low, in or out, fast, curve, or slow.

To fool the hitter—there's the rub. With an assortment at his disposal, a pitcher tries to adapt the delivery, as well as the pitch, to the hitter's weakness. Pitchers may have distinct forms of delivery and work differently on a given hitter; a pitcher throws overhand, three-quarter overhand (which is about midway between overhand and sidearm), side arm, or underhand. A crossfire is an emphasized sidearm pitch thrown against the forward foot as the body leans to the same side as the pitching arm at the time of the motion and delivery. Not the least important part of the delivery is the body follow-through to get more stuff on the pitch and to take pressure off the arm. Having determined the hitter's weakness, the pitcher can throw to spots—for example, "high neck in," low outside, or letter high. But he never forgets that, with all his equipment, he is trying to throw the hitter off his timing—probably the best way to fool him, to get him out. Without varying his motion, he throws a change-of-pace fastball or curveball, pulls the string on his fastball, slows up, takes a little off or adds a little to his fast-ball.

Just as there are speed kings, so there are hitters without an apparent weakness. They have unusual vision, power, and great ability to coordinate these in the highest degree. They are the ranking, top hitters who hit everything in the strike zone well—perhaps one type of pitch less well than another. To these hitters the pitcher throws his best pitch and leaves the result to the law of averages. Joe DiMaggio straddles in a spread-eagle stance with his feet wide apart and bat already cocked. He advances his forward foot only a matter of inches, so that, with little stride, he doesn't move his head, keeping his eyes steadily on the ball. He concentrates on the pitch; his weight equally distributed on both feet, he has perfect wrist action and power to drive the ball for distance. Mel Ott, on the other hand, lifts the front foot high just as the pitcher delivers the ball; he is not caught off balance or out of position, because he sets the foot down only after he has seen what type of pitch is coming. With DiMaggio's stance one must have good wrist action and power. With Ott's, there is a danger of taking a long step forward before one knows what is coming. But Mel does not commit himself.

Rogers Hornsby, one of the game's greatest right-hand hitters, invariably took his position in the far rear corner of the batter's box, stepped into the pitch, and hit to all fields equally well. Ty Cobb was always a step ahead of the pitcher. He must have been because he led the American League in hitting every year but one in the thirteen-year period 1907–19. He outstudied the pitcher and took as many positions in the batter's box as he thought necessary to counteract the type of motion and pitch he was likely to get. He adapted his stance to the pitcher who was then on the mound; for Red Faber, whose spitball broke sharply down, Cobb stood in front of the plate; for a curveball left-hander, Ty took a stance behind the plate in order to hit the curve after it broke, because, as Ty said, he could see it break and get hold of it the better. For Lefty O'Doul, one of the greatest teachers of hitting in the game, there are no outside pitches. Lefty stands close to the plate; his bat more than covers it; he is a natural right-field pull hitter. Babe Ruth, because of his tremendous, unequaled home-run power, and his ability to hit equally well all sorts of pitches with a liberal stride and a free swing, and consistently farther than any other player, has demonstrated that he had the greatest coordination and power of any hitter ever known. Ted Williams, of the Boston Red Sox, the only current .400 hitter in the game, completely loose and relaxed, has keen enough eyes never to offer at a bad pitch; he has good wrist and arm action, leverage, and power. Jimmie Foxx, next to Babe Ruth as a home-run hitter, steps into a ball, using his tremendous wrists and forearms for his powerful, long and line drives. These hitters do not lunge with the body; the front hip gives way for the swing, and the body follows through.

III

The game is carried back and forth between the pitcher and the hitter. The hitter notices what and where the pitchers are throwing. If the pitcher is getting him out consistently, for example, on a curve outside, the hitter changes his mode of attack. Adaptability is the hallmark of the big-league hitter. Joe Cronin, playing manager of the Red Sox, has changed in his brilliant career from a fastball, left-field pull hitter to a curveball and a right-field hitter, to and fro through the whole cycle and back again, according to where the pitchers are throwing. He has no apparent weakness, hits to all fields, and is one of the greatest "clutch" hitters in the game. *Plus ça change, plus c'est la même chose.*

Like Walter Johnson, Lefty Grove was a fastball pitcher, and the hitters knew it. The hitters looked for this pitch; Lefty did not try to fool them by throwing anything else, but most of them were fooled, not by the type of pitch, but by his terrific speed. With two strikes on the hitter, Lefty did throw his curve at times, and that, too, led almost invariably to a strikeout. In 1935, Lefty had recovered from his first serious sore arm of the year before. Wear and tear, and the grind of many seasons, had taken their toll. Now he had changed his tactics, and was pitching curves and fastballs, one or the other. His control was practically perfect. On a day in that year in Washington, Heinie Manush, a great hitter, was at bat with two men on the bases. The game was at stake; the count was three balls and two strikes. Heinie stood there, confident, looking for Lefty's fastball. "Well," thought Heinie, "it might be a curve." Lefty was throwing the curve more and more now, but the chances with the count of

three-and-two were that Lefty would throw his fastball with everything he had on it. Fast or curve—he couldn't throw anything else; he had nothing else to throw. Heinie broke his back striking out on the next pitch, the first forkball Grove ever threw. For over a year, on the sidelines, in the bullpen, between pitching starts, Lefty had practiced and perfected this pitch before he threw it, and he waited for a crucial spot to use it. Lefty had realized his limitations. The hitters were getting to his fastballs and curveballs more than they used to. He wanted to add to his pitching equipment; he felt he had to. Heinie Manush anticipated, looked for, guessed a fastball, possibly a curve, but Lefty fooled him with his new pitch, a forkball.

Here was the perfect setup for outguessing a hitter. Lefty Grove's development of a third pitch, the forkball, is the greatest example in our time of complete successful change in technique by one pitcher. When a speed-ball pitcher loses his fast one, he has to compensate for such loss by adding to his pitching equipment. Lefty both perfected his control and added a forkball. Carl Hubbell's screwball, practically unhittable at first, made his fastball and curve effective. Lefty Gomez, reaching that point in his career where he had to add to his fastball and curveball, developed and threw his first knuckle ball this year. Grove, Gomez, and Hubbell, three outstanding left-handers—Grove and Gomez adding a forkball and a knuckle ball respectively to their fastballs and curveballs when their speed was waning, Hubbell developing a screwball early in his career to make it his best pitch and to become one of the game's foremost southpaws—so you have the build-up of great pitchers.

At first, the superspeed of Grove obviated the necessity of pitching brains. But, when his speed began to fade, Lefty turned to his head. With his almost perfect control and the addition of his forkball, Lefty now fools the hitter with his cunning. With Montaigne, we conceive of Socrates in place of Alexander, of brain for brawn, wit for whip. And this brings us to a fascinating part of the pitcher–hitter drama: Does a hitter guess? Does a pitcher try to outguess him? When the pitching process is no longer mechanical, how much of it is psychological? When the speed of a Johnson or a Grove is fading or gone, can the pitcher outguess the hitter?

IV

We know that the pitcher studies the strength and weakness of every hitter and that the hitter notes every variety of pitch in the pitcher's repertory; that the big-league hitter is resourceful, and quick to meet every new circumstance. Does he anticipate what the pitcher is going to throw? He can regulate his next pitch arbitrarily by the very last-second flick of the wrist. There is no set pattern for the order of pitches. Possible combinations are so many that a formula of probability cannot be established. He may repeat the fastball or curveball indefinitely, or pitch them alternately; there is no mathematical certainty what the pitch will be. There is no harmony in the pattern of a pitcher's pitches. And no human being has the power of divination.

But does this prevent a hitter from guessing? Does he merely hit what he sees if he can? Is it possible for a hitter to stand at the plate and use merely his vision, without trying to figure out what the pitcher might throw? The hitter bases his anticipation on the repertory of the pitcher, taking into account the score of the game, what the pitcher threw him the last time at bat, whether he hit that pitch or not, how many men are on base, and the present count on him. The guess is more than psychic, for there is some basis for it, some precedent for the next move; what is past is prologue.

The few extraordinary hitters whose exceptional vision and power to co-ordinate must be the basis for their talent can afford to be oblivious of anything but the flight of the ball. Hughie Duffy, who has the highest batting average in baseball history (he hit .438 in 1894), or Rogers Hornsby, another great right-hand hitter, may even deny that he did anything but hit what he saw. But variety usually makes a hitter think. When Ty Cobb changed his stance at the plate to hit the pitcher then facing him, he anticipated not only a certain type of motion but also the pitch that followed it. He studied past performance. Joe DiMaggio hit a home run to break Willie Keeler's consecutive-games hitting record of forty-four, standing since 1897, and has since carried the record to fifty-six games. In hitting the home run off Dick Newsome, Red Sox pitcher, who has been very successful this year because of a good assortment of pitches, Joe explains: "I hit a fastball; I knew he would come to that and was waiting for it; he had pitched knucklers, curves, and sinkers." Jimmie Foxx looks for a particular pitch when facing a pitcher—for example, a curveball against a notorious curveball pitcher—and watches any other pitch go by. But when he has two strikes he cancels all thought of what the pitcher might throw; he then hits what he sees. Jimmie knows that if he looks for a certain pitch and guesses wrong, with two strikes on him, he will be handcuffed at the plate watching the pitch go by. Hank Greenberg, full of imagination, has guessed right most of the time—he hit fifty-eight home runs one year.

Just as Lefty Grove perfected control of his not-so-speedy fastball and curve, and added the forkball to give him variety, so even the outstanding hitters have to change their mode of attack later when their vision and reactions are not quite so sharp as they used to be.

V

The catcher squatting behind the hitter undoubtedly has the coign of vantage in the ballpark; all the action takes place before him. Nothing is outside his view except the balls-and-strikes umpire behind him—which is at times no hardship. The receiver has a good pair of hands, shifts his feet gracefully for inside or outside pitches, and bends his knees, not his back, in an easy, rhythmic motion, as he stretches his arms to catch the ball below his belt. The catcher has to be able to cock his arm from any position, throw fast and accurately to the bases, field bunts like an infielder, and catch foul flies like an outfielder. He must be adept at catching a ball from any angle, and almost simultaneously tagging a runner at home plate. The catcher is the Cerberus of baseball.

These physical qualifications are only a part of a catcher's equipment. He signals the pitcher what to throw, and this implies superior baseball brains on his part. But a pitcher can put a veto on a catcher's judgment by shaking him off and waiting for another sign. The game cannot go on until he pitches. Every fan has seen a pitcher do this—like the judge who kept shaking his head from time to time while counsel was arguing; the lawyer finally turned to the jury and said, "Gentlemen, you might imagine that the shaking of his head by His Honor implied a difference of opinion, but you will notice if you remain here long enough that when His Honor shakes his head there is nothing in it." (Judges, if you are reading, please consider this *obiter*.) One would believe that a no-hit, no-run game, the acme of perfection, the goal of a pitcher, would satisfy even the most exacting battery mate. Yet, at the beginning of the seventh inning of a game under those conditions, "Sarge" Connally, White Sox pitcher, said to his catcher, "Let's mix 'em up; why don't you call for my knuckler?" "Sarge" was probably bored with his own infallibility. He lost the no-hitter and the game on an error.

Of course, no player monopolizes the brains on a ball club. The catcher gives the signals only because he is in a better position than the pitcher to hide them. In a squatting position, the catcher hides the simple finger, fist, or finger-wiggle signs between his legs, complicating them somewhat with different combinations only when a runner on second base in direct line of vision with the signals may look in, perhaps solve them, and flash back another signal to the hitter.

Signal stealing is possible in many ways. The most prevalent self-betrayals are made by the pitcher and catcher themselves. Such detection requires the closest observation. A catcher, after having given the signal, gets set for the pitch; in doing so he may unintentionally, unconsciously, make a slight move—for example, to the right, in order to be in a better position to catch a right-hander's curveball. But more often it is the pitcher who reveals something either to the coaches on the base lines or—what is more telling—to the hitter standing in the batter's box.

The pitcher will betray himself if he makes two distinct motions for two different pitches—as, for example, a sidearm delivery for the curve and over-hand for the fast ball. A pitcher may also betray himself in his windup by raising his arms higher for the fastball than for the curve. In some cases, his eyes are more intent on the plate for one pitch than for another. Usually the curve is more difficult to control. If a pitcher has to make facial distortions, they should be the same for one pitch as for another.

A pitcher covers up the ball with his glove as he fixes it, to escape detection. Otherwise, he may reveal that he is holding the ball tighter for a curve than for a fastball, or even gripping the stitches differently for one than for the other. Eddie Collins, all-time star second baseman, was probably the greatest spy on the field or at bat in the history of the game. He was a master at "getting" the pitch for himself somewhere in the pitcher's manipulation of the ball or in his motion. This ability in no small part helped make him the great performer that he was.

Ballplayers would rather detect these idiosyncrasies for themselves, as they stand awaiting the pitch, than get a signal from the coach. The coach, on detecting something, gives a sign to the hitter either silently by some move—for instance, touching his chest—or by word of mouth—"Come on," for a curve. But this is dangerous unless the coach detects the pitches with 100 percent accuracy. There must be no doubt. Many times, in baseball, a club knows every pitch thrown and still loses. The hitter may be too anxious if he actually knows what is coming, or a doubt might upset him. And there is always the danger of a pitcher's suspecting that he is "tipping" himself off. He then deals in a bit of counterespionage by making more emphatic to the opposition his revealing mannerism to encourage them, only to cross them up at a crucial time.

The whole club plays as a unit to win. The signs that the pitcher and catcher agree on reflect the collective ideas, the judgment of all the players on how to get the opposition out. Preventing runs from scoring is as important as making them. The players know how the pitcher intends to throw to each opponent. They review their strategy before game time, as a result of which they know how the battery is going to work, and they play accordingly. The shortstop and second baseman see the catcher's signs and get the jump on the ball; sometimes they flash it by prearranged signal to the other players who are not in a position to see it. The outfielders can then lean a little, but only after the ball is actually released.

He is a poor catcher who doesn't know at least as well as the pitcher what a hitter likes or doesn't like, to which field he hits, what he did the last time, what he is likely to do this time at bat. The catcher is an on-the-spot witness, in a position to watch the hitter at firsthand. He has to make quick decisions, bearing in mind the score, the inning, the number of men on the bases, and other factors.

VI

Pitchers and catchers are mutually helpful. It is encouraging to a pitcher when a catcher calls for the ball he wants to throw and corroborates his judgment.

The pitcher very seldom shakes a catcher off because they are thinking alike in a given situation. By working together they know each other's system. Pitchers help catchers as much as catchers do pitchers. One appreciative catcher gives due credit to spitballer Red Faber, knuckle-baller Ted Lyons, and fastballer Tommy Thomas, all of the Chicago White Sox, for teaching him, as he caught them, much about catching and working with pitchers. Bill Dickey, great Yankee catcher, will readily admit that Herb Pennock taught him battery technique merely by catching a master and noting how he mixed up his pitches. Ray Schalk, Chicago White Sox, and Steve O'Neill, Cleveland Indians, were two of the greatest receivers and all-round workmen behind the plate in baseball history. Gabby Hartnett and Mickey Cochrane stood out as hitters as well as catchers, Mickey being probably the greatest inspirational catcher of our time.

The catcher works in harmony with the pitcher and dovetails his own judgment with the pitcher's stuff. He finds out quickly the pitcher's best ball and calls for it in the spots where it would be most effective. He knows whether a hitter is in a slump or dangerous enough to walk intentionally. He tries to keep the pitcher ahead of the hitter. If he succeeds, the pitcher is in a more advantageous position to work on the hitter with his assortment of pitches. But if the pitcher is in a hole—a two-and-nothing, three-and-one, or three-and-two count—he knows that the hitter is ready to hit. The next pitch may decide the ball game. The pitcher tries not to pitch a "cripple"—that is, tries not to give the hitter the ball he hits best. But it is also dangerous to overrefine. Taking the physical as well as the psychological factors into consideration, the pitcher must at times give even the best hitter his best pitch under the circumstances. He pitches hard, lets the law of averages do its work, and never second-guesses himself. The pitcher throws a fastball through the heart of the plate, and the hitter, surprised, may even take it. The obvious pitch may be the most strategic one.

The pitcher may throw overhand to take full advantage of the white shirts in the bleacher background. Breaking balls are more effective when thrown against the resistance of the wind. In the latter part of a day, when shadows are cast in a stadium ballpark, the pitcher may change his tactics by throwing more fastballs than he did earlier in the game.

The players are not interested in the score, but merely in how many runs are necessary to tie and to win. They take nothing for granted in baseball. The idea is to win. The game's the thing.

The University of Southern California baseball program, headed by coach Ron Dedeaux, has been highly successful in NCAA play and as a feeder of top-level talent to the major leagues. Fred Lynn, Don Buford, Ron Fairly, Steve Kemp, Dave Kingman, Roy Smalley, Rich Dauer—all are USC products. And Trojan pitchers include Tom Seaver, Bill Lee, Steve Busby, and Jim Barr—yet none of them won as many collegiate games as Bruce Gardner. The All-American Baseball Player of the Year in 1960, Gardner wanted more than anything to pitch in the big leagues. The dream died, and with it the dreamer.

IRA BERKOW and
MURRAY OLDERMAN

An American Tragedy

Los Angeles Police Department
Death Report: File #71-045 104
Date/Time deceased discovered: June 7, 1971. 0900 hours
Interviewing officers: Det. Richard Ortiz, Det. George Kellenberger
   Officers notified of possible suicide at Bovard Athletic Field (baseball field), University of Southern California campus.
   Officers observed deceased lying on his stomach on the grass. Deceased was in an open area of the baseball field approx. 18 ft. n/w of the pitcher's mound. Both hands were partially under the face and neck, with the left hand clutching a Smith & Wesson .38 spcl. rev., 3″ barrel.
   The deceased had a gunshot wound to the left temple with an exit wound in the right temple. The body was rigid. The bullet that passed thru the head could not be located.
   Next to the body, officers found a laminated plaque with the deceased's name on it, naming him as All-American Baseball Player of the Year for 1960. Under the right portion of the body clutched in the right hand was a laminated plaque of a B.S. degree from Univ. of So. Calif. issued to Bruce Clark Gardner.
   Approx. 3 ft. from body toward pitcher's mound was full-page typewritten statement taped to smooth wood board and resembling the laminated plaques. The note indicated possible suicide. It was unaddressed and unsigned.

At six o'clock that morning, Bruce Cameron, a USC caretaker, had seen a body lying prone on the baseball infield, but he didn't approach it. He thought it was a student sleeping off a drunk. A couple of hours later, he and Mitharu Yamasaki, another campus caretaker, came closer. At Heritage Hall, where the USC athletic offices are housed, Virgil Lubberden, who often got to work early, saw them through a window. Jess Hill, then director of athletics, told his assistant to see what was going on.

"He was sprawled out, face down," Lubberden recalled. "I didn't realize at first it was Bruce. It was just unbelievable when I found out who it was."

At the Glasband–Willen Mortuary on Santa Monica Boulevard in Los Angeles, the crowd of mourners was so huge—about 500—that nearly half of them had to stand outside during the funeral service for Gardner.

Marty Biegel, the basketball coach at Fairfax High School, which Gardner had attended, delivered the eulogy with tears in his eyes. "Why? Dear God, explain to us why a thirty-two-year-old man like Bruce, so young, who had so much to give to so many, takes his life."

Bruce Clark Gardner won more games—forty—than any pitcher in USC history, including Tom Seaver, Bill Lee, Jim Barr, and Steve Busby. Before he ever pitched in a varsity game, he was offered a $66,500 bonus by the Chicago White Sox. He was handsome, intelligent, sensitive, and articulate. In junior high and high school, he was president of the student body. He was a talented pianist and entertainer. Nearly everyone who knew him came away feeling better for it.

Ron Mix, an All-American football player at USC and an All-Pro with the San Diego Chargers, knew Gardner well in college. "Bruce was a guy who seemingly had everything that God could bestow on one person," remembered Mix, now an attorney. "He was very bright—one of the top students in our class. He was a first-rate, decent person. If you could design your own life, what you'd like to be, you'd come up with a Bruce Gardner."

And yet, one June night nine years ago, Bruce Gardner, with most of his life left to live, walked out to the pitcher's mound at Bovard Field and put a bullet through his head.

In retrospect, it really ended for Gardner seven years earlier when he was released by Salem (Oregon) of the Northwest League. In 1960, fresh out of USC, he had signed a modest bonus contract of $12,000 with the Los Angeles Dodgers. The next year in the minors he won twenty games. Then he hurt his arm. By 1964, his professional baseball career was over. At twenty-five, Bruce Gardner, who had been brilliantly successful all his young life, considered himself a failure.

He returned home to Los Angeles, his lifelong dream of making the major leagues shattered—a dream he once had every reason to believe would become reality. Now lost, confused, his future unclear, Gardner began to feel frustration and bitterness.

Until now, Gardner's lengthy suicide note was never made public. Nor were the contents of his four thick, meticulously kept scrapbooks—15 × 13 art-form black Naugahyde-covered books with twenty-ring acetate pages—which he started to keep at seventeen.

At first, the scrapbooks tell a love story between Gardner and life. There are numerous photos of his parents, of young Betty Fegen, a pretty, twenty-five-year-old blond when she met Joe Gardner, and dark-haired, round-faced Joe ("robust, singing, smiling, friendly," wrote Gardner).

Betty and Joe married in 1937. Joe worked in an automotive parts store, and later started his own gas station. Gardner was born October 30, 1938. Baby pictures and photos of Gardner with his parents—he resembled his father—dominate the early pages. Happy childhood, happy family.

And then, suddenly, a funeral notice: "In memory of Joseph J. Gardner." Under it, Gardner wrote: "March 3, 1941, my father, Joe Gardner, died of strep throat, probably complicated by his own rheumatic fever as a boy"—and, ironically—"his death just preceded the use of penicillin."

Gardner included in his scrapbooks a poem—"The love and heart of my father"—composed when Gardner was nine:

> When he had a heart
> When he had a soul
> God had to take my
> Father to his goal
>
> I dreamed of him too
> and when I was
> two years old he
> had to go to his
> goal. And after seven years
> I saw his grave.
>
> My father was
> very kind and he
> loved everybody that
> was good and he said,
> Never do anything that
> you will be sorry for,
> and his last words were

God bless you, and I
hope he did.

This is the end
of my story.
So, so long.

Despite his father's death, his boyhood seemed full and joyous—Cub Scouts, Halloween costumes, singing in a synagogue choir. And, at ten, he began to write about what would be the love and consuming passion of his life: baseball.

October, 1948: "Today was Halloween," he wrote. "I went trick or treating. I also thought about baseball. I made believe that I was the second Babe Ruth. When *The Babe Ruth Story* came to a local theater, I went in at two and came out after midnight. I sat through the main feature twice just to watch the Babe three times."

And later: "I had seen someone in school with a Marty Marion glove and I thought it was the greatest. I remember pulling my mother by the arm to the sporting goods store. No one was ever more willing to drop everything to play baseball than I was."

And at twelve, in 1950: "Ever since I have been playing baseball, it has been my ambition to one day be in the big leagues."

He was becoming a standout sandlot pitcher, as well as a model student. He wrote original poems, won "posture" contests, represented his school in city-wide oratorical contests, and was elected president of the student body of Bancroft Junior High in 1953.

"The election would be decided by the candidates' speeches," Gardner wrote. "I was last. This helped make the difference, because their weaknesses built up the dramatic strength of my speech. The scuffling during their speeches turned to silence during mine. I could feel the riveted attention to the last sentence. I won."

He also played the piano—at least partially out of a sense of commitment as the only child of a widowed mother. "After my dad's death, her life became a sacrifice," Gardner captioned one photo of his mother, who was working as a secretary at Temple Israel. "She went without things for herself so that I could have a baseball glove, piano lessons, braces on my teeth and a million other things. May I die on the spot if I try to forget it."

And he added: "I can't imagine how much different it would have been for mother if dad had lived."

When Gardner was about ten, Samuel Fegen, Betty's father, came to live with them in their two-floor, three-bedroom apartment in the primarily Jewish Fairfax district of Los Angeles. An orthodox Jew born in Russia who achieved

prosperity through real estate investments in the U.S., Fegen was a strict man who would get up every morning at four, tuck his fringed prayer shawl into his black pants, and walk to the synagogue to pray.

Under his grandfather's influence, Gardner was bar-mitzvahed, an occasion he describes glowingly. But this is the last mention of religion in the scrapbooks.

Meanwhile, there was growing tension in the home. "The grandpa was always accusing Bruce of stealing, of doing something wrong," recalled Barry Martin Biales, who would become one of Gardner's best friends, the executor of his estate and, ultimately, the owner of his scrapbooks. "Bruce would get upset, being accused of things he never did. And his mother, she was very frugal. There was a lock on the telephone. It was like a twilight zone in that house."

Not surprisingly, Gardner sought support outside the home—usually in the form of father figures. He found several, invariably baseball coaches—Bob Malcolm, his junior high school coach; Frank Shaffer, his coach at Fairfax High; and Tony Longo, father of his friend, Mike Longo, and coach of Gardner's American Legion team. "I practically raised Bruce," Tony Longo would say later. In the summers, Gardner's friends had a routine: meet at school, go to the beach, play baseball at a local park. But Gardner would skip the beach to wait for Longo to take him to play baseball.

Gardner's devotion to baseball was paying dividends. He gained a reputation as a left-handed pitching star in sandlot, American Legion, and high-school ball. Large crowds watched and cheered him.

Although he did not have a blazing fastball, he did have pinpoint control. And his concentration was intense. Art Harris, a boyhood friend and teammate, recalled: "There was always the sense of Bruce being a loner. When he was pitching, he seemed like a stranger in a crowd."

Something Gardner especially liked, he wrote, "was to pitch quickly, to force the action by pouring strikes past the hitter." He put himself on a strenuous running program, and he felt this gave him unmatched endurance and the capacity to work quickly. Friends remembered him running up the steps of the Fairfax bleachers in 90-degree heat in a sweat suit. "I honestly believe I ran more than any athlete in the history of Fairfax," he wrote.

In high school, Gardner was an honor student (he would finish seventy-sixth in a class of 403 in a school with a high academic reputation), student body president, honorary Mayor of Los Angeles for a day, and a piano player and singer who entertained at school assemblies.

Larry Wein, a neighbor and later a high school coach, remembered one incident. "Every kid grows up looking for a hero. In my case, it was Bruce Gardner. In fact, he was a hero for a lot of kids. I lived across the street from Fairfax, and I remember one time I was out on the track, running with my father. Bruce came over and asked if he could work out with us. That blew my mind. I mean, my hero was asking if he could work with us."

Gardner's high school career was a stream of successes. He made the varsity at sixteen, was 11–2 as a junior, and 18–1 in his senior year, leading his team into the city finals.

Major-league scouts came to his games. One was Harold (Lefty) Phillips of the Dodgers, considered a highly astute judge of baseball talent (he later managed the California Angels). Some time after Gardner's senior year in high school, Phillips filed the following confidential scouting report: "Has good stuff for eighteen-year-old but might be as good now as he ever will be. Real intelligent boy—might be too smart, know-it-all type. With a little more pitching and knowledge and experience should go into AA or at best AAA."

The Dodgers were anxious to sign him, even sending Larry Sherry—a former Fairfax High School pitching star and then a minor leaguer in the Dodger farm system—to persuade Gardner. But Gardner had already turned down an offer from the Pittsburgh Pirates of $4,000, and the Dodgers' offer had not been enough to keep him from college. On the advice of high school coach Shaffer and his mother, he had opted for an athletic grant-in-aid to USC.

A primary reason for attending USC, only 10 miles from his home, was Rod Dedeaux, the finest college baseball coach in the country. Dedeaux's sales pitch—that he'd work to get Gardner a bonus later and that a college education was worth $100,000—made sense to Betty Gardner. She was part of a tradition that found solace and power in learning. Sports, at best, were harmless diversions; at worst, a waste of time.

Gardner, in his desire to attach himself to an older man, sensed Dedeaux would fill the void. A graying, paunchy ex-ballplayer, he had become a wealthy trucking magnate in L.A. But, like Gardner, Dedeaux loved baseball first. That accounted for his USC salary—$1 a year. He pursued the job with fervor: "I have one set of rules—do everything absolutely right." With his devotion to discipline and a methodical approach to all things, Gardner seemed a perfect match for Dedeaux.

The freshman team at USC was coached by Joe Curi, which was fine for Gardner. "Curi loved me because I didn't complain and I was always ready," he wrote. "I was 10–0 for the season and held the USC varsity to a 0–0 tie. I was USC's freshman athlete of the year over my teammate Ron Fairly and shotputter Dave Davis. I was quickly becoming the best unsigned prospect in the United States."

This, it seemed, was likely to change quickly. Bob Pease, Gardner's manager on a sandlot team and a bird dog for the White Sox, recommended him to Hollis Thurston, Chicago's top scout on the West Coast. Gardner, accompanied by Tony Longo, was flown to Chicago for a tryout.

Gardner threw to a catcher in the bullpen at Comiskey Park. The big leagues. For twenty minutes, Thurston, Longo, manager Al Lopez, general manager John Rigney and farm director Glen Miller watched the 6-foot-1-inch, 185-pound southpaw.

Then Thurston turned to Longo and said, "We'll take him." He mentioned a big bonus figure. Longo said, "You'll have to talk to his mother." Gardner was only eighteen, and needed his mother's consent to sign.

The big number was $66,500, enormous in 1957. Gardner rushed home to tell his mother the news. Betty Gardner was not moved.

"Bruce came over to my house to talk with my father, who he was very close to," said Biales. "He looked sad. He told us about the offer, and said his mother wouldn't let him sign. My father said, 'Are you kidding? That kind of money doesn't come along every day.' Bruce said he had pleaded with his mother. I remember him saying, 'I was in tears. I asked her to, please, just sign it. I can go to school in the off-season. I'm ready now.' "

Longo couldn't believe it. But he understood. "Bruce was a good boy, the kind of kid you want for your own. He had fights with his mother, but who hasn't? When it was done, he listened to her. It's not like today. When a parent told you to do something, you did it."

Apparently, Mrs. Gardner was influenced greatly by Dedeaux, who emphasized the value of a college education—and that Gardner would get an even better deal after he graduated as a star. "I didn't approve of his signing, because I felt he needed security for the future. I wanted to help him become a success and make a lot of money. The trouble, I suppose, was that he felt I was interfering with his goal." (Betty Gardner remembers her son fondly—"he was magic, a wonderful, adorable person"—but finds it too painful to say much more about him now.)

Several of Gardner's USC teammates would leave school after signing major-league contracts, including Ron Fairly and Len Gabrielson. But Gardner, the dutiful son, stayed and, on the surface, seemed happy. "I don't know of anyone who enjoyed college more than Bruce," said Dedeaux.

Star athlete, excellent student, popular with the coeds, handsome. Gardner tried out for a bit part in the campus play, *Damn Yankees*. He won the lead—playing Joe Hardy, the man who loved baseball more than anything else in life—and was a hit. He had never sung or danced on stage before.

On the field, Gardner made All-League in each of his three varsity years. In his last two (27–4), he made All-NCAA District 8, and, in his final year, he was All-American. In 1960, he was named Player of the Year after leading the Trojans to the final game of the College World Series (USC lost).

And he liked and respected Dedeaux. Don Buford, a USC teammate and later a major leaguer: "Most of the guys who played for Rod felt the same way about him. Playing for Rod was, in some ways, like playing for a major-league manager, he was that good. But most of us looked on him as more than a coach. We relied on his judgment, even in personal matters. Bruce and I were only children. Both our fathers died when we were young, and we were both raised by our mothers. We didn't talk about it much, but, in some ways, it created a bond between us."

Dedeaux remembered Gardner as a friend. "One of the finest boys we ever had. There was never a more cooperative guy in any way."

In 1958, the season after not being allowed to accept the White Sox bonus, Gardner wasn't satisfied with his performance. He wrote: "I had my first poor year. I won almost all my games—13–1, with a 2.62 ERA—because we scored so many runs. But I lost a good deal off my fastball, probably because of losing so much weight." (Gardner had dropped 15 pounds to 170.)

There is a photo of Gardner, customary smile on his face, with three other USC pitchers. Next to the photo, he wrote in his scrapbook: "I look happy on the outside, but I'm thinking, 'What am I doing here? I should be in professional ball now, establishing my credentials.' "

He also wrote about leaving the practice field terribly upset. "I was running away. But who to? My grandfather? My mother? Rod Dedeaux?"

On May 21, 1958, Phillips amended his scouting file on Gardner: "Poor rotation on curve and hangs lots of breaking balls. Poor deception on change-up. His stuff is inconsistent. Poor pitching rhythm. Question his mental setup, don't believe he will stay with the game if the going gets tough. He has gone backward."

During Gardner's senior year, his grandfather died, which caused some family problems. His grandfather's will had been changed shortly before his death, leaving everything to Betty Gardner and nothing to his other daughter and three sons. (Two cousins estimated the inheritance at more than $100,000, although Mrs. Gardner wouldn't confirm the figure.)

"Bruce went to see his aunt and uncle," recalled Biales, "and they didn't want him in the house. 'Go tell your mother to give us the thousands she took,' they told him.

" 'Why blame me?' he said.

" 'We don't want you showing up anymore,' they said."

This disturbed Gardner, who had a great sense of family. Growing up without a father, he had clung to his relatives. But as he was hurt, so he would turn around and exhibit kindness to others. "He'd be at a party," Biales said, "and he'd see a wallflower, a plain girl sitting off by herself. 'That's unfair,' he'd say. 'She's not having a good time.' And he'd ask her to dance."

After Gardner's senior year, Phillips upgraded the scouting report: "Tall, rawboned, long arms, good agility. Best fastball tails away high and outside. Sharp-breaking curve. Should be signed for somewhere in the amount of the first-year draft price." Translation: a bonus of $12,000, to be paid out in three $4,000 installments. Gardner agreed; Phillips signed him.

Gardner was smiling in newspaper photos of the signing, but he later wrote: "I cried that night. I had thrown away three baseball seasons. I had thrown away a very important amount of money. And though I had a college degree, I couldn't see its importance. I was older, and there was something wrong with my arm. It took me a long time to warm up the last few games at USC."

The severity of his arm problem was never spelled out, but the arm was strong enough for him to enter professional baseball at the highest level of the minor leagues, the Dodgers' AAA team in Montreal in the International League.

Oddly enough, however, by major-league standards he was less of a prospect than after his freshman year. At eighteen, he didn't have the outstanding fastball. But he might have developed one. At twenty-one, he didn't have that fastball, and he never would.

Dedeaux thought it was a good deal anyway. "If he had signed after his freshman year," said the USC coach, "he would never have been sent to a AAA team. He'd have started much lower in the minors."

Perhaps. But the White Sox might have taken special care of him, bringing him along properly to protect their investment.

Montreal was a rude awakening. "He goes to Montreal," said Biales, "which is like forty-two games behind, and they had all these greasy old ballplayers. Bruce is knocking on hotel doors, 'Hello, this is Bruce Gardner reporting.'

" 'Get the hell out of here, you punk kid. I got a broad in here.' He had to sleep in the lobby. You know, they broke him in at Montreal. He had been a virgin. The guys said, 'Hey, we got to take care of this kid.' So they took him out and got him laid.

"Some people wonder if he was a homosexual, and couldn't face that fact in his macho sports world. If he was, I never knew it. He loved women, loved their bodies. He had a lot of affairs as he got older."

To the hardened veterans of pro ball, Gardner must have seemed vulnerable. Clean-cut, seemingly naive, a musician, college kid. There were few collegians in pro baseball then, and only a few had degrees, as Gardner did. Many players had not finished high school. Some veteran managers had not even attended high school.

Gardner wrote to Dedeaux: "Boy, what a difference. Pro ball isn't the glamorous life everybody thinks it is."

Johnny Werhas, a USC teammate who later played for the Angels and the Dodgers, felt that a lot of baseball people simply didn't understand Gardner. "They thought he was an oddball. But I tell you, he was way ahead of his time. He was eating health foods way before the fad. He went to chiropractors before anyone else. Once he removed all the hair on his left arm, as an experiment, to cut down wind resistance. People laughed, but years later swimmers like Mark Spitz and other athletes were doing the same thing." He also stood on his head doing yoga in the dugout. He said it brought more blood to his pitching arm.

After some undistinguished appearances at Montreal, where his record was 0–1, he reported for his first spring training at Dodgertown in Vero Beach, Florida, in 1961. The facilities were first-rate, but the caliber of baseball minds did not impress Gardner. "I can't believe these people", Gardner told Biales. "The only smart guy I met there was Walter O'Malley." O'Malley owned the Dodgers and once gave Gardner $100 for playing his favorite song on the lounge piano.

That first spring, Gardner still had not gotten over a case of mononucleosis. "Mononucle-what?" said one of the coaches. "Get out there and run. When I was your age, Gardner, I never had this mono-stuff you're talking about." Gardner's response? "Go tell Roy Campanella when you were his age, you never got in an auto accident." Campanella, the great Dodger catcher, was paralyzed for life after an auto mishap.

Gardner, who was supposed to be assigned to Greenville in AA classification, was sent instead to Reno of the California League. Class C. "What a waste,"

Gardner told a friend. "I'll probably win forty games. I should be pitching AAA ball."

Gardner was 20–4 at Reno. In his Dodger scouting report, Reno manager Roy Smalley described Gardner: "Excellent attitude, exceptional aptitude. Improving steadily, has endurance, good fielder, hits well, mentally tough. Has a chance to make majors." Smalley did not mention Gardner's occasional habit of standing on his head in the dugout, sometimes while the National Anthem was being played.

The official 1962 program of the Dodgers lists a handful of players with exceptional promise on their minor-league clubs. One was Gardner: "Former Trojan Bruce Gardner topped the California League in four departments. His 20–4 record gave him top victory total, and best percentage (.833). He also pitched most complete games, eighteen, and was the ERA leader with 2.82."

After the season ended, Gardner went to Fort Ord, California, to fulfill a military obligation. He was to serve six months and be out in time for spring training. But the Cold War escalated into the Berlin Crisis, active duty rosters were frozen, and Gardner injured his arm on maneuvers—possibly one time when he fell off a truck. Finally released in July, he was assigned to Spokane, a AAA team in the Pacific Coast League.

At the time, his mother was staying with one of Gardner's paternal aunts in Oakland. She begged him to take her along to Spokane. He didn't want to, but he couldn't stand to see her cry. So he piled everything he had in the world—including his mother—into his car and took off. He met the team on the road in Seattle and sent his mother on in the loaded car to Spokane to find an apartment.

Gardner had made $600 a month in Reno. He expected a minimum raise to $800 and thought he would probably get $1,000. He received a new contract for $700. And that wasn't the worst of it. "I came into Spokane at seven in the morning—and there my mother was in the car packed to overflowing and no place to go," he wrote. Apparently, only two places met Betty Gardner's standards of frugality. "One was a dingy basement apartment. The other was a *fucked* up, dilapidated Chinese hotel. I put my hand over my forehead and eyes and just sat still. I gave up. We took the Chinese hotel. I went to sleep on an empty, unmade cot and later got up and went to the ballpark like a POW. This was early August, 1962, and around this time Marilyn Monroe committed suicide. And this idea for the first time entered and cemented itself in my mind." It was also the first time Gardner had used any profanity in his writings.

He finished 1–5 in Spokane. There were hysterical shouting matches with his mother in which Gardner dredged up old hurts about not signing the big bonus contract. He was suffering, his arm hurt, and he was failing as a pitcher.

"I didn't sleep nights," he wrote. "Instead, I took piano lessons in Spokane. After each game I would go to the studio and beat the piano until morning. I even smoked cigarettes for the first time. Then I could go back to the Chinese hotel and sleep all day on that shitty cot."

Spokane manager Preston Gomez's succinct report on Gardner: "Says arm hurts. So have to wait for him to get better before make determination."

There is still vagueness about the origins of his arm problem. But it was clear the snap in his pitches was diminishing. So was his confidence as he prepared for another season. He wrote: "In spring training, Tommy Lasorda didn't even say hello. [The year before, Lasorda had held Gardner up as an example of how to throw the difficult 'drop' curve.] It's a game of survival of the fittest. A twenty-game winner fits. A one-game winner doesn't. My pitching was forced. I had trouble getting anything on the ball."

During his years in the minors, there is no mention of his father in the scrapbooks. Two photographs put in about this time are noteworthy, though. One shows Gardner's father in a dark suit, buttoned up, smiling, with his arm around a friend. In the photo directly below, taken more recently, Gardner is posed and dressed identically—with his arm around the son of his father's friend.

In 1963, he was assigned to Salem (Oregon) in Class A, pitched poorly, and was sent to Great Falls (Montana) in the Pioneer League. His last night in Salem was spent with a girl named Jo. "It was the most beautiful time I'd ever had. In the morning she brought her baby over (from a previous marriage), made breakfast. I dreamed of life as it should be, packed everything I owned again into the car and traveled to Great Falls."

There, getting by on guile, he was 10–4 with a 4.07 ERA. And the dream of a major-league career persisted. That December he sent Christmas cards with a picture of himself in a Dodger uniform.

Betty Gardner still worried about her son. Early in 1964, she wrote to Fresco Thompson, vice-president of personnel for the Dodgers:

May I introduce myself? I am Bruce Gardner's mother. Confidentially, I am concerned about my son. Could you give me any information about his future with the Dodgers? How fast is his ability as a pitcher? How is he progressing, etc.?

I am very proud of my son and eager to help him make good. He is very ambitious and loves baseball very much. I wonder if there is anything I can do to help him achieve his aspirations.

P.S. Of course, I would not want Bruce to know that I am writing to you as he may think I am being too forward.

Thompson responded:

You are, undoubtedly, aware that Bruce began his professional career by winning 20 and losing 4 in 1961. For some reason, he has been unable to recapture the form which he showed in 1961.

At spring training in 1962, he indulged in self-diagnosis and self-treatment of real and imaginary ills. On two occasions, I personally went to his room to see why he had not reported for practice. Each time I found him in bed with what he had diagnosed as a respiratory condition. He was treating himself despite the fact that we had a full time Doctor and Registered Nurse on the premises at all times.

He then began visiting chiropractors in Vero Beach and elsewhere for soreness in his arm. Mrs. Gardner, in all my baseball experience, I have never heard of one of these bone-poppers curing a baseball player of anything.

Baseball is a difficult and demanding taskmaster. One must, during the baseball season, apply himself solely and diligently to becoming a ballplayer. This I do not think Bruce does at all times. With most youngsters in the Dodger Organization, baseball is the end. With Bruce, this is not so; baseball is a means to an end. What that end is no amount of probing and delving has uncovered.

Gardner discovered these letters in 1968 and put them in his scrapbooks. He wrote: "Boy, oh boy. Some of the things she says in that letter sure hurt. 'Proud of my son and eager to help him make good.' How come we never discussed this? She didn't seem proud in 1957. It's a little late now.

"But Fresco's answers are as ridiculous as my mother's questions. 'How fast is his pitching ability?' Her main question was 'etc.' That's Jewish for 'I don't know what I'm interested in asking so you tell me.'

"So he tells her that I was sick in 1962. Since I was actually sick during 1961, that's also the year I had my successful season. He forgets I was in the Army in 1962. Then I suppose he convinced my mother I wasn't really dedicated. Fresco had a real talent for: thinking, over-eating, over-drinking and using the word 'taskmaster'."

Gardner's last training camp was in 1964 at Vero Beach. "Bruce was the hardest working guy I ever saw," said Jimmy Campanis, his catcher that final season. "He would run and run and run." But he broke an ankle practicing slides and wasn't ready to pitch again until early summer, when he reported to Salem. A rule of thumb among major-league teams is three years to rise in the minors. Salem was Gardner's last chance.

"Good kid," recalled his last manager, Stan Wasiak. "Hard worker, high-class boy. But sometimes I got the feeling he thought he was above me, in intellectual status."

At the ballpark, Gardner struggled to a 2–2 record in nineteen appearances, finished none of his three starts, and had an earned-run average of 5.40. An old USC teammate, Marcel Lachemann, played in the same league that year and thought Gardner pitched "almost like an amateur. It was sad watching it." He was nearly twenty-six years old, a faded prospect.

"I was up in the press box late one night after a game," remembered Bob Schwartz, sports news editor of Salem's morning newspaper, the *Oregon Statesman*. "I saw Bruce on the field, fully dressed. He was standing on the mound. I'm sure he didn't know I was there. He smoothed the rubber with his foot, then walked around the mound. I went back to work. When I had finished, he was gone."

In a confidential Dodger report, a scout wrote: "Has no future." Gardner concurred. "My arm could only take an inning," he wrote. "Damaged by now." But he felt bitterness toward the Dodger organization: "Too many kinds of people that can't be decent unless you're leading the bandwagon."

From the scrapbooks: "Notice of Official Release. September 30, 1964. You are officially notified of the non-disposition of your contract. You are released unconditionally. Fresco Thompson."

Gardner now faced the classic dilemma of the former pro athlete, the one-time star: What do you do when the cheers stop, when the lifelong dream collapses? Whom could he blame? Whom could he strike back at? He was not a violent person. He never even threw at a hitter. He remembered when Marilyn Monroe committed suicide, how he felt. One day, about a month after he was released, Gardner went to Vernon, a small town near Los Angeles, and bought a .38 Smith & Wesson blue-steel pistol in a pawn shop.

He told Biales: "I went home to plan to shoot myself, but the phone rang and got my mind off it."

Biales was stunned. "Are you serious?"

"Yeah," said Gardner. "Everything's so low. The baseball's over and there's nothing left for me."

On June 4, 1965, Betty Gardner, now having frequent shouting matches with her son, again wrote to Fresco Thompson:

My son seems so unhappy at the end result of his baseball career.

I hate to see him so unhappy. It is partially due to a scout making a high offer one day and reneging the next day, that has caused Bruce to be this way.

I think perhaps if he could in any way work with baseball (which has been his dream since he was 10 years old) that he would not now be so depressed. Do you think there is any phase of the game he could fit into?

Thompson replied two weeks later:

I am indeed sorry that Bruce appears to be so unhappy due to the fact that he is now out of baseball.

I must say that Bruce has absolutely no one to blame but himself for his present predicament. We gave Bruce every opportunity to take full advantage of his God-given baseball talents. He appeared, however, to have many other things on his mind.

I regret that I cannot advise you of some other phase of the game in which he might fit. Professional baseball is an exacting taskmaster and in order to succeed, a full-time effort is required.

Gardner wrote: "Now my career is over. Eight years late and now my mother is concerned. My mother's philosophy is to get concerned when it's too late. But create the predicament by not using reason beforehand. She says a scout reneged. I guess because I didn't sign. He didn't renege. She shouted, 'No,' at me. I'm afraid the shadows of Rod Dedeaux in the wings made her unable to move in any direction.

"Quit bothering the wrong man [Fresco Thompson], mother! Looking back, I don't see what I could have done differently except to quit baseball earlier. My life was taken away."

Outwardly, Gardner seemed to adjust. He was a real-estate salesman, then sold mutual funds. He dressed nattily and flashed jewelry. In 1968, he won a trip to Bermuda and the next year was awarded another trip—to Puerto Vallerta, Mexico—for his sales success.

There he fell in love with a "beautiful, intelligent and charming girl" from Vancouver named Donna. He wrote a song about her the first day he met her, "with the sound of xylophone and mariachi in my mind."

> . . . there wasn't anything such as tomorrow
> They would wine and dine and laugh,
> And the day just seemed like half;
> She was the essence of his life—
> such a madonna.
> But when it came time to leave,
> How his soul would ache and grieve;
> It tore his heart to have to say, Mañana Donna, mañana Donna,
> It's so hard to be apart,
> For you have entered in my heart,
> Life is too short to want to say,
> mañana Donna . . .

He visited her in Canada but soon concluded, "Her enthusiasm didn't equal mine."

There were other girls—exotic Latins he met in some of the strip joints in which he played the piano—and for a time there was a serious liaison with a slim blond named Pat. But they all faded, too. He complained he could never get the girl he wanted.

In 1970, his mutual funds career collapsed because of a slump in the market. Friends and relatives who had invested with him lost money—and he felt real guilt about it. He trained to become a bank manager for a savings company, but he was let go after four months. He was told he didn't have the background for the position.

"In the last two weeks of 1970, I became very despondent and thought of ending my life, which hasn't been a rare thought for me for over a decade now," he wrote.

His cousin, Paul Fegen, remembered Gardner's disillusionment with life "because he couldn't make of himself what everyone else thought he should have. He was disappointed that he couldn't make money, because in school he was always the hero. He was like an aging actor who no longer could get parts. With Bruce, it happened suddenly."

Gardner still maintained an interest in baseball, and often went to games at Dodger Stadium with Biales. He would sit high behind home plate, watch the pitcher intently, and say, "That should be me out there." Periodically, he visited the Dodger clubhouse to look up old teammates who had made it—Campanis, Lefebvre, Werhas, Fairly. "I didn't sense any bitterness or envy in him," said Werhas. "He seemed happy for me."

So to the world at large, Gardner maintained a smile. And he still went out of his way to extend a kindness. In December of 1970, he organized a surprise party for the managers of his apartment building, Arthur and Virginia Searles. He wrote a letter to the apartment building owner, Mr. Meltzer, describing the good job they did. The Searleses framed the letter.

"But do you know what else Bruce did?" Virginia Searles would later ask rhetorically. "He deliberately sent the invitation to Mr. Meltzer a day late, so he wouldn't be there. Mr. Meltzer wasn't the friendly type, and Bruce felt he didn't appreciate us as much as he should. When Mr. Meltzer called me, he said, 'I would have come to the party but I got the letter a day late.' All of us in the building thought it was a wonderful joke."

To earn a steady living, Gardner took a job as a physical education and health teacher at Dorsey High School in southwest Los Angeles. It's a predominantly black school, with a small percentage of Oriental students. Gardner also coached the junior varsity baseball team to a 13–2 record, winning a championship for the first time in the school's history.

The star of the jayvee squad was Vassie Gardner, no relation. Vassie Gardner is black. He was a pitcher; he is now an outfielder with Chattanooga of the Southern League.

"Mr. Gardner reminded me of the coach on the TV program, *White Shadow*—only he was years ahead of it, and he was for real," said Vassie Gardner. "We were mainly a black team, and it was hard for me to believe a white guy would really care for me. He thought I had the potential to make the major leagues. But I was running loose on the streets. He'd call my house to make sure I was all right. Once he asked me to move in with him. He'd kind of adopt me.

"Guys used to joke around, say Mr. Gardner's funny. A faggot. Because of the way he walked. Real straight. But he wasn't effeminate. He scared the hell out of me when he got mad.

"One day, I was late for practice. He told me to take a lap around the field. I told him I wasn't going to do it. Oh, did he get angry. So I said, 'Well, I better run a lap.' About halfway, I ducked behind a backstop on the other side of the field. As soon as I stopped, I felt someone grab me from behind. It was Mr. Gardner; he'd been running behind me. He wrestled me to the ground. He was strong. And he began hitting me in the stomach. Playfully, not really hurting me. 'I'm tired of your bullshit,' he told me. 'You're going to start doing things right, and you're going to get your ass out here and become a ballplayer.'

"He talked about his career. Something messed it up, a bad arm. He was my man. I wish he was still living. It happened too fast; I was just getting to know him."

Ironically, at the same time he was having this kind of impact on his players, Gardner was telling friends and relatives how he hadn't found anything worth doing, how useless he felt. And aimless.

Jim Lefebvre, his teammate at Salem and then with the Dodgers, saw him sitting alone in the box seats in Dodger Stadium one day in 1971. "I went over to him and asked him how he was doing. He said, 'Oh, okay.' I asked him what he was up to, and he told he was coaching junior high school. I asked how he liked it. He said, 'It's not what I want to be doing.' His eyes had a vacant quality. He seemed alone, inside himself."

On the first Thursday in June of 1971, his boyhood buddy, Art Harris, saw Gardner at Dodger Stadium at the city high-school-baseball championship game. "Good," Art thought to himself, "he's with some other people." Harris was sensitive to Gardner's loneliness. Then Harris spotted Dedeaux and Casey Stengel, a close friend of Dedeaux, walking down the aisle together. "Bruce turned around and saw Dedeaux," Harris said. "Rod gave him the usual, 'Hi, Tiger.' Bruce's face turned as white as a gym towel. Looking back, I know now that he was already planning to kill himself."

Bruce Gardner, sensitive and dedicated, wasn't trained to handle failure. When Al Campanis, the Dodgers' vice-president for personnel (and father of

Gardner's teammate, Jimmy), was asked what he remembered most about Gardner, he said:

"He didn't win."

On Friday afternoon, June 4, 1971, Vassie Gardner was playing basketball in the Dorsey gym and turned to see his coach staring at him. "He was just standing and watching me," he said. "I never saw that stare before. I guess he knew he was going to go away."

Gardner stayed in all of Saturday and Saturday night. He fastidiously arranged his bookshelves. In his bedroom, there was a neat pile of *Playboy* magazines, which would later shock one of his aunts. His clothes in the closet were hung meticulously in sections—pants, suits, coats. Stacks of record albums neatly flanked his stereo. The blond wood furniture was dusted. The seascape oil painting on the wall behind the stereo was perfectly straight. The lid of the piano was pulled down over the keys.

On Sunday, Virginia Searles saw Gardner neatly folding his wash in the laundry room. She said, "Good morning, Bruce." He said, "Good morning." That was it. She knew Gardner was a private person, though friendly. If he didn't want to say anything more, that was fine.

That was the last time anyone saw Bruce Gardner alive.

At 11:30, Arthur Searles made his nightly security check around the building. He noticed that Gardner's Buick LeSabre was parked in an odd place. The driveway had eighteen individual carports on each side, with Gardner's spot designated No. 1, his apartment number. He always parked it there. Perfectly. This night, the car was parked on the incline at the end of the driveway. Since Searles saw no light in Gardner's apartment, he decided not to knock. Gardner—"such a thoughtful neighbor"—would take care of the problem the next day.

At that moment, Gardner was probably lying in bed in the dark. Apparently, he had made the decision at least as far back as Friday. Ken Bailey, the tennis coach, had seen Gardner grading books for his four gym classes. Bailey thought it was odd. School didn't close for two weeks.

Sometime after midnight, it is presumed, Gardner rose from his bed and began his final preparations:

The chronology is uncertain, but he probably sat down at his Remington manual typewriter to type his suicide note. He poured himself a shot of Scotch. He kept the liquor for guests, because he never drank. But in times of distress, he would often do something out of character—like the time in Spokane when an argument with his mother drove him to his first cigarette. As he typed up two copies of the suicide note—and a will, which he left in the roller—he drank some more. (He would eventually consume the equivalent of four highballs, according to the coroner's report.) The will gave most of his $3,000 estate to Biales. He left $1 to his mother.

Gardner then placed one copy of the suicide note into the last page of his scrapbook, and carefully taped the other note onto a wooden board.

He washed his glass and returned the bottle of Scotch to the cabinet.

He shaved, brushed his dark brown curly hair—cut short because he didn't like the way it kinked.

He put on a tan sport shirt with thin collar, a black sweater, blue-striped slacks, and black loafers. Then he slipped into a brown corduroy jacket with leather buttons.

He gathered the three plaques he would carry with him: the baseball All-American certificate, his USC diploma, the suicide note.

From the back of his top drawer in the bedroom, he removed the pistol and put it in his jacket pocket.

Before leaving, he made his bed. A detective would say later that the apartment was so tidy it looked as if Gardner had been expecting guests.

He picked up the plaques, closed the lights, walked outside, and double-locked the door. It was cool in Los Angeles for a June morning, 57 degrees. He buttoned his jacket. It was about three A.M.

He put the three plaques in the car, and backed out onto Cattaraugus Avenue.

The route he usually took was through a quiet neighborhood of small, single-story homes to the Santa Monica Freeway. The divided concrete strip is invariably quiet at that hour. On the left are the lights of Beverly Hills and the Hollywood hills. Two of his closest cousins, Paul Fegen and Arlene Rosenthal, were asleep in large homes in the high section—the kind of luxurious homes Gardner never had. He drove past the Fairfax Avenue turnoff, exit to the neighborhood in which he was the big star. He drove past La Brea, the exit he would normally take to Dorsey High School. The exits rolled by—Crenshaw, Arlington, Normandy, and finally Vermont and the turnoff to USC. He almost certainly clicked the right-turn signal. He was a careful driver, never got a ticket, followed all the rules of the road.

At Jefferson Boulevard, he would turn left, then right on McClintock to the USC campus. The security guardhouse, built on a small island at the entrance, was empty. He turned into 34th Street and parked halfway down the block. Bovard Field was only 300 yards away. It was quiet.

Gardner got out of the car with his three plaques, the gun in his pocket. He walked past Founders Hall, then through the slightly dewy hedge to the baseball field. The gate was locked. He climbed over the wooden fence, probably at its lowest point—along left field—where it was 7 feet high.

The moon was three nights short of full, and it cast a bright light, creating shadows on the field. Gardner walked across the moist grass to the pitcher's mound, surrounded by empty stands which were once filled with fans cheering for him. He placed the suicide note on the grass at the edge of the circle. He walked a few feet more and lay down, halfway to second base. He lay straight. When they found him, he wouldn't be crumpled and awkward. His right elbow cradled the All-American plaque and his degree. With his pitching hand, he removed the pistol from his jacket pocket, then raised it to his temple.

Only the typewritten note nearby would be left to explain.

Let my blood be the pathetic proof to those who have heard Rod Dedeaux say that a college education is worth $100,000 more in a man's lifetime. Because it is so deceitfully true. The man who starts at $800 a month versus the one who starts at $600 a month will wind up, after forty years, with $100,000 more.

And isn't that enough reason to shatter the hopes and dreams of an eighteen-year-old boy who has the opportunity to sign into professional baseball with offers high in five figures?

To keep him in college, don't let him believe that he could do anything with that kind of money but squander it. Don't ask what it is the boy wants to accomplish. Because he might tell you that he would like to go into professional baseball, especially in light of the fact that many who know baseball have regarded him very highly. And that it's his love.

Then don't look too carefully at the facts. Don't think that a good student—president of Bancroft Junior High and Fairfax High—with the determination of a winning miler, captain and three-year cross-country runner, and the excellence of an All-City pitcher, could possibly have the wherewithal to make decisions concerning his own life.

Since he is too young to sign for himself, scare his mother. It's even easier, because his father passed away when the son was three. Let the mother feel that her boy will be wandering skid row if he leaves college. So that when he begs her to let him sign, she has nothing but shouts of "no." Do all these things carefully, Rod Dedeaux, and you will have an All-American. And his mother will get her vicarious college degree. Don't let any of his advantages get in the way of your National Championship.

He'll have graduated before your half-truths become the realities of his place in the world. And then he'll wonder where is the magic in the education you don't seek, and why so much energy is compulsively wasted in containing his bitterness and moving one foot in front of the other to get to each day's meaningless job. Where his $800 a month won't buy the home he's never had, meet the friends he's never entertained, nor call the mother he never wants to see. To what direction have the fragments of his broken heart discarded his ability to give and receive love?

But given another thirty-two years—in retirement he'll be able to look back with that overpowering joyful knowledge that some people in their work-a-day world jobs didn't earn the $100,000 more that he did in his. And that's when he'll hug his diploma and die of unhappiness. But somehow I don't need to wait anymore for that day. I reached it years and years ago.

I saw no value in my college education. I saw life going downhill every day and it shaped my attitude toward everything and everybody. Everything and every feeling that

I visualized with my earned and rightful start in baseball was the focal point of continuous failure. No pride of accomplishment, no money, no home, no sense of fulfillment, no leverage, no attraction. A bitter past, blocking any accomplishment of a future except age.

I brought it to a halt tonight at thirty-two.

The 1980s have wrought a queasy new turn on the alumni reunion: a curdled-fantasy baseball camp for the old-boy set, complete with now-rotund heroes of yore. Was Dorian Gray ever on a baseball card? Or Ricardo Montalban? Never mind—only a determined spoilsport would find this frolic a downer. Boys of winter, play on.

ROY BLOUNT, JR.

We All Had a Ball

I have a T-shirt and two sweat shirts that say "I PLAYED BASEBALL AGAINST THE 1969 CUBS." This intro lets me get on with the rest of the story. "Hello, my name is Blat, Blong, Bough—whatever, it doesn't matter—and the very fact that Ferguson Jenkins was playing me deep enough to catch a ball hit 350 feet tells you something" is how I usually begin.

"Excuse me?" people reply.

"I hit a ball 350 feet," I say.

"Where?"

"Pulled it dead to left. It was caught—over the shoulder, but still, he must have been playing me pretty deep—by Ferguson Jenkins. He was in left at the time. You know how guys over thirty-five are; they like to live out their fantasies, and Jenkins probably always wanted to rob a sportswriter of extra bases. Earlier in camp, he called me—just a minute, I think I have the exact wording somewhere . . . here it is: 'A good hitter.' O.K., you *could* say that's the kind of thing he might say to his nephew, but still. . . ."

"No, I mean where, like in, what park?"

"Scottsdale Stadium. Arizona. Which was strangely appropriate, because. . . ."

"Oh. Thin air."

Thin air. I may have to get another T-shirt that says "I HIT A BASEBALL 350 FEET AND WHY IS IT THAT EVERYONE'S REACTION IS 'THIN AIR'?" The whole trouble with my baseball career, and my life, is that my T-shirts have to have too many words on them.

My game shirt, the authentic Chicago away uniform shirt I was wearing when I hit the ball 350 feet, has only one word on it: "CUBS." The All-Star Baseball School's weeklong camp last month for men over thirty-five, which culminated with a game against some of the '69 Cubs, was the closest I will come to fitting myself into that word, that one round patch.

How close was that?

What? Who are *you* with?

This was an oft fantasized experience you had, right? So this is your oft fantasized interview.

About time.

You weren't satisfied with your press coverage at the camp?

No. *Time* magazine unaccountably attributed my 350-foot shot to Art Lessel, a sixty-three-year-old pilot.

Yeah, but what about the thin air?

I'll tell you about thin air. Thin air is when Randy Hundley, who was one of the former Cubs I played against, pops a ball incalculably high into what we call the Big Arizona Sky. Being camped under a fly in Arizona is like looking over the side of a boat after a camera you just dropped into Lake Michigan. And I'll tell you something else about thin air. Thin air is when I, the third baseman, fresh from the triumph of hitting a ball 350 feet, find myself in the position of having to come to grips with a pop-up that resembles the average person's concept of a pop-up about as much as Ralph Sampson resembles your gym teacher.

In other words, a tough chance.

But that's not all. To try to catch it, I have to drift toward the same spot where, in 1970, I had my darkest day as a sportswriter, when Leo Durocher—who managed the Cubs then and was managing them again in this game—branded me as the anti-Cub right there in front of the whole team. Anyway, I miss it.

Really? The pop-up? Why do you miss it?

I don't miss it now. I missed it then. And three days later it's on national TV. At least my friends and I think that's me we see, though I find out much later it's some other guy missing a different pop-up. But by then, the damage to my psyche and reputation had been done.

What were you called? You and the other sixty-two men over thirty-five who, for $2,195 each, lived out a boyhood dream by working out with major leaguers?

"Campers." I would have liked "prospects" better. By the way, two or three guys under thirty-five slipped in. Can you imagine how far I would have hit the ball if I'd been their age? I'm forty-one! True, I never hit a ball that far when I *was* under thirty-five. That was the longest ball I ever hit in my life. And maybe the last. What a way to go out! But what if I'm getting better? What if I have yet to come into my oft fantasized-own? Baseball! You just won't let go! I might say, however, that it was never my boyhood dream to miss a pop-up in front of thousands of people.

The All-Star School, which is operated by Hundley and Chicago entrepreneur Allan Goldin, usually instructs kids, right?

Yes, we were the historic first middle-aged campers. And we seem to have struck a chord. Every television network was all over us. Another Cub camp, also in Scottsdale, is planned for April, and a company called Baseball Fantasies Fulfilled has announced an April camp in Tempe featuring old Dodgers.

How did the Cub camp work?

Very well. We had the Scottsdale facilities that the Cubs formerly used for spring training, and we were drilled in fundamentals by '69 Cubs Hundley, Jenkins, Billy Williams, Ron Santo, Ernie Banks, Glenn Beckert, Jim Hickman, Rich Nye, Ken Rudolph and Gene Oliver, and by slightly later-vintage Cubs José Cardenal and Steve Stone. The old Cubs also played with us in intrasquad games. Nobody wanted to look like a jerk in front of them. Take away the Cubs and the camp would have degenerated into middle-aged doctors, lawyers, brokers, and businessmen rolling around on the ground fighting over whose bat it was. There should be Cubs at the U.N.

And on the last day of camp, in Scottsdale Stadium—where the fences are all deeper than 350 feet—before around 4,200 fans and a host of media folks who don't really care about the longest ball a person ever hit in his entire life, the old Cubs beat us 23–6.

Does that mean you were seventeen runs short of being as good as a team of major leaguers, one of whom, Jenkins, is still active, and, incidentally, is 6 feet 5 inches and is the guy who caught your soaring drive over his shoulder?

It's hard to say. I do know that I came within about 15 inches of catching what you would call a major-league pop-up. I remember thinking to myself, while drifting over toward the spot in foul territory where I first met Durocher in 1970, "Oh, well, God, I guess . . . mine." Privately, I hoped that Jimmy Stuart, a commodities trader in Chicago who won the plaque for Most Aggressive Camper, would hustle pushily over from shortstop and call me off of it, and I would've given him a look of annoyance and let him have it. But he didn't.

I looked up at that thing. And what struck me was, "This pop-up doesn't care who I am." Also, the sun was in my eyes. "The sun is in my eyes," I thought. "And I *still* don't know what made Durocher say what he said in

1970. And anyway, what in the hell am I supposed to do with this thing? I'm a writer. I'm forty-one years old. And I was never all that good when I was twenty-one. And it's not even really spring yet. The pop-ups are ahead of the third basemen. And . . ."

And you missed it. . . . Could you give us an idea of what a typical day in camp was like?

Thank you for changing the subject. First of all, we take a bus from our hotel to the '69 Cubs' spring workout fields (now used by the Giants) on Hayden Road, where we enter a dressing room and don big-league uniforms. Right? Most of us would have been willing to die at that point. All right, my pants were too big. But if angels offered me a golden robe, would I say, "Only if you've got it in a 44 long"? And the old Cubs are sitting around telling stories about Durocher, their manager in '69 (as well as '70, when I met him), and how hard he was on nonregulars, whom he referred to as "the rest of you bleep." There was the time Lee Thomas went up to pinch-hit and Durocher sat on the bench saying, "Look at that bleep bleep bleep. He can't run, he can't hit, I don't know why the bleep bleep bleep I got him. Look at him! He's going to pop up." And sure enough, Thomas popped up. Durocher swore for several minutes, then turned to Ted Savage and told him to pinch-hit next. "Why should I go up there," said Savage, "and subject myself to abuse?"

Would you say you were subjected to big-league baseball without the abuse?

Well, to some extent. In all candor, I would have to say that this was where the $2,195 came in. Half of that may have been for overhead and the other half for not having Durocher come in until the end of the week. But there was some abuse, after all. There were all those reporters. And aerobics.

Aerobics were led by Susie Warren, who is what you might call lithe. And she made us campers do terrible things with our bodies, to music. Cardenal would accompany us, using a bat as a baton and crying *"No más! No más!"* Otherwise, the Cubs grunted and groaned with the rest of us. I have found it possible to live a normal life without reflecting upon the fact that I have hamstrings. I did not find this possible while performing aerobics.

Hamstrings a-twang, we would leave Susie and take on the easier part of the day: playing hardball. We would divide into five squads and rotate from field to field and Cub to Cub. Williams showed me that I'd been holding a bat wrong all my life. You're supposed to hold it up in the forward, or fingers, part of the hand, not back up against the pad. Because when—or if—you hit a ball thrown at big-league batting-practice speed with the bat held back up against your pad, your right pad, if you bat right-handed, turns various shades of blue. This subject arose when I asked Williams why I had developed indigo hand.

It was Santo who explained why I'd developed it on my left hand, too. That was because I've been holding the glove wrong all my life. You're supposed to hold it so that the ball always hits in the webbing, he said. This was a piece of advice I was unable to use. I feel I'm doing well when I catch a ball with any part of the leather. Playing third base, I also developed indigo shoulder, chest, and thigh.

Hickman and Jenkins also explained to me that I'd been holding the ball wrong all my life. If you hold it along the seams, it veers. This is what Jenkins usually does, because as a pitcher he usually wants it to veer. This is what Hickman never did, because as a fielder he didn't want it to. This is what I, as a fielder, have often done down through the veers.

There are a great many intangibles in baseball, aren't there?

Yes, and I wonder whether I will ever get a feel for them.

What else would you do on a typical day of training, after finding out that you've always been holding everything wrong?

Go back to the dressing room. Sit around sweaty. Take a shower with a member of the Hall of Fame, Banks, who's saying, "There is a vast reservoir of potential in all of us waiting to be tapped!" Stiffen up. Walk out toward the bus like somebody who just got off a horse. Yet feel *primed*. Feel *bodily*.

And go back to the hotel and sit in the whirlpool with the Cubs. Santo tells about the time Rogers Hornsby went through the Cubs' minor-league camps checking out all the hitters. Hornsby called a bunch of them together in some bleachers and went down the rows. The first guy was black. "You better go back to shining shoes," Hornsby said, "because you can't hit." And he said more or less the same thing to one prospect after another. Santo and Williams were sitting together. "If he says that to me," Santo said to Williams, "I'm going to cry." And Hornsby came to Williams. "You," Hornsby said, "can hit in the big leagues right now." And he said the same thing to Santo.

Later, Santo was up in the bigs, in the All-Star Game. "And there are McCovey and Aaron and Mays, and Ron Santo, and some photographer is taking a picture of us together!" Santo says, beaming. We beam with him. Not only campers but also Cubs are returned to their youth.

Would you say that rejuvenation was a theme of the camp?

Yes. But also fading. The '69 Cubs, you know, were the team that blew the National League East title to the Miracle Mets. The Cubs looked as if they were going to run away with it. Until September. On the first day of camp, Hundley gave Stone, who was to be our coach in the big Friday game against the Cubs, a chance to address us. "Just stay close to them till Thursday," Stone advised. "These are the '69 Cubs. They fade."

I asked Banks how he knew when it was time to retire. "You lose your quickness," he said. "And you hear whispers. Rumors. 'He used to make that play.' 'He used to hit that pitch.' Or maybe they don't say anything, but you can see it when they look at you. You can see it in their eyes."

That sounded like what I had been going through since I was twelve. In my last Little League season I was pretty good, but since then it has been only flashes. Moments. Inklings of what it feels like to be a player.

Did you have any of those inklings with the Cubs?

I had so many inklings, I may never sort them out. "You look like you've played some ball," Hundley told me, and to give you some idea how that made me feel, here's a story. A reporter at the camp overheard some of the Cubs saying that Ken Schwab, a fifty-five year-old Illinois grain-farm owner, looked pretty good. After asking another camper to point out Schwab, the reporter went up to another person he thought had been indicated and said, "Hey, the Cubs are saying you look pretty good." The guy nearly fainted. "My lifelong dream!" he cried. "You can't imagine what this means to me. For a big-league player to say, 'Irvin Singletary looks pretty good!' " (I have changed his name.) Here's how I felt: 1) "I have played some ball! I *have* played some ball. I must have! All those years, some of the time, anyway, that was actually *ball* I was playing!" And 2) *"Me?"*

Then, too, there were simpler moments. Grounder hit at me, bing-bing-tapocketta, it's in my glove, I'm up with it smoothly, throwing, zip, it's over to the first baseman chest high, a couple of murmurs among the campers: "Got an arm."

"Don't throw too hard too soon," Santo tells me. And the next day he asks me, "How's your hose?"

It wouldn't have sounded much sweeter if it had been Jessica Lange asking.

How was your hose?

My hose was there, all right. My hose wasn't dead.

You sound surprised.

The irony of all this is that before the opportunity to play with the Cubs arose, I had planned to retire from organized ball. I had given Willie Stargell, who is my age, the chance to hang it up first. I didn't want to steal any of his thunder. This spring I was going to make a simple announcement.

There had been certain telltale signs. For instance, when the slo-pitch softball team that you think you belong to fails to inform you that the season is under way, you begin to wonder. That happened two seasons ago. Then, too, I had doubts about my hose.

The one thing I've had in baseball was an arm from third base. Aside from a tendency to hit, at best, singles to right and on defense to stare off into space, I've been, since Little League, a classic third baseman: too slow to run or to hide. And when the ball bounced off some part of my body, I could pick it up and make that throw. If my hose wasn't out of sorts.

Also, I could never hit slo-pitch softball pitching, which was the only kind I seemed likely to face again. I don't like a pitch that goes way up in the air. When I go to bed at night and either pitch or bat myself to sleep, I see curves, sliders, screwballs, and hummers. I can't hit pitching that I never see in my dreams.

You were going to confine yourself to fandom, then?

No, I thought I might go on as a sort of pitcher in the rye. Throwing batting practice to the young. You groove the ball to somebody, and he or she hits it on the nose and you both feel good. And so do people watching. It's like a comedy act. And it's interesting, because you can fail at it. In Scottsdale I threw BP to Santo, and I pressed too hard and didn't get the ball where he or I wanted it, and he kept popping it up. I got the feeling he was pressing, too, trying to hit pitches he should've laid off so I wouldn't feel bad. I pressed harder. It was like strained conversation. I wonder whether something like that wasn't going on between the '69 Cubs in the stretch, when they let each other down.

Do you have much experience throwing batting practice?

Ah. At the highest level of serious competition I reached, high school, that was my forte. Somebody once told me he'd run into my old high school coach, Ray Thurmond, who remembered me as a pitcher. I was, of course, a third baseman, but it was at throwing batting practice that I shone. I wore a hole in my right high-school baseball shoe throwing BP without a pitcher's toe. Those are the spikes I wore against the Cubs.

The shoes of a congenial player, a giving player.

Many people might prefer that their old coach remember them the way Durocher remembers Eddie Stanky, as one of those "scratching, hungry, diving ballplayers who come to kill you."

That's the kind of player I wanted to be. Scrappy. I remember the only time I ever broke up a double play. I was playing intramural softball, in college. Hit the second baseman just right, flipped him up into the air. Didn't hurt him, though. I actually think he enjoyed it, too. This is a terrible thing for someone who pretends to understand serious ball to say, but my deepest desire in sports isn't to win but to share a good time. Maybe that's why Durocher seemed outraged at the very sight of me, that day in 1970.

This was the incident that occurred over in foul territory near the third-base dugout, where you missed the pop-up?

I wish you wouldn't keep harping on that pop-up. To me, if I *catch* a pop-up that goes as high as the Washington Monument, that's news. Or if I hit a ball 350 feet. But to my critics and friends, the idea of me camped not quite under a pop-up, and tilting slightly to the left, and tilting slightly farther to the left, and then the ball coming down well beyond my grasp—that's their idea of something worthy of comment. What people usually say to me now, if I'm unable to start the conversation off on the right note, is, "I hear that you missed a pop-up."

I'm sorry. There are so many other things I wanted to ask you. Like, how did you prepare for the Cubs?

For the first time in my life, I worked out. I hate to work out. You have an angel on one shoulder saying "Go, go, go" and a devil on the other saying "Stop, stop, stop," and there you are in between, bored to death with the whole argument and wallowing in sheer, but not pleasant, kinesthesia.

I like to play ball. A ball takes you out of yourself. Of course, if you miss a ball, you snap back into yourself pretty quick, but then you have a lot to talk over with yourself. Even while you are out of yourself, you can be narrating semiconsciously. "He can still hit," you can be saying, referring to yourself in the third person. "Ball was in on him but he got that bat head out in front. . . ." The main reason I cover sports is so I can keep the vocabulary of my semiconscious narration up-to-date.

Now looming ahead of me was a shot at living that narration. I was there to write about it, sure, but it meant a lot more to me than that. So, do you know what I did? I lifted weights. Not only do I not like lifting weights, I deplore it. However, a person doesn't get many chances later on in life to whang a well-pitched baseball or to snag a well-hit one. A person doesn't want to come back from such a chance to report to his family, "I was overpowered."

My son has 10-pound dumbbells lying around the house. I started pumping them and swinging them and going through throwing and batting motions with them, and I didn't stop even when my daughter would collapse—her prerogative—in helpless laughter. I also split two cords of firewood down to the biggest pile of kindling in Massachusetts.

When you first encountered the wily hardball in Arizona, how did you feel?
Overpowered.

A hardball is a thing that, when you have not seen one with steam on it in many years, is upon you before you know it. And in the field I was lost in the complexity of hops. Grounders were like logarithms. Also, I didn't seem to hinge in the same places I used to. And my throwing was so zipless the first day that it moved me to compose a blues song:

> I used to have a rifle,
> I used to have a gun.
> Lord, Lord.
> I used to have a rifle,
> I used to have a gun.
> Now that ball floats over
> Like a cinnamon bun.

But you said your hose wasn't dead.
Several things happened. One is that our trainer, Harry Jordan, manipulated my arm and discovered that the tendon over the funny bone had popped out. At least that's what he claimed. He popped it back in. I've never heard of anyone being plagued by funny-bone-tendon problems before, but I know that as he worked, Harry made terrific deep crunching noises in his throat that served to keep some of the faint-hearted campers out of the training room altogether, so I'm willing to believe that Jordan was a funnybonologist.

Another thing that kept me going early in camp was my chewing. I was chewing good. I talked chewing on a knowledgeable basis with Jenkins, who bites right into an open can of snuff with his lower front teeth. I could chew with the big boys. I even chewed during aerobics. This helped.

Also, nobody was yelling at anybody. The spirit of Durocher wasn't in the camp. I don't respond to being yelled at. It distracts me from yelling at myself.

Then, too, I had all of my clichés working.

I thought sportswriters are supposed to eschew clichés.
Sportswriters, yes. Ballplayers use them to hone their concentration.

I was being interviewed by a TV crew. Most campers were interviewed so many times that they eventually stopped calling their wives to tell them to turn on the VCR.

"Are you feeling the pressure?" I was asked.

"Nah," I lied. "When the bell rings, the juices will flow."

And I spat. Television likes visual touches. If you want to get a statement heard and seen all across the land, remember to spit right after making it.

Then, all of a sudden, I picked up a ball the way the first caveman picked up the first good fist-sized rock. And I felt my hose start to fill with water again. I felt leaner, stronger, springier, *glad* to have hamstrings. The downside of this was that my pants became even baggier. But I wore a psychic T-shirt that said "PLAYING MYSELF INTO SHAPE."

And then you went on a tear, right?

No. Then I reached my nadir. I thought I had reached my nadir years ago, several times, but in the very first intrasquad game I hit another new low.

Because I let the guys down. "We are here," Banks had announced one day behind the batting cage, "to ameliorate the classic polarization of the self-motivated individual and the ideology of the group."

Excuse me. Did Banks say things like that often?

Banks said things that came from the Big Arizona Sky. When someone asked him whether he felt he had come along too soon, before the days of astronomical baseball salaries, he said, "No. Wish I'd been born sooner. With the philosophers. Days of Plato, and Socrates, and Alexander Graham Bell." When I asked him what would be a thrill for him, comparable to the thrill we campers were getting, he said, "To sing in the Metropolitan Opera."

What Banks most often said was, "*Veez*-ualize yourself hitting a home run!"

"Ernie," said a camper, "I thought we were just supposed to meet the ball, and it would take care of itself."

"No," he said. "It won't. It will not take care of itself. You have to see yourself inside the ball when it is in the pitcher's hand, and you're thinking, 'Time to take a long ride.'"

But don't change the subject. I'm ready to discuss my nadir.

You have a lot of heart as an interviewee, you know that?

Yes, but in the first intrasquad game, I made several plays of the kind that kill infield chatter. Here I was feeling, "Give me Jimmy Stuart and Bob Margolin and Bill Mitchell and Dennis Albano and Wally Pecs (best ballplayer's name in camp) and Dennis Ferrazzano and Tim Tyers and Scott Mermel and George Altemose and Dave Schultz and Steve Heiferman and the Arnold, Crawford, and Patti brothers, and I could take on anybody in the world." And what do I do in the first intrasquad game? I drop a line drive hit right at me. A third basemen who can't catch a line drive at his sternum is as dependable as a frog that can't balance on a lily pad. And I let an easy grounder go under my glove. That's like letting a baby's head bob around. And Margolin, who in real life runs a vanity press but is no one's vanity catcher, whips a throw down to nip a guy stealing third, but I don't dig it out of the dirt. In Arizona a lot of thin air can get between a person and the ball—and between a person and his mates, even if they don't yell at you.

And the first time at bat, I dribble into a double play. The next time, Stone is pitching. "Can you hit a curveball?" he asks me.

"No," I say.

He throws me a curveball.

And you miss it?

No. Worse. I take it on the inside corner. And this is what I hear, from Oliver on the other bench: "That's a hanger, Roy." I've just taken a hanging curveball for a strike! What Stone has done is throw me a curve that I could hit. And I took it! That's like Jack Benny giving you a straight line and you saying, "Oh. Excuse me. I wasn't listening."

Like I say, nobody yelled at us campers, but every now and then one of the big-leaguers would give us a quiet, chastening line, like, "Got to have that one," or, "That's where we need you, big man." The social fabric. The ideology of the group.

The next pitch from Stone isn't a hanger. Not a curve. It's down the pipe. And I go after it. "All right!" I think.

The ball intersects with my bat about three inches from my hands. It pops weakly to the catcher. I feel as if I've reached out for a proffered ice-cream cone and found it in my armpit. "Well," I think, "I am losing my mind."

That was your nadir?

Yes. It didn't help that I had margarita tongue from the night before.

Ah, I've always wondered about the big-league night life. What did you do that night?

For one thing, talked to Cardenal about creekus.

What are creekus?

"You know, creekus," Cardenal said. "Little things." He made sawing motions with his arms like a cricket producing sounds. "One time in Chicago I come to the park with my eyes swollen shut. 'Cause I couldn't sleep. 'Cause creekus was in my room all night. So I can't play. And Mike Royko in the paper, ohhh, he got on me.

"And last night in my room? Creekus again. I find seven of them behind the toilet. I kill them all. I go back to bed. I hear more creekus. I turn the light back on. I find five creekus behind the television. I call the desk. 'You got to send the exterminator!' If Royko had been there! I could have shown him creekus!"

But, you came back from that nadir, right?

Let me put it this way. The next evening I'm in the coffee shop. I eat a well-earned sandwich. I sign the check. And there's a place on the check for "comments." So I write, "I went three-for-five today." There not being much room, I didn't bother to add, "and fielded flawlessly."

What turned you around?

After my nadir, I talked to Stone. He told me about his Cy Young season with Baltimore in 1980, after which he had nothing left. "I threw over 60 percent breaking balls," he said. "I knew it would ruin my arm, but I was winning fifteen games in a row. One year of twenty-five and seven is worth five of fifteen and fifteen." Before a game, he said, he would take a Percodan if he felt he would need it in addition to the four aspirin he would routinely take every three innings. And he kept breaking off those hooks.

"Well," I sighed, "your straight one was too tough for me."

"No, that was my forkball," he said.

"Oh!" I said. My heart leapt. "What does it do?"

"Drops off like a spitball and moves in on you. Nobody can hit it."

No wonder you didn't hit it.

Precisely. Not only that, but I'd had a real major-league experience. I'd popped up a forkball. The next day, when we played our next intrasquad game, I was ready.

Would you like to tell us about it?

Single to right off Dr. Harry Soloway, the Chicago shrink who became nationally famous by telling the *Today* show that he wasn't giving any more interviews because the last reporter he talked to called him "the most inept ballplayer I have ever seen, man or boy." Except for his fame, a single to right off Dr. Harry Soloway is not an enduring achievement, but a solid single is a solid single. Then, off Cardenal, I ground out and single up the middle. Then, off Beckert, I fly to left. I'm pulling the ball!

A portent. For the 350 . . .

Although I don't realize it at the time. But now we get down to the last inning. Bases loaded. Beckert, who has been moving painfully and saying, "Now I remember why I retired," wants to get the game over. He's working in and out on me. This feels like actual baseball! Three and two. Comes in with a high, tight fastball. Too close to take. I foul it back. This is probably a thrill for Beckert, too: a second baseman getting a chance to work on a hitter. He delivers a funny-looking pitch on the outside corner.

And what do you do with it?

Rip it. On a line. But not a straight line. More satisfying than that. A line like a scimitar blade. Over the first baseman's head, and it *bites* the ground three feet fair. It goes blisteringly on its way, and I say to it, "Burn!"

A double. And such a double! I am most of the way to third when I see the runner ahead of me running toward me. Fortunately, he's heading back toward third, not second. He has become conservative and decided he can't score. But this is such a double that I am able to turn around and go 70 feet back into second standing up. I have hit the equivalent of a triple and a half.

That must have been a thrill.

I'll tell you the thrill. The thrill is what Beckert exclaims.

What does Beckert exclaim?

Beckert exclaims, "How did you hit that pitch?" He turns to Jenkins, who's umpiring. "Slider right on the outside corner!" he says. "And I had him set up!"

"I was looking for it," I reply.

"That's right!" says Jenkins. "That's a good hitter."

Wow! You were looking for it?

No. I lied. The truth was I had found my strength as a hitter. Which turned out to be very similar to my strength as a defensive back in football—which is that I am too slow to take a fake. My strength as a hitter, I now realize, is that I haven't got sense enough to be set up. Why do you think a person becomes a writer? It's because he can never figure anything out until afterward. In baseball down through the years I've often been trying, during the seventh inning, to figure out what happened in the fifth. And what happened was that I wasn't paying attention because I was wondering what I did wrong in the third. And what I did wrong in the third was boot one because I was thinking, "I've got to concentrate with every fiber of my being. Hmm, interesting phrase. I wonder what all the fibers of my being in concert would look like? A nice wool shirt?" Oh, those rare great moments in sports when my mind isn't working and my body is!

Another thing I do in this game is throw four guys out with my hose. My mind is a blank then, too.

Did you talk your triple and a half over with Beckert and Jenkins later?

No, not exactly. But I will say this. In my time I'd exchanged various glances with ballplayers. And a major-league manager once mistook me for a member of the Hall of Fame. That was when I called Billy Martin on the phone, and hearing my voice, he cried, "Mick? Mick? Is it the Mick?" He thought I was Mickey Mantle. When he realized I wasn't, we were both very disappointed.

But I had never exchanged a glance with a ballplayer that contained any hint that I, too, was a part of the actual ballplaying experience. One time, a Venezuelan sportscaster, Juan Vené, and I told Manny Sanguillen, when he was catching for the Pirates, that we had played baseball on opposing press teams.

"Softball?" asked Sanguillen.

"No, hardball."

Sanguillen was one of the most gracious ballplayers I've ever met. But Sanguillen shook his head and said, "You guys!"

That evening in Scottsdale after the second intrasquad game, I exchanged glances with Beckert and Jenkins that, to me—and I am talking in terms of diamond experience now—contained a hint of "us guys."

Tell me. This is another thing I have always wondered about. Do you ballplayers put your pants on one leg at a time, like everybody else?

I can only speak for myself. The answer in my case is: not always. After that intrasquad game, I got tired putting one leg on, stopped for a while and worked on the other one.

But you were ready for the big game the next day in Scottsdale Stadium?
Did I tell you I hit a ball 350 feet?

In passing, but tell me more about it.
I have always gotten on well with veterinarians. Rich Nye, who won twenty-six games in the big leagues, is now a veterinarian. If I didn't live so far from Des Plaines, Illinois, I'd send my dogs to him. Nye threw me a good pitch to hit.

Every camper got one at bat in the big game. By the time I got up, in the ninth or tenth of many innings, it had become clear that a few winded old Cubs are better than wave after fresh wave of old brokers, law professors, and salesmen. The crowd was diminished and restive.

"Representing *Sports Illustrated*," blared the loudspeaker, "Ray" and a mispronunciation of my last name. I strode to the plate and realized I didn't have on a helmet. I ran back and got one. I strode to the plate and realized that the flap covered the wrong ear. I ran back and got a left-eared one. Fan reaction indicated a doubting of my expertise. I dug in.

"Coming right down the middle," said Rudolph, who was catching.

All you selfless, unrecognized batting-practice pitchers out there, Keep it up! Your service will be repaid. Someday a veterinarian will lay one in there for you. In practice, Nye had shown me his real 80-mile-per-hour fastball, which I nearly hit. This one was a notch slower. Later he said he wished he'd thrown it harder; I would have cleared the fence. But I'll take my 350 feet, and the sound of a crowd that came to scoff and stayed to eat its heart out.

Anything else you'd like to say?
Yeah. I got my longest hit ever against a team managed by Leo Durocher.

Did I tell you about the first time I met Leo? It was in Scottsdale Stadium in the spring of 1970 that I, a cub reporter, innocently introduced myself to him. And he, standing outside the third-base dugout, pointed his finger at me and began to address, at the top of his lungs, the players who, a few months before, had been the '69 Cubs: "I want everybody to hear this! I'm not talking to this guy! I'm not saying a word!"

Just before he disappeared under the stands, he turned and added, "And he knows why!"

I didn't then and don't now. But it got to me. I loved baseball, and Durocher went all the way back through Willie Mays and Coogan's Bluff and the Gashouse Gang to Ruth. I couldn't shake the feeling that there must be something about me that didn't fit into the national pastime.

Did you ever run into Durocher again?

Not until camp week thirteen years later. At the banquet after the big game, he took the occasion to make an emotional talk. He confessed why the '69 Cubs folded: "They didn't give me 100 percent."

What a thing to say at this point! Would the man never let up?

"They gave me 140 percent." Ah. The Cubs had pressed. Durocher was conceding that he'd chewed on them too hard.

He also apologized publicly for embarrassing Santo nastily in a celebrated 1971 clubhouse meeting. After the banquet, Durocher and Santo embraced.

Durocher didn't apologize to me. He glared at me once but with no hint of recognition. He had relieved me, however, of one burden. I still don't know

---

ROY ALTON BLOUNT JR.
Name pronounced Blunt.

Born Oct. 4, 1941, at Indianapolis, Ind.
Height, depends. Weight, depends.
Throws and bats righthanded.
Hobby—Raising mixed-breed dogs.
Attended Vanderbilt University, Nashville, Tenn., and
Harvard University, Cambridge, Mass.

Year Club	League	Pos.	B.A.
1951—Tigers†	Little	OF	.063
1952—Tigers	Little	OF	.179
1953—Tigers	Little	3B	.320
1954—‡	(Did not play)		
1955—Pels	Babe Ruth	3B	.213
1956—Pels	Babe Ruth	3B	.265
1956—Decatur High B-Team ...	Region 4-AA	3B	.213
1957—Decatur High B-Team ...	Region 4-AAA	3B	.270
1958—Decatur High Varsity § .	Region 4-AAA	3B	.000
1959—Decatur High Varsity x .	Region 4-AAA	3B-1B	.000
1960–70— ‡	(Did not play)		
1971—Sports Illustrated vs. NY Press in Yankee Stadium, one game		C	.500
1972—NY Press vs. Venezuelan Press in Venezuela, three games y		3B	.400
1973—NY Press vs. Venezuelan Press in Yankee Stadium, one game z		2B	.500
1974— ‡	(Did not play)		
1983—All-Star Campers vs. each other and '69 Cubs, three games a		3B	.375
			——
Totals (In major league stadium or uniform)			.409
(Not in major league stadium or uniform) ...			.201

† Nearly everyone else was bigger.
‡ On temporary inactive list.
§ Not very many at bats.
x Hardly any at bats.
y Wore New York Yankee and Met uniforms.
z Wore Yankee uniform.
a Wore Chicago Cub uniform. (Got to keep it. For $80.)

what made me anathema, but I do know it wasn't my fault that the Cubs didn't win in '69.

"Winning the pennant that year might have been anticlimactic for the kind of love we had on that team," said emcee Gene Oliver from the podium. However that may be, in 1969 Durocher seems, oddly enough, to have forged a team that couldn't win but did learn how to share a good time.

So you have no complaints?

No complaints? No complaints? What madman built a stadium whose fences are nowhere shorter than 355 feet?

Let me quote to the you the testimony of Steve Stone, and also of longtime Chicago baseball writer Richard Dozer, now of *The Phoenix Gazette*, who was as much of an official scorer as we had: "The ball is out in Fenway."

But . . . the air in Fenway isn't thin.

Yeah, and Hundley's pop-up doesn't go nearly so high, and I catch it and toss it over to Leo.

Reggie is large, he contains multitudes. If he sings a song of himself, who is to gainsay? Unfortunately, in recent years has come a horde of detractors who delight in his outfield misplays, his off-field mishaps, and his decline at the bat (his 1983 average of .194, while exceeding his self-proclaimed I.Q. of 160, fell short of his weight). And yet Reggie remains confident, if somewhat subdued. As Ol' Diz said, if you can do it, it ain't braggin' . . . and Mr. October has done it. Does Reggie go to Cooperstown? Does Frankie go to Hollywood? Of course; the question surely was answered long ago. Thomas Boswell is one of the game's most thoughtful writers; this essay originally appeared in his *Washington Post* column and was later collected in *How Life Imitates the World Series*.

THOMAS BOSWELL

Mr. October

Mark Twain said that politicians, old buildings, and prostitutes become respectable with age. Reggie Jackson would like to make it a foursome.

It isn't easy for a hurricane to become its own calm eye, but the former Buck Tater Man is trying. After years of straining to be the straw that stirs the drink, it has dawned on Jackson that, perhaps, he is the drink that is getting stirred.

When you go to the movies and get sued, when you walk to your car and get accused of battering a child, when you sit in your car and somebody walks up and points a revolver at your nose from six-inch range, it makes you wonder who's getting stirred. When your house burns down, it makes you wonder who's in control. When you foul off a sacrifice bunt and get suspended for insubordination, when you jog in from the outfield and your manager is waiting in the dugout to punch you, or when you step in a hole and disable yourself for a month, it makes you wonder about your luck, about your approach to things.

All this, and much more, has happened since Jackson came to the New York Yankees in 1977. From clubhouse fights, to an IRS-audit brouhaha, to banner headlines screaming, GUNMAN FIRES AT REGGIE ON MANHATTAN STREET, Jackson has never lacked for somber subjects to mull in his idle, thoughtful hours.

Slowly, he has changed. And is still changing. Like any fine protagonist in fiction, Jackson alters, grows, learns, regresses, doubles back, stakes out new ground before our eyes.

Jackson has not outlined his new position—his new image, as he perhaps unwisely chooses to call it—in any single way, but rather in a dozen ways. "I must take off my black hat . . . I have to control my tongue . . . I have to substantiate my thoughts rather than just raise hell . . . You have to sell yourself and politic a little in this life . . . I have to stop getting into things too deep . . . I don't want to offend . . . It's good to feel wanted and respected . . . Part of the trouble with Billy [Martin] was that I misunderstood his wants."

These snippets of conciliation, these bons mots of a once-burned, twice-shy man, are extracts from Jackson's conversation—all said within fifteen minutes. If the New York Yankee slugger suddenly has to go on the disabled list, no one should have to ask why. It'll be a slipped disc; this is a man spending a lot of time bending over backward. Jackson seems to be a man in the midst of a long, gradual, yet uneasy personal transition. His locker in the New York clubhouse is in the corner, almost hidden, as though he were an animal gone to earth. If Jackson now feels most comfortable with his back protected by a wall, he has good reason.

From his first day in pinstripes, Jackson was baseball's King Midas of fame, its Hester Prynne of sluggers with a dollar sign on his chest. Everything he touched turned to instant celebrity. Since Aesop, men have been warned to be careful when they make a wish. It just might come true. Jackson asked the free-agent genie for millions of dollars, a candy bar named after him, and a Yankee uniform.

And, brother, did he get it!

A passion for fame, for a lasting place in folklore, is perhaps the most easily comprehended, and the most easily excused, of vanities. Yet Jackson, who hit more homers than any man in baseball during the first fourteen full years of his career (424 from 1968 through 1981), is seldom judged generously. Few exceptional athletes have had to hear the words "fraud" and "phony" applied to themselves so often, even by teammates.

"Reggie is an average player," said Baltimore's average pitcher Jim Palmer after Jackson left Baltimore.

"Reggie Jackson has never done anything in his life that was not for effect. He's a total phony," said pitcher Bill Lee, perhaps proving the adage that we say of others those things that apply best to ourselves.

"Reggie is a charlatan, but a charlatan with credentials," said pitcher Don Sutton. "He cons people and sells himself, but he produces."

After the greatest slugging World Series in history in '77, what was Jackson's reward? His manager, Martin, platooned him against southpaws, batted him

seventh, and put a slew-footed catcher in his right-field position. What other star was ever treated so preposterously, yet remained so relatively silent? "I never pay any attention to anything Reggie says anyway," said Martin, while still Yankee skipper. "Why should I? His teammates don't."

Jackson's basic difficulty, one that may take him years to solve, is that, like politicians and poets on a grander scale, Jackson does not live a life in the conventional, everyday sense. He manufactures a legend, a personal history, with himself and his exploits at the center. Jackson's sin is that he has always been uniquely bad at hiding this conscious myth-making process. Baseball elects its heroes for life by bleacher plebiscite, not by self-appointment. The old game has never forgiven Jackson for proclaiming himself a "superstar"—the one-word title of his autobiography—before his public and peers had time to come to the same conclusion.

The irony, of course, is that with each year, with each new accomplishment, it becomes more obvious that Jackson is, and always has been, everything he claimed. The most elementary Jackson statistic—his glory in a nutshell—is that in those mere fourteen seasons he has been the cleanup hitter and offensive leader on nine division champions and five world champions. That alone, without a single personal stat, ought to be enough for Cooperstown.

Even when Jackson knows that his feats should speak for themselves, even when he knows that humility is the right card to play, he has always tipped his hand. He can mix hokum and genuine insight, subtle phrasing and pathetic bombast like no other star. Few men match his knack for having a good idea, then mopping the floor with it. If Jackson discussed the Bill of Rights long enough, he'd make you want to repeal it.

Yet this marathon philosophizer is the soul of pith. Who else in baseball says, "It was an insurance homer; that's why I hit it halfway to the Prudential Building," or "I hit it so far my eyes weren't good enough to see it land. That one had some voltage." Of all the athletes in all American sports, perhaps none has so much fun making phrases, or gets himself in so much trouble doing it. Jackson's epigrams—"hitting against Nolan Ryan is like eating soup with a fork"—are a mixture of image-laden Baptist preaching and a college-educated mind. The cruelest epithet that trails Jackson through the years is Mickey Rivers's taunt: "Reginald Martinez Jackson—white man's first name, Spanish middle name, and a black man's last name. No wonder you don't know who the hell you are." The truth is that, consciously or not, Jackson has chosen to meld and blend all the strains in his background, all the cultural lineages that he can draw upon from ghetto to campus to Park Avenue, and contain them in one personality. The result is often a brilliant blend of street-wise cynicism, tangy language, and the genuine worldliness of a man who has read some good books and seen a lot of great places.

It is impossible for such a man not to put a high value on his own opinions. No one ever mastered the tricks of the limelight game better than Jackson— the places to be, the times to be there, the expression to have on your face, if you want the microphones, the notepads, and the cameras to gather.

"I know how to answer questions," says Jackson. "I know how to tell the truth, but not hurt too many feelings . . . I can recognize a colorful quote . . . I don't think ballplayers understand the trouble they could save themselves if they paid attention to how to give an interview . . . I am aware that I sell myself and promote myself. Sometimes you do or say something for effect. But the real reason I have a good press is that I treat interviewers like people. In other words, I treat them the way I am not treated."

Of all Jackson's traits, the one which is most resented is his off-hand ability to steal headlines. In a prosaic locker room, he stands out like a walking poem. The most difficult task for Jackson as he matures will probably be the need to muzzle himself, renouncing the great pleasure he takes in ruminating. Already, it seems, he no longer seeks attention in the little ways that rankle other players. When he is not sedulously avoiding the media line of fire, he is driving the wordsmiths away with kindness, channeling the conversation to dull baseball labor topics or the like.

It may be Jackson's misfortune that the new Reggie, when he is eventually noticed, will be mistaken for a Madison Avenue concoction by a man who, after selling candy bars, jeans, VWs, and cologne, can certainly take care of repackaging and selling himself. It is probably more accurate that Jackson is simply showing the flip side of himself that has always been there, that has always been the best side of him, but also the least noticed.

"I didn't really know what I was getting into when I came to New York. I never guessed how tough this town was," he says. "It's a city that loves visiting celebrities and treats them great. Makes you want to come here. If they see you two days a year, you're royalty. If they see you every day, you're a bum."

How dramatically tunes change. When Jackson came to New York, former teammate Ken Holtzman predicted, "He'll love it. Reggie just soaks up attention. His desire for fame may be insatiable." Even Jackson, the spring after his three-homer Series game in '77, said, "You can't get too much of a good thing; I don't understand that idea. I wanted to come to the Yankees. I wanted to hit five home runs in a World Series. I've earned everything I've got. It's been hectic, sure. It's been hard. But it's been a pleasure."

However, like Midas, Jackson has had second thoughts about his good New York fortune. It is bitterly ironic that Jackson should have found Apple fans so hard to satisfy. Within big-league dugouts, Jackson is categorized as a player best appreciated by those who see him every day. But it takes an eye.

"Reggie's not a difficult player to manage, 'cause he's what you call a 'hard' player," says Baltimore's Earl Weaver. "He hustles, runs everything out, hates to embarrass himself. He'll take a guy out on the double play, or run into a wall, making a sliding catch. His whole career he's missed games because of 'hustle' injuries.

"Most important, he can reach a special level of concentration in the key situations that win games—just like Frank Robinson. And, kinda like Frank, when the score's 9–2 either way, his concentration lapses and he gives away at bats or makes a meaningless error. That may hurt his batting average or his fielding average, but it don't hurt his team none," said Weaver.

"Reggie's a curious person and he's a person who likes to be shown the respect he's earned. He'll ask you why you made a certain move that involved him, which is unusual, 'cause most players don't give a damn. You explain it. You teach him somethin' maybe he didn't know. He nods. He appreciates it."

Jackson is delighted with this synopsis of The Care and Feeding of Reggie as seen by The Certified Genius. "I loved playing for Earl Weaver [in '76]," said Jackson. "Now I could play for the little Weave. That man will chew you out, read you the riot act down to the ground, and then forget all about it."

Jackson's most endearing trait, but one that few people see, is that he respects anyone who will challenge him, force him to defend his position cogently, cut through the bluster. "Earl's right, he's right," says Jackson. "I give away at bats, I'm careless. Last night, I wasn't 'in' the game until the sixth inning. The cold weather distracted me . . . took my mind off business. Maybe that's an area where I can improve as I get older."

Like anyone with a true talent, Jackson searches for people who can spot his genuine flaws. Changing, improving as he ages, achieving a middle ground where all sides of his nature are put in perspective are now priorities for Jackson. One step in that direction was the short tenure of Dick Howser as Yankee manager. "Dick shows a lot of respect for me, makes me feel wanted," said Jackson, who, at thirty-four under Howser, had his best season since he was twenty-three. "He knows people, tries to understand them," adds Jackson, who, like the gifted child in class, is a devil when he must demand attention, but an angel when he gets it. "I'd go out of my way not to offend Howser because I think he's a fair man."

About the unfairnesses of the past, Jackson has learned to remain mute: every time he has talked, he has lost. "I don't think Billy is gone for good. I think he'll be back as manager of the Yankees. I can't explain why. I just think so," says Jackson with the same reverse-English assurance as the golfer who roots for his putts by yelling, "Don't go in the hole . . . don't you dare go in the hole!"

Of the other fellow in the old Yankee vicious triangle, Jackson says, "I have to realize that Steinbrenner's never been late with a paycheck. A professional athlete has to accept responsibilities. I've always understood that, but I thought it applied to staying in shape, bearing down every game. I understand now that it also means controlling your tongue, not being too disparagingly critical of the owner.

"Maybe I'm just seeing the other side—the side of the people who run things. I represent companies [in commercials] and accept their money, so I have a responsibility to project an image, to come across as a person who substantiates his thoughts, not as some guy who's blowing off again."

No project could be more difficult or against-the-grain for Jackson than this reining-in process. Just look at him. He wears his uniform like a star—tight, muscles bulging, top button of shirt open. He runs distinctively, bent forward, a picture of barely controlled power. He seems to carry a stage with him everywhere. It is as difficult for him not to mention his alleged 160 IQ as it is hard for him to remember not to flash his wallet full of $100 bills. And, everywhere, he runs into those who want to prick his balloon, like Rivers the day he cackled, "Reggie says he's got an IQ of 160. Out of what? A thousand?"

Even if Jackson's intelligence quotient doesn't test out a little above Mozart's and a tad below Voltaire's, Jackson has always wanted to run in the intellectual fast lane, or at least, somewhere near it. He loves the big words and the complicated issues, wants very much—perhaps too much—to have an opinion on all the topics he thinks a smart man should have one on. He can't resist a pretentious subject any more than he can lay off the fastball in his wheelhouse—even if it's a ball. So he'll always strike out plenty.

Most ballplayers, most people probably, would be inflamed if anyone wrote such things about them. Jackson once walked up to me with a story I had written. He pointed to the paragraph just above this one—word-for-word the same—and, shaking his head, said, "So true," then walked away.

It's not easy being a man who is embarrassed by short home runs.

For Jackson, the struggle continues to be all things. He wants to be compassionate, simple, religious. But he wears gold chains and owns a fleet of kingly cars. He loves being his team's player representative. No star warms more genuinely to the "noblesse oblige" of losing money in a strike since it benefits other marginal players who really need a union. The anomaly of being a millionaire labor spokesman is just his style.

It is not a rare psychological bent to want to be both the cop and the robber, the oppressed and the oppressor, the hero and the villain, the object of love as well as hate, the loner who is also the leader. But it is wearisome, this always swinging for the parking lot, always changing costumes and masks so that every role in the play can be yours. It is so much easier to be undisciplined, to fly in all directions at once, to satisfy all the different appetites and personalities in one half-forged mind. But even for such a man, the time comes when he must choose among all the characters in the cast of his soul.

The campaign for quiet respectability and calm affection shown aging future Hall of Famers has already begun. "I want very much to be in the Hall of Fame. I'd kind of like to wait until the room is empty at night and go in once to look at the plaque. I worry some that I've made enemies, that I have a reputation that might hurt my chances. I think 500 homers and 1,500 RBIs would prevent that."

What distinguishes the great player, the man in the Hall?

"The pride," says Jackson, "that makes a player believe that he's better than the rest."

Reggie Jackson says these words like a boy bringing home a drawing from school, one that has "A-plus" written in the corner. Perhaps he really doesn't mean to boast. What he wants, and still so seldom gets, is a measured, unhysterical response. Neither the rabid cheers nor boos that are supposed to be his fuel, but rather a friendly, honest appraisal that indeed his hard work has been found worthy.

Ball Four is to my mind the best baseball book ever written principally by a player; only Cap Anson's *A Ball Player's Career* comes close. Len Shecter (represented solo later in this volume) was the shaping force behind Bouton's words, but the words are recognizably Bouton's—this is not a ghosted job. The tempest that followed publication in 1970 left Bouton a pariah of the baseball world, shunned by players and management alike; even today he is invited to no old-timers' games. What was obscured amid all the controversy surrounding the book was Bouton's remarkable comeback. A twenty-one-game winner as a fastball pitcher for the Yankees of 1963, he hurt his arm and won only nine games in his last four years in New York. With his career seemingly finished, he hooked on with the expansion Seattle Pilots as a knuckle-balling reliever and appeared in seventy-three games in 1969. Even more remarkable, after dropping out of the majors after a weak 1970 season, he bobbed up again eight years later, starting and winning a game for the Atlanta Braves. Here, the memorable conclusion to *Ball Four*.

JIM BOUTON

The Grip

In the winter I always find myself remembering more good things than bad. And in many ways 1969 was a great season. I began it as a minor leaguer trying a new style and a new pitch and finished as a genuine gold-plated, guaranteed-not-to-tarnish major leaguer again. My seventy-three appearances for Seattle and Houston were fifth in the majors, and my two wins, three losses, and two saves say something—although I'm not sure what.

The pettiness and stupidity were exasperating, sometimes damaging. And it's going to be a long winter before I can enjoy having had my shoes nailed to the clubhouse floor. New levels of noncommunication were reached. Still, there were rewards. There were enough laughs in the bullpen and in the back of the bus to make me eager for a new season. I met a lot of people I'll feel warmly toward for the rest of my life. Observing and recording my experiences for this book taught me a great deal not only about others but about myself. (I'm not sure I liked everything I learned, but learning is often a painful experience.)

I lucked out with five great roommates: Gary Bell, Bob Lasko, Mike Marshall, Steve Hovley, and Norm Miller. I went the whole season without an injury. I traveled the country in both leagues. And I saw the look in my son Mike's face when I came back from a road trip and he turned his big eyes up at me and said shyly, "Hey Dad, you're Jim Bouton, aren't you?"

I enjoyed living in the Great Northwest for most of a season, and I'm sad that Seattle didn't keep its franchise. A city that seems to care more for its art museums than its ballpark can't be all bad.

The team will play in Milwaukee next season, and it will be a new team in every respect. Even before the franchise could be shifted, Marvin Milkes, operating on the theory that when you make a mistake you make a change, made a lot of changes. Joe Schultz was fired and signed on as coach in Kansas City, moving in considerably below Lou Piniella in the team's pecking order. Piniella, groomed for oblivion in the first weeks of spring training with Seattle, became Rookie of the Year in Kansas City, hitting .282. Sal Maglie, Ron Plaza, Eddie O'Brien, and Frank Crosetti were also fired. As this is written only Crosetti has hooked on—with Minnesota.

Fred Talbot, Diego Segui, Ray Oyler, George Brunet, Don Mincher, and Ron Clark were all traded to Oakland for some warm bodies. Dooley Womack was released, Merritt Ranew was sent to the minors, and Mike Marshall, sold to Houston, will be back with me this spring. Gary Bell, released by the White Sox, was signed by Hawaii. Hope he can handle *mai tais*.

Houston traded Curt Blefary to the Yankees for Joe Pepitone and we will have all spring to practice Joe's pickoff sign. Wade Blasingame was sent to the minors. Ted Williams of the MFL was Manager of the Year and the Fat Kid won Most Valuable Player.

I did not win Comeback of the Year, but I went to a local sports banquet the other night and took a bow from the audience. As I watched the trophies being handed out, my mind wandered and I saw myself being called up to the dais and accepting the Fireman of the Year award for 1970.

And then I thought of Jim O'Toole, and I felt both strange and sad. When I took the cab to the airport in Cincinnati I got into a conversation with the driver, and he said he'd played ball that summer against Jim O'Toole. He said O'Toole was pitching for the Ross Eversoles in the Kentucky Industrial League. He said O'Toole is all washed up. He doesn't have his fastball anymore, but his control seems better than when he was with Cincinnati. I had to laugh at that. O'Toole won't be trying to sneak one over the corner on Willie Mays in the Kentucky Industrial League.

Jim O'Toole and I started out even in the spring. He wound up with the Ross Eversoles and I with a new lease on life. And as I daydreamed of being Fireman of the Year in 1970, I wondered what the dreams of Jim O'Toole are like these days. Then I thought, would I do that? When it's over for me, would I be hanging on with the Ross Eversoles? I went down deep and the answer I came up with was yes.

Yes, I would. You see, you spend a good piece of your life gripping a baseball, and in the end it turns out that it was the other way around all the time.

The fashion in fans has changed, and so has the fashion in sportswriters. Both are cooler now. The hard-boiled, epigrammatic style of Cannon that was admired by Hemingway has fallen from favor. Nobody asked me, but . . . the great ones come back, and Cannon will. This, from the collection *Who Struck John?*

JIMMY CANNON

Gallery of Buffs

The baseball enthusiast, according to the standard image drama by editorial page and sports department cartoonists, is a fat man with a belly in his lap. The artists of journalism give him an insipid smile, put a hot dog in one hand and a bottle of soda pop in the other, and illuminate his pudgy features with ecstasy. The collar is crumpled by sweat and the shirt is unbuttoned at the throat. Usually, there is a damp handkerchief tied around his neck as a substitute for a scarf. Constant association with the species led me to make notes on various types I have encountered in ballparks.

The Gourmet: There is a pile of cracked shells on either thigh, and his coat lapels are covered with shreds of the nut. He usually picks the crisis in the ballgame to stand up and shake himself clean. The guy sitting next to him spends the next couple of innings trying to get the stuff out of his eyes.

The Dugout Spy: What occurs on the ballfield doesn't interest him; he ignores the action to concentrate on the players on the bench. He stares into the dugout, making snide remarks about the manager and the substitutes.

The Coach Hater: This fan loathes all coaches. The coach stands with his back to the stands, and the coach hater spends nine innings abusing him. He leaves the park for a failure unless the coach turns around to glare at him.

The Switcher: The switcher comes into the park to root for a team, but the score influences his affection. As soon as the club of his choice gets behind, he ridicules them.

The Brooder: If the shortstop kicks a ball on opening day, he bellows: "There goes the pennant!" He shouts this at every player who makes an error in every game he attends. The standing of the clubs doesn't motivate him. He yells it at Pittsburgh and the Yankees.

The Regretful Assessor: If a ball falls safely in the outfield, he smiles with a cruel contentment and says: "DiMaggio would of got it."

The Haberdasher: He behaves as though he were judging the ten best dressed men. Why, he wants to know, doesn't a big-league ballplayer pull up his pants? He doesn't know why players play in dirty uniforms and wonders why they don't change between innings.

The Fan Club: The fan club is interested in only one player. He talks constantly about his idol even when he is not involved in the play. He heckles all the other players but begs for fairness if his hero is not regarded with respectful noise by the neighbors.

The Coat Holder: The coat holder proclaims himself a ballplayer's closest friend. He may be a waiter in a lunch wagon where the athlete once had a cup of coffee. He might run an elevator in which the ballplayer took a ride. But he tells everyone what a great guy the player is and how close they are. The coat holder never brags of friendship with an obscure player. It is always the star.

The Brute: The brute beseeches the pitcher to hit the batter between the eyes. It is his contention that a pitcher who doesn't try to decapitate a hitter is yellow.

The Slider: The slider ducks through the special cops as soon as the game is over and slides into the nearest base.

The Actor: The actor doesn't glance at the game but watches the television camera. As soon as he thinks it is turned on him, he stands up and waves.

The Cynic: The cynic suspects every move a team makes. If there is a series of errors or a lot of hits, he turns to the guy alongside of him and asks: "You think they want to win?" If the fellow replies yes, the cynic says something like this: "Baseball is a business like everything else. What's good for the gate is good for baseball."

The Watchman: He is only concerned with the pitchers. If they step off the rubber or fake a guy back to a base, he shouts: "Balk!" There are more of these than any other kind.

The Optimist: Nothing is important if the other team does it. No matter what the score is, he has one comment. He bawls, "You lucky bum!"

The Poet: Over and over again, from the first to the last inning, he rumbles, "Well, well," no matter what happens.

This is an excerpt from the brilliant, scary novel *The Universal Baseball Association, Inc.: J. Henry Waugh, Prop.* It is a baseball book that is not about baseball, as could be said of Malamud's *The Natural* or Roth's *The Great American Novel*. Then again, Coover could well believe that baseball is not about baseball. J. Henry Waugh is a man obsessed with a table game he has invented: he may hold the dice, but the outcome of each roll of the bones brings genuine surprise and delight. Here, Pioneers' pitching phenom Damon Rutherford, son of the immortal Brock Rutherford, is one out shy of perfection against the rival Haymakers.

ROBERT COOVER

JHWH

Of course, it was just the occasion for the storybook spoiler. Yes, too obvious. Perfect game, two down in the ninth, and a pinch hitter scratches out a history-shriveling single. How many times it had already happened! The epochal event reduced to a commonplace by something or someone even less than commonplace, a mediocrity, a blooper worth forgetting, a utility ballplayer never worth much and out of the league a year later. All the No-Hit Nealys that Sandy sang about . . .

> No-Hit Nealy, somethin' in his eye,
> When they pitched low, he swung high,
> Hadn't had a hit in ninety-nine years,
> And then they sent him out agin
> The Pi-yo-neers!

Henry turned water on to wash, then hesitated. Not that he felt superstitious about it exactly, but he saw Damon Rutherford standing there on the mound, hands not on the rosin bag, not in the armpits, not squeezing the ball, just at his side—dry, strong, patient—and he felt as though washing his hands might somehow spoil Damon's pitch. From the bathroom door, he could see the kitchen table. His Association lay there in ordered stacks of paper. The dice sat there, three ivory cubes, heedless of history yet makers of it, still proclaiming Abernathy's strikeout. Damon Rutherford waited there. Henry held his breath, walked straight to the table, picked up the dice, and tossed them down.

Hard John Horvath took a cut at Rutherford's second pitch, a letter-high inside curve, pulled it down the third-base line: Hatrack Hines took it back-handed, paused one mighty spellbinding moment—then fired across the diamond to Goodman James, and Horvath was out.

The game was over.

Giddily, Henry returned to the bathroom and washed his hands. He stared down at his wet hands, thinking: he did it! And then, at the top of his voice, "WA-*HOO!*" he bellowed, and went leaping back into the kitchen, feeling like he could damn well take off and soar if he had anyplace to go. "*HOO-HAH!*"

And the fans blew the roof off. They leaped the wall, slid down the dugout roofs, overran the cops, flooded in from the outfield bleachers, threw hats and scorecards into the air. Rooney hustled his Haymakers to the showers, but couldn't stop the Pioneer fans from lifting poor Horvath to their shoulders. There was a fight and Hard John bloodied a couple noses, but nobody even bothered to swing back at him. An old lady blew him kisses. Partly to keep Rutherford from getting mobbed and partly just because they couldn't stop themselves, his Pioneer teammates got to him first, had him on their own shoulders before the frenzied hometown rooters could close in and tear him apart out of sheer love. From above, it looked like a great roiling whirlpool with Damon afloat in the vortex—but then York popped up like a cork, and then Patterson and Hines, and finally the manager Barney Bancroft, lifted up by fans too delirious even to know for sure anymore what it was they were celebrating, and the whirlpool uncoiled and surged toward the Pioneer locker rooms.

"Ah!" said Henry, and: "*Ah!*"

And even bobbingly afloat there on those rocky shoulders, there in that knock-and-tumble flood of fans, in a wild world that had literally, for the moment, blown its top, Damon Rutherford preserved his incredible equanimity, hands at his knees except for an occasional wave, face lit with pleasure at what he'd done, but in no way distorted with the excitement of it all: tall, right, and true. People screamed for the ball. Royce Ingram, whose shoulder was one of those he rode on, handed it up to him. Women shrieked, arms supplicating. He smiled at them, but tossed the ball out to a small boy standing at the crowd's edge.

Henry opened the refrigerator, reached for the last can of beer, then glanced at his watch: almost midnight—changed his mind. He peered out at the space between his kitchen window and the street lamp: lot of moisture in the air still, but hard to tell if it was falling or rising. He'd brooded over it, coming home from work: that piled-up mid-autumn feeling, pregnant with the vague threat of confusion and emptiness—but this boy had cut clean through it, let light and health in, and you don't go to bed on an event like this! Henry reknotted his tie, put on hat and raincoat, hooked his umbrella over one arm, and went out to get a drink. He glanced back at the kitchen table once more before pulling the door to, saw the dice there, grinned at them, for once adjuncts to grandeur, then hustled down the stairs like a happy Pioneer headed for the showers. He stepped quickly through the disembodied street-lamp glow at the bottom, and whirling his umbrella like a drum major's baton, marched springily up the street to Pete's, the neighborhood bar.

> N-o-O-O-o Hit Nealy!
> Won his fame
> Spoilin' Birdie Deaton's
> Per-her-fect game!

The night above was dark yet the streets were luminous; wet, they shimmered with what occasional light there was from street lamps, passing cars, phone booths, all-night neon signs. There was fog and his own breath was visible, yet nearby objects glittered with a heightened clarity. He smiled at the shiny newness of things springing up beside him on his night walk. At a distance, car head lamps were haloed and taillights burned fuzzily, yet the lit sign in the darkened window he was passing, "DIVINEFORM FOUNDATIONS: TWO-WAY STRETCH," shone fiercely, hard-edged and vivid as a vision.

The corner drugstore was still open. A scrawny curly-headed kid, cigarette butt dangling under his fuzzy upper lip, played the pinball machine that stood by the window. Henry paused to watch. The machine was rigged like a baseball game, though the scores were unrealistic. Henry had played the machine himself often and once, during a blue season, had even played off an entire-all-UBA pinball tourney on it. Ballplayers, lit from inside, scampered around the basepaths, as the kid put english on the balls with his hips and elbows. A painted pitcher, in eternal windup, kicked high, while below, a painted batter in a half-crouch moved motionlessly toward the plate. Two girls in the upper corners, legs apart and skirts hiked up their thighs, cheered the runners on with silent wide-open mouths. The kid was really racking them up: seven free games showing already. Lights flashed, runners ran. Eight. Nine. "THE GREAT AMERICAN GAME," it said across the top, between the gleaming girls. Well, it was. American baseball, by luck, trial, and error, and since the famous playing rules council of 1889, had struck on an almost perfect balance between offense and defense, and it was that balance, in fact, that and the accountability—the beauty of the records system which found a place to keep forever each least action—that had led Henry to baseball as his final great project.

The kid twisted, tensed, relaxed, hunched over, reared, slapped the machine with a pelvic thrust; up to seventeen free games and the score on the lighted panel looked more like that of a cricket match than a baseball game. Henry moved on. To be sure, he'd only got through one UBA pinball tourney and had never been tempted to set up another. Simple-minded, finally, and not surprisingly a simple-minded ballplayer, Jaybird Wall, had won it. In spite of all the flashing lights, it was—like those two frozen open-mouthed girls and the batter forever approaching the plate, the imperturbable pitcher forever reared back—a static game, utterly lacking the movement, grace, and complexity of real baseball. When he'd finally decided to settle on his own baseball game, Henry had spent the better part of two months just working with the problem of odds and equilibrium points in an effort to approximate that complexity. Two dice had not done it. He'd tried three, each a different color, and the 216 different combinations had provided the complexity, all right, but he'd nearly gone blind trying to sort the colors on each throw. Finally, he'd compromised, keeping the three dice, but all white, reducing the total number of combinations to 56, though of course the odds were still based on 216. To restore—and, in fact, to intensify—the complexity of the multicolored method, he'd allowed triple ones and sixes—1–1–1 and 6–6–6—to trigger the more spectacular events, by referring the following dice throw to what he called his Stress Chart, also a three-dice chart, but far more dramatic in nature than the basic ones. Two successive throws of triple ones and sixes were exceedingly rare—only about three times in every two entire seasons of play on the average—but when it happened, the next throw was referred, finally, to the Chart of Extraordinary Occurrences, where just about anything from fistfights to fixed ball games could happen. These two charts were what gave the game its special quality, making it much more than just a series of hits and walks and outs. Besides these, he also had special strategy charts for hit-and-run plays, attempted stolen bases, sacrifice bunts, and squeeze plays, still others for deciding the ages of rookies when they came up, for providing details of injuries and errors, and for determining who, each year, must die.

A neon beer advertisement and windows lit dimly through red curtains were all that marked Pete's place. Steady clientele, no doubt profitable in a small way, generally quiet, mostly country-and-western or else old hit-parade tunes on the jukebox, a girl or two drifting by from time to time, fair prices. Henry brought his gyrating umbrella under control, left the wet world behind, and pushed in.

"Evening, Mr. Waugh," said the bartender.

"Evening, Jake."

Not Jake, of course, it was Pete himself, but it was a long-standing gag, born of a slip of the tongue. Pete was medium-sized, slope-shouldered, had bartender's bags beneath his eyes and a splendid bald dome, spoke with a kind of hushed irony that seemed to give a dry double meaning to everything he said— in short, was the spitting image of Jake Bradley, one of Henry's ballplayers, a Pastimer second baseman whom Henry always supposed now to be running a bar somewhere near the Pastime Club's ballpark, and one night, years ago, in the middle of a free-swinging pennant scramble, Henry had called Pete "Jake" by mistake. He'd kept it up ever since; it was a kind of signal to Pete that he was in a good mood and wanted something better than beer or bar whiskey. He sometimes wondered if anybody ever walked into Jake's bar and called him Pete by mistake. Henry took the middle one of three empty barstools. Jake— Pete—lifted a bottle of VSOP, raised his eyebrows, and Henry nodded. Right on the button.

The bar was nearly empty, not surprising; Tuesday, a working night, only six or seven customers, faces all familiar, mostly old-timers on relief. Pete's cats scrubbed and stalked, sulked and slept. A neighborhood B-girl named Hettie, old friend of Henry's, put money in the jukebox—old-time country love songs. Nostalgia was the main vice here. Pete toweled dust from a snifter, poured a finger of cognac into it. "How's the work going, Mr. Waugh?" he asked.

"Couldn't go better," Henry said and smiled. Jake always asked the right questions.

Jake smiled broadly, creasing his full cheeks, nodded as though to say he understood, pate flashing in the amber light. And it was the right night to call him Jake, after all: Jake Bradley was also from the Brock Rutherford era, must have come up about the same time. Was he calling it that now? The Brock Rutherford Era? He never had before. Funny. Damon was not only creating the future, he was doing something to the past, too. Jake dusted the shelf before

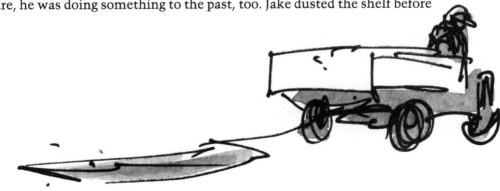

putting the cognac bottle back. He was once the middle man in five double plays executed in one game, still the Association record.

Hettie, catching Henry's mood apparently, came over to kid with him and he bought her a drink. A couple molars missing and flesh folds ruining the once-fine shape of her jaw, but there was still something compelling about the electronic bleat her stockings emitted when she hopped up on a barstool and crossed her legs, and that punctuation-wink she used to let a man know he was in with her, getting the true and untarnished word. Henry hadn't gone with her in years, not since before he set up his Association, but she often figured obliquely in the Book and conversations with her often got reproduced there under one guise or another. "Been gettin' any hits lately?" she asked, and winked over her tumbler of whiskey. They often used baseball idiom, she no doubt supposing he was one of those ballpark zealots who went crazy every season during the World Series and got written up as a character—the perennial krank—in the newspapers, and Henry never told her otherwise. Since she herself knew nothing at all about the sport, though, he often talked about his Association as though it were the major leagues. It gave him a kind of pleasure to talk about it with someone, even if she did think he was talking about something else.

"Been getting a lot," he said, "but probably not enough." She laughed loudly, exhibiting the gaps in her teeth. "And how about you, Hettie, been scoring a lot of runs?"

"I been scorin', boy, but I ain't got the runs!" she said, and whooped again. Old gag. The other customers turned their way and smiled.

Henry waited for her to settle down, commune with her drink once more, then he said, "Listen, Hettie, think what a wonderful rare thing it is to do something, no matter how small a thing, with absolute unqualified utterly unsurpassable *perfection!*"

"What makes you think it's so rare?" she asked with a wink, and switching top knee, issued the old signal. "You ain't pitched to me in a long time, you know."

He grinned. "No, but think of it, Hettie, to do a thing so perfectly that, even if the damn world lasted forever, nobody could ever do it better, because you had done it as well as it could possibly be done." He paused, let the cognac fumes bite his nostrils to excuse the foolish tears threatening to film his eyes over. "In a way, you know, it's even sad somehow, because, well, it's done, and all you can hope for after is to do it a second time." Of course, there were other things to do, the record book was, above all, a catalogue of possibilities...

"A second time! Did you say *perfection* or *erection?*" Hettie asked.

Henry laughed. It was no use. And anyway it didn't matter. He felt just stupendous, not so exultant as before, but still full of joy, and now a kind of heady aromatic peace seemed to be sweeping over him: ecstasy—yes, he laughed to himself, that was the only goddamn word for it. It was good. He bought another round, asked Pete: "How is it you stay in such good shape, Jake?"

"I don't know, Mr. Waugh. Must be the good Christian hours I keep."

And then, when the barkeep had left them, it was Hettie who suddenly turned serious. "I don't know what it is about you tonight, Henry," she said, "but you've got me kinda hot." And she switched top knee again: call from the deep.

Henry smiled, slowly whirling the snifter through minute cycles, warming the tawny dram in the palm of his hand. It was a temptation, to be sure, but he was afraid Hettie would spoil it for him, dissipate the joy and dull this glow, take the glory out of it. It was something he could share with no one without losing it altogether. Too bad. "It's just that nobody's bought you two straight drinks in a long time, Hettie," he said.

"Aw," she grumbled and frowned at her glass, hurt by that and so cooled off a little. To make up for it, he ordered her a third drink. He'd had enough, time to get back, had to make it to work in the morning, old Zifferblatt had been giving him a hard time for weeks now and just looking for a chance to raise hell about something, but Pete poured him one on the house. Not every day you pitched perfect games and got VSOP on the house. "Thanks, Jake," he said.

"Henry, hon', gimme some money to put in the jukebox."

Coins on the bar: he slid them her way. Stared into his snifter, saw himself there in the brown puddle, or anyway his eye.

> It was down in Jake's old barroom
> Behind the Patsies' park;
> Jake was settin' 'em up as usual
> And the night was agittin' dark.
> At the bar stood ole Verne Mackenzie,
> And his eyes was bloodshot red . . .

"The Day They Fired Verne Mackenzie": Sandy Shaw's great ballad. Dead now, Verne. First of the game's superstars, starting shortstop on Abe Flint's Excelsiors back in Year I, first of the Hall of Famers. But he got older and stopped hitting, and Flint, nice a guy as he was, had to let him go. And they all knew how Verne felt, even the young guys playing now who never knew him, because sooner or later it would be the same for them. Hettie leaned against him, head on his shoulder, humming the jukebox melodies to herself. He felt good, having her there like that. He sipped his brandy and grew slowly melancholy, *pleasantly* melancholy. He saw Brock the Great reeling boisterously down the street, arm in arm with Willie O'Leary and Frosty Young, those wonderful guys—and who should they meet up with but sleepy-eyed Mose Stanford and Gabe Burdette and crazy rubber-legged Jaybird Wall. Yes, and they were singing, singing the *old* songs, "Pitchin', Catchin', Swingin' " and "The Happy Days of Youth," and oh! it was happiness! and goddamn it! it was fellowship! and boys oh boys! it was significance! "Let's go to Jake's!" they cried, they laughed, and off they went!

"Where?" Hettie mumbled. She was pretty far along. So was he. Didn't realize he had been talking out loud. Glanced self-consciously at Pete, but Pete hadn't moved: he was a patient pillar in the middle of the bar, ankles and arms crossed, face in shadows, only the dome lit up. Maybe he was asleep. There was only one other customer, an old-timer, still in the bar. The neon light outside was probably off.

"To my place," he said, not sure it was himself talking. Could he take her up there? She leaned away from his shoulder, tried to wink, couldn't quite pull it off, instead studied him quizzically as though wondering if he really meant it. "Hettie," he whispered, staring hard at her, so she'd know he wasn't kidding and that she'd better not spoil it, "how would you like to sleep with . . . Damon Rutherford?"

She blinked, squinted skeptically, but he could see she was still pretty excited and she'd moved her hand up his pantleg to the seam. "Who's he?"

"Me." He didn't smile, just looked straight at her, and he saw her eyes widen, maybe even a little fear came into them, but certainly awe was there, and fascination, and hope, and her hand, discovering he could do it, yes, he could do it, gave a squeeze like Witness York always gave his bat for luck before he swung, and she switched knees: *wheep!* So he paid Jake, and together—he standing tall and self-assured, Hettie shiveringly clasped in his embrace—they walked out. As he'd foreseen, the neon light was out; it was dark. He felt exceedingly wise.

"What are you, Henry?" Hettie asked softly as they walked under the glowing nimbus of a mist-wrapped street lamp. His raincoat had a slit in the lining behind the pocket, and this she reached through to slip her hand into his coin pocket.

"Now, or when we get to my place?"

"Now."

"An accountant."

"But the baseball? . . ." And again she took hold and squeezed like Witness York, but now her hand was full of coins as well, and they wrapped the bat like a suit of mail.

"I'm an auditor for a baseball association."

"I didn't know they had auditors, too," she said. Was she really listening for once? They were in the dark now, next street lamp was nearly a block away, in front of Diskin's. She was trying to get her other hand on the bat, gal can't take a healthy swing without a decent grip, after all, but she couldn't get both hands through the slit.

"Oh, yes. I keep financial ledgers for each club, showing cash receipts and disbursements, which depend mainly on such things as team success, the buying and selling of ballplayers, improvement of the stadiums, player contracts, things like that." Hettie Irden stood at the plate, first woman ballplayer in league history, tightening and relaxing her grip on the bat, smiling around the spaces of her missing molars in that unforgettable way of hers, kidding with the catcher, laughing that gay timeless laugh that sounded like the clash of small coins, tugging maybe at her crotch in a parody of all male ballplayers the world over, and maybe she wasn't the best hitter in the Association, but the Association was glad to have her. She made them all laugh and forget for a moment that they were dying men. "And a running journalization of the activity, posting of it all into permanent record books, and I help them with basic problems of burden distribution, remarshaling of assets, graphing fluctuations. Politics, too. Elections. Team captains. Club presidents. And every four years, the Association elects a Chancellor, and I have to keep an eye on that."

"Gee, Henry, I didn't realize! . . ." She was looking up at him, and as they approached the street lamp, he could see something in her eyes he hadn't seen there before. He was glad to see it had come to pass, that she recognized—but it wouldn't do when they got to bed, she'd have to forget then.

"There are box scores to be audited, trial balances of averages along the way, seasonal inventories, rewards and punishments to be meted out, life histories to be overseen." He took a grip on her behind. "People die, you know."

"Yes," she said, and that seemed to excite her, for she squeezed a little harder.

"Usually, they die old, already long since retired, but they can die young, even as ballplayers. Or in accidents during the winter season. Last year a young fellow, just thirty, had a bad season and got sent back to the minors. They say his manager rode him too hard." Pappy Rooney. Wouldn't let go of the kid. "Sensitive boy who took it too much to heart. On the way, he drove his car off a cliff."

"Oh!" she gasped and squeezed. As though afraid now to let go. "On purpose?"

"I don't know. I think so. And if a pitcher throws two straight triple ones or sixes and brings on an Extraordinary Occurrence, a third set of ones is a beanball that kills the batter, while triple sixes again is a line drive that kills the pitcher."

"Oh, how awful!" He didn't tell her neither had ever happened. "But what are triple sixes, Henry?"

"A kind of pitch. Here we are."

Even climbing the stairs to his place, she didn't want to release her grip, but the stairway was too narrow and they kept jamming up. So she took her hand out and went first. From his squat behind the box, the catcher watched her loosening up, kidded her that she'd never get a walk because they could never get two balls on her. Over her shoulder, she grinned down upon him, a gap-tooth grin that was still somehow beautiful. Anyhow, she said, I *am* an Extraordinary Occurrence, and on that chart there's no place for mere passes! The catcher laughed, reached up and patted her rear. "You said it!" he admitted, letting his hand glide down her thigh, then whistle up her stocking underneath the skirt. "An Extraordinary Occurrence!"

She hopped two steps giddily, thighs slapping together. "Henry! I'm ticklish!"

He unlocked the door to his apartment, switched on a night light in the hall, leaving the kitchen and Association in protective darkness, and led her toward the bedroom.

"We're at your place," she said huskily when they'd got in there, and squeezed up against him. "Who are you now?" That she remembered! She was wonderful!

"The greatest pitcher in the history of baseball," he whispered. "Call me . . . Damon."

"Damon," she whispered, unbuckling his pants, pulling his shirt out. And "Damon," she sighed, stroking his back, unzipping his fly, sending his pants earthward with a rattle of buckles and coins. And "Damon!" she greeted, grabbing—and that girl, with one swing, he knew then, could bang a pitch clean out of the park. *"Play ball!"* cried the umpire. And the catcher, stripped of mask and guard, revealed as the pitcher Damon Rutherford, whipped the uniform off the first lady ballplayer in Association history, and then, helping and hindering all at once, pushing and pulling, they ran the bases, pounded into first, slid into second heels high, somersaulted over third, shot home standing up, then into the box once more, swing away, and run them all again, and "Damon!" she cried, and "Damon!"

Has there ever been a better baseball biography than *Babe?* No, not even Creamer's admirable *Stengel*. The subtitle of *Babe* is "The Legend Comes to Life"; here the life ends, heartbreakingly, although the legend will live always. Today, fifty years after Ruth played his last major-league game, no one has come along to challenge his position as the game's greatest player. Roger Maris and Henry Aaron have surpassed his home-run records, but Ruth remains the nonpareil, an American hero more implausible than Paul Bunyan and more beloved than any but Lincoln.

ROBERT W. CREAMER

"Joe, I'm Gone"

Colonel Ruppert died in January 1939. Ruth visited him in the hospital as he lay dying and was touched when Ruppert, who had never called him anything but Ruth, whispered, "Babe, Babe." Gehrig was dying, and at the Lou Gehrig Day ceremonies at Yankee Stadium on July 4th, Babe ended their long antagonism by impulsively putting his arm around Gehrig and hugging him.

Time was closing in. Playing golf with Ben Curry at Leewood, Ruth said, "I feel terrible," and lay down on the grass near the sixteenth tee. "His face was almost blue," Curry recalled. A car was brought out and Ruth was driven to the clubhouse, where he lay down on a bench and asked for a glass of water. A doctor had been called, and Curry was afraid to let him have anything before the doctor got there. He put a sip of water in a glass and gave it to him. Ruth said, "Damn it, give me a glass of water," and began to lift himself. He was given a full glass of water and drank all of it and drank another. After the doctor checked him out, he rested for a while and that night felt fine.

But it was apparently a mild heart attack, and a year or so later he had another. Late in 1941, he was invited to appear in *Pride of the Yankees*, a movie about Gehrig. His weight was nearly 270, and he dieted strenuously in order to be down to presentable size when work on the film began early in

1942. He lost 40 pounds in a few months and became edgy and irritable. He had a minor but frightening auto accident in December that depressed him terribly, an odd thing for a man who had been in so many accidents. He caught a bad cold, and early in the New Year, suffering from the cold and nervous exhaustion, he was taken from his apartment on a stretcher and sent to the hospital. He recovered quickly and was off hunting for a few days before going to California for the movie.

In Hollywood he worked hard on the Lou Gehrig movie and did a fine natural job of acting, even to the point of putting his fist through a Pullman car window in a pennant celebration scene. But the stringent working schedule demanded by the film combined with his own normally late hours did not mesh well. He caught another cold and it developed into pneumonia. Again he was hospitalized and for a day or so was reported to be near death. But he was out of the hospital in two weeks, and by the end of April, with the movie finished, was home in New York, healthy and playing golf.

During World War II, he did work for the Red Cross, bought $100,000 worth of war bonds, made appropriate comments about Hitler and Mussolini and the Japanese, voted against Franklin Roosevelt, and appeared frequently at benefits. He played a series of three golf matches with Ty Cobb for war charities, losing the first, winning the second, and losing the third. In August 1942, he appeared at a benefit affair in Yankee Stadium, where he batted against Walter Johnson. It was his first time in the Stadium as a player since 1934, and he was as excited as a kid about it, making sure his uniform was clean and pressed, his spiked shoes shined. Johnson threw seven pitches before Ruth lifted a high fly into the stands in right. The ball curved foul, but Ruth, always a showman, accepted it as a home run and ran around the bases while the crowd cheered. In May 1943, he was in uniform again for a game between two teams from the armed forces, both studded with professional players. Babe pinch-hit and walked. A couple of months later he managed a servicemen's team in another benefit at Yankee Stadium and put himself in as a pinch hitter against Johnny Sain. He hit one long foul and then walked. A pinch runner came out from the dugout, but Ruth waved him off. The next man singled and Ruth moved to second, but he pulled up lame and puffing. He accepted the pinch runner then and half walked, half jogged off the field. It was his last appearance in a formal game.

He was in the hospital toward the end of the war for a cartilage operation on his knee. After the war he let his hope of managing come alive again. The Ruppert estate sold the Yankees to a syndicate headed by MacPhail, and Barrow was no longer running the team. Ruth phoned MacPhail and asked him for the job of managing the Yankees' Newark farm club. It was an embarrassing retreat from his long-held position that he was a big leaguer who did not have to go back to the minors as an apprentice, but he was being realistic. MacPhail said he would get back to him. There was no answer for a few weeks and then a letter came.

"That's bad news," Ruth said. "When it's good news, they telephone."

MacPhail did not want Ruth and told him so in a polite, circuitous note that ended with a plea for Babe to become involved in a sandlot baseball program sponsored by the city of New York. That was the final humiliation. He went back to golf, bowling, and hunting.

In May 1946, when Jorge Pascual was trying to build up the Mexican League by enticing American major leaguers with offers of huge salaries, Ruth spent two weeks in Mexico City as Pascual's guest. He was called El Rey Jonronero in the Mexican newspapers. Now past fifty, he said quite plainly that he doubted he would sign any sort of a contract with Pascual, but he had a fine time anyway. He went to a bullfight, played golf, got sunburned, saw a few ballgames, swung at a couple of pitches in batting practice. He met fifty-eight-year-old Armando Marsans, a Cuban who had been an American League outfielder thirty years earlier when Ruth was still a pitcher. "You remember me?" asked Marsans, and Ruth's face lit up. "Sure I do," he said, and he did. Not the name, but the man. Marsans was managing in one of the games Ruth saw, and when he refused to take a pitcher out of a game despite a rally by the other

team, Ruth approved. "That's right," he called out. "Let him stay in there."

Because of the major leagues' antipathy for Pascual and the Mexican League, Ruth was asked if anyone tried to persuade him not to visit Mexico. "No," Babe said, "nobody asked me not to come. But that doesn't make any difference. I go where I please anyway."

Several months later Ruth began to complain of extreme pain over his left eye. He thought it was a sinus headache, but it hurt so much that in November he entered French Hospital in New York for a thorough examination. Not much attention was paid—he had been in and out of hospitals so often—but this time it was deadly serious. He had a malignant growth in the left side of his neck, in such a position that it nearly encircled the left carotid artery. When he was operated on, nerves had to be severed and the artery tied off, which adversely affected the left side of his head, including his larynx. Most of the cancerous growth was removed but some could not be, and he was given radiation treatment to control it.

The disease and its treatment debilitated him. He could not eat and had to be fed intravenously. He was in French Hospital for three months and lost 80 pounds. When he was discharged in February 1947, he went to Florida to rest in the sun. He regained enough strength to play golf a few times and go fishing, but the seriousness of his condition was evident in his appearance. In March, A. B. (Happy) Chandler, the new commissioner of baseball (Judge Landis died in 1944), declared that Sunday, April 27, would be Babe Ruth Day in the major leagues. Ceremonies were held in all the parks, but the most significant was in Yankee Stadium.

Ruth returned to New York in time to be at the Stadium for his day. He wore his familiar camel's hair overcoat and camel's hair cap, but he was thin, his color a bad yellowish tan, his voice a disheartening croak. Almost 60,000 people were in the Stadium. There was the usual plethora of speeches, including one from a thirteen-year-old who represented boys' baseball. Ruth spoke too, bending forward slightly from the hips to bring his mouth close to the microphone. His speech was extemporaneous.

"Thank you very much, ladies and gentlemen," he began, the awful voice sounding even harsher as it came from the loudspeakers. "You know how bad my voice sounds. Well, it feels just as bad. You know, this baseball game of ours comes up from the youth. That means the boys. And after you've been a boy, and grow up to know how to play ball, then you come to the boys you see representing themselves today in our national pastime. The only real game in the world, I think, is baseball. As a rule, some people think if you give them a football or a baseball or something like that, naturally, they're athletes right away. But you can't do that in baseball. You've got to start from way down, at the bottom, when you're six or seven years old. You can't wait until you're fifteen or sixteen. You've got to let it grow up with you, and if you're successful and you try hard enough, you're bound to come out on top, just like these boys have come to the top now.

"There's been so many lovely things said about me, I'm glad I had the opportunity to thank everybody. Thank you."

He smiled and waved to the crowd and walked slowly to the Yankee dugout.

The unexcised part of the tumor continued to grow, and Ruth was in extreme discomfort through the spring of 1947. He did not know what was wrong with him, and no one told him. Considine said, "Those who knew him best, Mel Lowenstein and Paul Carey, and Claire, believed that if he knew he had terminal cancer, it would destroy him. He'd go right out the window." For a time Ruth thought his teeth were infected, and he would wince with pain and mutter, "These damn teeth."

He was in constant pain that had to be relieved with morphine. He tried to work with Considine on his autobiography, but when he could not recall something he was trying to remember, he would break off the conversation and say, "Let's get the hell out of here and go hit a few." They would get into Ruth's Lincoln Continental and drive to the butcher shop on Ninth Avenue. Instead of ordering a steak to take to the golf course, Ruth would buy chopped meat, since he could not chew. In the shop he would pick up a cleaver and playfully threaten the butchers. "I'm going to chop your goddamned heads off," he'd say, to their evident delight. A girl, a nurse, would usually meet him in the butcher shop and ride out to the golf course, where she would walk around with them while they played. Sometimes at the club he felt so bad he would have only a soft-boiled egg, and he had trouble swallowing that. One day he looked at the egg in his misery and said, "To think of the steaks." For a time he continued to play eighteen holes, but as he grew weaker his games grew shorter. One day he teed up his ball, swung well, and hit the ball cleanly. It carried straight down the fairway, but for only about 90 yards. Ruth stood on the tee watching it and cried, cursing through the tears.

By June 1947 the pain had become so bad that his doctors decided to treat the cancer with an experimental new drug, a synthetic relative of folic acid, part of the vitamin B complex. Treatment began on June 29, and Ruth showed such remarkable improvement that in September a paper on his case was read at an International Cancer Congress meeting in St. Louis. He began to travel around the country doing promotional work on American Legion baseball for the Ford Motor Company. He also had Lowenstein draw up papers creating The Babe Ruth Foundation, which was designed to help underprivileged children. Late in September, MacPhail put on another Babe Ruth Day at Yankee Stadium to raise funds for the Ruth Foundation, and Babe was there to watch an old-timers' game played by Ty Cobb and Tris Speaker and others. He had hoped to be strong enough to be able to pitch an inning, but he was not.

His dramatic improvement was apparently only a temporary remission of the cancer, and he continued painfully ill. When Ruth was in Cincinnati for the Ford people, Waite Hoyt and his wife visited him in his hotel. Claire met them at the door and brought them into the living room of the suite where Ruth was sitting on a couch, his head down, nodding from the sedatives he was taking. On the table in front of him was a bottle of beer, which, Hoyt said, he drank for food. Babe lifted his head wearily.

"I'm glad to see you," he whispered.

They talked for a while, but he appeared so exhausted that Hoyt decided he and his wife should leave.

"We'd better go, Jidge."

Ruth nodded. "I am kind of tired," he said.

The Hoyts stood up to go, but Ruth whispered, "Wait a minute." Painfully, he got to his feet and went into the kitchen. From the refrigerator he took a small vase with an orchid in it and brought it back to the living room.

"Here," he said to Mrs. Hoyt. "I never gave you anything."

On Sunday, June 13, 1948, the Yankees celebrated the twenty-fifth anniversary of Yankee Stadium, and Ruth was invited to be there along with other members of the 1923 Yankees. Sick as he was, he was delighted with the idea. The Yankees held a banquet for all the old players at Ruppert's brewery the night before the game, but Ruth was not well enough to attend that. There was concern that he might not be at the Stadium either on Sunday because it was a dank, rainy day. But he came. The other old Yankees were already in the locker room when he arrived.

"Here he is now," one of them said in a low voice, and Ruth came in slowly, helped by Paul Carey and Frank Dulaney, his male nurse. His face split into a grin, a shriveled caricature of the beaming one he used to have, and in his croaking voice he spoke to his old teammates, calling most of them by their nicknames. Dulaney helped him take off his street clothes and put on his uniform. The old teammates stayed away until he had his uniform on, and so did the photographers. Then they began to take pictures, with Ruth posing willingly. The old Yankees were gathered together for a group photograph. Ruth, stooped, smiling, stood in the middle of the back row. Joe Dugan, standing half behind him, had a hand on his shoulder, and so did Wally Pipp.

The old-timers began to go out onto the field, and Ruth, accompanied by Dulaney and Carey, followed slowly down the runway to the dugout. It was early, and Ruth paused in the runway, a topcoat slung over his shoulders to keep off the chill. "I think you'd better wait inside," said Dulaney. "It's too damp here." Ruth was led back to the clubhouse and stayed there until it was nearly time for him to appear on the field. Then he came down the runway again and into the dugout, where room was made for him on the bench. Mel Harder, a Cleveland coach who had pitched against Ruth, came over to say hello.

Ruth said hoarsely, "You remember when I got five-for-five off you in Cleveland and they booed me?"

Harder smiled.

"Line drives," Ruth croaked, "all to left field. And they booed the shit out of me."

All the other old-timers had been introduced, the applause from the big crowd rising and falling as each name was called. It was time for Ruth. He got to his feet, letting the topcoat fall from his shoulders, and took a bat to use as a cane. He looked up at the photographers massed in front of the dugout. His name rang out over the public address system, the roar of the crowd began and, as W. C. Heinz wrote, "He walked out into the cauldron of sound he must have known better than any other man."

He walked slowly, and he was smaller than Babe Ruth should have been. He paused for the photographers, leaning on the bat, looking up at the crowded tiers of people. Near home plate he was met by Ed Barrow, a month past his eightieth birthday, who hugged him. At the microphone Ruth spoke briefly, saying how proud he was to have hit the first home run in the Stadium and how good it was to see his old teammates. When the ceremonies were over and the other old players trotted out to their positions for a two-inning game, Ruth left the field at Yankee Stadium for the last time. He was helped down into the dug-out and back along the runway to the clubhouse. The topcoat was put over his shoulders again, and he kept it on in the clubhouse. He felt chilly. The glow of the excitement was wearing off. Dugan, who played only one inning of the old-timers' game, came into the clubhouse.

"Hiya, Babe," Dugan said, sitting down next to him.

"Hello, Joe."

"Can you use a drink?"

"Just a beer."

A small bar had been set up in a corner of the locker room, and Dugan got a drink for himself and a beer for Ruth and brought them back. They sat there a while, sipping their drinks.

"How are things, Jidge?" Dugan asked.

"Joe, I'm gone," Ruth said. "I'm gone, Joe."

He started to cry, and Dugan did too.

A week or so later, Ruth was in the hospital again. He did not want to go, and when it was time to leave for the hospital he refused to get out of bed. Frank Dulaney said, "He was in terrible pain. I tried to cajole him, but he shook his head. He wouldn't get up. I sat on the side of his bed and talked to him. I said, 'If you were my father, I'd make you go.' He got up then."

As Dulaney helped him up the steps of Memorial Hospital, Ruth said, "Isn't this hospital for cancer?" Dulaney answered, "Cancer and *allied* diseases." Ruth grunted.

He never was told he had cancer, but he certainly knew it, at least toward the end. When Jim Peterson took Connie Mack to visit him, Ruth said, "Hello, Mr. Mack. The termites have got me."

Ruth was ambulatory in the hospital, and when he felt strong enough he would go out for a drive. Early in July, he paid his last visit to Baltimore, flying down for a charity game. It was rained out, but he had a chance to talk to Roger Pippen, who had been with him in Fayetteville in 1914. Back in his hospital room he watched baseball on television, a relatively new phenomenon, and was pleased by visits and mail. He received hundreds of letters every day. A few would be read to him and he would rasp his reaction. May Singhi Breen, a onetime radio star who, with her husband, the songwriter Peter DeRose, was close to Claire and Babe, took on the job of seeing to it that all the mail was answered. Many contained requests for autographs, and on days he felt well Ruth would ask for "my cards." These were postcards with his photograph, and he would sign a hundred or so at a time to keep a supply on hand. President Truman phoned him, and Betty Grable, whom he had met and liked in Hollywood, sent him a bottle of pine-scented cologne. He wanted the cologne in his bath water each day and sometimes he would grunt to Dulaney, "Toss a little around the room, Frank."

The last rites of the Catholic Church were administered on July 21, but Ruth rallied again after that. He left the hospital on the evening of July 26 to attend the premiere of *The Babe Ruth Story*. He was very uncomfortable watching the film and left well before it was over. He seemed content back in the hospital, and he never left it again. "All my obligations are over," he said. "I'm going to rest now. I'm going to take it easy."

In August, his condition steadily deteriorated. Claire stayed in a room across the hall, usually attended by a friend or by Julia or Dorothy. Few visitors were admitted, but Ruth, even though he was unable to say much, relished the visits. Paul Carey phoned Ford Frick one day and told him Babe would like to see him. Frick said the hospital was like a three-ring circus, with reporters and photographers waiting, and the deathwatch across the hall. He spoke to Claire for a moment and then went into the room.

"It was a terrible moment. Ruth was so thin it was unbelievable. He had been such a big man, and his arms were just skinny little bones and his face was so haggard. When I came in he lifted his eyes toward me and raised his right arm a little, only about three or four inches off the bed, and then it fell back again. I went over to the bed and I said, 'Babe, Paul Carey said you wanted to see me.' And Ruth said, in that terrible voice, 'Ford, I always wanted to see you.' It was just a polite thing to say. I stayed a few minutes and left and I spoke to Claire again across the hall and then I went home and the next day he was dead."

What is a muffin game? It is an 1860s travesty of baseball perpetrated by inept, out-of-shape, middle-aged supporters of an amateur club's first nine. A muffin muffed—he could not catch, or throw, or hit—but he could enjoy himself, and he certainly could entertain others. In the days when baseball was new, it was common to stage a muffin match after the regular contest had concluded. The delightful account below by one "Q. K. Philander Doesticks" appeared in *The Hartford Courant* of October 10, 1866, and may describe the "Great Muffin Game" held four months earlier between Hartford and Waterbury. By the way, the Pitchman is a pitcher, the Catchman a catcher, and the players are termed "monkeys" because of their gaudy uniforms.

Q. K. PHILANDER DOESTICKS

A Muffin Game

I squared myself, raised my big stick, and told the Pitchman to pitch in. He did so. The first ball came like a cannon shot, but I dodged it neatly. The next one hit me plump in the breast. I dropped the stick and asked him what he did that for. Cap told me to pick up the stick again and try to hit the ball. Did so. When I saw the ball coming, I poked my stick at it, but didn't hit it. The truth was I wasn't prepared to have it come so fast. Told the Pitchman to give me a fair ball, an easy one; then all the fellows laughed. Then I got mad—punched the stick at the next ball—didn't hit it; punched again—all the fellows yelled "Run, run—run you muffin! Run you diabolical fool, run! Run, I tell you!—" About this time I started to run; didn't look which way I went; ran into the Catchman, who stood behind me; bowled him over on his head. "Not that way—run, run," everybody yelled again. Changed my course; tumbled over the Umpire, and tangled my legs in his chair. Veered about, and dashed furiously against our Captain and caught a dim vision of his heels in the air, as I started on a new course, and backed into a sturdy policeman. Then tumbled over one of the base bags; some fellows yelled to "Stop!", others, "Run, run!" Started once more; dashed into a crowd of spectators and upset about a dozen; then pitched into the game keepers; finally ran into the fence, and fell all in a heap into a frog hole. When I was picked up, everything was spinning around the sky and the ballground was all mixed up; the policeman seemed to be floating in the air, and all the monkeys to be whirling round at a terrific rate among the clouds; while the spectators, the bases, the bags, the officers, the wagons, the clubhouse, the trees, bushes, and frog pond seemed to be joining in a frantic jig on the double quick, only ten times faster than any double quick ever executed. When I came to my senses, found everybody shrieking with laughter, and calling me "the dashedest muffin that ever held a club." My nose was bleeding, my elbows skinned, my hair full of burdocks, and my monkey clothes covered with mud and frog-spawn. Cap came over and soon as he could stop laughing long enough to speak, he said, "Well, of all the dashed muffins I ever saw, you are the dashedest!" I didn't wait for any more compliments, but went home.

For this ripping yarn I am indebted to my friend Fred Ivor-Campbell of Providence, who read it in that city's *Sunday Journal* in 1979 and fortunately saved it. Before being picked up by the Associated Press, Bill Doyle's deft profile appeared in the Holyoke *Transcript-Telegram*.

BILL DOYLE

Ticket Taker Talks Technique

Every Holyoke Millers player hopes to make the major leagues someday, and the team's head ticker taker has the same aspiration.

"My dream is to be a big-league ticket taker," admits Bill Kane of 38 Kane Rd.

Kane, a science teacher at Holyoke High School in the off-season, is in his rookie year as a Mackenzie Field ticket taker. He says he has worked hard to improve his ticket-tearing skills to get a chance to rip in the big leagues.

"I can rip from either side," said the 6 foot, 160 pounder, who claims only one thing has prevented him from making the jump to the majors.

"I have no experience with turnstiles whatsoever, and I think that's what's holding me back," he said.

Millers' general manager Tom Kayser thinks the rookie has plenty of potential. "He's got the style and he's got the personality, but he's a little weak in ticket tearing speed," Kayser noted. "His hand—eye coordination is off."

While Kane dreams of ripping in the majors, he doesn't have stars in his eyes.

"If I'm not there by the time I'm thirty, I'll have to reassess my future," said Kane, who will turn thirty in October. "I'm not getting any younger. When you get to be thirty, you have to realize you may never tear a ticket in the bigs."

Tearing tickets isn't easy, but Kane has it down to a science. One of the trickiest ticket tears is a multiple ticket rip.

"We just call it 'multiple' in the business," said Kane.

A multiple occurs when a ticket taker is handed more than one ticket to tear at the same time. "You must fold the tickets together and give them one quick rip," said Kane.

The only thing trickier than a multiple ticket rip is a double multiple rip. A double multiple rip is ripping two stacks of two or more tickets at once.

But, there's more to being a ticket taker than ripping. After ripping the ticket in half, a ticket taker must make sure he gives the rain check back to the fan and places the other half in the ticket box. Early in the season, Kane often became confused and gave the wrong half back to the fan.

Kane said he practices his ticket tearing by "tearing up the *Transcript* at home, but only after I read it."

Part of the job is being pleasant to incoming fans. Kane said he greets the fans with one of two phrases as he rips their tickets—"Enjoy the game" or "Don't kick the dirt."

Kane said he has wanted to be a minor-league ticket taker since he attended a game at the now-demolished Pynchon Park in Springfield as a boy.

"I idolized the ticket taker there," said Kane. "He was incredibly fast and sure-handed. And, he was tall."

Kane got his chance at ripping professional tickets after a one-year stint tearing for Holyoke Trade High School basketball games in 1976.

Kane's father, Ed, is also a ticket taker at Miller games. Ed has been shipped to the back gate while Bill rips at the busier Beech Street entrance. "They've decided to go with youth," said Kane.

Kane thinks ticket tearing just may run in the family's blood.

"My two-year-old son Chris tears up a lot of stuff at home," said Kane. "He might have what it takes."

Ticket takers have to stay relaxed during a game.

"I do stretching exercises because I don't want to run the risk of pulling a finger," he said.

Kane has managed to avoid injury so far this season, but admits he shares every ticket taker's fear—hangnails.

If Kane doesn't get his shot in the big leagues, he could settle for ripping tickets at movie theaters. But it wouldn't be the same.

"This is the American pastime," he said.

Open *The Baseball Encyclopedia* to the register of all the 13,000-odd men who have played even a minute of major-league baseball; first among these is Henry Aaron. He is also first in career home runs, and this is the one that put him over the top: Number 715. Aaron's previous homer, the one that tied the Babe, had come amid a swirl of controversy: Braves' management had considered benching him for the opening series in Cincinnati to insure maximum hometown promotional punch, but Commissioner Bowie Kuhn ordered the Braves to play Aaron, who diplomatically socked only the one homer on enemy soil.

JOSEPH DURSO

Aaron Hits 715th, Passes Babe Ruth

ATLANTA, April 8—Henry Aaron ended the great chase tonight and passed Babe Ruth as the leading home run hitter in baseball history when he hit No. 715 before a national television audience and 53,775 persons in Atlanta Stadium.

The forty-year-old outfielder for the Atlanta Braves broke the record on his second time at bat, but on his first swing of a clamorous evening. It was a soaring drive in the fourth inning off Al Downing of the Los Angeles Dodgers and it cleared the fence in left-center field, 385 feet from home plate.

Skyrockets arched over the jammed stadium in the rain as the man from Mobile trotted around the bases for the 715th time in a career that began a quarter of a century ago with the Indianapolis Clowns in the old Negro leagues.

It was 9:07 o'clock, thirty years after Ruth had hit his 714th on his first swing of the bat in the opening game of the season.

The history-making home run carried into the Atlanta bullpen, where a relief pitcher named Tom House made a dazzling one-handed catch against the auxiliary scoreboard. He clutched it against the boards, far below the grandstand seats, where the customers in "Home Run Alley" were massed, waiting to retrieve a cowhide ball that in recent days had been valued as high as $25,000 on the auction market.

So Aaron not only ended the great home run derby, but also ended the controversy that surrounded it. His employers had wanted him to hit No. 715 in Atlanta, and had even benched him on alien soil in Cincinnati.

The commissioner of baseball, Bowie Kuhn, ordered the Braves to start their star yesterday or face "serious penalties." And tonight the dispute and the marathon finally came home to Atlanta in a razzle-dazzle evening.

The stadium was packed with its largest crowd since the Braves left Milwaukee and brought major-league baseball to the Deep South nine years ago. Pearl Bailey sang the National Anthem; the Jonesboro High School band marched; balloons and fireworks filled the overcast sky before the game; Aaron's life was dramatized on a huge color map of the United States painted across the outfield grass, and Bad Henry was serenaded by the Atlanta Boy Choir, which now includes girls.

The commissioner was missing, pleading that a "previous commitment" required his presence tomorrow in Cleveland, and his emissary was roundly booed when he mentioned Kuhn's name. But Governor Jimmy Carter was there, along with Mayor Maynard Jackson, Sammy Davis, Jr., and broadcasters and writers from as far away as Japan, South America, and Britain.

To many Atlantans, it was the city's festive premiere of *Gone With the Wind* during the 1930s, when Babe Ruth was still the hero of the New York Yankees and the titan of professional sports. All that was needed to complete the evening was home run No. 715, and Aaron supplied that.

The first time he batted, leading off the second inning, Aaron never got the bat off his shoulder. Downing, a one-time pitcher for the Yankees, wearing number 44, threw a ball and called strike and then three more balls. Aaron, wearing his own number 44, took first base while the crowd hooted and booed because their hometown hero had been walked.

A few moments later, Henry scored on a double by Dusty Baker and an error in left field, and even made a little history doing that.

It was the 2,063rd time he had crossed home plate in his twenty-year career in the majors, breaking the National League record held by Willie Mays and placing Aaron behind Ty Cobb and Ruth, both American Leaguers.

Then came the fourth inning, with the Dodgers leading by 3–1 and the rain falling, with colored umbrellas raised in the stands and the crowd roaring every time Aaron appeared. Darrell Evans led off for Atlanta with a grounder behind second base that the shortstop, Bill Russell, juggled long enough for an error. And up came Henry for the eighth time this season and the second this evening.

Downing pitched ball one inside, and Aaron watched impassively. Then came the second pitch, and this time Henry took his first cut of the night. The ball rose high toward left-center as the crowd came to its feet shouting, and as it dropped over the inside fence separating the outfield from the bullpen area, the skyrockets were fired and the scoreboard lights flashed in 6-foot numerals: "715."

Aaron, head slightly bowed and elbows turned out, slowly circled the bases as the uproar grew. At second base he received a handshake from Dave Lopes of the Dodgers, and between second and third from Russell.

By now two young men from the seats had joined Aaron, but did not interfere with his 360-foot trip around the bases and into the record books.

As he neared home plate, the rest of the Atlanta team had already massed beyond it as a welcoming delegation. But Aaron's sixty-five-year-old father, Herbert Aaron, Sr., had jumped out of the family's special field-level box and outraced everybody to the man who had broken Babe Ruth's record.

By then the entire Atlanta bullpen corps had started to race in to join the fun, with House leading them, the ball gripped tightly in his hand. He delivered it to Aaron, who was besieged on the grass about 20 feet in front of the field boxes near the Braves' dugout.

Besides the ball, Henry received a plaque from the owner of the team, Bill Bartholomay; congratulations from Monte Irvin, the emissary from Commissioner Kuhn, and a howling, standing ovation from the crowd.

The game was interrupted for eleven minutes during all the commotion, after which the Braves got back to work and went on to win their second straight, this time by 7–4. The Dodgers, apparently shaken by history, made six errors and lost their first game after three straight victories.

"It was a fastball, right down the middle of the upper part of the plate," Downing said later. "I was trying to get it down to him, but I didn't and he hit it good—as he would."

"When he first hit it, I didn't think it might be going. But like a great hitter, when he picks his pitch, chances are he's going to hit it pretty good."

Afterward the Braves locked their clubhouse for a time so that they could toast Aaron in champagne. Then the new home run king reflected on his feat and on some intimations that he had not been "trying" to break the record in Cincinnati.

"I have never gone out on a ballfield and given less than my level best," he said. "When I hit it tonight, all I thought about was that I wanted to touch all the bases."

When is a homer that is not a homer a homer? When George Brett hit it off Goose Gossage in the ninth inning of a game played on July 24, 1983. Remember? The two-out, two-run homer sent the Royals into the lead 5–4—but only momentarily, for when the Yankees called Brett's bat to the attention of umpire Tim McClelland, he ruled that the pine tar was unacceptably high, invalidated the homer, and declared Brett out and the game over. Kansas City protested, and four days later American League President Lee MacPhail reversed the umpires' ruling: he restored the homer and the Royals' lead, and ordered that the bottom of the ninth inning be completed on an open date in the schedule, since the Royals and Yanks had concluded their seasonal animosities. On August 18, little more than a thousand fans came to witness the anticlimactic end of the game. This is one of "Glenn Eichler's All-Star Magic Tips" from *National Lampoon*.

GLENN EICHLER

George Brett's Vanished and Restored Homer

WHAT THE AUDIENCE SEES: In what appears to be a smooth, single movement, you hit a game-winning home run. The audience, enchanted, applauds—but wait! After some patter between the opposing team and the umpires, the run vanishes and you lose the game! The clapping dies out—only to double in strength when the run and the win mysteriously reappear.

HOW IT'S DONE: This is a particularly satisfying effect in that no sleight is necessary, and what the audience perceives as a magician's "gimmick" later turns out to be a clever bit of misdirection. Before your presentation, coat two-thirds of your bat with a funny-looking foreign substance (I recommend Louis Tannen's Magician Pine Tar #3). This is the "excuse" the umpire needs to vanish the home run. On closer inspection, both the audience and the league president will realize that the substance could not affect your hitting—and as they do, the run will suddenly rematerialize! A sophisticated electronic scoreboard that "goes wacky" during the trick will only heighten the hilarity!

EFFECT: The professional magician knows that some not necessarily "artful" tricks should be included in his repertoire for the sake of "flashiness." This effect can be particularly useful toward the end of a boring season, and doubles in its impressiveness if used against a team of overpaid shitheads.

CAVEATS: The main problem with this effect is in gauging how quickly to restore the home run; if you wait too long, the first part of the trick may be forgotten by the audience. I suggest that during the interval between the vanish and the restoration, you keep interest alive by cursing at reporters, physically attacking opposing players, and featuring your bat in overnight-courier ads.

These sardonic, gritty lines were published in Robert Fitzgerald's 1943 volume of poetry titled, eerily, *In the Rose of Time*. The fly ball that was made into a triple—maybe Cobb would have caught it in time, as in time Rose would catch him.

ROBERT FITZGERALD

Cobb Would Have Caught It

In sunburnt parks where Sundays lie,
Or the wide wastes beyond the cities,
Teams in gray deploy through sunlight.

Talk it up, boys, a little practice.

Coming in stubby and fast, the baseman
Gathers a grounder in fat green grass,
Picks it stinging and clipped as wit
Into the leather: a swinging step
Wings it deadeye down to first.
Smack. Oh, attaboy, attyoldboy.

Catcher reverses his cap, pulls down
Sweaty casque, and squats in the dust:
Pitcher rubs a new ball on his pants,
Chewing, puts a jet behind him;
Nods past batter, taking his time.

Batter settles, tugs at his cap:
A spinning ball: step and swing to it,

Caught like a cheek before it ducks
By shivery hickory: socko, baby:
Cleats dig into the dust. Outfielder,
On his way, looking over shoulder,
Makes it a triple. A long peg home.

Innings and afternoons. Fly lost in sunset.
Throwing arm gone bad. There's your old ballgame.
Cool reek of the field. Reek of companions.

Is the reserve clause legal? That was the question confronting Curt Flood in 1970 when he wrote this article for *Sport*, and it is the question he went on to confront unsuccessfully in the courts. On June 19, 1971, after two losses in lower courts, the star center fielder suffered a 5–3 defeat in the Supreme Court in his attempt to overturn the ninety-year-old clause. By refusing a trade from the Cardinals to the Phillies he gave up the 1970 season, and with it his $100,000 salary; relinquished any hope of a career in baseball management; and cut short, at age thirty-two, a career that might have earned him a place in the Hall of Fame. Financial need compelled him to return to baseball with the Washington Senators in early 1971, but his skills and concentration had faded; after only thirteen games he left for good. Players now commonly make a million dollars a year and in some cases more than twice that, but few could even name their benefactor—their emancipator. If ballplayers are free men today, they have Curt Flood to thank.

CURT FLOOD

Why I Am Challenging Baseball

This winter, on a warm and bright day in San Juan, Puerto Rico, I walked into a meeting at the Americana Hotel. Seated in the room, waiting to listen to me, were the player representatives of the big-league clubs—people like Reggie Jackson, Tom Haller, Jim Bunning, Tim McCarver, Joe Torre, Bob Clemente, Dal Maxvill. There were twenty-six ballplayers in all, the executive board of the Major League Baseball Players Association. Now I was going to try to tell them why I planned to challenge baseball's reserve clause in a case that could revolutionize the structure of baseball and stop twenty-four millionaire owners from playing God with thousands of ballplayers' lives.

I knew what I was risking. I might well not play the 1970 season. I might lose a salary of $90,000 a year—and maybe triple that, because I might never play a game of baseball again. I am only thirty-two and last year I hit .285 for the Cardinals, but I was aware that if I challenged the reserve clause in the courts, I could be blacklisted by every big-league team.

Yet I felt I had to accept the risks and I had come here to Puerto Rico to ask for the players' help and support. For twenty minutes I spoke to the players. I told them why I thought the reserve clause was bad for the players, for you—the fans—and for the game.

People later told me it was an emotional speech, and I guess it was. I said things that had been building up inside my chest for thirteen years, ever since a day in a ballpark in Maracaibo, Venezuela, when a nineteen-year-old ballplayer got a telegram that told him he had been traded.

At the time—1957—I belonged to the Cincinnati Reds. I hadn't wanted to come to Venezuela to play winter ball. But after two good years in the Reds' minor-league system, I'd been told I had the best chance of making the big club if I could learn to play third base.

So, the dutiful ballplayer, I went to a strange country to field groundballs off my chest. And there, sitting on a stool in the clubhouse, I got a long telegram from the Reds telling me I had been traded to the St. Louis Cardinals.

I stared at the telegram for maybe a half hour. I was shocked by the suddenness of the trade and uncertain now about myself, wondering: What do you have to do to make it in baseball? I had put two good years back to back. I had done everything they had asked. Now this.

I'd always known it wasn't going to be easy for me to make the big leagues. I was 5 feet 9 inches, 150 pounds, and black, and naturally you have doubts. Now I had to start with a strange new organization. It was like leaving a family you had grown up with and moving in with a family you had never met. I felt I was starting all over again in baseball, very much alone, insecure, and in a word, scared.

Later, when the numbness wore off, there was disappointment. I had grown up with Frank Robinson, played with him on Oakland streets when I was six years old. I'd run on those same streets with Vada Pinson when I was nine. Robinson and I were in the same outfield one year at McClymonds High School, then Pinson and I played together. Now Frank was the Reds' regular right fielder. Coming up the minor-league ladder was Vada Pinson and I was right behind him. Nothing would have thrilled me more than to have played alongside my old hometown buddies, Frank Robinson and Vada Pinson.

Someone playing God had dictated otherwise, and now I was the property of the Cardinals. Again the dutiful ballplayer, I reported to the Cardinals in the spring of 1958 and I won a job that year, a job I kept for twelve years. They were good and happy years for me, and my salary climbed close to the $100,000 mark, the highest any ballplayer who wasn't a pitcher or a home run hitter ever had received in baseball.

They were also good and happy years for the Cardinals and their owner, Mr. Gussie Busch. In three of five years—from 1964 to 1968—the Cardinals were National League champions and twice world champions.

But all during my years as a Cardinal I saw things happening that reminded me of that afternoon in the Maracaibo clubhouse when I'd felt for the first time the blunt impact of the reserve clause on my life. The reserve clause involves more than the trading and selling of human beings like sheep or cattle or, if you will, slaves. (I've been asked how a $90,000-a-year ballplayer can be a slave; I've answered that even a well-paid slave is still a slave.) As much as the trading and selling bothered me, what also made me see the inside were off-shoots of the reserve-clause situation that demean a man's dignity and strike directly at his rights as a human being.

There are a number of things that many fans and some ballplayers do not understand about the reserve clause. First of all, there is no reserve clause as such in a baseball player's contract. What there are, rather, are a multiplicity of provisions that chain a ballplayer to a club for life or until his contract is sold to another club. "If you don't play for me," a general manager can tell a ballplayer, "you don't play for anybody."

Many players first comprehend what the so-called reserve clause is all about when they come into the general manager's office to negotiate a raise.

"I had a good year," the ballplayer says. "I'd like a $5,000 raise."

"Well and good," says the general manager. "But we are not going to pay you that much money. And if you don't like it, you can quit playing baseball and find some other way of making a living."

The words are rarely that pointed or direct, but the implication is clear when a player is bargaining for more money: he must take the owner's last offer or not play at all. In that kind of a situation the ballplayer is obviously a second-class citizen. He knows it, and the baseball establishment knows it, and he is treated accordingly: with a paternal pat on the head when he stays in line, with the back of the hand when he doesn't. I know of no other employee in America today who is treated in such a degrading manner.

I never had to look beyond the Cardinal clubhouse, or my own locker, to see how the reserve clause degraded us all. One Sunday afternoon in a game against New York, I tried to break up a double play. The Mets' little shortstop, Bud Harrelson, tried to get out of my way, but he landed on my leg with his spikes. He cut a ten-inch wound from my knee to my thigh. They patched me up and I finished the game.

After the game, they put stitches on the wound and gave me an antitetanus shot. The shot knocked me loopy and all night long I was nauseous and dizzy, the leg stiff and painful. I finally got to sleep at six in the morning.

I knew that the Cardinals had scheduled a banquet for noon the next day and all the players were supposed to be there. But since the Cardinals knew how sick I'd been in the clubhouse, I was sure I wasn't expected to attend.

I got up about two in the afternoon and arrived at the park at around 3:30 or so. I found a note in my locker to see the general manager.

When I walked into his office, he said, "Missing that banquet will cost you $250."

"You don't understand," I said. I had already undressed to my shorts, and I showed him the stitched-up leg.

"No excuses," he said.

I paid the $250. I should not have had to put up with something like that, no man should. But because of the reserve clause, I could not say, "I quit," and still remain in baseball.

There was a time Bob Howsam, then our general manager, chewed out one of the players in the newspapers, claiming the player wasn't hustling. Every man on the club knew that the player hustled. If that player could have said, "I don't have to take this; I am a man and I am going somewhere else," you know damn well that Howsam would not have criticized him in public. But because the ballplayer was owned by one man—and one man only—he had to take it.

In the spring of 1969, every ballplayer on the Cardinals had to take it. The owner, Gussie Busch, invited his board of directors and all of the press to hear him chew us out in our clubhouse. On that day, millions of Americans learned in the newspapers that we had been publicly bawled out by our boss for being fat calves asking for too much money, that we were angering fans by not giving them autographs and annoying the press by refusing to be interviewed.

Certainly it is a boss's right to chew out his employees. But in public? I have about thirty employees working for me in my various businesses in St. Louis and I wouldn't think of dressing down one in front of another. But we had to listen silently and accept this public scolding of grown men, because we wouldn't say, "I quit," and walk away.

On that spring day, Gussie Busch spoke to a team that had come within one game of winning two straight world championships. I am convinced that the

1969 Cardinals placed on the field the nine best ballplayers in the world when Bob Gibson was pitching. But on that day last spring, Mr. Busch destroyed the intangible this team had—its unity and its feeling of pride in being a part of the Cardinal organization. We never got over that.

By the late summer of 1969, I was sure the Cardinals were going to trade me. I recalled what I had promised myself after I had been traded at nineteen—that I would never permit myself to be traded again.

I had spent twelve years in St. Louis. I had made my home there, built up my name and a thriving photographic and art business. Last year, Curt Flood's Art and Photo Studio photographed 83,000 St. Louis pupils for pictures to be used in school yearbooks. We plan to set up other Curt Flood Studios with franchise agreements. I also own a photo-finishing plant as well as real estate in St. Louis. It would make no sense to endanger those businesses by leaving St. Louis to spend six months playing baseball in a faraway city.

Near the end of the season I thought: If they trade me, I will quit. I thought at the time I had no other recourse, even though I had often talked about the reserve clause and how unfair it was. Why couldn't a ballplayer, say after ten years of service, be declared a free agent? He would likely sell himself for the next year to the team he had played for the year before, because he'd want to play in a city where he was making a name for himself. But if the salary and working conditions weren't right, he could do what any truck driver, lawyer, artist or workman can do—quit and go to work for someone else.

In my conversations with other players about the clause, I had said, "The reserve clause is either constitutional or unconstitutional. I never heard of anything that is half-constitutional."

Ninety-nine percent of the ballplayers I talked to agreed something should be done about the clause. But many had been so impressed by the owners' propaganda—that the reserve clause is the "backbone" of baseball—that they were afraid what would happen if it were ruled unconstitutional.

"Maybe we'd be cutting our own throats," I heard ballplayers say. "Maybe the game would be ruined."

You can't blame a guy who is making $50,000 a year for worrying that his job might suddenly disappear.

My answer to those ballplayers was this: Don't believe the owners' propaganda. "The reserve clause," I said, "exists for two reasons. One, to cut down the money the ballplayers get; and two, to give a feeling of power to men who like to play God over other people's lives."

In the back of my noggin, I believe, there was always the feeling that one day I would be the one to test the reserve clause. At thirty-two—and I may be inflating my ego here—I think I have the capabilities, the resources, and the integrity to challenge the clause in the courts without giving in to pressure.

During the closing days of the 1969 season, though, it was not in my conscious mind to test the clause. I guess I was too concerned wondering where I was going to be traded and what I was going to say if I was traded—whether I really had the courage to say, "I quit."

I got the news about the trade one afternoon by phone. I have known Bing Devine, the Cardinal general manager, for much of thirteen years, and he has been good to me and I think I have made a few dollars for him. He didn't call. One of the lower-echelon people in his office called and, with a voice that sounded like a tape-recording, he told me I had been traded to Philadelphia along with Tim McCarver, Joe Hoerner, and Byron Browne for Richie Allen, Cookie Rojas, and Jerry Johnson.

The next day I received a scrap of paper in the mail. It was from the Cardinals and it read: "Dear Mr. Flood: You have been Sold/ Traded/ Released/ Optioned."

Only the "Traded" box hadn't been blocked out, meaning I had been traded. That scrap was my official notice from the Cardinals telling me I was gone. Somehow, I thought, after twelve years of playing as best as I could for this club, someone might have written a note saying thanks and goodbye.

I phoned Bing Devine and told him I didn't want to leave St. Louis. Later I met with John Quinn of the Phillies and I explained to him that I had nothing against Philadelphia, but I had put twelve years of my life in St. Louis and I couldn't just yank up those twelve years and walk away.

I went off to Copenhagen, a place I dearly love, for a three-week vacation, still not knowing what I should do: quit, or take the $90,000 and try to keep my business in St. Louis while playing in Philadelphia.

When I returned to St. Louis I went to see my good friend and lawyer, Allan Zerman, in his office. We talked for a while and finally I said, "I have no other alternatives—it's either quit or go to Philadelphia."

Allan said quietly, "There is one other alternative."

Right away I knew what he meant. We talked about it, each of us getting more excited. I called Marvin Miller, the executive director of the Baseball Players Association. I flew to New York and told him I was thinking about testing the reserve clause in the courts.

Right from the start Marvin tried to discourage me. "If you go ahead with this," he told me, "forget any ideas you have about ever being the first black manager. Or even a coach or a scout—forget it." He talked about blacklisting and how long the legal proceedings could take—two or more years—and how much the legal fees would cost. He reminded me that even with a good case, I might lose. He emphasized how much I could lose in salary—maybe $200,000 or more.

He told me to mull over my decision. As Marvin said later, he was playing devil's advocate so he could be sure I understood how immense a task I was facing in taking on the baseball establishment. He also wanted to be sure I was sincere.

Allan and I thought about it for about a week. Sitting one night in a St. Louis restaurant, we added up all the pros and cons for the last time, looked at each other, and decided our decision was go.

At Marvin Miller's invitation I flew to Puerto Rico to speak to the executive board of the Players Association, asking for their help. After telling them much of what I have told you—how the reserve clause demeans every player as a man and cheats him as an employee—I answered questions.

Some of the players, I knew, were understandably skeptical about my motives. In the past, other players have used this facade—an attack on the reserve clause—to get money out of the owners in salary or as an out-of-court settlement.

One of the players, I've forgotten who, asked me, "If after you start this suit, someone comes knocking at your door and offers you a million dollars to withdraw the suit, what will you do?"

I looked at the man and I said, "I can't be bought."

Perhaps that convinced them. Anyway, after I had left the room, the twenty-six players voted unanimously to support me publicly, to help pay my legal expenses, and to help me get the best available counsel. A few days later, Marvin Miller contacted former Supreme Court Justice Arthur Goldberg, who, after studying the matter and meeting with me, agreed to represent me.

I flew home from Puerto Rico proud I had the backing of the players. I hope I will have the backing of the fans. I think my fight can help them to see better baseball. Right now we play 162 games and every ballplayer knows that is too many. Too often we plod onto the field, tired men going through the motions, while Joe Fan who has paid $5 for his seat thinks he is seeing big-league baseball. He isn't. He is being cheated. The ballplayers know it and the owners know it too.

Each year the Cardinals make a St. Louis–San Francisco–Houston–Los Angeles swing. We would be up and down in the air like yo-yos. When we got to Los Angeles, we'd be exhausted. Some of us checked how all the teams who made that swing had done, over a two-year period, in the first game of their series with the Dodgers. Over two years the opposition had scored an average of *less than two runs*.

Do you think it is accidental that Dodger owner Walter O'Malley plays a big hand in drawing up the National League schedule?

If we win this fight over the reserve clause, O'Malley and the other owners are going to have to let the players have a voice in drawing up the schedules. We will be a stronger position to demand a shorter schedule that doesn't cheat the fan.

Are we right in challenging the legality of the reserve clause? Let me answer you this way. Suppose you are an accountant. One day your boss says to you, "Joe, we are moving you to the other coast. Now don't worry. We'll pay your expenses, you'll get the same salary you're getting here, and maybe more."

"But I don't want to go 3,000 miles away from my family and friends," you say. "I don't want to tear up roots."

"Of course you can quit and get another job," your boss says. "But we've got this reserve clause in your contract, you know. You can't work ever again as an accountant if you quit working for us."

"But accounting is the only business I know," you say.

"Sorry," says your boss.

What would you do? As an accountant and as a man? You know what I am doing. Maybe now you can understand why I feel I have to do it—as a ballplayer and as a man.

A picture may be worth a thousand words, but these few words convey what a thousand pictures cannot—the *feel* of the game. From *The Orb Weaver*, issued in 1953.

ROBERT FRANCIS

The Base Stealer

Poised between going on and back, pulled
Both ways taut like a tightrope-walker,
Fingertips pointing the opposites,
Now bouncing tiptoe like a dropped ball
Or a kid skipping rope, come on, come on,
Running a scattering of steps sidewise,
How he teeters, skitters, tingles, teases,
Taunts them, hovers like an ecstatic bird,
He's only flirting, crowd him, crowd him,
Delicate, delicate, delicate, delicate—now!

This piece was written in the heat of one of the greatest pennant races ever, by one of the game's brightest, freshest reporters. Coming into this crucial four-game series at Fenway, where they had lost to the Yankees only twice in two years, the Red Sox were clinging to a four-game lead with twenty-four left to play. On July 19, they had enjoyed a fourteen-game margin, but then the Yanks fired Billy Martin, brought in Bob Lemon, and went on a tear that reduced the Boston lead to six games by the end of the month. There things stood until September, when the Boston Massacre marked the point at which the teams crossed paths; by mid-September the Red Sox were 3½ games out and presumed dead. However, they then displayed enormous heart, winning twelve of their final fourteen to storm into a final-day tie for the division lead. And then, to a Boston steeped in the sorrows of yesteryear, came Bucky Dent.

PETER GAMMONS

The Boston Massacre

The man had on a gray Brooks Brothers suit, which made him look for all the world as if he were Harvard '44, and he was leaning over the railing of the box next to the Red Sox dugout. "Zimmer!" he screamed, but Don Zimmer just stared dead ahead. The score at that point in last Friday night's game was 13–0 in favor of the Yankees and except to change pitchers a few times the Red Sox manager hadn't moved in three hours. He had stared as Mickey Rivers stood on third just two pitches into the game. He had stared as, for the second straight night, a Yankee batter got his third hit before Boston's ninth hitter, Butch Hobson, even got to the plate. He had stared as the Red Sox made seven errors. And now he stared as the man kept screaming his name.

"I've been a Red Sox fan for twenty years," the man hollered. "A diehard Red Sox fan. I've put up with a lot of heartaches. But this time you've really done it. This time my heart's been broken for good." Finally Zimmer looked up, just as security guards hauled the man away.

From Eastport to Block Island, New Englanders were screaming mad. Only a couple of weeks before, the Red Sox had been baseball's one sure thing, but now Fenway Park was like St. Petersburg in the last days of Czar Nicholas. Back in July, when Billy Martin still sat in the Yankee manager's office and

New York was in the process of falling fourteen games behind the Sox, Reggie Jackson had said, "Not even Affirmed can catch them." But by late last Sunday afternoon, when the 1978 version of the Boston Massacre concluded with New York's fourth win in a row over the Red Sox, the Yankees had caught them. And the Yanks had gained a tie for first in the American League East in such awesome fashion—winning sixteen of their last eighteen, including the lop-sided victories that comprised the Massacre—that Saturday night a New Yorker named Dick Waterman walked into a Cambridge bar, announced, "For the first time a first-place team has been mathematically eliminated," and held up a sign that read: NY 35–49–4, BOS 5–16–11. Those figures were the combined line score of last weekend's first three games. The disparity between those sets of numbers, as much as the losses themselves, was what so deeply depressed Red Sox fans. "It's 1929 all over again," mourned Robert Crane, treasurer of the Commonwealth of Massachusetts.

The Red Sox and Yankees began their two-city, seven-game, eleven-day showdown in Boston last Thursday—it will continue with three games this weekend in New York—and it quickly became apparent that this confrontation would be quite different from their six-game shoot-out in late June and early July. On that occasion the Red Sox had beaten the Yanks four times and opened up a lead that appeared insurmountable. Back then the Yankees had so few healthy bodies that Catcher Thurman Munson was trying to become a right fielder, and one day a minor league pitcher named Paul Semall drove from West Haven, Connecticut, to Boston to throw batting practice. Had the New York brass liked the way he threw, Semall would have stayed with the Yankees and become a starter. By midnight, Semall was driving back to West Haven, and soon thereafter injuries became so rife among New York pitchers that reserve first baseman Jim Spencer was warming up in the bullpen.

Rivers, the center fielder and key to the Yankee offense, had a broken wrist. Both members of the double-play combination, Willie Randolph and Bucky Dent, were injured and out of the lineup. To complete the up-the-middle collapse, Munson was playing—sometimes behind the plate and sometimes in right—with a bad leg, and the pitching staff had been reduced to *Gong Show* contestants. Paul Semall got gonged. Dave Rajsish got gonged. Larry McCall got gonged. Catfish Hunter, Ed Figueroa, Dick Tidrow, Ken Clay, Andy Messersmith, and Don Gullett were all hurt or soon to be injured. Only the brilliant Ron Guidry stayed healthy. Almost singlehandedly he kept the bottom from falling out during July and early August.

Then, as the regulars gradually began getting back into the lineup, the blow-up between owner George Steinbrenner and Martin occurred. Martin resigned on July 24, and the next day Bob Lemon, who had recently been canned by the White Sox, took over. "The season starts today," Lemon told the Yankees.

"Go have some fun." Considering the disarray in New York during the preceding year and a half, that seemed a bit much to ask. So was catching Boston. No American League team had ever changed managers in midseason and won a championship. "Under Lemon we became a completely different team," says Spencer. "If Martin were still here, we wouldn't be," snaps one player. "We'd have quit. Rivers and Jackson couldn't play for him. But Lemon gave us a fresh spirit. We kept playing. We looked up, and Boston was right in front of us." The fact that a suddenly revived Hunter had won six straight, that Figueroa had regained health and happiness, that Tidrow had again become hale and that rookie right hander Jim Beattie had returned from the minors with his self-confidence restored didn't hurt.

And while the Yankees arrived in Boston 30–13 under Lemon and 35–14 since July 17—the night they fell fourteen games behind—the Red Sox had been stumbling. They were 25–24 since July 17. Their thirty-nine-year-old leader, Carl Yastrzemski, had suffered back and shoulder ailments in mid-July, and then he pulled ligaments in his right wrist that left him taped up and in and out of the lineup. He had hit three homers in two months. Second baseman Jerry Remy fractured a bone in his left wrist on August 25 and had not appeared in the lineup thereafter.

Catcher Carlton Fisk had been playing with a cracked rib, which he said made him feel as if "someone is sticking a sword in my side" every time he threw. Third baseman Butch Hobson has cartilage and ligament damage in both knees and bone chips in his right elbow. The chips are so painful that one night he had to run off the field during infield practice; his elbow had locked up on him. When New York came to town, he had a major-league-leading thirty-eight errors, most of them the result of bad throws made with his bad arm. Right fielder Dwight Evans had been beaned on August 29 and was experiencing dizziness whenever he ran. Reliever Bill Campbell, who had thirty-one saves and thirteen wins in 1977, had suffered from elbow and shoulder soreness all season.

The injuries tended to dampen Boston's already erratic, one-dimensional offense, which relies too heavily on power hitting even when everyone is healthy. They also ruined the Sox defense, which had been the facet of play most responsible for giving the Red Sox a ten-game lead over their nearest challenger, Milwaukee, on July 8. No wonder the pitching went sour, with Mike Torrez going 4–4 since the All-Star Game, Luis Tiant 3–7 since June 24, and Bill Lee 0–7 since July 15. And as Boston awaited its confrontation with the Yankees, it lost three out of five to Toronto and Oakland and two of three in Baltimore. The Sox' only lift came in Wednesday's 2–0 win over the Orioles. Tiant pitched a two-hitter that night, and Yaz, his wrist looking like a mummy's, hit a two-run homer. It was one of only two hits the Sox got off Dennis Martinez.

As play began Thursday night at Fenway Park, the Red Sox lead had dwindled to four games with twenty-four to play. "We'll be happy with a split," Lemon said. By 9:05 P.M. Friday—during the third inning of Game 2—Lemon turned to pitching coach-scout Clyde King and said, "Now I'll only be happy with three out of four." Right about then *The Washington Post*'s Tom Boswell was writing his lead: *"Ibid*, for details, see yesterday's paper." The details were downright embarrassing to the Red Sox.

The embarrassments had begun with a Hobson error in the first inning Thursday. Then a Munson single. And a Jackson single. Zap, the Yankees had two unearned runs. After giving up four straight singles to start the second inning, Torrez went to the showers. Munson had three hits—and the Yankees seven runs—before Hobson got his first at bat in the bottom of the third. After the seventh inning, someone in the press box looked up at the New York line on the scoreboard—2–3–2–5–0–1–0—and dialed the number. It was disconnected. When the game ended, the Yankees had twenty-one hits and a 15–3 victory.

New York's joy was tempered by two injuries. Hunter left the game with a pulled groin muscle in the fourth, too soon to get the victory, though the Yanks were leading 12–0. "The bullpen phone rang and six of us fought to answer it," said Clay, who won the phone call and the game. Hunter, it turned out, would probably miss only one start. In the sixth inning, Munson was beaned by Dick Drago. Though dizzy, Munson said he would be behind the plate Friday. "He smells blood," Jackson said.

The next night, the Yankees not only drained Boston's blood but also its dignity. Rivers hit rookie right hander Jim Wright's first pitch past first baseman George Scott into right field. On the second pitch, he stole second and cruised on into third as Fisk's throw bounced away from shortstop Rick Burleson. Wright had thrown two pitches, and Rivers was peering at him from third base. Wright went on to get four outs, one more than Torrez had; he was relieved after allowing four runs. His replacement, Tom Burgmeier, immediately gave up a single and walk before surrendering a mighty home run by Jackson.

Beattie, who in his Fenway appearance in June had been knocked out in the third inning and optioned to Tacoma in the sixth, retired eighteen in a row in one stretch, while the Red Sox self-destructed in the field. Evans, who had not dropped a fly in his first five and three-quarters years in the majors, dropped his second one of the week and had to leave the game. "I can't look up or down without getting dizzy," he said. Fisk had two throws bounce away for errors. Rivers hit a routine ground ball to Scott in the third and beat Scott to the bag, making him three-for-three before Hobson ever got up. The game ended with a 13–2 score and the seven Red Sox errors.

"I can't believe what I've been seeing," said King, who has watched about forty Red Sox games this season. "I could understand if an expansion team fell apart like that, but Boston's got the best record in baseball. It can't go on." On Saturday afternoon, Guidry took his 20–2 record to the mound. It went on.

This was to be the showdown of the aces. Dennis Eckersley, 16–6, was 9–0 in Fenway and had not been knocked out before the fifth inning all season. He had beaten the Yankees three times in a twelve-day stretch earlier in the year. When he blew a third strike past Jackson to end the bottom of the first, he had done what Torrez and Wright had not been able to do—shut the Yankees out in the first inning.

"It looked like it was going to be a 1–0 game, what with the wind whipping in and Eckersley looking like he'd put us back together," said Zimmer. After Burleson led off Boston's first with a single, Fred Lynn bunted. Guidry, who could have cut down Burleson at second, hesitated and ended up throwing to first. Then Dent bobbled Jim Rice's grounder in the hole for an infield single. Two on. But Guidry busted fastballs in on the hands of Yastrzemski and Fisk, getting them out on a weak grounder and called third strike, respectively. Despite leadoff walks in the next two Boston at bats, the Sox hitters were finished for the day. Rice's grounder would be their second and last hit of the afternoon.

Yastrzemski seemed to lift his catatonic team in the fourth with a twisting, leaping catch on the dead run that he turned into a double play. But three batters later, with two on and two out, all that Yaz and Eckersley had done to heighten Boston's morale unraveled when Lou Piniella sliced a pop fly into the gale in right center.

"It must have blown a hundred feet across, like a Frisbee coming back," says Eckersley. Lynn came in a few steps but he had no chance. Burleson made chase from shortstop, Scott took off from first. The ball was out of reach of both. Rice, who was playing near the warning track in right, could not get there. Frank Duffy, the second baseman, did, but when he turned and looked up into the sun he lost sight of the ball. It landed in front of him. It was 1–0. After an intentional walk to Graig Nettles, Dent dunked a two-strike pitch into left for two more runs. "That broke my back," said Eckersley. By the time the inning had ended, Eckersley was gone. There had been another walk, an error, a wild pitch, and a passed ball. Seven runs had scored. "This is the first time I've seen a first-place team chasing a second-place team," said NBC's Tony Kubek.

Guidry had not only become the second left-hander to pitch a complete game against the Red Sox in Fenway all season, but also was the first lefty to shut them out at home since 1974. "Pitchers are afraid to pitch inside here," he said. "But that's where you've got to."

The victory brought Guidry's record to 21–2, his earned-run average to 1.77, and his strikeouts to 220; it also brought the New York staff's ERA to 2.07 over the last twenty-six games. "They must be cheating," said Lynn. "Those aren't the same Yankees we saw before. I think George Steinbrenner used his clone money. I think those were Yankee clones out there from teams of the past."

"These guys are—I hope you understand how I use the word—nasty," said Jackson. "This is a pro's game, and this team is loaded with professionals. Tough guys. Nasty."

"This is two years in a row we've finished like this, so it must say something about the team's character," Tidrow said. Before Lemon took over, the only times the word "character" was used in the Yankee clubhouse it was invariably followed by the word "assassination."

With the 7–0 loss figured in, the Red Sox had lost eight out of ten. In those games they had committed twenty-four errors good for twenty unearned runs. Twice pop-ups to shallow right had dropped, leading to two losses and ten earned runs.

Tiant had been the only starting pitcher to win. Evans, Scott, Hobson, and Jack Brohamer, who most of the time were the bottom four in the batting order, were twelve for 123—or .098. "How can a team get thirty-something games over .500 in July and then in September see its pitching, hitting, and fielding all fall apart at the same time?" wondered Fisk.

After being bombarded in the first three games, all that the Red Sox could come up with in their effort to prevent the Yankees from gaining a first-place tie on Sunday was rookie lefthander Bobby Sprowl. In June, while the Sox were

beating the Yankees, Sprowl was pitching for the Bristol Red Sox against the West Haven Yankees.

Clearly he was not ready for their New York namesakes. He began by walking Rivers and Willie Randolph, lasted only two-thirds of an inning, and was charged with three runs. The most damaging blow came after Sprowl gave way to reliever Bob Stanley, who promptly yielded a single to Nettles that drove in two runners whom Sprowl had allowed to reach base. The Yankees would build a 6–0 bulge before coasting to an eighteen-hit, 7–4 victory. Suddenly, New York not only had a psychological edge on the Red Sox, but it also had pulled even with them in the standings.

"It's never easy to win a pennant," said Yastrzemski. "We've got three weeks to play. We've got three games in Yankee Stadium next weekend. Anything can happen." He stared into his locker. Anything already had.

Andrew Marvell wrote three centuries ago in "The Garden" (not alluding to the outfield): "The Mind, that Ocean where each kind / Does streight its own resemblance find; / Yet it creates, transcending these, / Far other Worlds, and other Seas; / Annihilating all that's made / To a green thought in a green Shade." Green is the eternal color—the color of spring, the color of hope, and the color of baseball. Yale's president and ardent fan wrote this loving essay in 1977.

A. BARLETT GIAMATTI

The Green Fields of the Mind

It breaks your heart. It is designed to break your heart. The game begins in the spring, when everything else begins again, and it blossoms in the summer, filling the afternoons and evenings, and then as soon as the chill rains come, it stops and leaves you to face the fall alone. You count on it, rely on it to buffer the passage of time, to keep the memory of sunshine and high skies alive, and then just when the days are all twilight, when you need it most, it stops. Today, October 2, a Sunday of rain and broken branches and leaf-clogged drains and slick streets, it stopped, and summer was gone.

Somehow, the summer seemed to slip by faster this time. Maybe it wasn't this summer, but all the summers that, in this my fortieth summer, slipped by so fast. There comes a time when every summer will have something of autumn about it. Whatever the reason, it seemed to me that I was investing more and more in baseball, making the game do more of the work that keeps time fat and slow and lazy. I was counting on the game's deep patterns, three strikes, three outs, three times three innings, and its deepest impulse, to go out and back, to leave and to return home, to set the order of the day and to organize the daylight. I wrote a few things this last summer, this summer that did not last, nothing grand but some things, and yet that work was just camouflage. The real activity was done with the radio—not the all-seeing, all-falsifying television—and was the playing of the game in the only place it will last, the enclosed, green field of the mind. There, in that warm, bright place, what the old poet called Mutability does not so quickly come.

But out here on Sunday, October 2, where it rains all day, Dame Mutability never loses. She was in the crowd at Fenway yesterday, a gray day full of bluster and contradiction, when the Red Sox came up in the last of the ninth trailing Baltimore 8–5, while the Yankees, rain-delayed against Detroit, only needing to win one or have Boston lose one to win it all, sat in New York washing down cold cuts with beer and watching the Boston game. Boston had won two, the Yankees had lost two, and suddenly it seemed as if the whole season might go to the last day, or beyond, except here was Boston losing 8–5, while New York sat in its family room and put its feet up. Lynn, both ankles hurting now as they had in July, hits a single down the right-field line. The crowd stirs. It is on its feet. Hobson, third baseman, former Bear Bryant quarterback, strong, quiet, over 100 RBIs, goes for three breaking balls and is out. The goddess smiles and encourages her agent, a canny journeyman named Nelson Briles.

Now comes a pinch hitter, Bernie Carbo, one-time Rookie of the Year, erratic, quick, a shade too handsome, so laid back he is always, in his soul, stretched out in the tall grass, one arm under his head, watching the clouds and laughing; now he looks over some low stuff unworthy of him and then, uncoiling, sends one out, straight on a right line, over the center-field wall, no cheap Fenway shot, but all of it, the physics as elegant as the arc the ball describes.

New England is on its feet, roaring. The summer will not pass. Roaring, they recall the evening, late and cold, in 1975, the sixth game of the World Series, perhaps the greatest baseball game played in the last fifty years, when Carbo, loose and easy, had uncoiled to tie the game that Fisk would win. It is 8–7, one out, and school will never start, rain will never come, sun will warm the back of your neck forever. Now Bailey, picked up from the National League recently, big arms, heavy gut, experienced, new to the league and the club; he fouls off two and then, checking, tentative, a big man off balance, he pops a soft liner to the first baseman. It is suddenly darker and later, and the announcer doing the game coast to coast, a New Yorker who works for a New York television station, sounds relieved. His little world, well-lit, hot-combed, split-second-timed, had no capacity to absorb this much gritty, grainy, contrary reality.

Cox swings a bat, stretches his long arms, bends his back, the rookie from Pawtucket, who broke in two weeks earlier with a record six straight hits, the kid drafted ahead of Fred Lynn, rangy, smooth, cool. The count runs two-and-two, Briles is cagey, nothing too good, and Cox swings, the ball beginning toward the mound and then, in a jaunty, wayward dance, skipping past Briles, feinting to the right, skimming the last of the grass, finding the dirt, moving now like some small, purposeful marine creature negotiating the green deep, easily avoiding the jagged rock of second base, traveling steady and straight now out into the dark, silent recesses of center field.

The aisles are jammed, the place is on its feet, the wrappers, the programs, the Coke cups and peanut shells, the detritus of an afternoon; the anxieties, the things that have to be done tomorrow, the regrets about yesterday, the accumulation of a summer: all forgotten, while hope, the anchor, bites and takes hold where a moment before it seemed we would be swept out with the tide. Rice is up, Rice whom Aaron had said was the only one he'd seen with the ability to break his records, Rice the best clutch hitter on the club, with the best slugging percentage in the league, Rice, so quick and strong he once checked his swing halfway through and snapped the bat in two, Rice the Hammer of God sent to scourge the Yankees, the sound was overwhelming, fathers pounded their sons on the back, cars pulled off the road, households froze, New England exulted in its blessedness, and roared its thanks for all good things, for Rice and for a summer stretching halfway through October. Briles threw, Rice swung, and it was over. One pitch, a fly to center, and it stopped. Summer died in New England and like rain sliding off a roof, the crowd slipped out of Fenway, quickly, with only a steady murmur of concern for the drive ahead remaining of the roar. Mutability had turned the seasons and translated hope to memory once again. And once again, she had used baseball, our best invention to stay change, to bring change on. That is why it breaks my heart, that game—not because in New York they could win because Boston lost; in that, there is a rough justice, and a reminder to the Yankees of how slight and fragile are the circumstances that exalt one group of human beings over another. It breaks my heart because it was meant to foster in me again the illusion that there was something abiding, some pattern and some impulse that could come together to make a reality that would resist the corrosion; and because after it had fostered again that most hungered-for illusion, the game was meant to stop, and betray precisely what it promised.

Of course, there are those who learn after the first few times. They grow out of sports. And there are others who were born with the wisdom to know that nothing lasts. These are the truly tough among us, the ones who can live without illusion, or without even the hope of illusion. I am not that grown-up or up-to-date. I am a simpler creature, tied to more primitive patterns and cycles. I need to think something lasts forever, and it might as well be that state of being that is a game; it might as well be that, in a green field, in the sun.

Here the noted paleontologist observes biology at play on the fields of Eden: time and change mark baseball after all. Are baseball players better than ever? Or did giants walk the earth in the good old days, never since equaled? No question provokes more angry words around the hot stove or at meetings of the Society for American Baseball Research—it approaches sacrilege to suggest that Ruth and Gehrig batted largely against patsies or that Cy Young would not have won 511 games against modern opponents. Sabermetricians (those dedicated to the coldly logical and statistical analysis of the game) have employed various methods of comparing the old-time player to the current model, none altogether satisfying. Gould's argument is different from but parallel to those of analysts Richard Cramer and Dallas Adams. They find a steady rise throughout baseball's history in the skill of the average player, thus making it ever more difficult to exceed the norm by the stupendous margins achieved by such batters as Ruth and Cobb or such pitchers as Radbourn and Johnson.

STEPHEN JAY GOULD

The Extinction of the .400 Hitter

I wish to propose a new kind of explanation for the oldest chestnut of the hot stove league—the most widely discussed trend in the history of baseball statistics: the extinction of the .400 hitter. Baseball aficionados wallow in statistics, a sensible obsession that outsiders grasp with difficulty and ridicule often. The reasons are not hard to fathom. In baseball, each essential action is a contest between two individuals—batter and pitcher, or batter and fielder—thus creating an arena of truly individual achievement within a team sport.

The abstraction of individual achievement in other sports makes comparatively little sense. Goals scored in basketball or yards gained in football depend on the indissoluble intricacy of team play; a home run is you against him. Moreover, baseball has been played under a set of rules and conditions sufficiently constant during our century to make comparisons meaningful, yet sufficiently different in detail to provide endless grist for debate (the "dead ball" of 1900–20 versus the "lively ball" of later years, the introduction of night games and relief pitchers, the changing and irregular sizes of ball parks, nature's own versus Astroturf).

No subject has inspired more argument than the decline and disappearance of the .400 hitter—or, more generally, the drop in league-leading batting averages during our century. Since we wallow in nostalgia and have a lugubrious tendency to compare the present unfavorably with a past "golden era," this trend acquires all the more fascination because it carries moral implications linked metaphorically with junk foods, nuclear bombs, and eroding environments as signs of the decline of Western civilization.

Between 1901 and 1930, league-leading averages of .400 or better were common enough (nine out of thirty years) and achieved by several players (Lajoie, Cobb, Jackson, Sisler, Heilmann, Hornsby, and Terry), and averages over .380 scarcely merited extended commentary. Yet the bounty dried up abruptly thereafter. In 1930, Bill Terry hit .401 to become the last .400 hitter in National League; and Ted Williams's .406 in 1941 marked the last pinnacle for the American League. Since Williams, the greatest hitter I ever saw, attained this goal—in the year of my birth—only three men have hit higher than .380 in a single season: Williams again in 1957 (.388, at age thirty-nine, with my vote for the greatest batting accomplishment of our era), Rod Carew (.388 in 1977), and George Brett (.390 in 1980). Where have all the hitters gone?

Two kinds of explanation have been offered. The first, naive and moral, simply acknowledges with a sigh that there were giants in the earth in those days. Something in us needs to castigate the present in the light of an unrealistically rosy past. In researching the history of misconduct, I discovered that every generation (at least since the mid-nineteenth century) has imagined itself engulfed in a crime wave. Each age has also witnessed a shocking decline in sportsmanship. Similarly, senior citizens of the hot stove league, and younger fans as well (for nostalgia seems to have its greatest emotional impact on those too young to know a past reality directly), tend to argue that the .400 hitters of old simply cared more and tried harder. Well, Ty Cobb may have been a paragon of intensity and a bastard to boot, and Pete Rose may be a gentleman by comparison, but today's play is anything but lackadaisical. Say what you will, monetary rewards in the millions do inspire single-minded effort.

The second kind of explanation views people as much of a muchness over time and attributes the downward trend in league-leading batting to changes in the game and its styles of play. Most often cited are improvements in pitching and fielding, and more grueling schedules that shave off the edge of excellence.

Another explanation in this second category invokes the numerology of baseball. Every statistics maven knows that following the introduction of the lively ball in the early 1920s (and Babe Ruth's mayhem upon it), batting averages soared in general and remained high for twenty years. League averages for all players (averaged by decade) rose into the .280s in both leagues during the 1920s and remained in the .270s during the 1930s, but never topped .260 in any other decade of our century. Naturally, if league averages rose so substantially, we should not be surprised that the best hitters also improved their scores.

Still, this simple factor cannot explain the phenomenon entirely. No one hit .400 in either league during 1931–40, even though league averages stood twenty points above their values for the first two decades of our century, when fancy hitting remained in vogue. A comparison of these first two decades with recent times is especially revealing. Consider, for example, the American League during 1911–20 (league average of .259) and 1951–60 (league average of .257). Between 1911 and 1920, averages above .400 were recorded during three years, and the leading average dipped below .380 only twice (Cobb's .368 and .369 in 1914 and 1915). This pattern of high averages was not just Ty Cobb's personal show. In 1912 Cobb hit .410, while the ill-fated Shoeless Joe Jackson recorded .395, Tris Speaker .383, the thirty-seven-year-old Nap Lajoie .368, and Eddie Collins .348. By comparison, during 1951–60, only three league-leading averages exceeded Eddie Collins's fifth-place .348 (Mantle's .353 in 1956, Kuenn's .353 in 1959, and Williams's .388, already discussed, in 1957). And the 1950s was no decade of slouches, what with the likes of Mantle, Williams, Minoso, and Kaline. A general decline in league-leading averages throughout the century cannot be explained by an inflation of general averages during two middle decades. We are left with a puzzle. As with most persistent puzzles, what we probably need is a new *kind* of explanation, not merely a recycling and refinement of old arguments.

I am a paleontologist by trade. We students of life's history spend most of our time worrying about long-term trends. Has life gotten more complex through time? Do more species of animals live now than 200 million years ago? Several years ago, it occurred to me that we suffer from a subtle but powerful bias in our approach to the explanation of trends. Extremes fascinate us (the biggest, the smallest, the oldest), and we tend to concentrate on them alone, divorced from the systems that include them as unusual values. In explaining extremes, we abstract them from larger systems and assume that their trends have self-generated reasons: if the biggest become bigger through time, some powerful advantage must attach to increasing size.

But if we consider extremes as the limiting values of larger systems, a very different kind of explanation often applies. If the *amount of variation* within a system changes (for whatever reason), then extreme values may increase (if total variation grows) or decrease (if total variation declines) without any special reason rooted in the intrinsic character or meaning of the extreme value itself. In other words, *trends in extremes* may result from systematic changes in amounts of variation. Reasons for changes in variation are often rather different from proposed (and often spurious) reasons for changes in extremes considered as independent from their systems.

Let me illustrate this unfamiliar concept with an example from my own profession. A characteristic pattern in the history of most marine invertebrates is called "early experimentation and later standardization." When a new body plan first arises, evolution seems to try out all manner of twists, turns, and variations upon it. A few work well, but most don't. Eventually, only a few survive. Echinoderms now come in five basic varieties (two kinds of starfish, sea urchins, sea cucumbers, and crinoids—an unfamiliar group, loosely resembling many-armed starfish on a stalk). But when echinoderms first evolved, they burst forth in an astonishing array of more than twenty basic groups, including some coiled like a spiral and others so bilaterally symmetrical that a few paleontologists have mistaken them for the ancestors of fish. Likewise, mollusks now exist as snails, clams, cephalopods (octopuses and their kin), and two or three other rare and unfamiliar groups. But they sported ten to fifteen other fundamental variations early in their history.

This trend to a shaving and elimination of extremes is pervasive in nature. When systems first arise, they probe all the limits of possibility. Many variations don't work; the best solutions are found, and variation diminishes. As systems regularize, their variation decreases.

From this perspective, it occurred to me that we might be looking at the problem of .400 hitting the wrong way round. League-leading averages are extreme values within systems of variation. Perhaps their decrease through time simply records the standardization that affects so many systems as they stabilize. When baseball was young, styles of play had not become sufficiently regular to foil the antics of the very best. Wee Willie Keeler could "hit 'em where they ain't" (and compile a .432 average in 1897) because fielders didn't yet know where they should be. Slowly, players moved toward optimal methods of positioning, fielding, pitching, and batting—and variation inevitably declined. The best now met an opposition too finely honed to its own perfection to permit the extremes of achievement that characterized a more casual age. We cannot explain the decrease of high averages merely by arguing that managers invented relief pitching, while pitchers invented the slider—conventional explanations based on trends affecting high hitting considered as an independent phenomenon. Rather, the entire game sharpened its standards and narrowed its ranges of tolerance.

Thus I present my hypothesis: the disappearance of the .400 hitter is largely the result of a more general phenomenon—a decrease in the variation of batting averages as the game standardized its methods of play—and not an intrinsically driven trend warranting a special explanation in itself.

To test such a hypothesis, we need to examine changes through time in the difference between league-leading batting averages and the general average for all batters. This difference must decrease if I am right. But since my hypothesis concerns an entire system of variation, then, somewhat paradoxically, we must also examine differences between *lowest* batting averages and the general average. Variation must decrease at both ends—that is, within the entire system. Both highest and lowest batting averages must converge toward the general league average.

I therefore reached for my trusty *Baseball Encyclopedia*, that *vade mecum* for all serious fans (though, at more than 2,000 pages, you can scarcely tote it with you). The encyclopedia reports league averages for each year and lists the five highest averages for players with enough official times at bat. Since high extremes fascinate us while low values are merely embarrassing, no listing of the lowest averages appears, and you have to make your way laboriously through the entire roster of players. For lowest averages, I found (for each league in each year) the five bottom scores for players with at least 300 at bats. Then, for each year, I compared the league average with the average of the five highest and five lowest scores for regular players. Finally, I averaged these yearly values decade by decade.

In the accompanying chart, I present the results for both leagues combined— a clear confirmation of my hypothesis, since both highest and lowest averages approach the league average through time.

Our decrease toward the mean for high averages seems to occur as three plateaus, with only limited variation within each plateau. During the nineteenth century (National League only; the American League was founded in 1901), the mean difference between highest average and league average was 91 points (range of 87 to 95, by decade). From 1901 to 1930, it dipped to 81 (range

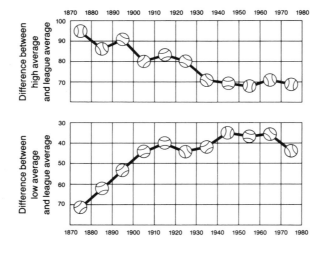

THE DECLINE IN EXTREMES

of only 80 to 83), while for five decades since 1931, it has averaged 69 (with a range of only 67 to 70). These three plateaus correspond to three marked eras of high hitting. The first includes the runaway averages of the 1890s, when Hugh Duffy reached .438 (in 1894) and all five leading players topped .400 in the same year. The second plateau includes all the lower scores of .400 batters in our century, with the exception of Ted Williams (Hornsby was tops at .424 in 1924). The third plateau records the extinction of .400 hitting.

Lowest averages show the same pattern of decreasing difference from the league average, with a precipitous decline by decade from 71 to 54 points during the nineteenth century, and two plateaus thereafter (from the mid-forties early in the century to the mid-thirties later on), followed by the one exception to my pattern—a fallback to the forties during the 1970s.

Nineteenth-century values must be taken with a grain of salt, since rules of play were so different then. During the 1870s, for example, schedules varied from sixty-five to eighty-five games per season. With short seasons and fewer at bats, variation must increase, just as, in our own day, averages in June and July span a greater range than final-season averages, several hundred at bats later. (For these short seasons, I used two at bats per game as my criterion for inclusion in statistics for low averages.) Still, by the 1890s, schedules had lengthened to 130–150 games per season, and comparisons to our own century become more meaningful.

I was rather surprised—and I promise readers that I am not rationalizing after the fact but acting on a prediction I made before I started calculating—that the pattern of decrease did not yield more exceptions during our last two decades, because baseball has experienced a profound destabilization of the sort that calculations should reflect. After half a century of stable play with eight geographically stationary teams per league, the system finally broke in response to easier transportation and greater access to almighty dollars. Franchises began to move, and my beloved Dodgers and Giants abandoned New York in 1958. Then, in the early 1960s, both leagues expanded to ten teams, and in 1969 to twelve teams in two divisions.

These expansions should have caused a reversal in patterns of decrease between extreme batting averages and league averages. Many less than adequate players became regulars and pulled low averages down (Marvelous Marv Throneberry is still reaping the benefits in Lite beer ads). League averages also declined, partly as a result of the same influx, and bottomed out in 1968 at .230 in the American League. (This lamentable trend was reversed by fiat in 1969 when the pitching mound was lowered and the strike zone diminished to give batters a better chance.) This lowering of league averages should also have increased the distance between high hitters and the league average. Thus I was surprised that an increase in the distance between league and lowest

averages during the 1970s was the only result I could detect of this major destabilization.

As a nonplaying nonprofessional, I cannot pinpoint the changes that have caused the game to stabilize and the range of batting averages to decrease over time. But I can suggest the sorts of factors that will be important. Traditional explanations that view the decline of high averages as an intrinsic trend must emphasize explicit inventions and innovations that discourage hitting—the introduction of relief pitching and more night games, for example. I do not deny that these factors have important effects, but if the decline has also been caused, as I propose, by a general decrease in variation of batting averages, then we must look to other kinds of influences.

We must concentrate on increasing precision, regularity and standardization of play—and we must search for the ways that managers and players have discovered to remove the edge that the truly excellent once enjoyed. Baseball has become a science (in the vernacular sense of repetitious precision in execution). Outfielders practice for hours to hit the cutoff man. Positioning of fielders changes by the inning and man. Double plays are executed like awesome clockwork. Every pitch and swing is charted, and elaborate books are kept on the habits and personal weaknesses of each hitter. The "play" in play is gone.

When the world's tall ships graced our bicentennial in 1976, many of us lamented their lost beauty and cited Masefield's sorrow that we would never "see such ships as those again." I harbor opposite feelings about the disappearance of .400 hitting. Giants have not ceded to mere mortals. I'll bet anything that Carew could match Keeler. Rather, the boundaries of baseball have been drawn in and its edges smoothed. The game has achieved a grace and precision of execution that has, as one effect, eliminated the extreme achievements of early years. A game unmatched for style and detail has simply become more balanced and beautiful.

In this lonely land of ours, where the beacon of individuality has guided us from the onset of nationhood, baseball has become the tie that binds. Where religion, family, class, even ideology unite people of other lands, here baseball is the lingua franca: it connects males across the barriers of class or age, as Donald Hall notes, and in its arcane ways lies the immigrant's sure path to becoming American. But what baseball does is apart from what it is, and like music or art, it is a thing of beauty for its own sake. This beautiful piece was published in the *National Review* in 1981.

DONALD HALL

Baseball and the Meaning of Life

Professor McCormick's suggestion is surely farfetched. Although dark-suited umpires may remind him of warlocks, although the pitcher's motion mimics dubious rituals, we must resist the suggestion that baseball retains elements of the Old Religion. We may admit the existence of Seasonal Parallels without lending credence to his speculations on the shape of home plate.

For baseball dies into the October ground as leaves fall obscuring basepath and pitcher's mound, littering empty dugouts and bullpens, flitting like spooked grounders over second base into the stiffening outfield grass. November rain expunges lime-powder foul lines from Centerville's Little League Park to Yankee Stadium, from Yakima to Bangor, from Key West to Iron Mountain. Soon in the north a colder powder, no less white, freezes diamond and foul territory together into an egalitarian alabaster plain below the cold green ranks of box, grandstand, and bleacher. The old game waits under the white; deeper than frozen grass, down at the frostline it waits. . . .

To return when the birds return. It starts to wake in the South, where it had never quite stopped, where winter is a doze of hibernation interrupted by sleepy, staggering, momentary wakenings, like bears or skunks in a northern thaw. The game wakes gradually, gathering vigor to itself as the days lengthen late in February and grow warmer; old muscles grow limber, young arms throw strong and wild, legs pivot and leap, bodies hurtle into bright bases *safe.* . . . Clogged vein-systems, in veteran oaks and left-fielders both, unstop themselves, putting forth leaves and line drives in Florida's March. Migrating north with the swallows, baseball and the grass's first green enter Cleveland, Kansas City, Boston.

Silly he may be, but on the whole we sympathize with Professor McCormick's imaginative anthropology (*The Bat and the Wand*. A. Doubleday. 60'6". Cooperstown. No date). At least we share the intuition that connects baseball with the meaning of life.

April baseball is tentative, exploratory, daring and timid together, poking a quivering finger into the risen year. May strengthens, sure-footed now, turning night into bright green day, springing with young manhood's energy and vanity toward the twilights of high summer. In June, the animal-plant, full-leaved and muscled with maturity, invites us to settle secure for a season.

We arrive at the ballpark early. The ballplayers have been here for hours, for BP and pepper and shagging outfield flies, as coaches with fungoes bang balls at the shins of shortstops, or raise cans of corn to the shallow outfield, or strike line drives off outfield walls and corners. We arrive and settle with scorecards and Cracker Jack and peanuts and Schlitz and hot dogs. There is a rasp in our voices, there is glory in our infant hearts, there is mustard on our T-shirts.

Soon the tunnel disgorges three young men in bright suits carrying gloves, then two more, then six. "Play catch?" one says to another. They sort themselves by twos, throwing baseballs hard at each other without effort, drawing ruler-straight lines like chalk-stripes between them. The soft pock of caught balls sounds in attentive ears.

The bullpen squad—a coach, a catcher, two longmen, two or three shortmen—ambles with fabulous unconcern, chewing as slowly as prize Holsteins, down the foul lines toward their condominium in right field. The ninth inning's fastballing superstar ace-reliefman is not among them, but back in the trainer's room lying flat on his back, reading *Swann's Way* or *Looney Tunes*, waiting to trot his urgent trot from dugout to bullpen at the start of the eighth, the game 1–1, the one-man cavalry alerted to threat of ambush at the mountain pass.

Anticipating cavalry, the organist assaults the score of "The Star-Spangled Banner," which we attempt to sing because of the fierce joy that fills us and threatens to choke our throats unless we loosen this joyful noise. Then we chew the song's ending, and lean forward to watch the young men assume the field in their vain uniforms, to hear "Play ball!" to allow the game's dance to receive our beings into its rhythms for two hours or three.

Ah, the game! The game!

But what of the meaning of life . . .

Baseball connects American males with each other, not only through bleacher friendships and neighbor loyalties, not only through barroom fights, but most importantly through generations. When you are small you may not discuss politics or union dues or profit margins with your father's cigar-smoking friends when your father has gone out for a six-pack; but you may discuss baseball. It is all you have in common, because your father's friend does not wish to discuss the Assistant Principal or Alice Bisbee Morgan. About the season's moment you know as much as he does; both of you may shake your heads over Lefty's wildness or the rookie who was called out last Saturday when he tried to steal home with two out in the ninth inning down by one.

And you learn your first lessons of the rainbow arc all living makes, but that baseball exaggerates. For when you are in sixth grade, the rook has fuzz on his face and throws to the wrong base; before you leave junior high school, he is a seasoned regular, his body filled out, his jowl rippled with tobacco; when you graduate from high school he is a grizzled veteran—even if you are not certain what grizzled means. In a few years, the green shoot becomes the withered stalk, and you learn the hill all beings travel by.

So Carl Yastrzemski enters his forty-second year. So Wilver Stargell's bones are stiff. While George Brett climbs the glorious mountain of his prime, all gut and muscle, his brother Ken watches with admiration and irony from the shadows of his quick sundown, who started the All-Star Game for the National League in 1974, his record thirteen and two, the lithe left arm bending sliders to catch the black—unbeatable, impervious, in his high stride hitting home runs from the ninth position. His brother George played AAA that year. That year somebody asked Ken Brett, "Why don't you play outfield when you're not pitching?" "Because they do not have that much money in Pittsburgh."

In 1980, Ken was released by the Dodgers, later signed on with George's KC as a long man in the bullpen. This year or next he will begin to make The Adjustment, as the players call it, when he leaves forever the game he doubtless began at the age of seven or eight. The light grows pale on the older players but never dwindles entirely away. . . . I remember Edd Roush, batting champion of 1917, ancient and glorious at an Old-timers' Game in 1975. Smokey Joe Wood, amazing fastballer of the 1912 Red Sox, signed autographs in Boston at a collectors' convention in 1980.

Let it be. Players age, and baseball changes, as veterans slide off by way of jets to Japan instead of buses to Spokane. Baseball changes, and we wish it never to change. Yet we know that inside the ball, be it horsehide or cowhide, the universe remains unaltered. Even if the moguls, twenty years from now, manage to move the game indoors and schedule twelve months a year, the seasons will remain implicit, like the lives of the players. Grow-lites do not legislate winter away. If the whole sport emigrates to Japan, baseball will remain a Zen garden.

For surely, as Professor McCormick fails to remind us, baseball sets off the meaning of life precisely because it is pure of meaning. As the ripples in the sand, in the Kyoto garden, organize and formalize the dust which is dust, so the diamonds and rituals of baseball create an elegant, trivial, enchanted grid on which our suffering, shapeless, sinful day leans for the momentary grace of order.

The lure for students of baseball history is the illusion that all that has ever happened is known or can be discovered. Witness Art Hill's interest in such a ballplaying cipher as Joe Cobb or W. P. Kinsella's in Moonlight Graham, a one-inning defensive replacement in 1905 whom he made a central figure in his novel *Shoeless Joe*. *The Baseball Encyclopedia* is more than a reference work: it is an ever-expanding Book of Life, for statistics are the vital part of baseball, the only tangible and imperishable remains of games played yesterday or a hundred years ago.

ART HILL

A Stroll Through
The Baseball Encyclopedia

John Paciorek, as every serious collector of baseball curiosa knows, is major-league baseball's leading lifetime hitter. No one ever hit for a higher average over an entire career. His career, which was all over before he reached his nineteenth birthday, consisted of one game for Houston in 1963, and it was quite remarkable as far as it went. He had three hits in three times at bat, walked twice, scored four runs and batted in three.

There are many other hitters with lifetime averages of 1.000, but most of them had only one time at bat. Among batters who never made an out, Paciorek's three for three is tops.

I have, as you can guess, been browsing through the record book, an utterly fascinating accumulation of baseball facts, ranging from the awe-inspiring to the ineffably trivial. Listed here is every man who ever played in a major-league game. Here is Ty Cobb, with his 4,191 hits and .367 lifetime batting average (both "unbreakable" records), right below Joe Cobb, who has no batting average at all. Consider Joe Cobb. The books tells us that he was born in Hudson, Pennsylvania, January 24, 1895, and died December 24, 1947; that he batted and threw right-handed; that he was 5 feet 9 inches tall and weighed 170 pounds, and that his last name was originally Serafin. All this for a man who appeared in one game for Detroit in 1918, apparently going to the plate once and getting a base on balls. In the matter of vital statistics, we know more about Joe Cobb than we do about Shakespeare. Shakespeare never played big-league baseball, so we know not whether he batted left or right (although some readers of the sonnets have pegged him as a switch hitter).

I marvel at the scope of these great baseball record books which have appeared in the past ten years or so, products of the computer age. They have conferred immortality of a sort on men whose names were lost to history for fifty years or more. And of each of them, however slender his record, it can be said, "He was a good ballplayer." If he hadn't been, he never would have been offered a big-league uniform, even for a day.

For me, the big books are also an exercise in nostalgia, recalling names I had forgotten countless years ago. But surely their most intriguing feature, to any genuine baseball zealot, is the small glimpses they offer of the lives of otherwise unknown performers, and the puzzling questions they often raise.

Take Bill Bergen, for example. There is a mystery surrounding him that may never be solved. He was no one-day player; quite the contrary. He came into the major leagues in 1901, when he was already twenty-eight years old, and managed to stick around for eleven years, although he hit over .200 just once. His lifetime batting average was a limp .170. The question is: why? Why was this incredibly bad hitter allowed to go to bat 3,116 times in major-league ball games? He was a catcher, and the assumption is that he must have been an awfully good one. My own theory is that his father owned the Brooklyn ball club, with which he spent most of his career.

Bergen, incidentally, was a teammate of three interesting players at Cincinnati in 1902, all of whom achieved fame (or something) with other teams. Harry Steinfeldt became the forgotten third baseman in the Chicago Cubs' infield immortalized in Franklin P. Adams's "Tinker to Evers to Chance." Sam Crawford was a twenty-two-year-old outfielder who hit .333 and then went on to Detroit, where he stayed for fifteen years, made the Hall of Fame, and collected the amazing lifetime total of 312 triples. No one but Cobb (Ty, not Joe), with 297, has ever come close to that figure, and he had almost 2,000 more at-bats than Sam.

The most remarkable player on that 1902 Cincinnati team, however, was Dummy Hoy, then forty years old and winding up a career that had begun in 1888. William Ellsworth (Dummy) Hoy was a deaf-mute who stood only 5 feet 4, but he had a lifetime batting average of .291, plus 607 stolen bases. He also was responsible for a small revolution in baseball tactics. The visual signals which are used by all teams were originally devised by Hoy's manager so he could communicate his wishes to him. Dummy Hoy died in 1961, just five months short of his 100th birthday. My father, as a very small boy, saw him play, I think. At least, he used to talk about him as if he had. Apparently, in those days, no one thought the name by which he was always identified at all demeaning.

Think about this. In 1906 the Chicago White Sox, the famous Hitless Wonders, were last in the league in hits, total bases, and team batting average. They produced a fraction over seven hits per game and had a grand total of six home runs! They also won the pennant and beat the Cubs in the World Series. The following year, they hit only five home runs, and in 1908 they achieved the seemingly impossible. In that year, playing 156 games, the White Sox hit three home runs (and still lost the pennant by just a game and a half). I feel reasonably sure this is the single-season record for futility in the power department.

Just as there are many batters with perfect batting averages, there are any number of pitchers in the book with won-lost records of 1.000—that is, they won at least one game and never lost one. The vast majority of them have 1–0 records, but there are more than a half dozen with 3–0 marks. The leader in this category is one Ben Shields, who must have been one of the luckiest pitchers ever to play the game. He won three games for the New York Yankees in 1925, kicked around the majors and minors for six years before resurfacing with the Philadelphia Phillies in 1931, where he won one game, despite giving up nine hits and seven walks in five innings of pitching. Over his career, he pitched a total of forty-one innings, during which he allowed fifty-five hits and twenty-seven walks and had an earned-run average of 8.34. But he was never charged with a loss. He is the only 4–0 pitcher in baseball history. (There have doubtless been several rookie pitchers with temporary 4–0 records, but they didn't know when to quit. Neither, apparently, did Ben Shields until it was forced upon him. But he got away with it.)

There is no mystery about Ben Shields. Plainly, the baseball gods favored him with one of their unpredictable smiles. And he hung around long enough to prove he wasn't good enough, perfect record notwithstanding. But what about the others, the dozens of 1.000 hitters and 1.000 pitchers (plus all the pitchers with 0.00 ERAs)? What happened to them? Their records are, I realize, deceptive, but still . . . when a man has fulfilled his obligation to perfection, why is he not then given another chance? Pure logic would dictate that there shouldn't be any 1.000 hitters or pitchers in the book. And yet there are too many to count. I wonder about them all.

There are, incidentally, only three pitchers in the book with "perfect perfect" records: won 1, lost 0, ERA 0.00. They are Nellie Rees (Washington, 1918), Paul Jaeckel (Cubs, '64), and Nestor Chavez (San Francisco, '67). The best of them was Jaeckel, who gave up only four hits in an eight-inning career. Where did he go? He is today only thirty-seven years old, and the Cubs might well consider giving him another chance.

But wait, here's a surprising development. There are, it's true, only three double-perfect pitchers *in the book*. But here's one who's not in the book. You'll remember him, though, if you're a baseball fan. The book I am using explains in the introductory notes that "men who were primarily non-pitchers are included in the pitcher register only if they pitched in five or more games." Rocky Colavito, he of the powerful biceps, 374 home runs and 1,159 RBI's, was beyond question a non-pitcher—primarily. But he pitched three innings of relief for Cleveland in 1958 and, ten years later, three more for the Yankees. In the latter game, he got the win over Detroit (and the Tigers went on to win the World Series that year). In all, Rocky pitched six innings, gave up only one hit, had an ERA of 0.00, won one and lost none. He was not only a "perfect perfect" pitcher, but the best of the lot. You might never have known that if I weren't an inveterate reader of small print.

One of the captivating features of the record book is the players' nicknames, especially those from the early part of the century. I am, first of all, stunned by the amount of research it must have taken to dig them up. No computer, it would seem, can be programmed to do that kind of work. But it is the names themselves, regardless of how they were uncovered, that stir the imagination. What do they mean?

No one would ask that question about such famous nicknames as those of Ty Cobb, who was called "the Georgia Peach," or Frank (Home Run) Baker. Cobb was from Georgia and was a peach of a player, and Baker earned his title by hitting two home runs in the 1911 World Series and banging out an average of seven per year over a career that spanned the great transition in baseball. (Baker broke in in 1908, the year the Chicago White Sox hit three home runs, and he was a teammate of Babe Ruth's in 1921 when the Babe hit fifty-nine.) But how, for example, did Dave Altizer of Pearl, Illinois, become known as "Filipino"? And why was little Arlie Latham, who played for six teams in three different leagues before the turn of the century, called "the Freshest Man on Earth"? (In 1909, evidently still fresh after a ten-year absence, Arlie Latham made a farewell appearance with the New York Giants at the age of forty-nine, and stayed long enough to steal his 791st base. It should be noted, however, that stolen bases before 1900 cannot be compared with twentieth-century steals since they were awarded on an entirely different basis.)

Names like Whitey, Hoss, Brickyard, Dapper Dan, and Big Bill are easily enough understood, and we can imagine how Benny (Earache) Meyer earned his designation. We can guess why Dirty Jack Doyle played for twelve different teams in seventeen years, too. Since he won 203 games, Al Orth (1895–1909) probably didn't mind being called "the Curveless Wonder," but what did Bill Lattimore do in his four-game stay with the 1908 Cleveland club to earn the title "Slothful Bill"? And how, in God's name, did Hub Perdue of the Boston Braves and St. Louis Cardinals (1911–15) come to be called "the Gallatin Squash"?

In the area of literary nicknames, there have been a number of "King" Lears and at least one "King" Lehr. More surprising, though, is Hal Janvrin, who played for several teams between 1911 and '22 and was called "Childe Harold." (Literary allusions are not common in baseball, but an interesting one comes along now and then. In recent years it has become fairly general to say of a poor infielder that he plays like the Ancient Mariner. That is, "he stoppeth one of three.")

Blue Sleeve Harper, Trolley Line Butler, Peaceful Valley Denzer, Dauntless Dave Danforth, Snooze Goulait, Buttermilk Tommy Dowd, Little All Right Ritchey, Sea Lion Hall. There's a story in every one of those names—undoubtedly in many cases a painfully dull one, but that's the chance you take. (Sea Lion Hall's baptismal name, incidentally, was Carlos Clolo. Figure that out.)

Finally, you may be interested to know that from 1908 to 1911, Albert Schweitzer (probably not the same one) played for the St. Louis Browns. His nickname was "Cheese."

Incredible but true. And how history might have altered if Fidel had gone on to become a New York Yanqui, or a Washington Senator, or even a Cincinnati Red.

DON HOAK with MYRON COPE

The Day I Batted
Against Castro

Cuba was an American baseball player's paradise when I played there in the winter of 1950–51. Later, as a major-league third baseman, I became one of the better-paid ballplayers, but I was just an $800-a-month minor leaguer when I went to Cuba.

There the Cienfuegos club paid me $1,000 a month plus $350 a month for expenses. I had a cottage apartment at the elegant Club Nautico on the beach near Havana. The rent, thanks to a reduced rate obtained by the owner of our team, was $150. The $150 included:

(a) A spacious living room with floor-to-ceiling windows; two bedrooms; two baths; a screened patio in the rear; a dazzling flower garden out front.

(b) A fine old Cuban lady named Eeta, who did my housekeeping and cooking. (I had to pay her bus fare.)

(c) A guard to watch over my apartment.

Late at night, after the baseball games were over, I fished off the coral reefs for yellowtails and eels. By day, I went scuba diving for lobster or napped on the beach or walked across the road to the golf course to shoot a round. Cuba was the best place in the world to play baseball.

But even in those days, the students at the University of Havana were politically restless. At the Havana ballpark they'd frequently interrupt our games by staging demonstrations on the field.

They would pour down from the stands and parade across the field carrying banners. They would set off firecrackers and blow horns and shout slogans for ten or fifteen minutes and then go back to their seats. The dictator, Fulgencio Batista, tolerated them, perhaps because he did not consider them a serious threat to his power. His police allowed them to spend their energies. As a matter of fact, Batista himself sometimes witnessed the demonstrations, for he attended many games. Surrounded by bodyguards, he would sit through the commotion with arms folded across his chest and just a trace of a smile at the corner of his lips.

Another regular customer at the park was Fidel Castro. He had just received his law degree from the university, but he remained a well-known and flamboyant leader of the students. As a baseball fan, he belonged in the nut category.

I knew Castro's face well and I suspected he was something of a wild man because of the company he kept. He often came to the park with a man named Pedro Formanthael, who played right field for the Marianao club. Pedro was about forty but an excellent ballplayer. He stood no more than 5 feet 10 but was built very solidly and could hit with power. He wore a great mustache and had a temper that was just as black. He always carried a pistol a foot long, and I wondered how he fit it into his jacket. Anyhow, he and Castro were great pals.

Our Cienfuegos club was playing Pedro Formanthael's team in the Havana park the night I came face to face with Castro.

It was approximately the fifth inning, as I recall, when the firecrackers went off. Up went the banners. The horns blared, and down from the stands came the students—perhaps 300 of them. As fate would have it, I had just stepped into the batter's box when all hell broke loose. "Here we go again," I thought as I stepped out of the box to await order.

But on this night the demonstration took an unexpected turn.

Castro marched straight out to the mound and seized a glove and ball from the Marianao pitcher, a tall Cuban whose name I can't recall. The pitcher shrugged and walked off the field.

Castro then toed the rubber, and as he did so his appearance on the mound was so ridiculous that I cannot forget a single detail of it. He wore no glasses then, but he did have a beard—a funny little beard at the point of his chin that he obviously had taken great care to groom. He was tall and rather skinny.

He wore a long-sleeved white shirt—a type of shirt many Cubans favored. It had pleats like a formal dress shirt and a square bottom which was worn outside the trousers. Castro also wore tight black slacks and black suede shoes with pointed toes. His footwear was almost dandy, and as I see pictures of today's Castro in army fatigues and combat boots I am amused by the contrast.

However, I don't suppose a guy in black suede shoes would stand very well at the head of a people's revolution.

Anyhow, Castro put on the glove and ordered the Marianao catcher—a Cuban veteran named Mike Guerra, who had played for the Washington Senators and Philadelphia Athletics—to catch his repertoire. Castro wound up with a great windmill flourish, whirling his pitching arm overhead about six times. Obviously he considered himself an ace hurler, as the sportswriters say. Left-handers as a breed are eccentric, but Castro, a right-hander, looked kookier than any southpaw I have known.

I figured, "Let him have his fun," and watched him throw half a dozen pitches. The crowd was in an uproar. The students, ranged along the foul lines, were dancing with glee.

Suddenly Castro stopped throwing, glared at me, and barked the Spanish equivalent of "Batter up!"

I looked at the umpire but he only shrugged. "What the hell," I said, and stepped into the batter's box. I was not particularly anxious to defy Castro and his mob, because I knew the Latin temper to be an explosive force. Also, Castro's gunslinging buddy, Pedro Formanthael, was throwing me dirty looks from right field.

Castro gave me the hipper-dipper windup and cut loose with a curve. Actually, it was a pretty fair curve. It had a sharp inside break to it—and it came within an inch of breaking my head.

"Ball one!" said the umpire. Castro marched forward a few paces from the mound and stared daggers at him. The students expressed considerable displeasure. The umpire suggested to me that I had better start swinging or he would be compelled to call me out on strikes.

But I glanced at those students on the foul line and thought, "If I swing hard I'm liable to line a foul down there and kill somebody." I had to think fast because Castro, his floppy shirt billowing in the evening breeze, was already into his windup—a *super* hipper-dipper windup this time. I thought he would take off for the moon.

Finally he cut loose with a fastball—a good fastball, a regular bullet.

It came at me in the vicinity of the shins. Fortunately, I was a pretty fair bat handler, so I came around on the pitch with a short golf stroke and lofted a pop-foul over the heads of the students on the third-base line. I figured the best thing to do was to tap soft fouls into the stands.

Castro's third pitch was another fastball. He really zinged it. It scorched its way straight for my eyeballs. I leaned away, gave my bat a quick lurch, and managed another pop-foul into the stands.

Castro had two strikes on me and he was stomping pompously around the mound as though he had just conquered Washington, D.C.

At that point, however, a new factor entered the picture. The Hoak temper.

I've got a wee trace of Comanche blood, you see, and I imagine I have a temper that can match any Latin's from Havana to Lima. To me, baseball is war. In 1956 I played winter ball in the Dominican Republic, where I pleased the fans by hitting .394 and sliding into bases like a maniac. I am known there, even to this day, as Crazy Horse. When I played for Pittsburgh, a broadcaster there named me The Tiger. Mind you, I don't care to fight Castro and 300 Cubans under any circumstances, but if I have a bat in my hands I know I won't be the only guy to get hurt.

So I turned to the umpire and announced, "I've got a major-league career and big money and good times ahead of me, and I am not going to stand here and let some silly punk in a pleated shirt throw at my skull. Now just get that idiot out of the game."

Here, still another factor entered the picture. The *umpire's* temper.

His name was Miastri and he was a fine umpire. He was such a firebrand that when he threw a player out of a game he often fined him on the spot, and when he fined a guy he would turn around and look up to the press box and announce the amount of the fine with vigorous hand signals. And now he had decided he, too, had had a bellyful of Castro.

He marched over to the *policía*, who were lazily enjoying the fun from the grandstands, and ordered them in no uncertain terms to clear the field. Down they came from the stands, riot clubs brandished at shoulder level.

A knot of cops moved briskly on pitcher Castro. Briefly, he made a show of standing his ground, but the cops shoved him off the mound. He shuffled meekly toward the third-base grandstands, like an impudent boy who has been cuffed by the teacher and sent to stand in the corner.

My final memory of him is one that somehow strikes me funny to this day. As he crossed the third-base line I happened to look at his shoes. He had dust on his black suede shoes.

Looking back, I think that with a little work on his control, Fidel Castro would have made a better pitcher than a prime minister.

A fabulous character recalls a fabled time in sport and sportswriting, especially that inexhaustible fount of hilarious stories, the Bambino. Richards Vidmer covered the Yanks and covered up for them, too—that was the code until Jim Brosnan lifted the veil in *The Long Season* (1960) and Jim Bouton vaporized it a decade later. The passage below is a portion of the chapter devoted to Vidmer in Jerome Holtzman's wonderful oral history of American sportswriting, *No Cheering in the Press Box* (1974).

JEROME HOLTZMAN

Richards Vidmer
Remembers

Richards Vidmer was not the garden variety sportswriter. Unlike many of his colleagues, he was an outstanding athlete: He played baseball at the minor-league level (under the name Widmeyer, to protect his college eligibility), and football at George Washington College; and he later coached football at St. John's University in Washington, D.C. He was also an accomplished equestrian and a scratch golfer. During his second marriage, to the daughter of a Borneo rajah, he broke the boredom of a life of ease by working as a golf pro. Not surprisingly, he was closer to the athletes than most of his peers and admitted, "I didn't hang around with the writers. The ballplayers were my friends."

Mr. Vidmer was the inspiration for the book Young Man of Manhattan, *a romantic novel about a playboy sportswriter. He more or less stumbled into newspaper work, starting on the Washington (D.C.) Herald, and is best remembered for his work in New York, first as a baseball writer for the* Times *and then at the* Herald Tribune, *where he succeeded the famous Bill Mc-Geehan and wrote a column titled "Down in Front." "The thing that saved my life in the newspaper business," explained Mr. Vidmer, "was that I never had any desire to have a drink until five o'clock, until after my work was done. Then, I could catch up with anybody.''*

The son of a highly decorated brigadier general who fought at San Juan Hill, Mr. Vidmer lived on army posts on four continents. For several years he was a mascot of the football teams at West Point, when Eisenhower, Patton, and Mark Clark were cadets. Mr. Vidmer survived an air collision during World War I, as a pilot, and during World War II was in intelligence, principally under assignment to General Eisenhower's headquarters. He now lives in Orlando, Florida, with his third wife, and is still dashingly handsome at the age of seventy-five.

Hell, I should have been dead twenty years ago. If I'd known I was going to live so long I would have taken better care of myself. I was careless, reckless. I've done things—well, I must have been crazy. Like one time in Philadelphia. I was on the twelfth floor in a hotel, in a corner room, and there was somebody I wanted to see in the next room—another guy. I'd been drinking. Instead of going around the corner and walking in through the door, I climbed out my window and crawled from one ledge to the other. Now, how stupid can you be?

I was what you might call either a playboy or a rounder. I suppose I was more of a playboy. I wasn't much of a rounder. I mean, I didn't get drunk and wind up in alleys or things like that, if that's what a rounder is. A playboy is a guy who takes life as it comes, has a good time, and enjoys himself. I've certainly enjoyed my life.

I was raised in the army. People ask me where I come from. Hell, I don't come from anywhere. I didn't have a home town. I've lived all over the world— Japan, Philippines, Iowa, Vermont, Texas. My father was a career officer. He wound up a general—in the cavalry. He was a captain during the time I was growing up. Whenever he went out on maneuvers or something like that, why, I'd go out with the troops.

He was the adjutant at West Point in 1912–13–14, when I was a brat around twelve years old. I was the mascot of the Army football team and the bat boy for the baseball team. They took me along on their trips. I had a card, had it for years, "Admit Bearer to Army Team Wherever It May Be."

One of my favorite conversation pieces is a magazine that I've got around here which West Point puts out three or four times a year, a rather ornate thing. Someone sent me this copy which was devoted primarily to Eisenhower. Ike played on the football team, and there's a picture of him with some of the other players. My favorite thing is to say, "Now find me." They search around looking at the players. They can't find me. But I'm the little fellow standing right next to Ike.

The fellows at West Point when I was up there, the cadets at that time, were big generals in the second war. Eisenhower, Bradley, Gerhardt, Aaker, Mark Clark. Hell, I knew Patton all through his life, more or less. And, of course, I served in both wars. Air Force. I was in an air collision during the first war. Miracle that I came out alive.

I was a sportswriter for thirty years, between the wars. I guess I was a romantic guy in those days. Everybody who comes around asks me if it was true that I married a rajah's daughter. It's true. She was the daughter of the Rajah of Sarawak. It's the northern portion of Borneo and embraces an area larger than England, Scotland, and Wales put together. The rajah owned the whole thing, and it was a very rich country.

There was this book, *Young Man of Manhattan*. It came out in the late 1920s, '27 or '28. It was written by Katharine Brush. She wrote seven or eight books. Some of what she wrote was racy stuff in those days, but it'd be tame today. She was a girl friend of mine. She built the book on me, what she knew of my character. It was a successful book. They made a movie out of it. Preston Foster played the male lead.

But it was all fictionalized, of course. Toby McLean was the hero of the book. He's a sportswriter—a playboy, always having a good time, but never getting down to real business. He's going with this girl, and she's always after him to write a book. "Write a book! Write a book!" And he procrastinates and tells her, "Okay, okay! Someday! Someday!" It's during Prohibition, of course, and he gets some bad liquor and goes blind. Then, while he's blind, he writes a book, dictating it all to her, and when it's published she puts the book into his hands, a very tender scene. And of course the book's a great success. Kay Brush was wonderful. Oh, she could write like hell.

The other sportswriters got a big kick out of it. Some people still call me Toby to this day.

I'll tell you the kind of writer I was. One day this editor called me—this was in New York, when I was doing the sports column for the *Herald Tribune*. He was from one of those highbrow magazines. What's the name of it? *The Atlantic Weekly?* No, *The Atlantic Monthly*, that's it. He said would I write a piece about Joe DiMaggio, and I said, "What kind of piece?"

He said, "Anything you want to do. We just want you to write a piece about Joe DiMaggio."

I said, "How much for how much?"

He said, "Well, three hundred dollars for twenty-five hundred or three thousand words."

"Sure, I'll do it. When do you want it?"

They didn't need it until the twenty-eighth of the month. This was about the third of the month. "Sure," I said. "No problem."

Of course, you know me. I could have sat down and written it then. But I just put it off. By God, the twenty-eighth arrives and he calls me up and says, "You know, we haven't gotten that piece from you yet."

"Hey, you haven't? Now wait a minute, I sent that up there yesterday by messenger. Wait! I'll see if it's gone." I let the phone hang there for a minute or two. Then I said, "No, it's still here where I left it. It hasn't gone out yet."

You know, I sat down and wrote that thing—three thousand words. Never even read copy on it. Got a messenger and set it up there, and the next day he called me up. I thought, "Oh, oh, here comes the rewriting."

I said, "Did you get the piece all right?"

"Oh, yes, we've got it. Just exactly what we wanted. Exactly."

I remember Bill Corum—he was an old friend of mine. We'd been on the copy desk together, when we were young fellows. Bill once said, "When you sit down and write something in a hurry, it's good. But when you sit down and labor over it, it stinks."

One time—this was when I was married to my first wife—I had been in Pittsburgh and had gotten back home late. I was asleep. She woke me up about eleven o'clock and said, "We've got to be down at so-and-so's at noon because there's a buffet luncheon and cocktails."

I thought, "Oh, Jesus," but I said, "All right" and we went. It was a good party. Bankers and brokers, and everybody having a lot of drinks and a good time. I never wrote on Sundays for Monday's paper. All of a sudden, it's about five o'clock, and I said, "This isn't Sunday. It's Armistice Day. It's Monday. I've got to write a column!"

So I blew out of there, jumped on the train to the city. On the way in I thought, "What the hell can I write that won't take much time?" I decided I'd write some Armistice Day poetry. So I kind of got it in my head, and when I got up there I knocked it out on a typewriter. It didn't fill a column, but did fill this much and it was something different. Very serious. Of course, I'm drunker than hell.

Son of a bitch, if Alexander Woollcott doesn't call me the next day wanting to know if he could put it on the air.

I don't know if you feel this way, but when you get through writing a column, do you think, "Jesus, that's good"? I wasn't that way. Almost every time I did a column, I said, "Well, Jesus, I'll write a better one tomorrow. That's the best I can do today." I always said that. But every day it was the same thing. I always thought I'd do better tomorrow.

But once in a while I'd write a column and I'd say, "Jesus, there's a dinger." Yet the ones that I felt stunk, I'd get a hundred letters, sometimes, saying that was a great column, and the ones I thought were great, I'd never hear a word. I was a bad judge, I guess.

I wasn't a good reporter. I always figured you could read a box score and know what happened. I still do. When I'd write a ballgame, I'd write about some particular thing, not: "In the first inning Gehrig singled to right, in the second inning Meusel tripled to center, and in the third inning so-and-so grounded into a double play." The hell with that.

Oh, I'd bring it all in—who won and the important plays—but I used to start my stories with some angle—like, well, there was the day the Yankees had the bases filled with two outs in the ninth inning and they sent Mike Gazella to pinch-hit. An awfully nice guy. Went to Lafayette. And he stood up there and got a base on balls to force in the winning run. So I started off, "He also serves who only stands and waits."

I played a lot of golf. I played every morning on the road. As a result, I was generally late to the ballgames. I'd get to the press box in the third inning and ask someone to fill me in. One time, in St. Louis, I got there pretty late in the game, maybe the fifth or sixth inning, and I asked Will Wedge—he was the baseball man at the *Sun*—if anything special had happened.

"Oh," he says, "Babe hit another home run," which was routine in those days. But he said they had broadcast on the loudspeaker that they wanted the ball back.

I said, "What for? Was it especially long or something?"

Wedge didn't know, but he said a little Italian kid had retrieved the ball and had given it to the Babe. Wedge gave me the kid's name.

Then I remember that Babe and Claire—that was his wife—and I had been to a movie a couple of nights before, and Babe happened to say, "Well, the next one I hit will be my five hundredth."

Now, you know what a big to-do there is today when a guy hits five hundred home runs. Writers and photographers follow him around for weeks. But Babe had just mentioned it casually. I was probably the only writer who knew it was his five hundredth.

So I sat down and wrote how Babe had hit this home run and this little kid in the alley, an Italian kid, had chased the ball, and how he'd been trying to get a ball all these years but he never got one because the bigger kids had always beaten him to it. Finally, he gets a ball, his big moment, and a cop comes up and says to the kid, "Come with me."

The kid's scared.

He says, "I ain't done nuthin', I ain't done nuthin'."

And the cop says, "Babe Ruth wants to see you."

Now the kid knows he's in trouble.

So they bring him into the Yankee dugout and Babe Ruth gives him five bucks and a brand-new ball.

That was my story for the next day, not the fact that the Yankees won 18–

4 or 9–1, or something like that. What the hell, you can see that in the box score. Hell, I'd have it moving. I'd have some drama in it, or romance, or some damn thing. Not like they do it today.

But don't get the wrong impression. I wasn't a big scoop artist. Christ, no! That's why I had so many friends. I never could see blowing the whistle on somebody just for a big headline, a one-day sensation. I'll give you an example.

The day Lou Gehrig took himself out of the lineup and went up to the Mayo Clinic, I wasn't traveling with the Yankees. I was writing a column then, and the Yankees were on the road when Lou took himself out. When the club came home I went into the clubhouse and said, "What the hell's the matter with you, Lou? When you going to get back in the lineup?" I was always kidding with him.

He said, "Wait a minute," and called this fellow over. It was his doctor. He said to the doctor, "Talk to him." And the doctor looked at Lou and Lou said, "Go ahead, tell him anything you want. He's my pal." And Lou walks away.

I asked the doctor, "What's the matter with Lou?"

The doctor told me he's got a creeping paralysis. Nobody knows what causes it. If they knew, they could cure it, or at least stop it.

"What are his chances?"

"Well," the doctor says, "there has been much progress made in paralysis these last few years because of President Roosevelt. We hope we'll discover the cause and cure it in time."

"Suppose you don't?"

"Well, I'd say two years is the limit."

I'm the only writer who knows what's the matter with Lou. But I didn't write it. And why the hell should I? The public has to be informed, my ass! None of the public's damned business as long as he plays ball or doesn't play. That's the way I felt and that's why Lou told the doctor he could level with me. Lou knew damn well I wasn't going to rush into print for the sake of a headline.

Then, maybe two weeks later, Jimmy Powers found out and he spreads it all over the *News*—saying how all of Lou's teammates are afraid to sit next to him in the dugout, and so on, which was a God damn lie. But it was sensational, all right.

I was always reticent about writing anything that was going to hurt somebody, and of course, I would never write anything told to me in confidence. I only read excerpts of the Bouton book. I thought it was damned interesting and amusing—and true. I had seen the same thing, or similar things, thirty years before. Sure, ballplayers are like that. All athletes are like that. For God's sake, all men are like that. But I just don't see where a public figure's private life is anybody's business.

Hell, I could have written a story every day on the Babe. But I never wrote

about his personal life, not if it would hurt him. Babe couldn't say no to certain things. Hot dogs was the least of 'em. There were other things that were worse. Hell, sometimes I thought it was one long line, a procession.

I remember once we were coming north, at the end of spring training. We used to barnstorm and stop at all the little towns. We traveled on the train. Babe and some of the other ballplayers and myself, we'd play bridge between the exhibition games, in the morning before they had to go to the ballpark, and then after the ballgame until the train left, generally about eleven o'clock that night. In those days they used to start games at one o'clock, or one-thirty. We'd be through by three, and we'd go back to the hotel to Babe's room and start playing bridge, and surer than hell the phone would ring. I'd always answer it.

"Is Babe Ruth there?"

And I'd say, "No, he's not here right now. This is his secretary. Can I tell him who called?"

"This is Mildred. Tell him Mildred called."

And I'd say, "Mildred"—and the Babe would shake his head, meaning no. Get rid of her.

I'd say, "I'm sorry, he's not here right now, but I'll tell him that you called."

Well, before I could finish, Babe would be across the room, grab the phone, and say, "Hello, babe, c'mon up."

He couldn't say no.

Up she'd come and interrupt the bridge game for ten minutes or so. They'd go in the other room. Pretty soon they'd come out and the girl would leave. Babe would say, "So long, kid," or something like that. Then he'd sit down and we'd continue our bridge game. That's all. That was it. While he was absent we'd sit and talk, wait for him.

One evening in Philadelphia I was in the dining room and Babe had me paged. I went to the phone and Babe said, "What are you doing tonight?"

I said, "Nothing in particular."

And he said, "Come up about nine o'clock, will ya?"

I didn't know what he wanted, but I went up there at nine o'clock. Babe was in his dressing gown. There was some whiskey and ice, soda and whatnot on the table. Babe always had a suite. We had two or three drinks and chatted away about a lot of crap. He talked about Joe McCarthy. Babe had ambitions to be a manager and he never liked McCarthy. He always said McCarthy was a dumb Irishman who didn't know anything. After about a half hour of this I saw a shadow at the door in the other room, the bedroom, and I said, "Say, Claire isn't down with you, is she?"

He says, "No, she didn't come down this trip."

So I says, "Have you got a doll in there?"

And he said, "Yeah."

"Jesus, Babe, why didn't you tell me? I've been sitting here chewing the fat with you, and all the time you've got a doll in there."

"No, no," he says. "That's why I wanted you to come up. I thought I'd need a rest."

Oh, sure, that sort of thing is funny, but I didn't think it would add anything to the public image of the Babe. The public already had a good picture of him.

If you weren't around in those times, I don't think you could appreciate what a figure the Babe was. He was bigger than the president. One time, coming north, we stopped at a little town in Illinois, a whistle stop. It was about ten o'clock at night and raining like hell. The train stopped for ten minutes to get water, or something. It couldn't have been a town of more than 5,000 people, and by God, there were 4,000 of them down there standing in the rain, just waiting to see the Babe.

Babe and I and two other guys were playing bridge. Babe was sitting next to the window. A woman with a little baby in her arms came up and started peering in at the Babe. She was rather good looking. Babe looked at her and went on playing bridge. Then he looked at her again and finally he leaned out and said, "Better get away from here, lady. I'll put one in the other arm. . . ."

"Discerning the De Facto Standards of the Hall of Fame," read the subhead when this piece appeared in *The 1980 Baseball Abstract.* At that time a self-published, typewritten book, it began to pierce the fog of myth and misunderstanding with which baseball brahmins robed themselves. The 1980 effort attracted a few hundred devoted readers; today *The Bill James Baseball Abstract* is commercially published and claims a readership well in excess of 100,000. It is not too much to say that James has revolutionized the way fans think about the game and the way professionals write about it. This essay, like a modern dictionary, is not prescriptive but descriptive—it does not attempt to weigh the justice of the Cooperstown election system but simply to determine what the implied standards are and how prospective candidates stack up against them.

BILL JAMES

What Does It Take?

I used to write a lot about the Hall of Fame. I wrote about how they could design more equitable election systems. I wrote about why the different boards inevitably used different standards. I wrote about the statistical illusions that tend to reinforce the Senile Ballplayers Committee in their inevitable belief that the Boys I played with were the best ever. Nobody paid any attention. I made up charts that demonstrated the New York bias in the Hall of Fame's composition. No New Yorkers called to resign. Eventually I gave it up. I dislike howling into the wind.

What never ceases to amaze me is the hold that this unremarkable institution has on the imagination of baseball fans. You go to a meeting of the Society for American Baseball Research, and every third word is Cooperstown. Every separate interest group scratches at the base of this one pedestal. The Committee on the Negro Leagues wants to get more old-time blacks into the Hall of Fame. The Committee on Stat Analysis wants to establish standards for election to the Hall of Fame. The Committee on the Minor Leagues feels unfulfilled until there exists a minor-league Hall of Fame. And everybody and his fourteen-year-old son wants to collar me and explain why Ross Barnes, Arky Vaughan, Johnny Mize, and Bob Elliott belong in the Hall of Fame. I get sick of hearing about it. The Negro Leagues are fascinating, stat analysis will obviously hold my interest. The minor leagues are a delicious memory, and even Ross Barnes might be interesting if you knew something about him. Why must all of these topics be submerged into a never-ending argument about who belongs in the Hall of Fame?

Men without voices rattle their cups, I suppose. And so, for three *Abstracts*, I have said hardly a word about the Hall of Fame—admirable restraint, I think, if I must say so myself. But it is a major subject of stat analysis, and one can't avoid it forever. The notion floats around that one can detect patterns among the random selections of the various committees, and in that way discern some sort of general standards for Hall of Fame selection. What I propose to do here is to try to get those standards down on paper, to make them add, and in that way to bring some hard evidence out about what it is that will make a record stand out when the memory of the man has cooled.

Understand, I am not in the least talking about what Hall of Fame standards *should be.* I am talking about what they *are.* De Facto standards, inferred from a study of who has made it and who hasn't. If we can build a prediction formula that will take the records of Enos Slaughter, Chick Hafey, Gil Hodges, and Ralph Kiner and tell us that from that group Hafey and Kiner are the Hall of Famers, then we will have, it seems to me, that much better of an understanding of what it takes to become a Hall of Famer. That understanding we can then apply to the records of contemporary players.

In some ways the system which results is far from being logical. The Hall of Fame prediction system (HOFPS) awards 8 points for each season that an outfielder hits .300, only 3 points for each season that he drives in 100 runs. As a statement of the relative value of hitting .300 and driving in 100 runs, this is asinine. But it is also what works. The fact is that Indian Bob Johnson, Del Ennis, Bob Elliott, and Gil Hodges, who have around thirty 100-RBI seasons among them, are *not* in the Hall of Fame, while a bunch of singles hitters who have had about the same number of .320 seasons are.

So then, the prediction system. Actually, I have two prediction systems, one for pitchers, one for outfielders. Both require 100 points. There are no partial or percentage qualifications; 100 points and you're in, 99 and you're out. I don't have anything for infielders or catchers; somebody who has the time is encouraged to try to develop something. Anyway, here's what I have:

Pitchers

1. Count 3 points for each season of fifteen or more wins.
2. Count 10 points for each season of twenty wins.
   a. 20–20 seasons (that is, seasons with both twenty wins and twenty losses) should be counted as fifteen-victory seasons.

b. Seasons are not to be counted in more than one win category—that is, twenty-victory seasons are not to be double-counted with the fifteen-victory seasons, nor thirty-victory seasons as also twenty-victory seasons.

3. Count thirty-win seasons at 1 point per win recorded.

4. Career wins are not counted before 150. After 150, count 1 point per three wins until 235. For example, count 1 point for 153–155 career wins, 11 points of 183–185. Count 1 point for each win above 235.

5. Count 2 points for each World Series *start*.

6. Count 3 points for each World Series *win*.

   a. Total points awarded for World Series performance are not to exceed 30.

7. Count 5 points for each season leading the league in ERA.

8. Count 5 points for each season leading the league in strikeouts.

9. Count 1 point for each .010 the pitcher's career won-lost percentage is above .500.

There are thirty-six pitchers from this century (not counting the Negro Leagues) who are in the Hall of Fame. There are thirty-five pitchers from this century who would be predicted to be in the Hall of Fame. There are thirty-three pitchers who are on both lists, thus the HOFPS makes three or five errors, depending on how you figure it. The two pitchers who are not in although they have 100 qualification points are Carl Mays, who has been informally blacklisted because he threw the pitch that killed Ray Chapman, and Hal Newhouser, whose records are (rightfully) discounted because they were posted with the aid of a war.

The three pitchers who are in although they lack 100 qualification points are Addie Joss, Pop Haines, and Rube Marquard, who are in for reasons that I will be kind enough not to speculate on. I will add that not only do these pitchers not have 100 points, they're not close, either. These, unless I missed somebody, are the only five pitchers from this century for whom the system fails to make a correct In/Out decision.

Obviously, the first set of numbers that I tried did not draw that line there. At a glance it is not really obvious why Rube Waddell (184–141) is in the Hall of Fame but Lon Warneke (193–121) is not, or why Jack Chesbro (199–127) is in but Ed Reulbach (185–104) is not. Among the most pronounced patterns in the taste of Hall of Fame voters is that they are much impressed by pitchers who were starters on championship teams, thus the points awarded for World Series performance (the same is true among other players.) But the key element in most cases is twenty-victory seasons. Well, you've got a choice: you can get in by winning twenty games every year, or you can get there by winning 235 or more total.

Among active pitchers and recently retired pitchers, totals of note include:

Pitcher (W–L)	Points Under Rule Number:									Total	In/Out
	1	2	3	4	5	6	7	8	9		
Gomez (189–102)	9	40	0	13	14	16	10	15	14	131	In
Lemon (207–128)	6	70	0	19	8	6	0	5	11	125	In
Chesbro (199–127)	6	40	41	14*	0	0	0	0	11	112	In
Rixey (266–251)	12	40	41	59	0	0	0	0	1	112	In
Walsh (194–130)	9	30	39	14	4	6	10	10	9	131	In
Dean (150–83)	3	30	30	0	8	6	0	20	14	111	In
Hoyt (237–182)	8	20	0	30	22	8	5	0	6	109	In
Pennock (241–162)	18	20	0	34	10	15	0	0	9	106	In
Waddell (184–141)	12	30	0	12*	0	0	10	35	6	105	In
Lyons (260–230)	9	30	9	55	0	0	5	0	3	102	In
Bender (210–128)	18	20	0	20	20	10	0	0	12	100	In
Derringer (223–212)	12	40	0	24	14	6	0	0	1	97	Out
Reynolds (182–107)	18	10	0	10	18	12	5	10	13	96	Out
Drysdale (209–166)	15	20	0	19	12	9	0	15	5	95	Out
Bridges (194–138)	6	30	0	14	10	12	0	10	8	94	Out
Shawkey (198–150)	12	40	0	16	10	3	5	0	6	92	Out
Coombs (158–110)	0	20	30	2	12	15	0	0	9	88	Out
Walters (198–160)	12	30	0	16	6	6	10	5	5	90	Out
Cicotte (210–148)	9	30	0	20	10	6	5	0	8	88	Out
Warneke (193–121)	15	30	0	14	6	6	5	0	11	87	Out
Ferrell (193–128)	3	60	0	14	0	0	0	0	10	87	Out
Bunning (224–184)	21	10	0	24	0	0	0	15	4	84	Out
Burdette (203–144)	18	20	0	17	12	12	5	0	8	92	Out
Reulbach (185–104)	12	30	0	11	10	6	0	0	14	83	Out

But also:

Mays (208–126)	6	50	0	19	14	9	0	0	12	110	Out
Newhouser (207–150)	9	40	0	19	6	6	10	10	8	108	Out
Marquard (204–179)	6	30	0	18	16	6	0	5	3	84	In
Haines (210–158)	5	30	0	20	8	9	0	0	7	79	In
Joss (160–97)	6	40	0	3	0	0	10	0	12	71	In

*Does not include pre-1900 accomplishments.

It is appropriate for those two to tie for the top spot. I was going to apologize for Luis Tiant's being shown as still needing a couple of points (6 wins would do it), because I thought he was an obvious in, but then I read that Bill Mead

Pitcher (W–L)	Points Under Rule Number:									Total
	1	2	3	4	5	6	7	8	9	
Seaver	18	50	0	28	8	3	25	15	13	160
Palmer	6	80	0	25	16	9	10	0	14	160
Gibson	15	50	0	44	18	12	5	5	9	158
Perry	24	50	0	72	0	0	0	0	6	152
Jenkins	9	70	0	40	0	0	0	5	7	131
Marichal	9	60	0	36	2	0	5	0	13	129
Hunter	6	50	0	24	18	15	5	0	7	125
Kaat	15	30	0	57	6	3	0	0	4	115
Carlton	15	40	0	25	2	0	5	10	8	105
Tiant	6	40	0	22	6	6	10	0	8	98
Lolich	18	20	0	22	6	9	0	5	3	83
Sutton	24	10	0	22	12	6	0	0	6	80
Niekro, P.	21	20	0	22	0	0	5	5	3	76
Ryan	12	20	0	5	0	0	0	35	1	73
Blue	9	30	0	2	10	0	5	0	8	64
Guidry	6	10	0	0	4	6	10	0	25	61
John	6	20	0	14	6	3	0	0	7	56
Richard	9	10	0	0	0	0	5	10	9	43

of SABR wrote an article in which he rated Tiant as a dark horse. I don't know how in the world he figured that. The contrast between his seat-of-the-pants analysis and the prediction formula is interesting; he has Ferguson Jenkins, with seven twenty-victory seasons and 247 career wins, in the same class with Mickey Lolich, in "more than even chance." Jenkins may have to wait a few years, like Robin Roberts, but he will obviously go, while Lolich is very unlikely to make it unless Hall of Fame standards drop markedly.

It should be noted that while Vida Blue (64 points) and Ron Guidry (61 points) look about even, this is not really true. Twenty-five of Guidry's points are "soft" points, which could be lost unless he is able to maintain a .756 lifetime won-lost percentage, which no one ever has. If he goes 12–12 in 1980, he will end the year with 55 points, six less than he has now. Blue, on the other hand, has crossed the magic "150" line above which career victory totals begin to help you, so if he goes 12–12 he will wind up the year with 67 points. If both were to go 21–10 and lead their leagues in ERA, Guidry would advance to 74 points, but Blue would leap to 87.

The system for outfielders delivers about the same degree of accuracy. Somehow I have misplaced my count of the number of outfielders from this century who are in the Hall of Fame, but it is about the same, somewhere around thirty. The system for outfielders makes, again, five errors. One of those, on Shoeless Joe Jackson, has nothing to do with statistics. Another, Richie Ashburn, probably will be changed within a few years; Ashburn is fully qualified and will eventually go. Two other players are figured as qualified but not in; both of them, interestingly enough, are players with impressive records, but records which are completely dwarfed by the company they keep. The names are Bobby Veach and Bob Meusel. One cannot think of Veach and Meusel without thinking about Crawford and Cobb and Ruth and Gehrig, and when you think about records like that, Veach and Meusel don't look so good. But they are, in fact, better than the records of many Hall of Famers. The fifth error is Harry Hooper, in for his defensive reputation, but far from being qualified as a hitter. And, again, I may have missed somebody:

Outfielders

1. Award 8 points for each season of hitting .300, 100 or more games, up to a limit of 60 points.
2. Award 15 points if the player has a lifetime batting average of .315 or better in 1,000 games.
3. Award 3 points per 100-RBI season.
4. Award 8 points per 200-hit season.
5. a. Award 4 points for each season leading the league in stolen bases.
   b. Award 5 points for each season leading in RBIs.
   c. Award 8 for leading in home runs.
   d. Award 12 for leading in batting.
6. Count 1 point per World Series Game Played, up to a limit of eighteen.
7. Add 10 points if the player has 3,000 career hits.
8. Add 10 points if the player has 400 career home runs.

There are 100 more players who just miss, but that's enough. I will leave the computation of the errors and the active outfielders for your idle moments, or mine. Perhaps in future *Abstracts* a list of the active players who are charting a Hall of Fame progression will be a regular feature. That, however, would require frequent updating of the system so as to continue to minimize errors. I have no idea how well the outfielder's system would adapt to other positions; I would guess very well at first and fairly well at third and second, but not very well at short and catcher. I haven't tried it.

Finally, I will offer my opinion with regard to the recurrent proposal that fixed statistical guidelines for Hall of Fame selection should be established. Explicit criteria, it is argued, would do two things: it would end the erosion

Player	Points awarded under rule number:											Total	In/Out
	1	2	3	4	5a	5b	5c	5d	6	7	8		
Wheat	60	15	6	24	0	0	0	12	12	0	0	129	In
Wilson	40	0	18	8	0	10	32	0	12	0	0	120	In
Snider	56	0	18	0	0	5	8	0	18	0	10	115	In
Manush	60	0	6	32	0	0	0	12	5	0	0	115	In
Combs	56	15	0	24	0	0	0	0	18	0	0	113	In
Waner, L.	60	15	0	32	0	0	0	0	4	0	0	111	In
Averill	60	15	15	16	0	0	0	0	3	0	0	109	In
Youngs	56	15	3	16	0	0	0	0	18	0	0	108	In
Roush	60	15	0	0	0	0	0	24	8	0	0	107	In
Kaline	60	0	9	8	0	0	0	12	7	10	0	106	In
Kiner	24	0	18	0	0	5	56	0	0	0	0	103	In
Carey	48	0	0	8	40	0	0	0	7	0	0	103	In
Hafey	48	15	9	0	0	0	0	12	18	0	0	102	In
Meusel, I.	48	0	12	16	0	5	0	0	18	0	0	99	Out
Walker, D.	60	0	6	0	0	0	8	12	12	0	0	98	Out
Slaughter	60	0	9	0	0	0	8	0	18	0	0	95	Out
Williams, K.	60	15	6	0	0	5	8	0	0	0	0	94	Out
Cramer	60	0	0	24	0	0	0	0	9	0	0	93	Out
Kuenn	60	0	0	16	0	0	0	12	4	0	0	92	Out

of standards that has already brought into the Hall too many second-rate stars, and it would end the "injustices" of players like Freddie Lindstrom and Pop Haines being inducted while obviously better players wait outside.

In my opinion, this is not the way. Justice? One cannot do an injustice to a bunch of numbers. One can deal unfairly with a man, with a memory perhaps, but not with lines of statistics. Such injustices as there are here have nothing to do with statistics, and will not be prevented by establishing statistical reference points.

The declining quality of Hall of Fame inductees, not to mention the fact that an increasing percentage of them are dead and forgotten, is caused by two things: 1) the system of multiple review boards, in which one takes up again the players who have already been passed over by the others, creates an in-evitable downward spiral, as the decisions of the latter reflect back on the standards of the former. 2) More importantly, fair judgments are prevented by favoritism, by passions, by PR campaigns and personal loyalties—all of the things which create the vortex of controversy which is both the strength and the liability of the institution. So long as people carry every grand and petty cause that they stumble over to bang on the door of Cooperstown, that door will continue to be battered. If you would save the institution, then consider in your judgments not only what is good for your favorite player, but what is good for the Hall itself.

But there is an even better reason not to have statistical standards, which is that there is no way in the world to evolve a set of standards which is as comprehensive, as complex, as fair, or as open to improvement as is human judgment. I have spent all of my life, sad as it may sound, learning to understand baseball records. If I couldn't make up standards which are fair and comprehensive, who could? And I don't feel that I could. There are simply too many things in the game of baseball which are not measured, are poorly measured, are still in the process of being measured. You could state that Mark Belanger over his career has won as many games by his glove as Joe DiMaggio did by his bat, and while we might not agree, there is no way in hell that anybody could prove you wrong. Statistical analysis is simply one more way of understanding the game of baseball. It is not our place to stand in judgment of the others.

The Boys of Summer is a warm, evocative book that has stood the test of time. Although some of the Brooklyn Dodgers have not—"the boys of summer in their ruin," from Dylan Thomas's verse—Carl Erskine assuredly has. The Dodgers of our boyhood grew old, a disquieting fact; better, we may have thought, to preserve them in our memories as they were, frozen in a baseball-card pose, so that we too might stay young forever. Roger Kahn showed us that heroes grown frail, retired from the fray, remain men . . . and in other, greater arenas, still heroes.

ROGER KAHN

Carl and Jimmy

The Erskines' den extends square and compact from the living room. The walls are busy with plaques and books. "Would you like to drink the present you brought?" Carl asked. It was after dinner. He went to a cabinet under a bookcase and produced three scrapbooks, bound in brown tooled leather. "Some old fellow kept these. We didn't know anything about them until I came back here to live.

"I was looking beyond baseball, beyond a lot of things, and I enrolled in Anderson College as a thirty-two-year-old freshman." Erskine tells stories with a sense of detail. "All right," he said. "Monday morning. Eight-o'clock class. The start of freshman English. I get to the building. I got these gray hairs. It's two minutes to eight when I walk in, a little scared. All of a sudden the room gets quiet." Erskine grinned. "They thought I was the professor.

"I got in about sixty-five credits before Dad died and for a lot of reasons I had to quit. Heck, I wasn't only a thirty-two-year-old freshman. I became a thirty-six-year-old dropout."

Betty went for a Coke and a drink, and the ceremony of scrapbooks began. "Here's one of yours," Erskine said. "How does it read?" He had opened to the World Series strikeout story:

A crowd of 35,270 fans, largest ever to squeeze and elbow its way into Ebbets Field for a series contest, came to see a game the Dodgers had to win. They saw much more. They saw a game of tension, inescapable and mounting tension, a game that offered one climax after another, each more grinding than the one before, a game that will be remembered with the finest.

"John Mize," Erskine said, "was some hitter. But he had a pretty good mouth, too. All afternoon I could hear him yelling at the Yankee hitters. 'What are you doing, being suckers for a miserable bush curve?' Then he's pinch-hitting in the ninth and I get two strikes. Wham. John Mize's becomes the strikeout that breaks the record."

"On a miserable bush curve?"

"A sweet out."

"Here's the Scotch," Betty said. "And a Coke for you, Carl."

"But I wasn't out of it," Erskine said. He was sitting forward on a plush chair, his face furrowed with thought. "After Mize, I had to pitch to Irv Noren. I walked him. All right. Now here comes Joe Collins. I forget the record. All I can think is that the right-field wall is 297 feet away and Collins is a strong left-handed hitter who has struck out four times. Baseball is that way. One swing of the bat. He hits the homer. He scores two runs. He goes from goat to hero. He wins it all. Collins had the power and I'm thinking, 'Oh brother, he can turn this whole thing around for himself.'

"That's in my head. What I didn't know is over on the Yankee bench Mize and the others have been kidding Collins. They tell him the World Series goat record is five strikeouts. One more and his name goes into the book forever.

"He goes to the plate entirely defensive. He's choking up six inches on the bat. He's using it like a fly swatter.

"I get two strikes on him real fast. Still, I have this fear of the short porch in right. The last pitch I throw is a curve and it's a dandy. It snaps off and it's about ankle-high. So help me, he swings straight down. He beats it into the ground and gets enough of the ball to nub it back to me. I get my record. Think of the two minds. It ends with me scared to death of the long ball and Collins scared to death of striking out. He doesn't get to hit the long ball and I don't get to strike him out." Erskine grinned and refilled our glasses.

"A great thing about our family comes ten years later. It's 1963. Sandy Koufax goes out and strikes out fifteen Yankees. We're living here then, but we see it on television. And one of the boys, looking real blue, says, 'Don't feel sad, Dad. You still hold the record for *right-handers*.'

"All of the kids give pleasure, in different ways, the older boys, Susan, Jimmy. It's hard for some to understand that Jimmy is fun. Heck, we had an Olympics for all the retarded kids of Madison County and Jimmy won a big event."

"What event was that, Carl?"

"Ballbounce. He bounced a basketball twenty-one times."

Erskine sipped at his Coke. "You wonder, of course. You look for guilt. When was he conceived? Was somebody overtired? Did you really want him? A few months along in pregnancy Betty got a virus and ran 103. Did that affect Jim? Whose fault is it? We've talked to scientists and doctors and you know what mongolism is? A kind of genetic accident. There's an extra chromosome there that can come from mother or father and no one has any idea why, except that illness or being tired doesn't seem to have anything to do with it. You establish that, a man and his wife, and go on from there. You're not alone. Jimmy isn't alone. There are three thousand retarded children just here in Madison County, and when we came back to live here, there wasn't any place for them. I'm on a committee. We've set up schools. We're making beginnings."

Easy in his den, sitting against his louvered bookcases, the son of the Middle Border let his mind range. "The Erskines are Scots. It would have been my

great-great-great-grandfather who settled in Virginia, and then moved on to Boone County, Indiana. That's sixty miles west. I remembered my Scottish background once in the Ebbets Field clubhouse when a lady wrote me a letter. She lived in Scotland and had seen my picture in a magazine. I must be Scottish and a relative of hers. I looked just like her Uncle Willie."

"Willie Erskine?"

"Or something."

"How do Presbyterian Scots become Indiana Baptists?"

"Easy. The Baptists take anybody."

He got up and brought in a dish of nuts and picked up his story. "When my father was very small—Dad, if he were living, would be eighty-six years old—near the end of the nineteenth century, the Erskines left Boone County and moved here. Anderson was a center of glass-blowing, and there was a natural-gas industry. My family had swampy farmland in Boone County they'd gotten for twenty-five cents an acre. Now it's been drained, and it's really valuable. But there are Scots and there are Scots. My family sold the land for twenty-six cents an acre, or maybe twenty-four.

"The auto industry came to Anderson long ago and General Motors tied in with an electrical company called Remy Brothers. And that was Delco Remy, spark plugs and electrical systems. There are seventeen local plants. There's no one who's been here any time who hasn't worked part of his life—a year, a month, a week—for Delco Remy.

"My Dad was real interested in baseball, and I guess I had the most promise of his three boys. At night at the side of the house, there'd be four or five congregated for catch. It got to be quite a thing for these older people to play burnout with me. You know. Step closer and closer, keep throwing harder and harder. I'd hang in and end up with a bruised hand. At nine, I was pitching from sixty feet.

"It was Dad who showed me a curve. First he taught what *he* had: the old barnyard roundhouse. You threw it sidearm and it broke flat. No break at all, except sideways. When I was eleven, Dad bought a book on pitching. We're in the living room. Dad has the pitching book in his left hand, held open with a thumb, and he has a baseball in his right hand. He's reading, and very engrossed. The arm is carried back. The wrist is cocked. At this position you come forward with a snap and a spin of the fingers. He goes through the motion, staring at the book. He releases the baseball. The ball goes through the doorway to the dining room and into a big china cupboard with a glass front. It breaks the glass. It breaks the dishes. We stand there. Dishes keep falling out. My mother comes in." Erskine's eyebrows rose in merriment. "Maybe a year afterward my father said that was the best break he ever got on a curve."

It was the sort of boyhood Booth Tarkington memorialized with a romantic

Saturday Evening Post glow, but Erskine is an existential man. "I guess there wasn't any money," he said. "I needed a mastoid operation and for a long time I'd keep bringing laundry to the doctor's house. My mother was paying the surgeon by taking in his wash.

"Around 1930 there was a lynching thirty miles north in a town called Marion. The day after it happened, Dad drove me up and showed me where it was. Two Negroes had been taken out of the jail and hung in the jailyard. The bark was skinned off the tree where they were hung. I can still see that naked branch. There had been a scramble. People had made off with things as souvenirs. But there was a piece of rope. I saw a lynching rope before I was ten." His soft voice carried controlled horror.

"One Negro boy grew up in my neighborhood, Johnny Wilson. We played grade-school basketball together; he made all-state in high school and went on to the Globetrotters. He's a high-school coach today. Jumpin' Johnny Wilson ate maybe as many meals at my home as he did in his own. With a background like that, the Robinson experience simply was no problem. It was really beautiful in a way.

"Somewhere Jack said he appreciated help from some white teammates in establishing himself, but to me it goes the opposite. It's 1948. The Dodgers want me from Fort Worth. I'm twenty-one and scared. I don't know anybody on the big club. I cut their names from the newspapers when I was a kid. The team is in Pittsburgh. I walk into the Forbes Field dressing room carrying my duffel bag. Just inside the door Jackie Robinson comes over, sticks out his hand, and says, 'After I hit against you in spring training, I knew you'd be up here. I didn't know when, but I knew it would happen. Welcome.' "

Erskine's face lit. "Man," he said, "I'd have been grateful if anyone had said 'Hello.' And to get this not from just *any* ballplayer but from Jackie Robinson. I pitched that day and won in relief.

"Whenever Jack came to the mound, he always gave me the feeling he knew I could do the job. He just wanted to reassure me. Whatever words he used, the effect was: *There's no question about it. We know you can do it. Here's the ball. Get it done.* Times when I wasn't sure I could do it myself, he seemed to be.

"Now here's what bothers me. He wins a game. We go to the next town. We're all on the train, a team. But leaving the station, he doesn't ride on the team bus. He has to go off by himself. He can't stay in the same hotel. But I didn't do anything about it. Why? Why didn't I say, 'Something's wrong here. I'm not going to let this happen. Wherever he's going, I'm going with him.'

"I never did. I sat like everybody else, and I thought, 'Good. He's getting a chance to play major-league ball. Isn't that great?' And that's as far as I was at that time.

"Now I hear people putting him down. Black people. To Stokely Carmichael and Rap Brown, he's a period piece. When I hear that, I feel sorry for *them*. Carmichael and Brown can never understand what Robinson did. How hard it was. What a great victory.

"But he can understand them. He was a young black man once, and mad and hurt. He knows *their* feeling, and their ignorance must hurt him more."

In the little Indiana den, it is the old story of the father and the son, a startling sunburst over autumn haze, expressed by a father whose own son is robbed of expression.

Anderson, Indiana, site of the annual Church of God Camp Meeting, thirty thousand strong gathered within and about Anderson College's Styrofoam-domed amphitheater, dubbed "The Turtle" by undergraduates, is a community that takes pride in its parks. "There are thirty-eight in all," said Carl Erskine, the morning go-getter. He had risen early, driven Jimmy to school at the Methodist church on Jackson Street, phoned the insurance brokerage in which he is a partner, and stopped off at the First National Bank of Anderson, of which he is vice-president.

"I thought I'd show you a little of the town," he said at 10:30. "Then we can pick up Jimmy after class and the three of us can go to the Y." We crossed Dwight D. Eisenhower Memorial Bridge, fording the White River, and leading downtown. The old masonry structures of Anderson are yielding prominence. "That new one with the glass front is the bank. Next to it is the San Francisco Restaurant. This isn't San Francisco, or New York, but it isn't all that sleepy either. Now we'll head out toward the college."

A large library, donated by Charles E. Wilson of General Motors, stands near the Turtle. "I do a little radio sports show from here once a week, and I coach baseball," Erskine said.

"How do you move around?"

"You mean the limp? It's more embarrassing than anything else. When I was through with ball, I began to develop pains in my left hip, the hip you land on when you throw right-handed. The pains got worse and worse. My arm hurt every day for ten years, but *this* was agony. Finally I went to a local man, and he said I'd damaged a bone in the socket and the thing to do was to ease up. No running. No handball. I love handball. All right, I'm thirty-nine years and through, because the kicker is that he tells me if I do ease up, I only put off the wheelchair a few years. Whatever, a wheelchair is just ahead.

"When I was pitching and I had the constant arm pain, I went to Johns Hopkins and a famous surgeon said something was gone for good and I should pitch sidearm. But the only way I could get velocity and a good break was to come straight over. Saying pitch sidearm was really telling me don't pitch. I kept pitching overhand and it kept hurting, but I got a dozen years in the big leagues.

"This wasn't pitching. This was walking. I flew to the Mayo Clinic, and one of the surgeons there had worked out a procedure for rotating the bone in the hip socket. He said I could keep the pain and look all right. Or he could operate and stop the pain and leave me a limp." Erskine smiled as an irony stirred. "All the time I had bad pain, nobody knew. Now that I have the limp people keep coming up and asking if my leg hurts. With that limp they figure it must hurt bad and"—a thin, swift smile—"it's painless."

As we reached the Jackson Street Methodist church, boys and girls straggled out a doorway. The class for retarded children was letting out. One boy's head shook from side to side, flapping straight straw hair. A girl of eleven squinted through thick glasses. Someone was snorting. Jimmy Erskine saw his father and broke from the flagstone walk.

"Hello, Jim. Want to go swimming? Want to swim?"

"Ihmin," Jimmy Erskine said. "Ihmin." He jumped up and down with excitement.

A few blocks off, at the YMCA, Erskine put on gym clothes and dressed Jimmy. Carl and I shot baskets for twenty minutes. Erskine took one-hand set shots, as Indiana schoolboys did in 1945. Jimmy found a ball and bounced it. He bounced it three times, four times, five times. When he bounced it longer, he shouted with joy. Carl played a round of handball, his limp suddenly more noticeable. Jimmy sat next to me watching. "Hosh-uh," he said, and climbed into my lap. "Ihmin, Hosh-uh. Ihmin."

There were only three of us in the Y pool, warm, green, and redolent of chlorine. Carl swam with a smooth crawl. Jimmy splashed about, making little cries. "Swim, Jimmy," Carl said. "Show how you can swim."

Jim fell onto his stomach, thrashed his arms and floated for three strokes. Then he jerked over to his back and showed a wide grin.

"Attaboy, Jim."

"Hosh-uh," Jimmy said.

"Watch him jump in," Carl said. "Jump, Jim. Show us how you can jump into the water."

The little boy hurried to a ladder. His foot slipped at the lowest rung. Carl put a strong hand to Jim's right buttock and pushed. Jim stood by the side of the pool, took two deep breaths and jumped into a kind of dive. He struck the water hard, chest first.

"Good goin', Jim," Carl said.

Another grin split Jimmy Erskine's face. Praise delights him. He waded toward the ladder and, climbing for a second time, held a support with his left hand. Then to show his father that he knew how to learn, he placed his right hand on his own buttock. What Jimmy Erskine had learned, from his father's boost, was that one leaves a pool with a hand placed on a buttock.

After leisurely dinner at the San Francisco Restaurant, Carl asked, back in his small, warm den, if I remembered the World Series of 1952. The sun of October flooded my memory and I saw again the blue crystal sky and the three-colored playing field and shrill, excited people thronging to Yankee Stadium, and my father's walk, lurching with expectancy.

"I had first-class stuff," Erskine said. "Not much pain. The curve is sharp. We go into the fifth inning ahead four runs. Do you happen to remember the date? It was October 5. That was my fifth wedding anniversary. My control slips. A walk. Some hits. Mize rips one. I'm behind, 5–4. And here comes Dressen.

"I'm thinking, 'Oh, no. I got good stuff.' I look at Dressen coming closer and I think. The numbers are against me. October fifth. My *fifth* wedding anniversary. The *fifth* inning. I've given the Yankees *five* runs. Five must be my unlucky number.

"Charlie says to give him the ball. You weren't allowed to talk when he came out. He was afraid you might argue him into leaving you in, and you had to wait on the mound for the next pitcher, so's you could wish him good luck. Now Charlie has the ball. I'm through. The fives have done me in. Suddenly Dressen says, 'Isn't this your anniversary? Are you gonna take Betty out and celebrate tonight?'

"I can't believe it. There's seventy thousand people watching, as many as in all Anderson now, and he's asking what I'm doing that night. I tell him yes, I was planning to take Betty someplace quiet.

" 'Well,' Dressen says, 'then see if you can get this game over before it gets dark.' He hands me back the ball. I get the next nineteen in a row. We win in eleven. I took Betty out to dinner and we celebrated the first Series game I ever won."

"What do you think," I said, "your life would have been if you hadn't been a pitcher?"

"I don't know. It's like asking what my life would be without Jimmy. Poorer. Different. Who knows how?"

. . .Wooden shutters stand open behind Erskine's chair. Memories have poured, but night claws at the window. "Old Campy," Erskine says. Nine hundred miles away, Roy Campanella is sitting in a motorized wheelchair, with shriveled arms and withered stumps for legs.

"The worst thing I can imagine is what happened to Campy," Erskine said. He gazed at the ceiling. "Real intimacy develops between catcher and pitcher.

You work 120 pitches together every few days, after a while you think like one man.

"All right. Campy is hurt over the winter of 1957–58. That's the same winter the team moves to California. We start out playing in a football field, the Coliseum, with left real close, a China wall. You know how Campy used to hit high flies to left; as soon as I see the China wall, I think, 'Son of a buck, if Campy was well, he'd break Ruth's record, popping flies over that dinky screen.'

"We start badly. We get to Philadelphia. I'm supposed to pitch. It rains. Campy was born in Philadelphia. Whatever, I start thinking about him with his broken spine and I don't tell anybody anything, but I go to the station in the rain and take a train to New York. I find a cab and go to University Hospital. They say I can't see him. I persist. At last, okay.

"Now I'm the first person not family to visit, the first man who's come from the team.

"I get to his room. I'm still thinking of the short fence and Ruth's record. I open the door and there's a shrunken body strapped in a frame. I stand a long time staring. He looks back. He doesn't see just me. He sees the team. He starts to cry. I cry myself. He cries for ten minutes, but he's the one who recovers first. 'Ersk,' Campy says, 'you're player representative. Get better major medical for the guys. This cost me. Eight thousand dollars for just the first two days.'

"I say, 'Sure, Campy.'

" 'Ersk,' he says, 'you know what I'm going to do tomorrow? I'm working with weights and I'm going to lift five pounds.'

"I go there thinking of him breaking Babe Ruth's record, he's thinking of lifting five pounds. But he's enthusiastic. He starts to sound like the old Campy. He wants to know when I'm going to pitch. He's got some kind of setup where they turn the frame and he can watch TV. I'm going the next day in Philly if it doesn't rain, and he gets real excited. They'll be televising that one back to New York. 'I'll be watching, Ersk,' he says. 'Make it a good one.'

"I get out of there. By this time I'm pitchin' with a broken arm, but this one I got to win. I got to win it—I don't care if it sounds like a corny movie—for Roy.

"The next day I go out with my broken wing. I pitch a no-hitter for five innings. I end up with a two-hitter. I win it for Campy. That was the last complete game I ever pitched in the major leagues.

"I could look back and say I should have pitched a few more years. My arm doesn't hurt now. The game looks easy on television. But in 1959 I walked into the office of Buzzy Bavasi and told him I'd had enough. I was thirty-two years old and my arm was 110. It ached every day. Some of the time I could barely reach the plate. Buzzy said he'd put me on the voluntary retired list, and he went out to get his secretary to draw up the papers.

"I thought, *'This is it.'* And all of a sudden in Buzzy's office in Los Angeles I'm seeing myself in the Kenmore Hotel room with Branch Rickey thirteen years before. I can see it clear as my hand. I can see my Navy bell-bottoms. I see Rickey puffing smoke. I see the way Dad looked. I hear the sound of Rickey's voice. That's the beginning. And here, I think, in Buzzy's office is the end.

"I say to myself, *'Wait!* I don't want this to end. Shouldn't I go for one more start?' And then I say, 'No. I don't want one more start. I've given myself every opportunity. At thirty-two, after 335 games, I'm worn-out.'

"I say to myself, 'Remember the way you feel. Burn this in your mind. *Strong!* Five years from now when you're back in Indiana and you start saying, the way all old ballplayers start saying, I could play another year, conjure up this feeling you have now.' "

"Have you had to do that, Carl?" I said.

"Only about five hundred times."

Erskine turned out the lights. He went upstairs and looked into Jimmy's room. The little boy breathed noisily in sleep.

No. And there never was one like John Kieran, either. He began as a sportswriter with the *New York Times* in 1916 and in 1927 inaugurated that paper's first signed column, "Sports of the Times," later home to Arthur Daley and Red Smith. In 1938 he became an electronic "personality" as a panelist on the popular *Information Please* radio program. By the mid-1940s his interests had turned from bats and balls to birds and flowers; not long thereafter his *Natural History of New York City* (1953) won for him the prestigious Burroughs Medal. This column appeared the day after Ruth hit his sixtieth.

JOHN KIERAN

Was There Ever a Guy Like Ruth?

New York, Oct. 2, 1927—Some four months ago or more there was printed in this column a versified query: "Was there ever a guy like Ruth?" From time to time Yankee rooters suggested the reprinting of the query, and now that Babe Ruth has answered it, a recital of the old question may be in order. Here it is:

A Query.

You may sing your song of the good old days till the phantom cows come
    home;
You may dig up glorious deeds of yore from many a dusty tome;
You may rise to tell of Rube Waddell and the way he buzzed them through,
And top it all with the great fastball that Rusie's rooters knew.
You may rant of Brouthers, Keefe, and Ward and half a dozen more;
You may quote by rote from the record book in a way that I deplore;
You may rave, I say, till the break of day, but the truth remains the truth:
From "One Old Cat" to the last "At Bat," was there ever a guy like Ruth?
He can start and go, he can catch and throw, he can field with the very
    best.

He's the Prince of Ash and the King of Crash, and that's not an idle jest.
He can hit that ball o'er the garden wall, high up and far away,
Beyond the aftermost picket lines where the fleet-foot fielders stray.
He's the Bogey Man of the pitching clan and he clubs 'em soon and late;
He has manned his guns and hit home runs from here to the Golden
    Gate;
With vim and verve he has walloped the curve from Texas to Duluth,
Which is no small task, and I beg to ask: Was there ever a guy like Ruth?

As a matter of fact, there was never even a good imitation of the Playboy of Baseball. What this big, good-natured, uproarious lad has done is little short of a miracle of sport. There is a common axiom: They never come back. But Babe Ruth came back twice. Just like him. He would.

It takes quite a bit of remembering to recall that the great home run hitter was once the best left-handed pitcher in baseball. When he was a member of the Boston Red Sox team, he set a record of pitching twenty-nine scoreless innings in World Series competition.

Then he started to slip and everybody said the usual thing: "Good-bye Forever!" (copyright by Tosti).

Babe gathered in all the "Good-byes" and said: "Hello, everybody! I'm a heavy-hitting outfielder."

And he was. He set a league record of twenty-nine home runs in 1919 and then he came to New York and took the cover off the siege gun.

That was Ruth's first comeback. A mild one. Others had done that, and the Babe yearned to be distinguished even from a chosen few. He wanted to be the One and Only. He nearly knocked the American League apart with fifty-four home runs in 1920, and in 1921 he set the record at fifty-nine circuit clouts for the season.

"It will stay there forever," prophesied the conservatives.

For five years the record was safe enough. In his bland and childlike way the Babe fell afoul of disciplinary and dietary laws, with the result that he was barred from the diamond for lengthy stretches on orders from Judge Landis, Miller Huggins, and the Ruth family physician.

He set the record of fifty-nine home runs when he was twenty-seven years old. In the following years he failed to come within hailing distance of his high-water mark, and once again everybody said: "Good-bye Forever!" (copyright by Tosti).

The Babe's answer was, "Say au revoir, but not good-bye!" And G. Herman Ruth was as right as rain. It was "au revoir" for five seasons, and in the sixth season the big boy came back with a bang!

Supposedly "over the hill," slipping down the steps of Time, stumbling toward the discard, six years past his peak, Babe Ruth stepped out and hung up a new home run record at which all the sport world may stand and wonder. What Dempsey couldn't do with his fists, Ruth has done with his bat. He came back.

Put it in the book in letters of gold. It will be a long time before anyone else betters that home-run mark, and a still longer time before any aging athlete makes such a gallant and glorious charge over the comeback trail.

And in Conclusion.

You may rise and sing till the rafters ring that sad and sorrowful strain:
"They strive and fail—it's the old, old tale; they never come back again."
Yes, it's in the dope, when they hit the slope they're off for the shadowed
    vale,
But the great, big Bam with the circuit slam came back on the uphill
    trail;
Came back with cheers from the drifted years where the best of them go
    down;
Came back once more with a record score to wear a brighter crown.
My voice may be loud above the crowd and my words just a bit uncouth,
But I'll stand and shout till the last man's out: There was never a guy
    like Ruth!

This is the opening chapter to *Shoeless Joe*, the powerfully imagined, lyrical, thrilling first novel by a professor at the University of Calgary who each summer tours the United States in his beat-up Datsun, visiting ballparks. What explains the hold of Joe Jackson on the imaginations of those who never saw him play? Why do we continue to hear of groups petitioning to get Jackson off baseball's blacklist and into the Hall of Fame? Why, despite considerable evidence that he accepted money to do less than his best in the 1919 World Series, is he still regarded as baseball's amalgam of Candide, Sacco, and Vanzetti? Perhaps because he was illiterate, perhaps because he hit .375 to lead all batters in that Series *anyway*, perhaps because he was a rube in the den of city slickers. Beats me. If I had to make a case for one of the eight Black Sox, I'd make it for Buck Weaver.

W. P. KINSELLA

Shoeless Joe Jackson Comes to Iowa

My father said he saw him years later playing in a tenth-rate commercial league in a textile town in Carolina, wearing shoes and an assumed name.

"He'd put on fifty pounds and the spring was gone from his step in the outfield, but he could still hit. Oh, how that man could hit. No one has ever been able to hit like Shoeless Joe."

Three years ago at dusk on a spring evening, when the sky was a robin's-egg blue and the wind as soft as a day-old chick, I was sitting on the verandah of my farm home in eastern Iowa when a voice very clearly said to me, "If you build it, he will come."

The voice was that of a ballpark announcer. As he spoke, I instantly envisioned the finished product I knew I was being asked to conceive. I could see the dark, squarish speakers, like ancient sailors' hats, attached to aluminum-painted light standards that glowed down into a baseball field, my present position being directly behind home plate.

In reality, all anyone else could see out there in front of me was a tattered lawn of mostly dandelions and quack grass that petered out at the edge of a cornfield perhaps fifty yards from the house.

Anyone else was my wife Annie, my daughter Karin, a corn-colored collie named Carmeletia Pope, and a cinnamon and white guinea pig named Junior who ate spaghetti and sang each time the fridge door opened. Karin and the dog were not quite two years old.

"If you build it, he will come," the announcer repeated in scratchy Middle American, as if his voice had been recorded on an old 78-r.p.m. record.

A three-hour lecture or a 500-page guide book could not have given me clearer directions: Dimensions of ballparks jumped over and around me like fleas, cost figures for light standards and floodlights whirled around my head like the moths that dusted against the porch light above me.

That was all the instruction I ever received: two announcements and a vision of a baseball field. I sat on the verandah until the satiny dark was complete. A few curdly clouds striped the moon, and it became so silent I could hear my eyes blink.

Our house is one of those massive old farm homes, square as a biscuit box with a sagging verandah on three sides. The floor of the verandah slopes so that marbles, baseballs, tennis balls, and ball bearings all accumulate in a corner like a herd of cattle clustered with their backs to a storm. On the north verandah is a wooden porch swing where Annie and I sit on humid August nights, sip lemonade from teary glasses, and dream.

When I finally went to bed, and after Annie inched into my arms in that way she has, like a cat that you suddenly find sound asleep in your lap, I told her about the voice and I told her that I knew what it wanted me to do.

"Oh love," she said, "if it makes you happy you should do it," and she found my lips with hers. I shivered involuntarily as her tongue touched mine.

Annie: She has never once called me crazy. Just before I started the first landscape work, as I stood looking out at the lawn and the cornfield, wondering how it could look so different in daylight, considering the notion of accepting it all as a dream and abandoning it, Annie appeared at my side and her arm circled my waist. She leaned against me and looked up, cocking her head like one of the red squirrels that scamper along the power lines from the highway to the house. "Do it, love," she said as I looked down at her, that slip of a girl with hair the color of cayenne pepper and at least a million freckles on her face and arms, that girl who lives in blue jeans and T-shirts and at twenty-four could still pass for sixteen.

I thought back to when I first knew her. I came to Iowa to study. She was the child of my landlady. I heard her one afternoon outside my window as she told her girl friends. "When I grow up I'm going to marry . . ." and she named me. The others were going to be nurses, teachers, pilots, or movie stars, but Annie chose me as her occupation. Eight years later we were married. I chose willingly, lovingly, to stay in Iowa. Eventually I rented this farm, then bought it, operating it one inch from bankruptcy. I don't seem meant to farm, but I

want to be close to this precious land, for Annie and me to be able to say,
"This is ours."

Now I stand ready to cut into the cornfield, to chisel away a piece of our
livelihood to use as dream currency, and Annie says, "Oh, love, if it makes
you happy you should do it." I carry her words in the back of my mind, stored
the way a maiden aunt might wrap a brooch, a remembrance of a long-lost
love. I understand how hard that was for her to say and how it got harder as
the project advanced. How she must have told her family not to ask me about
the baseball field I was building, because they stared at me dumb-eyed, a row
of silent, thickset peasants with red faces. Not an imagination among them
except to forecast the wrath of God that will fall on the heads of pagans such
as I.

"If you build it, he will come."

He, of course, was Shoeless Joe Jackson.

> Joseph Jefferson (Shoeless Joe) Jackson
> Born: Brandon Mills, South Carolina, July 16, 1887
> Died: Greenville, South Carolina, December 5, 1951

In April 1945, Ty Cobb picked Shoeless Joe as the best left fielder of all time.
A famous sportswriter once called Joe's glove "the place where triples go to
die." He never learned to read or write. He created legends with a bat and a
glove.

Was it really a voice I heard? Or was it perhaps something inside me making
a statement that I did not hear with my ears but with my heart? Why should
I want to follow this command? But as I ask, I already know the answer. I
count the loves in my life: Annie, Karin, Iowa, Baseball. The great god Baseball.

My birthstone is a diamond. When asked, I say my astrological sign is hit
and run, which draws a lot of blank stares here in Iowa where 50,000 people
go to see the University of Iowa Hawkeyes football team while 500 regulars,
including me, watch the baseball team perform.

My father, I've been told, talked baseball statistics to my mother's belly
while waiting for me to be born.

My father: born, Glen Ullin, North Dakota, April 14, 1896. Another diamond
birthstone. Never saw a professional baseball game until 1919 when he came
back from World War I where he had been gassed at Passchendaele. He settled
in Chicago, inhabited a room above a bar across from Comiskey Park, and
quickly learned to live and die with the White Sox. Died a little when, as
prohibitive favorites, they lost the 1919 World Series to Cincinnati, died a lot

the next summer when eight members of the team were accused of throwing that World Series.

Before I knew what baseball was, I knew of Connie Mack, John McGraw, Grover Cleveland Alexander, Ty Cobb, Babe Ruth, Tris Speaker, Tinker-to-Evers-to-Chance, and, of course, Shoeless Joe Jackson. My father loved under-dogs, cheered for the Brooklyn Dodgers and the hapless St. Louis Browns, loathed the Yankees—an inherited trait, I believe—and insisted that Shoeless Joe was innocent, a victim of big business and crooked gamblers.

That first night, immediately after the voice and the vision, I did nothing except sip my lemonade a little faster and rattle the ice cubes in my glass. The vision of the baseball park lingered—swimming, swaying, seeming to be made of red steam, though perhaps it was only the sunset. And there was a vision within the vision: one of Shoeless Joe Jackson playing left field. Shoeless Joe Jackson who last played major-league baseball in 1920 and was suspended for life, along with seven of his compatriots, by Commissioner Kenesaw Mountain Landis, for his part in throwing the 1919 World Series.

Instead of nursery rhymes, I was raised on the story of the Black Sox Scandal, and instead of Tom Thumb or Rumpelstiltskin, I grew up hearing of the eight disgraced ballplayers: Weaver, Cicotte, Risberg, Felsch, Gandil, Williams, McMullin, and, always, Shoeless Joe Jackson.

"He hit .375 against the Reds in the 1919 World Series and played errorless ball," my father would say, scratching his head in wonder. "Twelve hits in an eight-game series. And *they* suspended *him*," Father would cry. Shoeless Joe became a symbol of the tyranny of the powerful over the powerless. The name Kenesaw Mountain Landis became synonymous with the Devil.

Building a baseball field is more work than you might imagine. I laid out a whole field, but it was there in spirit only. It was really only left field that concerned me. Home plate was made from pieces of cracked two-by-four embedded in the earth. The pitcher's rubber rocked like a cradle when I stood on it. The bases were stray blocks of wood, unanchored. There was no backstop or grandstand, only one shaky bleacher beyond the left-field wall. There was a left-field wall, but only about 50 feet of it, 12 feet high, stained dark green and braced from the rear. And the left-field grass. My intuition told me that it was the grass that was important. It took me three seasons to hone that grass to its proper texture, to its proper color. I made trips to Minneapolis and one or two other cities where the stadiums still have natural-grass infields and outfields. I would arrive hours before a game and watch the grounds keepers groom the field like a prize animal, then stay after the game when in the cool of the night the same groundsmen appeared with hoses, hoes, and rakes, and patched the grasses like medics attending to wounded soldiers.

I pretended to be building a Little League ballfield and asked their secrets and sometimes was told. I took interest in the total operation; they wouldn't understand if I told them I was building only a left field.

Three seasons I've spent seeding, watering, fussing, praying, coddling that field like a sick child. Now it glows parrot-green, cool as mint, soft as moss, lying there like a cashmere blanket. I've begun watching it in the evenings, sitting on the rickety bleacher just beyond the fence. A bleacher I constructed for an audience of one.

My father played some baseball, Class B teams in Florida and California. I found his statistics in a dusty minor-league record book. In Florida he played for a team called the Angels and, according to his records, was a better-than-average catcher. He claimed to have visited all forty-eight states and every major-league ballpark before, at forty, he married and settled down in Montana, a two-day drive from the nearest major-league team. I tried to play, but ground balls bounced off my chest and fly balls dropped between my hands. I might have been a fair designated hitter, but the rule was too late in coming.

There is the story of the urchin who, tugging at Shoeless Joe Jackson's sleeve as he emerged from a Chicago courthouse, said, "Say it ain't so, Joe."

Jackson's reply reportedly was, "I'm afraid it is, kid."

When he comes, I won't put him on the spot by asking. The less said the better. It is likely that he did accept money from gamblers. But throw the Series? Never! Shoeless Joe Jackson led both teams in hitting in that 1919 Series. It was the circumstances. The circumstances. The players were paid peasant salaries while the owners became rich. The infamous Ten Day Clause, which voided contracts, could end any player's career without compensation, pension, or even a ticket home.

The second spring, on a toothachy May evening, a covering of black clouds lumbered off westward like ghosts of buffalo, and the sky became the cold color of a silver coin. The forecast was for frost.

The left-field grass was like green angora, soft as a baby's cheek. In my mind I could see it dull and crisp, bleached by frost, and my chest tightened.

But I used a trick a grounds keeper in Minneapolis had taught me, saying he learned it from grape farmers in California. I carried out a hose, and, making the spray so fine it was scarcely more than fog, I sprayed the soft, shaggy spring grass all that chilled night. My hands ached and my face became wet and cold, but, as I watched, the spray froze on the grass, enclosing each blade in a gossamer-crystal coating of ice. A covering that served like a coat of armor to dispel the real frost that was set like a weasel upon killing in the night. I seemed to stand taller than ever before as the sun rose, turning the ice to eye-dazzling droplets, each a prism, making the field an orgy of rainbows.

Annie and Karin were at breakfast when I came in, the bacon and coffee smells and their laughter pulling me like a magnet.

"Did it work, love?" Annie asked, and I knew she knew by the look on my face that it had. And Karin, clapping her hands and complaining of how cold my face was when she kissed me, loved every second of it.

"And how did he get a name like Shoeless Joe?" I would ask my father, knowing the story full well but wanting to hear it again. And no matter how many times I heard it, I would still picture a lithe ballplayer, his great bare feet white as baseballs sinking into the outfield grass as he sprinted for a line drive. Then, after the catch, his toes gripping the grass like claws, he would brace and throw to the infield.

"It wasn't the least bit romantic," my dad would say. "When he was still in the minor leagues he bought a new pair of spikes and they hurt his feet. About the sixth inning he took them off and played the outfield in just his socks. The other players kidded him, called him Shoeless Joe, and the name stuck for all time."

It was hard for me to imagine that a sore-footed young outfielder taking off his shoes one afternoon not long after the turn of the century could generate a legend.

I came to Iowa to study, one of the thousands of faceless students who pass through large universities, but I fell in love with the state. Fell in love with the land, the people, the sky, the cornfields, and Annie. Couldn't find work in my field, took what I could get. For years, I bathed each morning, frosted my cheeks with Aqua Velva, donned a three-piece suit and snap-brim hat, and, feeling like Superman emerging from a telephone booth, set forth to save the world from a lack of life insurance. I loathed the job so much that I did it quickly, urgently, almost violently. It was Annie who got me to rent the farm. It was Annie who got me to buy it. I operate it the way a child fits together his first puzzle—awkwardly, slowly, but, when a piece slips into the proper slot, with pride and relief and joy.

I built the field and waited, and waited, and waited.

"It will happen, honey," Annie would say when I stood shaking my head at my folly. People looked at me. I must have had a nickname in town. But I could feel the magic building like a gathering storm. It felt as if small animals were scurrying through my veins. I knew it was going to happen soon.

One night I watch Annie looking out the window. She is soft as a butterfly, Annie is, with an evil grin and a tongue that travels at the speed of light. Her jeans are painted to her body, and her pointy little nipples poke at the front of a black T-shirt that has the single word RAH! emblazoned in waspish yellow capitals. Her red hair is short and curly. She has the green eyes of a cat.

Annie understands, though it is me she understands and not always what is happening. She attends ballgames with me and squeezes my arm when there's a hit, but her heart isn't in it and she would just as soon be at home.

She loses interest if the score isn't close, or the weather's not warm, or the pace isn't fast enough. To me it is baseball, and that is all that matters. It is the game that's important—the tension, the strategy, the ballet of the fielders, the angle of the bat.

"There's someone on your lawn," Annie says to me, staring out into the orange-tinted dusk. "I can't see him clearly, but I can tell someone is there." She was quite right, at least about it being *my* lawn, although it is not in the strictest sense of the word a lawn; it is a *left field*.

I have been more restless than usual this night. I have sensed the magic drawing closer, hovering somewhere out in the night like a zeppelin, silky and silent, floating like the moon until the time is right.

Annie peeks through the drapes. "There *is* a man out there; I can see his silhouette. He's wearing a baseball uniform, an old-fashioned one."

"It's Shoeless Joe Jackson," I say. My heart sounds like someone flicking a balloon with his index finger.

"Oh," she says. Annie stays very calm in emergencies. She Band-Aids bleeding fingers and toes, and patches the plumbing with gum and good wishes. Staying calm makes her able to live with me. The French have the right words for Annie—she has a good heart.

"Is he the Jackson on TV? The one you yell 'Drop it, Jackson' at?"

Annie's sense of baseball history is not highly developed.

"No, that's Reggie. This is Shoeless Joe Jackson. He hasn't played major-league baseball since 1920."

"Well, Ray, aren't you going to go out and chase him off your lawn, or something?"

Yes. What am I going to do? I wish someone else understood. Perhaps my daughter will. She has an evil grin and bewitching eyes and loves to climb into my lap and watch television baseball with me. There is a magic about her.

"I think I'll go upstairs and read for a while," Annie says. "Why don't you invite Shoeless Jack in for coffee?" I feel the greatest tenderness toward her then, something akin to the rush of love I felt the first time I held my daughter in my arms. Annie senses that magic is about to happen. She knows she is not part of it. My impulse is to pull her to me as she walks by, the denim of her thighs making a tiny music. But I don't. She will be waiting for me.

As I step out onto the verandah, I can hear the steady drone of the crowd, like bees humming on a white afternoon, and the voices of the vendors, like crows cawing.

A ground mist, like wisps of gauze, snakes in slow circular motions just above the grass.

"The grass is soft as a child's breath," I say to the moonlight. On the porch wall I find the switch, and the single battery of floodlights I have erected behind the left-field fence sputters to life. "I've tended it like I would my own baby. It has been powdered and lotioned and loved. It is ready."

Moonlight butters the whole Iowa night. Clover and corn smells are thick as syrup. I experience a tingling like the tiniest of electric wires touching the back of my neck, sending warm sensations through me. Then, as the lights flare, a scar against the blue-black sky, I see Shoeless Joe Jackson standing out in left field. His feet spread wide, body bent forward from the waist, hands on hips, he waits. I hear the sharp crack of the bat, and Shoeless Joe drifts effortlessly a few steps to his left, raises his right hand to signal for the ball, camps under it for a second or two, catches it, at the same time transferring it to his throwing hand, and fires it to the infield.

I make my way to left field, walking in the darkness far outside the third-base line, behind where the third-base stands would be. I climb up on the wobbly bleacher behind the fence. I can look right down on Shoeless Joe. He fields a single on one hop and pegs the ball to third.

"How does it play?" I holler down.

"The ball bounces true," he replies.

"I know." I am smiling with pride, and my heart thumps mightily against my ribs. "I've hit a thousand line drives and as many grounders. It's true as a felt-top table."

"It is," says Shoeless Joe. "It is true."

I lean back and watch the game. From where I sit the scene is as complete as in any of the major-league baseball parks I have ever visited: the two teams, the stands, the fans, the lights, the vendors, the scoreboard. The only difference is that I sit alone in the left-field bleacher and the only player who seems to have substance is Shoeless Joe Jackson. When Joe's team is at bat, the left fielder below me is transparent, as if he were made of vapor. He performs mechanically but seems not to have facial features. We do not converse.

A great amphitheater of grandstand looms dark against the sky, the park is surrounded by decks of floodlights making it brighter than day, the crowd buzzes, the vendors hawk their wares, and I cannot keep the promise I made myself not to ask Shoeless Joe Jackson about his suspension and what it means to him.

While the pitcher warms up for the third inning we talk.

"It must have been . . . It must have been like . . ." but I can't find the words.

"Like having a part of me amputated, slick and smooth and painless." Joe looks up at me and his dark eyes seem about to burst with the pain of it. "A friend of mine used to tell about the war, how him and a buddy was running across a field when a piece of shrapnel took his friend's head off, and how the friend ran, headless, for several strides before he fell. I'm told that old men wake in the night and scratch itchy legs that have been dust for fifty years.

That was me. Years and years later, I'd wake in the night with the smell of the ballpark in my nose and the cool of the grass on my feet. The thrill of the grass . . .''

How I wish my father could be here with me. If he'd lasted just a few months longer, he could have watched our grainy black-and-white TV as Bill Mazeroski homered in the bottom of the ninth to beat the Yankees 10–9. We would have joined hands and danced around the kitchen like madmen. "The Yankees lose so seldom you have to celebrate every single time," he used to say. We were always going to go to a major-league baseball game, he and I. But the time was never right, the money always needed for something else. One of the last days of his life, late in the night while I sat with him because the pain wouldn't let him sleep, the radio picked up a static-y station broadcasting a White Sox game. We hunched over the radio and cheered them on, but they lost. Dad told the story of the Black Sox Scandal for the last time. Told of seeing two of those World Series games, told of the way Shoeless Joe Jackson hit, told the dimensions of Comiskey Park, and how, during the series, the mobsters in striped suits sat in the box seats with their colorful women, watching the game and perhaps making plans to go out later and kill a rival.

"You must go," Dad said. "I've been in all the major-league parks. I want you to do it, too. The summers belong to somebody else now, have for a long time." I nodded agreement.

"Hell, you know what I mean," he said, shaking his head. I did indeed.

"I loved the game," Shoeless Joe went on. "I'd have played for food money. I'd have played free and worked for food. It was the game, the parks, the smells, the sounds. Have you ever held a bat or a baseball to your face? The varnish, the leather. And it was the crowd, the excitement of them rising as one when the ball was hit deep. The sound was like a chorus. Then there was the chug-a-lug of the tin lizzies in the parking lots, and the hotels with their brass spittoons in the lobbies and brass beds in the rooms. It makes me tingle all over like a kid on his way to his first doubleheader, just to talk about it."

The year after Annie and I were married, the year we first rented this farm, I dug Annie's garden for her; dug it by hand, stepping a spade into the soft black soil, ruining my salesman's hands. After I finished, it rained, an Iowa spring rain as soft as spray from a warm hose. The clods of earth I had dug seemed to melt until the garden leveled out, looking like a patch of black ocean. It was near noon on a gentle Sunday when I walked out to that garden. The soil was soft and my shoes disappeared as I plodded until I was near the center. There I knelt, the soil cool on my knees. I looked up at the low gray sky; the rain had stopped and the only sound was the surrounding trees dripping fragrantly. Suddenly I thrust my hands wrist-deep into the snuffy-black earth. The air was pure. All around me the clean smell of earth and water. Keeping my hands buried I stirred the earth with my fingers and I knew I loved Iowa as much as a man could love a piece of earth.

When I came back to the house Annie stopped me at the door, made me wait on the verandah and then hosed me down as if I were a door with too many handprints on it, while I tried to explain my epiphany. It is very difficult to describe an experience of religious significance while you are being sprayed with a garden hose by a laughing, loving woman.

"What happened to the sun?" Shoeless Joe says to me, waving his hand toward the banks of floodlights that surround the park.

"Only stadium in the big leagues that doesn't have them is Wrigley Field," I say. "The owners found that more people could attend night games. They even play the World Series at night now."

Joe purses his lips, considering.

"It's harder to see the ball, especially at the plate."

"When there are breaks, they usually go against the ballplayers, right? But I notice you're three-for-three so far," I add, looking down at his uniform, the only identifying marks a large S with an O in the top crook, an X in the bottom, and an American flag with forty-eight stars on his left sleeve near the elbow.

Joe grins. "I'd play for the Devil's own team just for the touch of a baseball. Hell, I'd play in the dark if I had to."

I want to ask about that day in December 1951. If he'd lived another few years things might have been different. There was a move afoot to have his record cleared, but it died with him. I wanted to ask, but my instinct told me not to. There are things it is better not to know.

It is one of those nights when the sky is close enough to touch, so close that looking up is like seeing my own eyes reflected in the rain barrel. I sit in the bleacher just outside the left-field fence. I clutch in my hand a hot dog with mustard, onions, and green relish. The voice of the crowd roars in my ears. Chords of "The Star-Spangled Banner" and "Take Me Out to the Ballgame" float across the field. A Coke bottle is propped against my thigh, squat, greenish, the ice-cream-haired elf grinning conspiratorially from the cap.

Below me in left field, Shoeless Joe Jackson glides over the plush velvet grass, silent as a jungle cat. He prowls and paces, crouches ready to spring as, nearly 300 feet away, the ball is pitched. At the sound of the bat he wafts in whatever direction is required, as if he were on ball bearings.

Then the intrusive sound of a slamming screen door reaches me, and I blink and start. I recognize it as the sound of the door to my house, and, looking into the distance, I can see a shape that I know is my daughter, toddling down the back steps. Perhaps the lights or the crowd have awakened her and she has somehow eluded Annie. I judge the distance to the steps. I am just to the inside of the foul pole, which is exactly 330 feet from home plate. I tense. Karin will surely be drawn to the lights and the emerald dazzle of the infield. If she touches anything, I fear it will all disappear, perhaps forever. Then, as if she senses my discomfort, she stumbles away from the lights, walking in the ragged fringe of darkness well outside the third-base line. She trails a blanket behind her, one tiny fist rubbing a sleepy eye. She is barefoot and wears a white flannelette nightgown covered in an explosion of daisies.

She climbs up the bleacher, alternating a knee and a foot on each step, and crawls into my lap silently, like a kitten. I hold her close and wrap the blanket around her feet. The play goes on; her innocence has not disturbed the balance. "What is it?" she says shyly, her eyes indicating she means all that she sees.

"Just watch the left fielder," I say. "He'll tell you all you ever need to know about a baseball game. Watch his feet as the pitcher accepts the sign and gets ready to pitch. A good left fielder knows what pitch is coming, and he can tell from the angle of the bat where the ball is going to be hit, and if he's good, how hard."

I look down at Karin. She cocks one green eye at me, wrinkling her nose, then snuggles into my chest, the index finger of her right hand tracing tiny circles around her nose.

The crack of the bat is sharp as the yelp of a kicked cur. Shoeless Joe whirls, takes five loping strides directly toward us, turns again, reaches up, and the ball smacks into the glove. The final batter dawdles in the on-deck circle.

"Can I come back again?" Joe asks.

"I built this left field for you. It's yours anytime you want to use it. They play 162 games a season now."

"There are others," he says. "If you were to finish the infield, why, old Chick Gandil could play first base, and we'd have the Swede at shortstop and Buck Weaver at third." I can feel his excitement rising. "We could stick McMullin in at second, and Eddie Cicotte and Lefty Williams would like to pitch again. Do you think you could finish center field? It would mean a lot to Happy Felsch."

"Consider it done," I say, hardly thinking of the time, the money, the back-breaking labor it would entail. "Consider it done," I say again, then stop suddenly as an idea creeps into my brain like a runner inching off first base.

"I know a catcher," I say. "He never made the majors, but in his prime he was good. Really good. Played Class B ball in Florida and California . . ."

"We could give him a try," says Shoeless Joe. "You give us a place to play and we'll look at your catcher."

I swear the stars have moved in close enough to eavesdrop as I sit in this single rickety bleacher that I built with my unskilled hands, looking down at Shoeless Joe Jackson. A breath of clover travels on the summer wind. Behind me, just yards away, brook water plashes softly in the darkness, a frog shrills, fireflies dazzle the night like red pepper. A petal falls.

"God, what an outfield," he says. "What a left field." He looks up at me and I look down at him. "This must be heaven," he says.

"No. It's Iowa," I reply automatically. But then I feel the night rubbing softly against my face like cherry blossoms; look at the sleeping girl-child in my arms, her small hand curled around one of my fingers; think of the fierce warmth of the woman waiting for me in the house; inhale the fresh-cut grass smell that seems locked in the air like permanent incense; and listen to the drone of the crowd, as below me Shoeless Joe Jackson tenses, watching the angle of the distant bat for a clue as to where the ball will be hit.

"I think you're right, Joe," I say, but softly enough not to disturb his concentration.

Is Ring Lardner a big-leaguer or a busher? This question dominated a 1985 literary convocation observing the centennial of his birth, as it has preoccupied Lardner's critics for generations. In 1925 Virginia Woolf (no baseball fan) wrote of *You Know Me Al*: "... he writes the best prose that has come our way.... With extraordinary ease and aptitude, with the quickest strokes, the surest touch, the sharpest insight, he lets Jack Keefe the baseball player cut out his own outline, fill in his own depths, until the figure of the foolish, boastful, innocent athlete lives before us." F. Scott Fitzgerald, on the other hand, deplored Lardner's subject matter: "However deeply Ring might cut into it, his cake had exactly the diameter of Frank Chance's diamond. Here was his artistic problem...." Take your choice: a deep cut into a cupcake or a thumbprint in the icing of a seven-layer job—the diamond of Frank Chance or a diamond as big as the Ritz. Here, busher Jack Keefe, having made the Chicago White Sox ca. 1914, fills in friend Al. Enjoy.

RING LARDNER

A Busher's Letters Home

St. Joe, Missouri, April 7.

FRIEND AL: It rained yesterday so I worked to-day instead and St. Joe done well to get three hits. They couldn't of scored if we had played all week. I give a couple of passes but I catched a guy flatfooted off of first base and I come up with a couple of bunts and throwed guys out. When the game was over Callahan says That's the way I like to see you work. You looked better to-day than you looked on the whole trip. Just once you wound up with a man on but otherwise you was all O.K. So I guess my job is cinched Al and I won't have to go to New York or St. Louis. I would rather be in Chi anyway because it is near home. I wouldn't care though if they traded me to Detroit. I hear from Violet right along and she says she can't hardly wait till I come to Detroit. She says she is strong for the Tigers but she will pull for me when I work against them. She is nuts over me and I guess she has saw lots of guys to.

I sent her a stickpin from Oklahoma City but I can't spend no more dough on her till after our first payday the fifteenth of the month. I had thirty bucks on me when I left home and I only got about ten left including the five spot I won in the poker game. I have to tip the waiters about thirty cents a day and

I seen about twenty picture shows on the coast beside getting my cloths pressed a couple of times.

We leave here to-morrow night and arrive in Chi the next morning. The second club joins us there and then that night we go to Cleveland to open up. I asked one of the reporters if he knowed who was going to pitch the opening game and he says it would be Scott or Walsh but I guess he don't know much about it.

These reporters travel all round the country with the team all season and send in telegrams about the game every night. I ain't seen no Chi papers so I don't know what they been saying about me. But I should worry eh Al? Some of them are pretty nice fellows and some of them got the swell head. They hang round with the old fellows and play poker most of the time.

Will write you from Cleveland. You will see in the paper if I pitch the opening game.

Your old pal, JACK

Cleveland, Ohio, April 10.

OLD FRIEND AL: Well Al we are all set to open the season this afternoon. I have just ate breakfast and I am sitting in the lobby of the hotel. I eat at a little lunch counter about a block from here and I saved seventy cents on breakfast. You see Al they give us a dollar a meal and if we don't want to spend that much all right. Our rooms at the hotel are paid for.

The Cleveland papers says Walsh or Scott will work for us this afternoon. I asked Callahan if there was any chance of me getting into the first game and he says I hope not. I don't know what he meant but he may surprise these reporters and let me pitch. I will beat them Al. Lajoie and Jackson is supposed to be great batters but the bigger they are the harder they fall.

The second team joined us yesterday in Chi and we practiced a little. Poor Allen was left in Chi last night with four others of the recruit pitchers. Looks pretty good for me eh Al? I only seen Gleason for a few minutes on the train last night. He says, Well you ain't took off much weight. You're hog fat. I says Oh I ain't fat. I didn't need to take off no weight. He says One good thing about it the club don't have to engage no birth for you because you spend all your time in the dining car. We kidded along like that a while and then the trainer rubbed my arm and I went to bed. Well Al I just got time to have my suit pressed before noon.

Yours truly, JACK

Cleveland, Ohio, April 11.

FRIEND AL: Well Al I suppose you know by this time that I did not pitch and that we got licked. Scott was in there and he didn't have nothing. When they had us beat four to one in the eight inning Callahan told me to go out and warm up and he put a batter in for Scott in our ninth. But Cleveland didn't have to play their ninth so I got no chance to work. But looks like he means to start me in one of the games here. We got three more to play. Maybe I will pitch this afternoon. I got a postcard from Violet. She says Beat them Naps. I will give them a battle Al if I get a chance.

Glad to hear you boys have fixed it up to come to Chi during the Detroit serious. I will ask Callahan when he is going to pitch me and let you know. Thanks Al for the papers.

Your friend, JACK

St. Louis, Missouri, April 15.

FRIEND AL: Well Al I guess I showed them. I only worked one inning but I guess them Browns is glad I wasn't in there no longer than that. They had us beat seven to one in the sixth and Callahan pulls Benz out. I honestly felt sorry for him but he didn't have nothing, not a thing. They was hitting him so hard I thought they would score a hundred runs. A right-hander name Bumgardner was pitching for them and he didn't look to have nothing either but we ain't got much of a batting team Al. I could hit better than some of them regulars. Anyway Callahan called Benz to the bench and sent for me. I was down in the corner warming up with Kuhn. I wasn't warmed up good but you know I got the nerve Al and I run right out there like I meant business. There was a man on second and nobody out when I come in. I didn't know who was up there but I found out afterward it was Shotten. He's the center fielder. I was cold and I walked him. Then I got warmed up good and I made Johnston look like a boob. I give him three fastballs and he let two of them go by and missed the other one. I would of handed him a spitter but Schalk kept signing for fast ones and he knows more about them batters than me. Anyway I whiffed Johnston. Then up come Williams and I tried to make him hit at a couple of bad ones. I was in the hole with two balls and nothing and come right across the heart with my fast one. I wish you could of saw the hop on it. Williams hit it right straight up and Lord was camped under it. Then up come Pratt the best hitter on their club. You know what I done to him don't you Al? I give him one spitter and another he didn't strike at that was a ball. Then I come back with two fast ones and Mister Pratt was a dead baby. And you notice they didn't steal no bases.

In our half of the seventh inning Weaver and Schalk got on and I was going up there with a stick when Callahan calls me back and sends Easterly up. I don't know what kind of managing you call that. I hit good on the training trip and he must of knew they had no chance to score off me in the innings they had left while they were liable to murder his other pitchers. I come back to the bench pretty hot and I says You're making a mistake. He says If Comiskey had wanted you to manage this team he would of hired you.

Then Easterly pops out and I says Now I guess you're sorry you didn't let me hit. That sent him right up in the air and he bawled me awful. Honest Al I would of cracked him right in the jaw if we hadn't been right out where everybody could of saw us. Well he sent Cicotte in to finish and they didn't score no more and we didn't either.

I road down in the car with Gleason. He says Boy you shouldn't ought to talk like that to Cal. Some day he will lose his temper and bust you one. I says He won't never bust me. I says He didn't have no right to talk like that to me. Gleason says I suppose you think he's going to laugh and smile when we lost four out of the first five games. He says Wait till to-night and then go up to him and let him know you are sorry you sassed him. I says I didn't sass him and I ain't sorry.

So after supper I seen Callahan sitting in the lobby and I went over and sit down by him. I says When are you going to let me work? He says I wouldn't never let you work only my pitchers are all shot to pieces. Then I told him about you boys coming up from Bedford to watch me during the Detroit serious and he says Well I will start you in the second game against Detroit. He says But I wouldn't if I had any pitchers. He says A girl could get out there and pitch better than some of them have been doing.

So you see Al I am going to pitch on the nineteenth. I hope you guys can be up there and I will show you something. I know I can beat them Tigers and I will have to do it even if they are Violet's team.

I notice that New York and Boston got trimmed to-day so I suppose they wish Comiskey would ask for waivers on me. No chance Al.

Your old pal, JACK

P. S.—We play eleven games in Chi and then go to Detroit. So I will see the little girl on the twenty-ninth.

Oh you Violet.

Chicago, Illinois, April 19.

DEAR OLD PAL: Well Al it's just as well you couldn't come. They beat me and I am writing you this so you will know the truth about the game and not get a bum steer from what you read in the papers.

I had a sore arm when I was warming up and Callahan should never ought to of sent me in there. And Schalk kept signing for my fastball, and I kept giving it to him because I thought he ought to know something about the batters. Weaver and Lord and all of them kept kicking them round the infield and Collins and Bodie couldn't catch nothing.

Callahan ought never to of left me in there when he seen how sore my arm was. Why, I couldn't of threw hard enough to break a pain of glass my arm was so sore.

They sure did run wild on the bases. Cobb stole four and Bush and Crawford and Veach about two apiece. Schalk didn't even make a peg half the time. I guess he was trying to throw me down.

The score was sixteen to two when Callahan finally took me out in the eighth and I don't know how many more they got. I kept telling him to take me out when I seen how bad I was but he wouldn't do it. They started bunting in the fifth and Lord and Chase just stood there and didn't give me no help at all.

I was all O.K. till I had the first two men out in the first inning. Then Crawford come up. I wanted to give him a spitter but Schalk signs me for the fast one and I give it to him. The ball didn't hop much and Crawford happened to catch it just right. At that Collins ought to of catched the ball. Crawford made three bases and up come Cobb. It was the first time I ever seen him. He hollered at me right off the reel. He says You better walk me you busher. I says I will walk you back to the bench. Schalk signs for a spitter and I gives it to him and Cobb misses it.

Then instead of signing for another one Schalk asks for a fast one and I shook my head no but he signed for it again and yells Put something on it. So I throwed a fast one and Cobb hits it right over second base. I don't know what Weaver was doing but he never made a move for the ball. Crawford scored and Cobb was on first base. First thing I knowed he had stole second while I held the ball. Callahan yells Wake up out there and I says Why don't your catcher tell me when they are going to steal. Schalk says Get in there and pitch and shut your mouth. Then I got mad and walked Veach and Moriarty but before I walked Moriarty Cobb and Veach pulled a double steal on Schalk. Gainor lifts a fly and Lord drops it and two more come in. Then Stanage walks and I whiffs their pitcher.

I come in to the bench and Callahan says Are your friends from Bedford up here? I was pretty sore and I says Why don't you get a catcher? He says We don't need no catcher when you're pitching because you can't get nothing past their bats. Then he says You better leave your uniform in here when you go out next inning or Cobb will steal it off your back. I says My arm is sore. He says Use your other one and you'll do just as good.

Gleason says Who do you want to warm up? Callahan says Nobody. He says

Cobb is going to lead the league in batting and basestealing anyway so we might as well give him a good start. I was mad enough to punch his jaw but the boys winked at me not to do nothing.

Well I got some support in the next inning and nobody got on. Between innings I says Well I guess I look better now don't I? Callahan says Yes but you wouldn't look so good if Collins hadn't jumped up on the fence and catched that one off Crawford. That's all the encouragement I got Al.

Cobb come up again to start the third and when Schalk signs for a fast one I shakes my head. Then Schalk says All right pitch anything you want to. I pitched a spitter and Cobb bunts it right at me. I would of threw him out a block but I stubbed my toe in a rough place and fell down. This is the roughest ground I ever seen Al. Veach bunts and for a wonder Lord throws him out. Cobb goes to second and honest Al I forgot all about him being there and first thing I knowed he had stole third. Then Moriarty hits a fly ball to Bodie and Cobb scores though Bodie ought to of threw him out twenty feet.

They batted all round in the fourth inning and scored four or five more. Crawford got the luckiest three-base hit I ever see. He popped one way up in the air and the wind blowed it against the fence. The wind is something fierce here Al. At that Collins ought to of got under it.

I was looking at the bench all the time expecting Callahan to call me in but he kept hollering Go on and pitch. Your friends wants to see you pitch.

Well Al I don't know how they got the rest of their runs but they had more luck than any team I ever seen. And all the time Jennings was on the coaching line yelling like a Indian. Some day Al I'm going to punch his jaw.

After Veach had hit one in the eight Callahan calls me to the bench and says You're through for the day. I says It's about time you found out my arm was sore. He says I ain't worrying about your arm but I'm afraid some of our outfielders will run their legs off and some of them poor infielders will get killed. He says The reporters just sent me a message saying they had run out of paper. Then he says I wish some of the other clubs had pitchers like you so we could hit once in a while. He says Go in the clubhouse and get your arm rubbed off. That's the only way I can get Jennings sore he says.

Well Al that's about all there was to it. It will take two or three stamps to send this but I want you to know the truth about it. The way my arm was I ought never to of went in there.

                                                    Yours truly, JACK

The author of *Blue Highways*, from which this snip of a story is taken, traveled the small towns and back roads of America (the blue lines on the road map), recording what he saw and heard. This uncharacteristically cogent barroom banter took place in Bagley, North Dakota. By the way, the Cease Funeral Home ranks right up there with New York City's Terminal Delicatessen (by the bus station), but still several notches below my local Sans Souci Funeral Parlor.

WILLIAM LEAST HEAT MOON

Beans

With a bag of blueberry tarts, I went up Main to a tin-sided, false-front tavern called Michel's, just down the street from the Cease Funeral Home. The interior was log siding and yellowed knotty pine. In the backroom the Junior Chamber of Commerce talked about potatoes, pulpwood, dairy products, and somebody's broken fishing rod. I sat at the bar. Behind me a pronghorn antelope head hung on the wall, and beside it a televised baseball game cast a cool light like a phosphorescent fungus. "Hear that?" a dwindled man asked. He was from the time when boys drew "Kilroy-Was-Here" faces on alley fences. "Did you hear the announcer?"

"I wasn't listening."

"He said 'velocity'."

"Velocity?"

"He's talking about a fastball. A minute ago he said a runner had 'good acceleration.' This is a baseball game, not a NASA shot. And another thing: I haven't heard anybody mention a 'Texas leaguer' in years."

"It's a 'bloop double' now, I think."

"And the 'banjo hitter'—where's he? And what happened to the 'slow ball'?"

"It's a 'change-up.' "

The man got me interested in the game. We watched and drank Grain Belt. He had taught high-school civics in Minneapolis for thirty-two years, but his dream had been to become a sports announcer. "They put a radar gun on the kid's fastball a few minutes ago," he said. "Ninety-three point four miles per hour. That's how they tell you speed now. They don't try to show it to you: 'smoke,' 'hummer,' 'the high hard one.' I miss the old clichés. They had life. Who wants to hit a fastball with a decimal point when he can tie into somebody's 'heat'? And that's another thing: nobody 'tattoos' or 'blisters' the ball anymore. These TV boys are ruining a good game because they think if you can see it they're free to sit back and psychoanalyze the team. Ask and I'll tell you what I think of it."

"What do you think of it?"

"Beans. And that's another thing too."

"Beans?"

"Names. Used to be players named Butterbean and Big Potato, Little Potato. Big Poison, Little Poison, Dizzy and Daffy. Icehouse, Shoeless Joe, Suitcase, The Lip. Now we've got the likes of Rickie and Richie and Reggie. With names like that, I think I'm watching a third-grade scrub team."

The announcer said the pitcher had "good location."

"Great God in hemock! He means 'nibble the corners.' But which of these throwing clowns nibbles corners? They're obsessed with speed. Satchel Paige—there's a name for you—old Satch could fire the pill a hundred and five miles an hour. He didn't throw it that fast very often because he couldn't make the ball cut up at that speed. And, sure as spitting, his pitching arm lasted just about his whole life."

The man took a long smacking pull on his Grain Belt. "Damn shame," he said. "There's a word for what television's turned this game into."

"What's the word?"

"Beans," he said. "Nothing but beans and hot air."

If Ring Lardner hated what the lively ball did to his game (see the final piece in this collection), imagine his horror at the billiard-baseball played today, especially in Seattle's Kingdome and the Minneapolis Metrodome. The first artificial turf appeared, as everyone knows, in Houston's Astrodome. What few recall, however, is that the Astros of 1965—their first season in the new domed stadium—played on God's own sod, nourished by God's own sunlight shining through the transparent dome. However, experience with day games revealed that outfielders could not track fly balls in the glare. Painting the dome solved that problem but killed the grass, thus "paving" the way for Monsanto's Astroturf in 1966. Eugene J. McCarthy—poet, politician, and baseball player—wrote this article for *The New Republic* of November 22, 1982.

EUGENE J. McCARTHY

Baseball? Boingball.

At the opening of the 1978 baseball season, I wrote optimistically . . . of the future of the game, . . . noting that despite the introduction of the livelier ball, despite the use of aluminum and plastic bats below the level of the major leagues, and despite Charlie Finley and Bowie Kuhn, the game seemed to be thriving. But after watching several games in the new Minneapolis Metrodome, and watching as much of the recent World Series between the Cardinals of St. Louis and the Brewers of Milwaukee as I could stand, I have begun to wonder whether the integrity of the game, and the validity of its statistics, can survive in an era of domed stadiums and the artificial turf they contain.

Actually, the domes would be all right if one could play in them on something other than artificial turf. It is the turf that changes the game. Even to call it artificial turf is to offend against language. In their natural state baseball diamonds were never said to be turfed. As one moved up the scale of baseball, one went from the sandlot, to the diamond with dirt infield and grass outfield, and finally to the diamond with grass infield, grass outfield, and dirt basepaths. There was no such thing as "turf," whether natural or counterfeit. In any case, the covering called "artificial turf" is not turf of any kind. It is not even a carpet or rug, but some kind of plastic conglomerate, possibly suitable for tennis, which, it seems, can be played on almost any surface: clay, grass, plastic, wood, rubber, cement, or ground glass.

I began to have doubts about the future of the game one night as I listened to a broadcast from the Minneapolis Metrodome. The Twins were not doing very well, not just that night but in season play. I had read that the owner and manager of the team had explained the poor play by saying that the team had been built up in anticipation of playing on grass in the old outdoor park, and that the team was not tailored to the conditions under which the dome game was being played—mostly the size and shape of the enclosure and the quality of the playing surface (plus a few minor adjustments such as learning how to catch balls that had hit loudspeakers or support cables). Yet as I listened to the broadcast, I was puzzled by the announcers' comments. They would say things like, "This is a pitchers' duel, a tight one. It's the bottom of the third inning, it's tied at five and five, each team has ten hits, but neither one has hit a home run." Or they would say, "It's a long fly. The outfielder is running in on it." Or, "The shortstop has just made a great leaping catch of a ground ball on the third hop."

When I saw my first game in the new facility, my confusion cleared up but my doubts deepened. Outfielders did indeed run in on long flies, hoping to catch the ball on the second or third rebound bounce rather than have it go over their heads on the first bounce off the turf after rebounding from the wall. Yet outfielders seldom charged a short fly, or even a "Texas Leaguer," but most often turned tail and raced for the wall, looking back over their shoulders for the first hop as the ball returned from the stratosphere.

The infield game was something else. Nothing normal about it. There were easy two-hop plays, and occasionally a ball might bounce three times in the infield, on a deep play, before it was handled. There were few good plays by traditional standards. Mostly it was brilliant grabs, errors, base hits through the infield, and base hits *within* the infield, especially from balls that hit resilient turf somewhere between home plate and the pitcher's mound and then sprang twenty or thirty feet into the air—the runner making it to first base while the infielder waited patiently for the ball to descend.

And then came this year's World Series. The games played in Milwaukee were played on grass. But in St. Louis, in an open stadium, in a city that has good annual rainfall, where grass grows well, and where the team owner, Gus Busch, could afford a good grounds keeper, the games were played on "the carpet." There were two wholly different kinds of game played, depending on the covering. The victor was not the Cardinals, but the turf. Ground balls that under normal circumstances could have been caught slithered through the infield for hits. Hits that should have been singles at most rolled to the wall for doubles and triples. High bouncers, hit by St. Louis batters schooled, by report, to hit down on the ball, sailed over the pitcher's head. The turf was so bad that it actually played better in the rain.

So much for the game. Bad enough. But more serious, in the long run, is the effect on the statistics.

It is obvious that if the statistics that have been kept for over a hundred years, giving stability and continuity to the game of baseball, are to have any objective historical relevance, new scoring principles and methods will have to be introduced to reflect the differences between games played on artificial turf and those played on grass. Hits, errors, earned runs, extra base hits— everything is of a different order. Certainly all of the basic statistics should be separated—batting, fielding, pitching. Those made on grass could be incorporated into the established record books, those made on turf kept separate. Balls that hit the ground within an arc, drawn and marked on the field at, say, thirty feet from home plate, and that are caught before they touch the ground to bounce a second time, could be treated as though they were simple fly balls. Two short outfielders might be introduced, allowed to move within a limited range, as some soccer players are restricted, and permitted to catch or stop only ground balls. I anticipate that unless rules are changed or the turf banned or improved, we may enter an era in which the positions of shortstop and second base, formerly occupied by quick, small men, such as Rizzuto, Lazzeri, Crosetti, Fox, and others of modest stature, will be filled by men who are seven feet tall, with long arms and great leaping abilities. Reach, not movement, will become the important attribute. Announcers, instead of saying of an infielder that he has great lateral movement, will say he has great vertical movement. And instead of praising outfielders who, like Willie Mays, could "go back and get them," we will revere outfielders for their ability to play the angles, the rebounds, the caroms.

The alternative is to turn off the television broadcasts of baseball games, as I did during the Series, and to amuse oneself playing Atari baseball, which Billy Martin likes, or the rival Intellivision, which George Plimpton says is better.

When the Philadelphia Phillies squared off against the Kansas City Royals in the World Series of 1980, they were the only one of the original sixteen major-league franchises never to have won a championship. James Michener, who had seen his hapless Phils come up empty for six decades, learned of their victory in midair, en route to Bangkok; thereupon he dashed off this nimble paean to the Phillies, claimants at last to their own World Sillies.

JAMES MICHENER

Lines Composed in Exaltation over the North Atlantic

When they launched their quest in the play-offs, the Phillies, always a team of infinite class, asked the city's revered musician, Eugene Ormandy, to throw out the ball for the first game, and a local scribbler to start the second.

Ormandy won his game, I lost mine, proving that the piccolo is mightier than the Smith-Corona. The flawless artistry displayed by the Phils in the series was due in large part to this graceful beginning.

While flying to Bangkok during the World Series, I was prompted to scribble a verse on hearing the pilot announce, "The Phillies won."

> Crash the cymbals, blare the trumpets,
> Wreathe their noble brows with laurel.
> Heap the festive board with crumpets
> And with decorations floral.
> They deserve the fairest lilies—
> Who? The Phillies.

Through the long dark years they stumbled
Scarred with deep humiliations
But our cheering never crumbled
And we kept our expectations.

Yes, we loved them for their sillies—
Who? The Phillies.

Triple plays that did not triple,
Strikeouts with the bases loaded.
Pitchers serving up the cripple,
All our hopes again exploded.
Are they not a bunch of dillies?
Who? The Phillies.

Far behind in early innings,
Doomed to tragedy eternal,
They turn losses into winnings
Through some holy fire internal.
They give enemies the willies—
Who? The Phillies.

Bang the drum and toot the oboes,
Dance until the earth has shaken.
Cheer, for our beloved hoboes
Have at last brought home the bacon.

Garland them with timeless lilies!
Although they are a bunch of dillies
Who give honest men the willies.
We still love them for their sillies—
Hail, The Phillies.

No, not exactly, though the legend here is uncommonly close to the mark. Jim Murray of the *Los Angeles Times*, by acclamation the dean of baseball columnists, wrote this in 1972. Has Babe Herman been ill-used by the press? Perhaps . . . but no more so than Yogi Berra. Let me tell you this one: the Dodgers went into the ninth inning at Forbes Field with a 2–1 lead over Pittsburgh. The Pirates put two men on base with two out, but then, as Pie Traynor looped a routine liner to center, their rally seemed to have fallen short. Herman charged the ball, fell on his face, and saw the ball whiz by as the winning runs crossed the plate. The crestfallen Dodgers trudged off the field in defeat. Manager Wilbert Robinson, ever the kindhearted soul, put his arm around Herman. "What happened, Babe?" he inquired tenderly. *"When?"* was Herman's reply. And if that story's not strictly true, well, it ought to be.

JIM MURRAY

Did Babe Herman Triple into a Triple Play?

History, Henry Ford said, is bunk. Or did he?

Did George Washington really throw a dollar across the Rappahannock? Was that midnight rider really Paul Revere? Or two guys from Springfield? Did Shakespeare really write those plays? Think Patrick Henry really said, "Give me liberty or give me death"? Or did he say, "Lemme outta here, you guys are nuts!"

It's the same in sports. Did Babe Ruth really call his shot in the World Series? Did Willie Keeler really say, "Hit 'em where they ain't"?

Men usually become legends posthumously. Nothing promotes the growth of a legend like the demise of anyone who might contradict it.

Which is why I sought out Babe Herman at the Dodgers' Old-timers' luncheon one day last season. Mention the name "Babe Herman" in any gathering of baseball fans and the smiles immediately come to the corners of the mouth. The old joke is revived, of the guy hollering down from the grandstand to the street, "The Dodgers have three men on base!" And the question comes up from the pedestrian below, "Which base?"

Babe Herman's life was a series of fly balls bouncing off his cap, sliding into occupied bases, passing base runners with his head down, starting to trot in from the outfield with only the *second* out with the bases loaded, right? The Flatbush Follies, right? The "Daffiness Boys." The Daffy of the Daffy Dodgers. The guy who came into the league a big-eared rookie in 1926 and left it still a big-eared rookie nineteen years later.

One of the most famous paragraphs in baseball literature was the one the late John Lardner wrote: "Floyd Caves Herman never tripled into a triple play, but he once doubled into a double play, which is the next best thing." Or, "Floyd Caves Herman did not always catch fly balls on the top of his head, but he could do it in a pinch."

Unfortunately, Babe Herman slides into this occupied base, too. "Now, I'll tell you the truth of that," he said doggedly the other day. "In the first place, they said I 'tripled into a triple play,' but there was one out so how could I do that? Also, they forget I hit in the winning run in that game. Now, here is what happened: DeBerry [Brooklyn catcher] was on third, Dazzy Vance [Brooklyn pitcher] was on second, and Chick Fewster [second baseman] was on first. We were playing the Braves and George Mogridge hung a curve, and I hit it four feet from the top of the wall in right. DeBerry scores to put us ahead 3–2, which we stayed in the top of the ninth. Vance runs halfway to third, then he runs around third, then he starts to run back. Fewster is on third, so he starts back to second.

"Now, I got the throw beat, and I slide into second. Safe. Right? So, now, somebody hollers to Jimmy Cooney, the shortstop, and he throws home. Al Spohrer chases Vance back to third. Now, I go to third on the rundown and, naturally, I slide into third. Safe. Right. Now, I was called out for passing Fewster, but Vance is on third and it's his bag by the rules. Spohrer begins tagging everybody—but I am already out. It's like sentencing a dead man. Now, there are only two out, but Fewster wanders out to right field to get his glove and Doc Gautreau, the Braves' second baseman, chases him and tags him out.

"You see, there never were three men on third exactly. See how everything gets mixed up?

"Now, the fielding was another thing they got all mixed up. Here I was playing first base all those years and, one day, Bizzy Bissonette gets sick and can't play right field. So I say, 'Hell, I'll play it.' You see, it was this awful sun field out there, the toughest sun field in the league, and, the sunset, which came through the opening of the roof there, made it worse. So, we didn't have flip glasses in those days and, when it got dark enough, the sky was murder, and when the ball was hit up, there was this black spot you had to pick out of the sun. What? Oh, the black spot was the ball and you can see sometimes how you could camp under the wrong spot."

Like, the Babe sometimes found himself waiting for a mosquito to come down and while waiting he would feel this Thunk! on the back of his head.

As you can see from the foregoing, covering Babe Herman wasn't the simple historical endeavor that the Thirty Years' War was and, given the limitations of the medium, I would stack Lardner's history with Toynbee's any old day. After all, not many guys come up with the bases loaded and one out and drive home one run and three runners to third base. Somebody probably should have said simply, "Herman then doubled to right to load the base."

The idea of a designated hitter may have been bandied about on the Elysian Fields of Hoboken or during the 1890s, when a "courtesy runner" was permitted to take the base for an ailing batter without necessitating that batter's removal from the game (isn't "courtesy hitter" a cuter appellation than "designated hitter"?). However, the idea is at least as old as the 1920s, when John McGraw was asked his opinion of it and replied that one might as well "go all the way and let a club play nine defensive players in the field and then have nine sluggers do all the hitting." Messrs. Okrent and Ringolsby can't both be right. No matter that Bowie Kuhn, in his Solomonic wisdom, permitted the leagues to split the baseball baby in two in 1973. No matter that a poll of all fandom, as Peter Ueberroth has contemplated, would figure to be similarly divided. Either the designated hitter is good baseball or it isn't. The two camps are well represented below.

DANIEL OKRENT and

TRACY RINGOLSBY

Ban the DH . . . Save the DH

Daniel Okrent writes:
Nineteen seventy-three was a momentous year in baseball. Roberto Clemente died on his relief mission to Nicaragua. Henry Aaron took his home run total to the Ruthian precipice, hitting number 713. For the first time in the game's history, total attendance passed 30 million. Salary arbitration was instituted. The Oakland A's won the second of three straight world championships.

Yet all these events were dwarfed by an occurrence of such immense proportion, of such stunningly negative effect, that the year can be remembered for nothing else. As 1861 saw the Union rent in two; as 1914 plunged the world into pain and horror, as 1929 marked the end of prosperity, the onset of a decade's gloom—as all these watershed years stand out for the world, so must 1973 stand out for baseball.

For it was the year of the plague: the introduction into the game's rules of the designated hitter.

WHAT HAPPENED TO MY GAME?

There is nothing that can be said on behalf of the designated hitter rule. The case against it is clear and uncorrupted. It has done nothing to enrich the game, and it has done so much to sully its immortal symmetry that it should not be allowed to remain in force one day longer.

Spreading swiftly throughout baseball, a metastasizing monstrosity, the DH has become so pervasive that the National League is the *only* baseball league in the Western world—professional or amateur, adult or child, male or female—that requires the pitcher to bat. As such, it is the only league in the Western world that truly plays *baseball*, and not some adulterated form of the game. In the NL (and in Japan's Central League, the one other redoubt of the classical game), teams run risks each time they allow a pitcher to bat. Managers hold their breath as great sluggers, consigned to left field or first base, gather beneath pop flies. Front office personnel work into the night every spring, trying to balance a lineup while knowing no one can be hidden within its folds.

National League teams, and the brand of baseball they play, also happen to embody the fundamental tenet that underlies the game and gives it its texture: that every talent carries with it a concomitant price. Did Mark Belanger's glove justify his bat? In saying yes, Earl Weaver each season took a risk. Does Hal McRae's bat disguise his glove and his arm? We will never know. Hal McRae does not play baseball. Hal McRae hits.

AN IMPROPER BALANCE

With the Nationals playing the traditional game and the American League a mutant version, we find the two leagues diverging in a sport whose beauty rests in comparisons. They are, in effect, playing two different games—not subtly different, as is the case with the National Football League's two conferences, but as dissimilar as the NFL game is from the one played in the Canadian Football League. The World Series, that true symbol of baseball's interaction, is now merely an awkward test, forcing one team to alter the way it has excelled over 162 games. Simple matters like comparative salaries and statistics now must carry an asterisk. Is a National League pitcher of particular skills worth more than a comparable American Leaguer because he must bat? Or, if this left fielder is a worse-than-average fielder, is the DH (who never makes an error, or never throws to the wrong base) worth *more?*

Consider as well the managers that this rule has wrought. Only ten years after the introduction of the DH, there are managers like the White Sox's Tony La Russa who have never run a game—in the majors, minors, or winter ball—in which the pitchers batted. Soon enough we will meet managers who have never *played* in such a game, at any level, from Little League on up. Will the time come when an American League manager will panic in a no-DH World

Series? It's already happened—to the Yankees' Bob Lemon when he hit for Tommy John in 1981. Will the time come when a manager will be confined to American League jobs because of the narrowness of his experience? It is virtually inevitable.

It is not enough, however, to base one's arguments on imbalance between the leagues or on the awkwardness of different playing rules in alternate World Series or on the potential effect of the DH on the permanent class of baseball managers. Obviously, it would be easier to install the DH in the National League rule book than to excise it from the rules of hundreds of other leagues. But expediency is not our goal. Let us examine the designated hitter on its merits.

I noted before that there is nothing at all that can be said to justify the DH rule. Lest you think my ears have been closed to the dissimulating cries of its proponents, I will attempt to dismiss each argument they use:

1. "It brings more offense into the game."
Let us leave unsaid whether offense alone is a virtue (show me someone who categorically prefers high-scoring games to pitchers' contests and I'll show you a San Diego Charger). In 1982, there were 18.11 hits per American League game, 17.57 per National League game. That's .54 hits per game difference—only .27 *per team* per game. Go to two baseball games. Soak up the sun. Enjoy the action. Drink a few beers. Then tell me whether one more hit—*one hit*—in those two games would have made them more or less enjoyable for you.

Tell me, as well, whether the ecstasy produced by that hit compares to the anxiety wrought when there's a man on second in the ninth inning of a tie game and a single is lined to left—to Don Baylor and his popcorn arm. Tell me whether Philadelphians still weep over Manny Mota's drive to the wall in

the third game of the 1977 playoffs, a drive that anyone but Greg Luzinski would have caught. Tell me, finally, whether our appreciation of baseball is enhanced or diminished by the pain of Luzinski's failure, the prospect of Baylor's challenge—by the subtlety of defense—as much as by the fireworks of offense.

2. *"It enables a team to use popular players who might otherwise not earn a place in the everyday lineup."*
Designated hitters who saw action in the second week of May included these immortals: Jorge Orta, John Wockenfuss, Ron Jackson, Dave Edler, Mickey Hatcher, and Johnny Grubb. Surely this rule was not invented to provide employment opportunities for Ron Jackson, who over his seven major league seasons has posted a .266 batting average and forty-eight home runs. Come to think of it, perhaps it was: the first DH in history was the mild and inoffensive Ron Blomberg of the Yankees.

Except for the occasional Baylor or McRae, the charismatic Reggie, or the freakish Luzinski, designated hitters are by and large fairly unexceptional hitters. The great athletes, the game's nonpareils, are fielders as well as hitters, and as such are the ones who genuinely bring fans to the park: Mike Schmidt, Gary Carter, Eddie Murray, Robin Yount—all Gold Gloves, platinum bats, and the most popular players in their cities.

3. *"It extends the careers of the biggest stars."*
Last April 24, just before his back began to act up yet again, forty-three-year-old Carl Yastrzemski was the DH for the Red Sox. That same day, for the Phillies, forty-two-year-old Pete Rose played right field, thirty-nine-year-old Bill Robinson played third, and forty-year-old Tony Perez—released by Boston because, apparently, he was too old and infirm even to DH—played first base, keeping alive his streak of playing in every Philadelphia game this season.

Perez is playing in 1983 because he deserves to play, not because he has been granted a senior citizen's discount pass. To his credit, when Willie Stargell's skills deteriorated to the level of Carl Yastrzemski's, he retired. If we want to watch our old heroes, let's watch them on Old-timers' Day. It is not cold-hearted to prefer that heroes still be able to play heroically.

4. *"It allows pitchers more complete games."*
Undeniable. However, it would serve us well to ask what the price of those complete games might be. The lamed Oakland pitchers whom Billy Martin threw to the wolves in 1980 would probably be pretty forthright about this. Catfish Hunter averaged 235 innings per year before the DH came along; in the four years following its introduction he averaged 300—and saw his career

crumble prematurely at age thirty-three. Three straight American League Cy Young Award winners—Steve Stone, Rollie Fingers and Pete Vuckovich—have seriously damaged their arms, perhaps irreparably, from overwork. The DH even creates strain for relievers. A Rich Gossage brought in to pitch the top of the eighth won't be removed for a pinch hitter in the bottom of the inning; under the sign of the designated hitter, the one-inning specialist starts going two or three. Over the course of a season, this can cripple a man who might appear three or four times a week.

5. *"It spares us the boredom, and the embarrassment, of watching pitchers hit."*

Is a pitcher's at bat necessarily boring? In my experience, when there's less than two out, a man on first and the pitcher at bat, something strange happens in the ballpark. Everybody knows that the pitcher will bunt—and the knowing focuses our attention. The park grows quiet, fans concentrate on the field, infielders charge the plate. The moment freezes. The bunt is, on its face, an exciting play; it is all the more so when the act is foreordained but the outcome is not.

Even if we concede that watching a pitcher hit is boring, this argument ill serves the most remarkable of baseball's athletes, namely those who can hit and pitch. Today the best hitting pitchers include Steve Carlton, Mike Krukow, and Tim Lollar; that they aren't bad pitchers either is very much to the point. They are better pitchers—they win more games—because they are good hitters. The best hitting pitchers a generation or two ago included Warren Spahn, Bob Lemon, Bob Gibson, Don Newcombe, and Don Drysdale (who occasionally even batted seventh or eighth in the order during his career). Those are three Hall of Famers, and two who've reached the Hall's doorstep. It isn't a coincidence.

6. *"Innovation vitalizes the game."*

The most specious argument of all, usually offered by football types or others who are fearful for the innate quality of the product *they* offer. Want more offense? Let's move first base 3 feet closer to home. Defense is boring? Let's tie the shortstop's shoelaces together. Stars are big draws? Bring back Whitey Ford and let him pitch from 40 feet. Change for its own sake in any endeavor is a questionable virtue; in baseball, where the lines of logic and continuity run back to the last major rule changes instituted in the late 1890s, it is specifically counterproductive.

There are some who say that the rule change that brought about the DH is partly responsible for the upsurge in baseball attendance over the past several years. If the DH is a help at the gate, why did the average National League club outdraw the average American League club by 150,000 fans last season? By 36,000 in strike-ridden 1981 and by nearly 200,000 in 1980?

I HAVE A DREAM

Proponents of the DH have never satisfactorily answered the sturdiest criticism of the institution—that it eliminates a manager's most fundamental, and most second-guessable, strategic dilemma, namely when to remove a pitcher. Why do they ignore this?

Could it be that the many strategic choices that fall solely upon National League managers do not appeal to these people? Do they not second-guess a manager who has left in a faltering pitcher because he leads off the next inning? Did that manager blow it by leaving him in, when he was fully aware that he had lost his best stuff—simply hoping that he could last the inning? Or should he have lifted that pitcher at the risk of having one of his relievers wasted on one batter, only to be removed in the bottom half of the inning in search of more runs. In this situation, the complexities that rest before a National League manager are just beginning. Once a manager has removed his relief pitcher for a pinch hitter, must he then remove another man—possibly one of his best defensive players, but a weak bat—so that he can hide his next pitcher in the batting order? And what of the sacrifice? If the manager's late-inning reliever is a good bunter, should a spot be found for him to bat in the next inning? Could the manager then move runners into scoring position and still keep this valuable reliever in the game?

Perhaps strategic choices, the subtle balance of a particular game, the dramatic content of the pitcher-batter confrontation—baseball's distinguishing characteristics—do not appeal to those in favor of the designated hitter.

Now, I don't mean to say that the American League general managers who continue to support the DH don't appreciate baseball; these gentlemen have built organizational strategies around developing (or retaining) purely offensive talents, and their work would be wasted if the DH were abolished now. But it is undeniable that, in their cases, necessity has mothered a bastard invention, a short-sighted view of the game that sacrifices its integrity for the sake of a silly and corrupting rule. It is worse when one considers that a rule specifically intended to be an experiment managed to become institutionalized by default. Within moments of the DH's tentative introduction back in 1973, as the pitchers who batted disappeared from the schools and colleges and minor-league systems, it too easily became a terrifying prospect to suddenly force them to bat once again. The experiment had become, to the American League, a strategic straitjacket. Having created Frankenstein, they were incapable of killing him.

I said at the outset that each day of the DH's continued existence was mortally wounding. Yet the DH cannot be easily obliterated without injuring a number of innocent parties. Thus, in the interest of those young pitchers who have not touched a bat since Little League (if then), and in acknowledgment of career choices made by professionals who no longer play defense, let the designated hitter rule live—for a period of time.

What baseball needs to do is declare that, effective opening day of 1988, the DH is dead. Watching the date approach, high schools will begin to revert to the classical nine-man lineup. Teams in the lower minors will begin to have their pitchers bat again, to train them for that approaching day when they will have no choice.

Young players like the White Sox's Ron Kittle will no longer arrive in the majors and be expected to learn a fielding position on the job, our fan dollars providing them with a tuition grant as they commit aggravated assault on simple fly balls. And the five-year waiting period will allow those once-great players now on the edge of decline to end their careers in the spotlight—not in the sideshow glare of that sad and distorted institution, the designated hitter.

Tracy Ringolsby writes:
Did you ever wonder why the National League is the only form of organized baseball—other than the Central League of Japan—that has not accepted the designated hitter? Well, wonder no more. It's stubbornness, plain and simple. After all, imagine what it would do to the ego of those National League owners to admit the junior circuit was right.

As every true baseball fan knows, the DH adds intrigue to the course of a game. It forces a manager to handle every decision separately and with solid rationale. Mostly, though, it serves its stated purpose—increased offense.

Let's get the statistics out of the way first. The DH has been in effect for ten years, and during that time it has undeniably helped perk up the production in the American League. Consider that during that decade, DHs have combined for a .259 batting average and produced 18,145 runs. National League pitchers, meanwhile, have hit .153 and produced less than a third as many runs (5,237). And if you're looking for home runs, the American League averaged one every thirty-seven at bats in 1982—thanks in part to one every twenty-nine times a DH came to bat—while the National League averaged a homer once every fifty-one trips.

So why all the fuss? Let's look at the arguments that are used to degrade the rule: it creates too much wear and tear on a pitcher's arm. It takes away from a manager's decision-making abilities. And, the most irritating of all, it's just not the way the game was meant to be played. Hogwash and more hogwash.

In the first two years of the DH, there was a modern-day high of American League pitchers who worked 250 innings or more (twenty-two in 1973 and twenty-three in 1974). But by the summer of 1982 that number had dropped to five, three less than the National League, which has two fewer teams.

Consider, too, that the percentage of complete games by American League pitchers has also declined during the DH decade. In the four years prior to the DH, American League pitchers completed 24.4 percent of their games. With the advent of the DH, that figure jumped to 31.6 in 1973 and to 33.5 by 1974. But it has dropped since then, hitting a recent-day low of 19.6 in 1982.

Sure, there have been a number of top American League pitchers to be sidelined by sore arms in recent years. But instead of classifying this malady as DH burnout, it could be more logically described as breaking ball burnout. The American League has the old ballparks, and old ballparks mean headaches for pitchers and pleasing nuances for hitters. As a result, American League pitchers tend to finesse their way to success. They can't rear back and fire fastballs, like their National League counterparts, fully aware that they have spacious pastures inside the fences where deep fly balls can be run down.

Those who claim that the DH limits managerial decision-making couldn't be further from the truth. In fact, it creates more pressures than ever when it comes to handling pitchers. An example: In the late innings of a National League ballgame, if a club is down a run and a man gets on base, the manager pinch hits for the pitcher. There are no questions asked; it's the move he has to make. Another example of brilliant National League managerial strategy: a pitcher is struggling in the middle of an inning, but he's due to lead off when his team comes to bat. So the manager stays with the hurler, forcing him to make pressure pitches that can really ruin an arm. He gives up the key hit, but the manager is not second-guessed. He was simply sparing the expense of using an extra pitcher by milking an extra out from one who had already lost his best stuff.

When a manager makes a pitching change in the American League, he has to be of firm conviction that he's bringing in a pitcher who can do the job better than the one he's replacing. Managing with the DH puts a premium on being able to handle pitchers. "You have to have the ability as a manager to say, 'This guy has had it,' and then take him out," says Baltimore pitching coach Ray Miller. "You have to have sound judgment of pitchers and what they are doing over the course of a game." In other words, you have to make pitching changes in the American League because you need to make a change, not because you need a run.

"You have to know the characteristics of your pitcher's stuff," adds St. Louis manager Whitey Herzog, who has managed both with the DH (in Kansas City) and without. "He might be rolling along and throwing a great game, but you can't get lulled to sleep by that. You have to be ready to make the move when he starts to lose something."

One of the refinements of managing with the DH that has developed over the last decade is the realization of the versatility it presents a manager in constructing a batting order.

By removing the pitcher from the line-up, a manager can blend the strengths of a nine-man hitting rotation. One of the outgrowths of this has been the "double-leadoff-man" theory, which simply means that it is as important to have speed at the bottom of the order as it is to have it at the top.

Before he had Willie Wilson to get things going in Kansas City, Herzog used to bat George Brett and Hal McRae one-two in his lineup. His speed men, Fred Patek and Frank White, hit eight and nine. By having Brett and McRae, his best hitters, lead off, he could get them more at bats, and after the first time around, he had them coming up right behind his fastest runners. "You only have a leadoff hitter the first time in the American League," Herzog says. "And your first hitter is never batting after a pitcher."

The DH continues to demand more strategy throughout the course of a game. How much soul-searching does it take for a manager to call for a sacrifice bunt when his pitcher comes to the plate with a runner on first? It's automatic, and worse, it's a defensive action to an offensive part of the game.

The one time true strategy does come into play in the National League is in the late innings of a tight game, when the manager pinch-hits for the hurler. That's when he must decide if he's going to make a double change, so that he can move the pitcher to a less important spot in the lineup. But with the DH that strategy is at work from the first inning on. What a pitcher-free lineup does is force a manager to consider all his options: do nothing, sacrifice, steal, or hit-and-run.

"It starts with your number six hitter," Herzog explains. "If he gets on base, you hit-and-run with your seventh hitter. Say he grounds out and moves the runner to second. If you've got a pitcher in the lineup, they'll pass your number eight hitter and go right to the pitcher. With the DH though, they've got to pitch to your hitters. It opens up a lot of things for you throughout your lineup."

It will open up more things once the American League managers are able to put a more complete offensive player in that role. Instead of following the pattern of using older players who are just hanging on as their DH, teams will eventually have to follow the lead of the Hal McRaes and Don Baylors. They are players who can contribute in many ways offensively. They don't clog up an offensive production line of which a DH is the foreman.

Isn't it time for those National League diehards to realize the pettiness of their arguments against the DH on "purist" grounds. It's so ironic for them to complain, when they believe in a league that has become the bastion of antiseptic ballparks and artificial playing surfaces.

Sure Abner Doubleday didn't include the DH in his rules. But don't tell me that Doubleday was thinking of double-knits, floodlights, television, and ersatz grass back when he decided that the bases should be 90 feet apart.

"Most people who talk about the sacrilege of the DH are National League owners whose teams play on artificial surfaces," Miller argues. "You talk about changing the game; I think any record that is set on artificial grass should have an asterisk next to it. Anyone who says the DH destroys the sanctity of the game, and plays on artificial grass is being sacrilegious himself, and a hypocrite." Now, all in favor say aye.

Of the making of lists there is no end. The impulse is irresistible, so why resist? Right. My ten favorite team names (six of them are major-league!): the Hunkidoris, Tip-Tops, Quicksteps, Skeeters, Innocents, Intrepids, Canaries, Orphans, Black Jokes, and Pearls. Or how about thirteen major leaguers better known in other lines of work: Johnny Berardino (actor), Frank Olin (industrialist), Arlie Pond (doctor), Byron Houck (cinematographer), Chuck Connors (actor), Sam Crane (sportswriter), Billy Sunday (evangelist), Vinegar Bend Mizell (congressman), Ted Lewis (university president), Al Lawson (aviator), John Tener (Pennsylvania governor), Fred Brown (U.S. senator), Joe Garagiola (announcer). Or twenty-two . . . AARGH!

PHIL PEPE and

ZANDER HOLLANDER

Name Calling

"Mr. President, as the nation's No. 1 baseball fan, would you be willing to name your all-time baseball team?"

When President Nixon not only said he would, but did, and made the sports pages of just about every newspaper in the country with his selections, that was an open invitation for everybody to get into the act.

In the interest of fair play, it seems only right that others be given equal time.

What follows are the teams politicians, statespeople, and other celebrities might have chosen if they had the time, the inclination, and the opportunity. The selections are hypothetical, but the players chosen are real people who actually played in the major leagues.

LEONID BREZHNEV

First base—Lefty O'Doul
Second base—Red Schoendienst
Third base—Red Rolfe
Shortstop—Pinky May

Outfield—Eric (The Red) Tipton
Outfield—Red Murray
Outfield—Lou (The Mad Russian) Novikoff
Catcher—Red Dooin
Pitcher—Lefty Gomez

DON VITO CORLEONE

First base—Joe Pepitone
Second base—Tony Lazzeri
Third base—Joe Torre
Shortstop—Phil Rizzuto
Outfield—Joe DiMaggio
Outfield—Rocky Colavito
Outfield—Carl Furillo
Catcher—Yogi Berra
Pitcher—Sal Maglie

FRANK BUCK

First base—Snake Deal
Second base—Nellie Fox
Third base—Possum Whitted
Shortstop—Rabbit Maranville
Outfield—Mule Haas
Outfield—Ox Eckhardt
Outfield—Goat Anderson
Catcher—Doggie Miller
Pitcher—Old Hoss Radbourn

e. e. cummings

first base—r. c. stevens
second base—a. j. mc coy
third base—i. i. mathison
shortstop—j. c. hartman
outfield—g. g. walker
outfield—j. w. porter
outfield—r. e. hildebrand
catcher—j. c. martin
pitcher—w. a. kearns

GOLDA MEIR

First base—Ron Blomberg
Second base—Rod Carew
Third base—Al Rosen
Shortstop—Eddie Feinberg
Outfield—Hank Greenberg
Outfield—Goody Rosen
Outfield—Cal Abrams
Catcher—Joe Ginsberg
Pitcher—Sandy Koufax

GOV. ALFRED E. SMITH

First base—Willie Smith
Second base—George Smith
Third base—Charlie Smith
Shortstop—Billy Smith
Outfield—Al Smith
Outfield—Reggie Smith
Outfield—Elmer Smith
Catcher—Hal Smith
Pitcher—Al Smith

JACK JONES

First base—Nippy Jones
Second base—Dalton Jones
Third base—Willie (Puddinhead) Jones
Shortstop—Cobe Jones
Outfield—Cleon Jones
Outfield—Ruppert Jones
Outfield—Fielder Jones
Catcher—Bill Jones
Pitcher—Randy Jones

LYNDON JOHNSON

First base—Deron Johnson
Second base—Don Johnson
Third base—Billy Johnson
Shortstop—Bob Johnson
Outfield—Alex Johnson

Outfield—Lou Johnson
Outfield—Indian Bob Johnson
Catcher—Cliff Johnson
Pitcher—Walter Johnson

SWEET GEORGIA BROWN

First base—Ike Brown
Second base—Jimmy Brown
Third base—Bobby Brown
Shortstop—Larry Brown
Outfield—Ollie Brown
Outfield—Bobby Brown
Outfield—Gates Brown
Catcher—Dick Brown
Pitcher—Mordecai (Three Finger) Brown

BETTY FRIEDAN

First base—Mary Calhoun
Second base—Sadie Houck
Third base—She Donahue
Shortstop—Lena Blackburne
Outfield—Gail Henley
Outfield—Baby Doll Jacobson
Outfield—Estel Crabtree
Catcher—Bubbles Hargrave
Pitcher—Lil Stoner

JAMES BEARD

First base—Juice Latham
Second base—Peaches Graham
Third base—Pie Traynor
Shortstop—Chico Salmon
Outfield—Soupy Campbell
Outfield—Peanuts Lowrey
Outfield—Oyster Burns
Catcher—Pickles Dillhoefer
Pitcher—Noodles Hahn

J. P. MORGAN

First base—Norm Cash
Second base—Don Money
Third base—Milton Stock
Shortstop—Ernie Banks
Outfield—Art Ruble
Outfield—Elmer Pence
Outfield—Bobby Bonds
Catcher—Gene Green
Pitcher—Jim Grant

NORMAN VINCENT PEALE

First base—Earl Grace
Second base—Johnny Priest
Third base—Frank Bishop
Shortstop—Angel Hermoso
Outfield—Dave Pope
Outfield—Hi Church
Outfield—Maurice Archdeacon

Catcher—Mickey Devine
Pitcher—Howie Nunn

JOHN COLEMAN

First base—Sunny Jim Bottomley
Second base—Nippy Jones
Third base—Gene Freese
Shortstop—Stormy Weatherly
Outfield—Hurricane Hazle
Outfield—Curt Flood
Outfield—Icicle Reeder
Catcher—Sun Daly
Pitcher—Windy McCall

JIMMY THE GREEK

First base—Frank Chance
Second base—Lucky Jack Lohrke
Third base—Charlie Deal
Shortstop—John Gamble
Outfield—Curt Welch
Outfield—Trick McSorley
Outfield—Ace Parker
Catcher—Candy LaChance
Pitcher—Shufflin' Phil Douglas

JOHN JAMES AUDUBON

First base—Andy Swan
Second base—Johnny Peacock
Third base—Jiggs Parrott
Shortstop—Chicken Stanley
Outfield—Ducky Medwick
Outfield—Goose Goslin
Outfield—Bill Eagle
Catcher—Birdie Tebbetts
Pitcher—Robin Roberts

FOSTER BROOKS

First base—Sherry Robertson
Second base—Mickey Finn

Third base—Billy Lush
Shortstop—Bobby Wine
Outfield—Jigger Statz
Outfield—Brandy Davis
Outfield—Half Pint Rye
Catcher—George Gibson
Pitcher—John Boozer

RAND-MCNALLY

First base—Frank Brazill
Second base—Chile Gomez
Third base—Frenchy Bordagaray
Shortstop—Sal Madrid
Outfield—Germany Schaefer
Outfield—Dutch Holland
Outfield—Clyde Milan
Catcher—Dick West
Pitcher—Vinegar Bend Mizell

QUEEN ELIZABETH

First base—Duke Carmel
Second base—Royal Shaw
Third base—Count Campau
Shortstop—John Knight
Outfield—Prince Oana
Outfield—Bris Lord
Outfield—Mel Queen
Catcher—Earl Averill
Pitcher—Clyde King

Just weeks before Jackie Robinson went to spring training in 1947 with the Brooklyn Dodgers, preparing to enter into the major leagues, the giant of Negro League baseball died. Josh, the black Babe Ruth—or was Babe the white Josh Gibson?—never got the chance to display his talents on a national stage. What might have been—not only for him, but for Cool Papa Bell, Oscar Charleston, Rube Foster, Pop Lloyd, Martin Dihigo, Judy Johnson, Buck Leonard, even the Satchel Paige and Monte Irvin of their primes? We will never know, but at least these men won eventual induction into the Baseball Hall of Fame, in no small measure because of the groundbreaking study of which this forms a chapter, *Only the Ball Was White*.

ROBERT PETERSON

Josh

> *There is a catcher that any*
> *big-league club would like to buy for*
> *$200,000. His name is Gibson . . . he*
> *can do everything. He hits the ball a*
> *mile. And he catches so easy he*
> *might as well be in a rocking chair.*
> *Throws like a rifle. Bill Dickey isn't*
> *as good a catcher. Too bad this*
> *Gibson is a colored fellow.*
> —Walter Johnson

There is a story that one day during the 1930s the Pittsburgh Crawfords were playing at Forbes Field in Pittsburgh when their young catcher, Josh Gibson, hit the ball so high and far that no one saw it come down. After scanning the sky carefully for a few minutes, the umpire deliberated and ruled it a home run. The next day the Crawfords were playing in Philadelphia when suddenly a ball dropped out of the heavens and was caught by the startled center fielder on the opposing club. The umpire made the only possible ruling. Pointing to Gibson he shouted, "Yer out—yesterday in Pittsburgh!"

Gibson fans of those years might concede that there was an element of exaggeration in the story, but not much. Josh Gibson was not merely a home run hitter; he was *the* home run hitter. He was the black Babe Ruth, and like the Babe a legend in his own time whose prodigious power was celebrated in fact and fancy. But while it is relatively easy to separate fact from fancy in Ruth's legend, Gibson's suffers from the paucity of certified records about the quantity and quality of his home run production. Old-timers credit Gibson with eighty-nine home runs in one season and seventy-five in another; many of them, of course, were hit against semipro competition.

Whatever the truth of these claims, a strong case can be made for the proposition that Josh Gibson, a right-hand batter, had more power than the great Babe. The clincher in the argument is the generally accepted fact that Gibson hit the longest home run ever struck in Yankee Stadium, Ruth's home for twelve seasons.

Baseball's bible, *The Sporting News* [June 3, 1967], credits Gibson with a drive in a Negro league game that hit just two feet from the top of the stadium wall circling the bleachers in center field, about 580 feet from home plate. It was estimated that had the drive been two feet higher it would have sailed out of the park and traveled some 700 feet!

Some old Negro league players say that Gibson's longest shot in Yankee Stadium struck the rear wall of the bullpen in left field, about 500 feet from the plate. But Jack Marshall, of the Chicago American Giants, recalls an epic blast by Gibson that went *out* of the stadium—the only fair ball ever hit out of the Yankees' park.

> In 1934, Josh Gibson hit a ball off of Slim Jones in Yankee Stadium in a four-team doubleheader that we had there—the Philadelphia Stars played the Crawfords in the second game; we had played the Black Yankees in the first game. They say a ball has never been hit out of Yankee Stadium. Well, that is a lie! Josh hit the ball over that triple deck next to the bullpen in left field. Over and out! I never will forget that, because we were getting ready to leave because we were going down to Hightstown, New Jersey, to play a night game and we were standing in the aisle when that boy hit this ball!

Both Ruth and Gibson played before the era of the tape-measure home run, when every long hit is carefully computed, almost to the inch. None of Ruth's towering smashes was ever officially measured, but the best guess of his longest is 550 feet. Only one of Gibson's home runs was ever measured. He was with the Homestead Grays in Monessen, Pennsylvania, one day in the late 1930s when he hit a homer of such impressive dimensions that the mayor ordered the game stopped and a tape measure applied. The result: 512 feet.

Unlike Babe Ruth, whose swing was awesome and whose body wound up like a pretzel when he missed the ball, Gibson's power was generated with little apparent effort. Judy Johnson, who was Gibson's first manager, said:

> It was just a treat to watch him hit the ball. There was no effort at all. You see these guys now get up there in the box and they dig and scratch around before they're ready. Gibson would just walk up there, and he would always turn his left sleeve.

And when Gibson raised his front foot, the infielders began edging backward onto the grass. If he met the pitch squarely and it came to them on one hop, they knew the ball would be in their glove before Gibson could drop his bat.

Josh Gibson was born December 21, 1911, in Buena Vista, Georgia, a village not far from Atlanta. His father scratched a bare living from a patch of ground outside the village. Josh, the first child of Mark and Nancy Gibson, was named Joshua after his grandfather.

At intervals of three years, two other children were born to the Gibsons: Jerry, who would follow Josh into professional baseball as a pitcher with the Cincinnati Tigers, and Annie. By 1923 the Gibson youngsters were growing up, and it became clear to Mark that if they were to have better opportunities than he had had he must join the swelling migration of black men to the North. And so, late that year, he went to Pittsburgh, where he had relatives, to find work. He quickly got a job as a laborer for Carnegie-Illinois Steel, which was later absorbed by U.S. Steel. In early 1924, Mark sent for his family. Josh was twelve years old when the Gibsons settled down in Pleasant Valley, a Negro enclave in Pittsburgh's North Side.

While equal opportunity was only a pleasant dream for a Negro boy in Pittsburgh, still, the change from the oppressive atmosphere of a southern small town was welcomed. "The greatest gift Dad gave me," Gibson said later, "was to get me out of the South."

Baseball was new to the migrant from Georgia, but he was soon the first one chosen for sandlot pickup games when he began demonstrating a talent for hitting the ball. He was always looking for a ballgame, to play or to watch, and he thought nothing of strapping on rollerskates and skating six miles downriver to Bellevue to see a game.

The young Josh did not care especially for football or basketball, the other neighborhood sports, but swimming caught his interest and as a teenager he brought home a number of medals from the city playground pools. At sixteen he was on his first uniformed baseball club—the Gimbels A.C., an all-Negro amateur team playing in Pittsburgh. He was already a catcher, as he would be throughout his career, except for an occasional game in the outfield.

His education was over. Josh had gone through fifth grade in the Negro school in Buena Vista and continued in elementary school in Pittsburgh. He dropped out after the completing the ninth grade in Allegheny Pre-Vocational School, where he learned the rudiments of the electrician's trade. He immediately went to work as an apprentice in a plant that manufactured air brakes. But by this time it was clear that Gibson's vocation would be baseball. He was nearing his full size of 6 feet 1 inch and 215 pounds. He had a moon-round, trusting face, a friendly disposition, and the body of a dark Greek god. His broad shoulders sloped down to tremendous arms, thick with muscle, and his barrel chest tapered in the athlete's classic mold to a deceptively slim-looking waist. Like his arms, Gibson's legs were heavily muscled.

For a Pittsburgh Negro boy who loved baseball, his goal would have to be the Homestead Grays. He could envy the Pirates' heroes of his youth—the Waners, Lloyd and Paul, and Pie Traynor and Burleigh Grimes and Rabbit Maranville—but he could not hope to step into their shoes. The next best thing was the Homestead Grays, who had started twenty years before in the steel town a few miles upriver and were beginning to emerge as a national Negro baseball power. They had Smoky Joe Williams and Johnny Beckwith and Sam Streeter and Vic Harris and Martin Dihigo—names that meant nothing to the typical Pirate fan but that loomed large in Negro baseball.

In 1929 and 1930, when the Grays were strengthening their position as one of the best Negro ballclubs in the country, Josh Gibson was catching for the Crawford Colored Giants of Pittsburgh. This was a semipro club that Josh had had a hand in organizing around a city recreation building in Pittsburgh's Hill District. The Crawfords (not to be confused with Gus Greenlee's powerhouse, which was formed in 1931) played other semipro clubs in and around Pittsburgh for a few dollars a game. No admission was charged for their games, and the collection rarely brought in more than fifty dollars, although crowds of 5,000, attracted by the growing awareness of Gibson's power at the plate, were not uncommon.

The Grays, naturally, soon heard of the big, raw slugger. Judy Johnson, who managed Homestead in 1930, said:

> I had never seen him play but we had heard so much about him. Every time you'd look in the paper you'd see where he hit a ball 400 feet, 500 feet. So the fans started wondering why the Homestead Grays didn't pick him up. But we had two catchers. Buck Ewing was the regular catcher, and Vic Harris, an outfielder, used to catch if we were playing a doubleheader.

In late July, the Kansas City Monarchs, Negro National League champions of 1929, came to Pittsburgh for a series with the Grays, bringing along their new portable lighting system. On July 25, the Grays and Monarchs were battling under these uncertain lights in Forbes Field. Johnson remembers:

> Joe Williams was pitching that night and we didn't know anything about lights. We'd never played under 'em before, and we couldn't use the regular catcher's signals, because if he put his hand down you couldn't see it. So we used the glove straight up for a fastball and the glove down—that was supposed to be the curve.
>
> Some way Joe Williams and the catcher got crossed up. The catcher was expecting the curve and Joe threw the fastball and caught him right there, and split the finger. Well, my other catcher was Vic Harris and he was playing the outfield and wouldn't catch. So Josh was sitting in the grandstand, and I asked the Grays' owner, Cum Posey, to get him to finish the game. So Cum asked Josh would he catch, and Josh said, "Yeah, oh yeah!" We had to hold the game up until he went into the clubhouse and got a uniform. And that's what started him out with the Homestead Grays.

Gibson got no hits that night, but he made no errors, either, and that was strange, for he was still a raw-boned eighteen-year-old and clumsy with the mitt. For the rest of that season, Johnson said, "Josh would catch batting practice and then catch the game, he was so anxious to learn. He wasn't much of a catcher then, but he came along fast."

Despite his shortcomings as a catcher, Gibson became an instant regular on the Grays, although he was often used in the outfield during his first year in top competition. His bat simply had to be in the lineup somewhere.

There remains a wide division of opinion among ballplayers who played with and against Gibson during his prime as to his skill as a catcher. Many maintain that he became a good receiver, but never a great one. They hold that he never learned to catch foul pop-ups, that his arm was adequate, but no more than that, and that as a receiver he was not in the same class with Bruce Petway, who threw out Ty Cobb twice trying to steal second in a series in Cuba in the winter of 1910, or Biz Mackey, whose career began in 1920 and spanned thirty years on top clubs, or Frank Duncan, Kansas City Monarchs catcher of the 1920s.

Walter Johnson's description of Gibson as a rocking-chair catcher with a rifle arm suggests otherwise. Joining Walter Johnson in his opinion that Josh was a superior catcher is Roy Campanella, who was beginning his career in professional baseball with the Baltimore Elite Giants in 1937, about the time Gibson reached his peak. Campanella said that Gibson was a graceful, effortless receiver with a strong, accurate arm. He was, said Campy, "not only the greatest catcher but the greatest ballplayer I ever saw."

The middle ground between these extreme opinions is held by Jimmie

Crutchfield, an outfielder who was a teammate of Gibson on the Pittsburgh Crawfords from 1932 through 1936:

> I can remember when he couldn't catch this building if you threw it at him. He was only behind the plate because of his hitting. And I watched him develop into a very good defensive catcher. He was never given enough credit for his ability as a catcher. They couldn't deny that he was a great hitter, but they could deny that he was a great catcher. But I know!

In 1931, Josh Gibson was an established star on the Homestead Grays. He was credited with seventy-five home runs that years as the Grays barnstormed around Pennsylvania, West Virginia, Ohio, and into the southern reaches of New York State, feeding the growing legend about the young black catcher who could hit the ball a country mile. The next year he was lured to the Pittsburgh Crawfords by the free-spending Gus Greenlee to form with Satchel Paige perhaps the greatest battery in baseball history. Gibson stayed with Greenlee's Crawfords for five summers, his fame growing with each Brobdingnagian clout. In 1934 his record was sixty-nine home runs and in the other years his homer production, although not recorded, was from all accounts similarly Ruthian. Or perhaps Gibsonian.

As Greenlee's dream of a baseball dynasty soured, Gibson jumped back to the Grays near the end of the 1936 season. In 1937 he was listed on the Crawfords' spring roster, but by mid-March he was described as a holdout. John L. Clark, Greenlee's publicity man, wrote in the *Pittsburgh Courier* that Greenlee and Rufus (Sonnyman) Jackson, Grays' co-owner, were discussing a trade in which Gibson and Judy Johnson (who had been the Crawfords' third baseman since 1932) would go to the Grays for catcher Pepper Bassett and any infielder, plus $2,500. Here is a measure of Negro baseball's finances. The game's greatest slugger—who was also the paramount drawing card (always excepting Satchel Paige)—and Negro baseball's most accomplished third baseman were to be traded for two journeymen players and $2,500.

That the story was in part a ploy to bring Gibson to terms is evident from Clark's faint praise of the slugger. He said that Gibson was an asset to any club, "but not the kind of asset that more colorful and less capable players might be. With all this ability, he has not developed that 'it' which pulls the cash customers through the turnstiles—although he has been publicized as much as Satchel Paige." Gibson's lack of color, plus a rumor that he had an offer to manage an unnamed club at a higher salary than Greenlee would offer, made it likely that a trade would be made, Clark wrote. Gibson did not come to terms with Greenlee and a trade went through: Gibson and Johnson for

Pepper Bassett and Henry Spearman. No money changed hands. Johnson did not report to the Grays.

And so Josh Gibson returned to the Homestead Grays, his first team. Spring training had hardly begun when he heard the siren call of the dollar to be made with Satchel Paige in the Dominican Republic. He heeded the call. The *Pittsburgh Courier* reported, most improbably, that Gibson had gone to Trujilloland with the consent of the Grays. In any event, he stayed only until July, returning in time to help the Grays win their first Negro National League championship.

For the next two years, Gibson's big bat was the piledriving punch on the strongest club in Negro baseball. Boasting Buck Leonard, Sam Bankhead, Vic Harris, and other sluggers in addition to Josh, the Grays dominated the league and toyed with their foes on the barnstorming trail. It was such a powerful and well-balanced team that it could survive the loss of Gibson and continue its mastery over the NNL in the 1940 and 1941 seasons after Gibson had jumped to the Mexican League. He earned $6,000 a season with Veracruz, according to the *Courier*, $2,000 more than he was paid by the Grays. If Cum Posey and Sonnyman Jackson had looked on with favor when he had gone to the Dominican Republic in 1937, they were not pleased by his contract-jumping in later years. They won a court judgment against Gibson for $10,000 and laid claim to his Pittsburgh home. But when he signed with the Grays for 1942, all was forgiven and they dropped the suit. Josh Gibson was at the height of his fame and near the peak of his incredible power, envied but popular with other Negro professional ballplayers, and the toast of Pittsburgh's black community. There was nowhere to go but down, and the slide would soon begin.

He had come into big-time Negro baseball twelve years before as a rookie of uncommon rawness, a young man so shy and retiring that when he visited in another player's home he spent the evening looking at his shoes. Now he was self-assured, the main attraction at any party, and he had developed a fondness for the bottle. Gibson's drinking never reached the point where he failed to show up for ballgames—or to hit with power—but in his final five seasons he was occasionally suspended for a few days for "failing to observe training rules," in Cum Posey's delicate phrase.

Another, more ominous, portent of the dark days ahead appeared when he began suffering from recurring headaches. On Jan. 1, 1943, he blacked out, lapsing into a coma that lasted all day and hospitalized him for about ten days. The diagnosis was a brain tumor. Doctors at Pittsburgh's St. Francis Hospital wanted to operate, but he would not permit it, according to his sister, Mrs. Annie Mahaffey. "He figured that if they operated, he'd be like a vegetable."

Gibson's knees, too, were giving him trouble, apparently the result of cartilage damage, and he was slowing to a snail's pace compared with his former speed. In his heyday, Gibson, despite his size, had been one of the fastest runners on the Grays. Yet, even while his troubles were pyramiding, Gibson was still the symbol of power. In 1944 he led the Negro National League in homers with six while batting .338 in 39 league games. The next year he was again home-run champion with eight and boasted a league-leading .393 average in 44 games. As a matter of course, he was chosen as the East's catcher in the East-West all-star games in 1944 and 1946. He missed the 1945 all-star game because it was played during one of his periodic suspensions for violating training rules.

Josh Gibson had played baseball the year-round every year from 1933 through 1945, spending the winter seasons in Puerto Rico, Cuba, Mexico, and Venezuela. His greatest thrill, he said, had been winning the batting title and the most-valuable-player award in the Puerto Rican League in 1941. (He was without doubt the most valuable player in the Negro National League for several seasons, but no MVP award was ever given in the NNL.)

Now, in the winter of 1946, his headaches and blackouts were increasing in frequency and severity, and for the first time since 1933 he stayed home in Pittsburgh. Outwardly, he remained a cheerful, easy-going giant, gregarious and friendly, and only his increasing attachment to liquor betrayed his concern about his illness. "He never got drunk so that he was staggering or anything like that," Mrs. Mahaffey recalled, "but still it worried you, because he wasn't really a drinking man."

On the evening of Jan. 20, 1947, Josh came home and told his mother that he felt sick. He said that he believed he was going to have a stroke. Mrs. Gibson said, "Shush, Josh, you're not going to have no stroke," but she sent him to bed. The family gathered around his bedside and waited for a doctor while Josh

laughed and talked. Then he sent his brother Jerry to the homes of friends to collect his scattered trophies and his radio and bring them home. "So Jerry came back about ten-thirty," Mrs. Mahaffey said, "and we were all laughing and talking, and then he had a stroke. He just got through laughing and then he raised up in bed and went to talk, but you couldn't understand what he was saying. Then he lay back down and died right off."

There are those who believe his death was caused by his disappointment at being denied the opportunity to play in the big leagues. Ted Page, an outfielder who was Gibson's teammate on the Crawfords, said, "Josh knew he was major-league quality. We would go to a major-league game if we had a day off. He was never the kind of a guy to say, 'I'm the great Josh Gibson,' but if he saw a player make a mistake he would say what should have been done, or he might say, 'I would have been expecting that.' "

Page said that Gibson never complained about the hard lot of the Negro professional.

> He wouldn't have traded his life for anything. One weekend, I remember, we played a twilight game at Forbes Field in Pittsburgh. Afterward we jumped in two cars and drove the 600 miles to St. Louis for a 2 P.M. game the next day. And the next day we drove 350 miles to Kansas City for a doubleheader. It was 110 in the shade, but he loved it. That night Josh and I were sitting on the back porch of the hotel and we saw a kid ballgame and we went and joined it. That's the kind of guy he was.

By the standards of Negro baseball, Gibson was well-paid for such labors. During the boom of the early 1940s, he was, next to Satchel Paige, the highest-salaried performer in the game, earning about $6,000 from the Homestead Grays for a five-month season and adding perhaps $3,000 in winter baseball. (A journeyman black player made about $1,250 for the summer and considerably less during the winter, if he played at all.) While Gibson's salary was higher than that of the average major-leaguer during this period, it was nowhere near that of white stars of his stature like Joe DiMaggio, Hank Greenberg, and Ted Williams.

Like them, he hit for a high average as well as for distance. Only for the last three years of his career are official records available, but they show him among the batting leaders in the Negro National League and suggest that in his prime he would have boasted a batting average not far below .400 against strong pitching.

As John L. Clark noted during Gibson's salary wrangle with the Crawfords in 1937, he was "colorless" in the same sense that Joe DiMaggio was. It was the colorlessness of perfection, the ability to do the difficult effortlessly. He loved the game and he played to win, but his performance excited only admiration and awe while Satchel Paige, with equally memorable though different skills, added to them a talent for showmanship. The result was that while hundreds went to the ballgame to see Gibson, thousands went to watch Paige.

Gibson died the year after Jackie Robinson had broken organized baseball's color line at Montreal and only months before Robinson would become the first Negro in the major leagues since Fleet and Weldy Walker in 1884. Gibson himself had had two tantalizing nibbles that suggested he might become the first to cross the line. In 1939, Wendell Smith of the *Courier* reported that Bill Benswanger, president of the Pittsburgh Pirates, had promised a trial for Josh and Buck Leonard, the Grays' slugging first baseman. Smith said Cum Posey had agreed to sell his two stars but Benswanger changed his mind. Benswanger's version was different. He said Cum Posey asked him not to sign Gibson because then other Negro stars would be taken and the Negro National League would be wrecked. In any case, no tryout was held.

A few years later, when the Homestead Grays were playing in Griffith Stadium regularly, Gibson and Leonard were called up to the Washington Senators' offices by Clark Griffith, the owner. "He talked to us about Negro baseball and about the trouble there would be if he took us into the big leagues," Leonard said. "But he never did make us an offer."

Griffith must have been sorely tempted to sign the two black men. His Senators were usually mired deep in the American League's second division, and when they were on the road he could look out of his office and watch Gibson and Leonard busting the fences in his park. In one game in 1943, Gibson hit three home runs there, one of them landing two feet from the top of the left-center-field bleachers, 485 feet from the plate. For the season, he belted eleven home runs to left field, the deep field in Griffith Stadium, playing there only once or twice a week, reportedly more than were hit to left in all American League action in that ballpark.

That Josh Gibson would have been one of baseball's superstars if the color line had been lowered earlier is beyond dispute. It is likely that he would have posed the most serious threat ever to Babe Ruth's lifetime record of 714 home runs in the major leagues.

Gibson did achieve a considerable measure of fame, parochial as it was, as the greatest hitter in Negro baseball. After Satchel Paige, his was easily the most famous name among black players. He is remembered with admiration, affection, and even wonder by old teammates and opponents alike, no small legacy for any man. Since Josh Gibson was not a man to pine for what might have been, perhaps the most fitting epitaph that could be devised was pronounced by Ted Page: "He was a big, overgrown kid who was glad for the chance he had. He loved his life."

Sam Rice retired in 1934 after batting .293, the *lowest* mark of his twenty-year career. He was only thirteen hits shy of 3,000, but in the days before recordmania, no one much cared—2,987 hits seemed a perfectly fine total. What folks did care about was the answer to baseball's great mystery: Did Sam Rice catch that ball in Game Three of the 1925 World Series, or did he not? Umpire Cy Rigler said he did, and that settled the ballgame but not the argument: Sam wasn't saying. He kept on not saying till the day he died, nearly half a century after the incident took place. And then . . .

SHIRLEY POVICH

A Voice from the Grave

Sam Rice's forty-nine-year secret has ended, with his own testimony from beyond the grave that he did, indeed, catch that long, homer-bound drive Earl Smith hit in the 1925 World Series between the Washington Senators and Pittsburgh Pirates.

The truth about the most disputed play in the seventy-one years of World Series history surfaced in a newly found testament written by Rice in 1965, "to be opened after my death."

The Washington outfielder died at eighty-four on October 13, 1974, having steadfastly refused to say unqualifiedly that he had made the catch on October 10, 1925, in Game Three of the Series. He long ago, however, had hinted he would put it in writing for the archives of the Baseball Hall of Fame.

Rice's document turned up the other day, but not at Cooperstown, New York, where Hall of Fame officials had combed the files for more than two weeks and were ready to dismiss reports of a Rice letter as unconfirmed rumor.

It surfaced in downtown New York City, at 30 Wall Street, where Paul S. Kerr, president of the Hall of Fame, has his office. Kerr, to whom the letter had been committed by Rice, was unaware that a search for the letter was under way.

Kerr made a ceremony of disclosing the contents of the letter left by Rice. Before witnesses, and as though ready to read a will, he slit open the envelope and recited its contents.

On that October Saturday almost fifty years ago, President and Mrs. Calvin Coolidge and 36,493 others jam-packed Griffith Stadium. Boy manager Bucky Harris made a defensive move that was prescient, after right fielder Joe (Moon) Harris singled home the run that gave the Senators their 4–3 lead in the seventh.

In the eighth, Harris replaced the slow moving Joe Harris as his right fielder, moved Sam Rice to that spot from center, and called in Earl McNeely as his center fielder.

Rice's speed (at thirty-five he may have still been the fastest man on the team) paid off for the Senators.

It took him into the path of Smith's swat into deep right center and he got a glove on it as man and ball crashed over the 3-foot fence into the seats. Rice and his trophy, or nontrophy, disappeared into the laps of the bleacher fans.

It was at least ten seconds before Rice disengaged himself to show the umpires a baseball in his glove.

In his letter, Rice described all the circumstances in the eighth inning of the game in which catcher Smith came to bat for Pittsburgh: "the ball was a line drive headed for the bleachers towards right center . . . I jumped as high as I could and back handed . . . but my feet hit the barrier . . . and I toppled . . . into the first row of bleachers . . . at no time did I lose possession of the ball."

Such was not the view of the Pirates, who protested loudly that Washington fans in the bleachers had replaced in Rice's glove the ball he had dropped. A score of Pittsburgh supporters in the bleachers offered affidavits that Rice did not hold the ball. The Senators won the game, 4–3, but lost the Series, four games to three.

For the remainder of his life, Rice helped to make mystery of the catch by refusing to make any comment except, "The umpire called him out, didn't he?" For the rest of his years, Rice's was the sardonic smile across the face of the baseball world.

It was at one of the annual, private dinners of members of the Baseball Hall of Fame at Cooperstown that Rice told fellow honorees that he had written his version of the catch, to be opened after his death.

Bill McKechnie, the Pirates' manager in 1925, was one of those to whom Rice confided in 1965 that he had written down his version of the catch. In a postscript, Rice wrote, "I approached McKechnie and said, 'What do you think will be in the letter.' His answer was, 'Sam, there was never any doubt in my mind but what you caught the ball.' "

McKechnie's agreement in 1965 that Rice had made the catch off Smith did not square with his opinion of the play on that October day in 1925.

According to *The Washington Post* account of the game, McKechnie was furious at the decision of umpire Cy Rigler in calling Smith out, and demanded that the other umpires overrule him. Like the other Pirates, McKechnie insisted that Rice had dropped the ball when he fell over the fence.

McKechnie, it was also reported in the *Post*, later took his protest to the box seat of Commissioner Kenesaw Mountain Landis, without success. Landis pointed out it was a judgment play that could not be appealed to him.

Rice's secret letter originally was supposed to go into his file at Cooperstown, but Hall of Fame officials have indicated that because of the public interest in it, it could have its own special display case.

The letter deposited by Rice with Kerr was actually inspired by the late Lee Allen, historian of the Hall of Fame. Allen refused to be content with Rice's evasion when questioned on the subject of the catch.

At each of Rice's visits to Cooperstown, Allen prodded Rice to make public his version of the disputed catch for the Cooperstown records.

When Rice refused to tell his secret, Allen pleaded, "You could at least leave us some kind of document to be opened after your death." It was this suggestion that Rice accepted.

Allen's death preceded Rice's, leaving many officials at Cooperstown unaware of the existence of the letter and fouling the search for it.

Rice was inducted into the Hall of Fame in 1963 by the special Old Timers' Committee, in recognition of his .322 lifetime batting average, his fame as a base stealer, and twenty years of consistent stardom in the American League.

He was more than the fielding star of the 1925 Series. His twelve hits led both teams at bat.

Over his twenty years in the American League, nineteen with Washington and one with Cleveland, Rice batted as high as .350 and .349, and was as great a threat on the bases as at bat. His sixty-three steals led the league in a year when Ty Cobb still was in his prime.

Rice was having a big year at bat in 1932 until late in the season, when his average slumped to a modest, for him, .323. Of course, he might have been tiring a bit near the season's end; he would be forty-one on his next birthday.

Barely 5 feet 10 and a mere 160 pounds, Rice was no overpowering figure in the batter's box. But he was the very model of a big-league hitter drawing a bead on a pitcher with malevolence aforethought.

An episode in Cleveland one year gave evidence of Rice's ability to manage his bat. A Cleveland pitcher, angered by a Washington home run, took a shot at the next batter, Rice, who was forced to hit the dirt. Dusting himself off,

Rice on the next pitch aimed a line drive and got him on the knee. Cleveland needed a new pitcher.

Later in the same game, another pitcher took a shot at Rice out of team loyalty, or some such. One pitch later, he was out of the game; Rice got him on the shin.

TESTIMONY OF SAM RICE: 'I HAD A DEATH GRIP ON IT'

Monday, July 26, 1965

It was a cold and windy day, the right field bleachers were crowded with people in overcoats and wrapped in blankets, the ball was a line drive headed for the bleachers towards right center. I turned slightly to my right and had the ball in view all the way, going at top speed and about 15 feet from bleachers jumped as high as I could and back handed and the ball hit the center of pocket in glove (I had a death grip on it). I hit the ground about five feet from a barrier about four feet high in front of bleachers with all my brakes on but couldn't stop so I tried to jump it to land in the crowd but my feet hit the barrier about a foot from top and I toppled over on my stomach into first row of bleachers, I hit my Adam's apple on something which sort of knocked me out for a few seconds but (Earl) McNeely arrived about that time and grabbed me by the shirt and pulled me out, I remember trotting back towards the infield still carrying the ball for about halfway and then tossed it towards the pitcher's mound. (How I have wished many times I had kept it.) At no time did I lose possession of the ball.

—Sam Rice

Most anyone's list of the five best baseball books ever written will include *The Glory of Their Times*, Larry Ritter's history of the early days of baseball as told by the men who played it. Indeed, such men as Red Barber and Stephen Jay Gould have called it the single greatest of all baseball books. I hasten to agree. The piece below has a curious history: it is a part of *The Glory of Their Times* and yet will not be found in that book. To interview the players, Ritter traveled some 75,000 miles in the early 1960s. His fascinating interview with former pitcher Marty McHale was taped in 1963 but inexplicably languished in the files of the Baseball Hall of Fame until 1982, when it became the centerpiece of the debut issue of a new baseball review, *The National Pastime*.

LAWRENCE S. RITTER

Ladies and Gentlemen, Presenting Marty McHale

Damon Runyon once wrote a story about me, saying this fellow McHale, who is not the greatest ballplayer that ever lived, is probably the most *versatile* man who ever took up the game. This was in the 1920s, after I had left baseball. So Johnny Kieran of *The New York Times* asked Babe Ruth about it, knowing he and I had been on the Red Sox together. Johnny said, "Marty played in the big leagues, he played football in college, he was on the track team, he was on the stage, he wrote for the Wheeler Syndicate and the *Sun*, he was in the Air Service"—and so forth. He went on listing my accomplishments until the Babe interrupted to say, "Well, I don't know about all those things, but he was the best goddamn singer I ever heard!"

You see, I sang in vaudeville for twelve years, a high baritone tenor—an "Irish Thrush," they called it then, and *Variety* called me "The Baseball Caruso." But even before vaudeville, before baseball even, I used to work in a lot of shows around Boston and made trips down to Wakefield, Winchester—minstrel shows, usually—and sometimes these little two-act sketches.

So when I joined the Boston club, a bunch of us—Buck O'Brien, Hughie Bradley, Larry Gardner, and myself—formed the Red Sox Quartette. After a while Gardner gave it up and a fellow named Bill Lyons stepped in. This Lyons was no ballplayer, but Boston signed him to a contract anyway, just to make the name of the act look proper. We were together three years, and when we broke up I was just as well satisfied because it was quite an ordeal keeping the boys on schedule. They just couldn't get used to that buzzer that tells you you're on next. They'd be a couple of minutes late and think nothing of it, but you can't *do* that in vaudeville, you know—you're *on*.

I did a single for about another three years, which was not very good—just good enough so that they paid for it—and then Mike Donlin and I got together. Now, you may not remember Mike, but he was—well, he was the Babe Ruth of his day. "Turkey Mike," they called him, because when he'd make a terrific catch or something he'd do a kind of turkey step and take his cap off and throw it up like a ham, a real ham; but he was a great one, he could live up to that stuff in the field or at the bat. His widow gave me some of his souvenirs: a gold bat and ball that were given to him as the most valuable player in 1905, some cuff links, and a couple of gold cups, one from the Giants and the other from the Reds. He hit over .350 for both of them.

Mike and I were together for five years, doing a double-entendre act called "Right Off the Bat"—not too much singing, Mike would only go through the motions—and we played the Keith-Orpheum circuit: twice in one year we were booked into the Palace in New York, and that was when it was the Palace, not the way it is now! They had nothing but the big headliners. When Mike left for Hollywood, I went back to doing a single. He made a bunch of pictures out there, and that's where he died.

Which did I like better, baseball or vaudeville? Well, I'd call it about 50–50. The vaudeville was more difficult, the traveling. Sure, you had to travel a lot in baseball, but you always had somebody taking care of your trunk, and your tickets and everything; all you had to do was get your slip, hop onto the train, and go to bed. When you got to the hotel your trunk was there. In vaudeville you had to watch your own stuff. I used to say to Mike, you're the best valet I know, because he was always on time with the tickets and had our baggage checks and everything all taken care of, right on the button all the time.

Of course, Mike and I wouldn't have been such an attraction if it hadn't been for baseball, so maybe I ought to tell you how I came to sign with the Red Sox in 1910. First of all, Boston was almost my hometown—I grew up in Stoneham, that's nine miles out, and if you took a trolley car and changed two or three times, you could get to the ballpark. Which I'd done only once—I only saw one big-league game before I played in one, and Cy Young pitched it; I wasn't really a Red Sox fan. But here comes the second reason for my signing: they gave me a *big* bonus. How big? Two thousand dollars, and back then that was money!

You see, that year for Maine University I had thrown three consecutive no-hitters, and the scouts were all over. I had a bid from Detroit, one from Pittsburgh, one from the Giants, and another from the Braves. And there was sort of a veiled offer from Cincinnati, which is an interesting story.

This Cincinnati situation, Clark Griffith was down there managing, and when I reported to the Red Sox, which was in June, following the end of the college term, his club was playing the Braves, over at Braves Field across the tracks from the Huntington Avenue park. Now, the Red Sox were on the road when I and some other college boys reported. We had signed, but the Red Sox didn't want us with them right away: they had to make room for us, they could only have so many players. So I remember that Griffith came over to the Red Sox park one morning to watch the boys work out. The clubhouse man told us we were all being watched—like you'd watch horses, you know, working out each morning, and he said if we wanted to stay with the club, better take it easy and not put too much on the ball and so on. See, the club usually asks waivers on the newcomers immediately upon reporting to see if anybody else is interested in them, and if so they can withdraw the waivers after a certain time.

I remember very definitely—I went out there and I was pitching to the hitters and I put everything I had on the ball, because after looking over that bunch of Red Sox pitchers I could see there was not much chance for a young collegian to crack that lineup.

At any rate, Griffith must have put in some claim, you see, because two days later I was on my way to Chicago to join the Red Sox. They had withdrawn the waivers. I joined them in Chicago and we went from there to Cleveland. I remember my pal Tris Speaker hurt his finger in Chicago and he was out for a few days, and Fordham's Chris Mahoney, who was an outfielder, a pitcher, and a good hitter, took his place.

He and I weren't the only college boys on that team, you know: Bill Carrigan, Jake Stahl, Larry Gardner, Duffy Lewis, Harry Hooper . . . even Speaker went to—not the University of Texas, but Texas Polyclinic, Polytechnic or something of that kind out there; only went for two years, but he went. And Ray Collins and Hughie Bradley, too. Buck O'Brien, he came the next year, he said, "I got a degree, I got a B.S. from Brockton." He said B.S. stood for boots and shoes, meaning that he worked in a factory.

Now, on this day in Cleveland we had Chris Mahoney playing right field, Harry Hooper moved over to center, and Duffy Lewis stayed in left, and Patsy Donovan put me in to pitch my first game in the big leagues against Joe Jackson and those Cleveland boys.

I wasn't what you'd call sloppily relaxed, but I wasn't particularly nervous, either. You see, I was one of the most egotistical guys that God ever put on this earth: I felt that I could beat anybody. I struck out ten of those Naps, including Jackson. The first time he was up, I had Joe two strikes, no balls, and I did something that the average big-league pitcher would never do. Instead of trying to fool him with a pitch, I stuck the next one right through there and caught him flat-footed. He never dreamed I'd do that.

So the next time up there the same thing happened. He hit a foul, then took a strike, and then Red Kleinow, an old head who was catching me, came out for a conference. He said, "What do you want to pitch him, a curveball?" And I said, "No, I'm going to stick another fast one right through there."

He said, "He'll murder it." Well—he did! Joe hit a ball that was like a shot out of a rifle against the right-field wall. Harry Hooper retrieved it in *left* center!

Yes, I had ten strikeouts, but I lost the ballgame. It was one of those sun-field things: a fellow named Hohnhurst was playing first base for Cleveland and, with a man on first, he hit a long fly to left-center field. Harry Hooper, who was in center this day, was dead certain on fly balls, but when Speaker was out there, as Harry said afterwards, he used to let Speaker take everything within range. Harry said he and Duffy Lewis didn't exactly get their signals crossed, but they were not sure as to who was going to take the ball.

Finally Duffy went for it, and just as he made his pitch for the ball the sun hit him right between the eyes and he didn't get his hands on the thing and the run, of course, scored, and Hohnhurst, the fellow who hit the ball—he got himself to second base. Ted Easterly got a single on top of that, and anyway, the score ended up 4–3. That was it.

I was supposed to be a spitball pitcher, but I had a better overhand curve, what they called a drop curve—you'd get that overspin on it and that ball would break much better than a spitter. I had what they call a medium-good fastball, not overpowering but good enough, and if you took something off your curve and your spitter, your fastball looked a lot better. For my slow one, the change-up as they call it now, I tried a knuckler but never could get any results with it, so I stole Eddie Karger's slow-breaking downer. He and I used to take two fingers off the ball and throw it with the same motion as we used for the fastball.

They still have those fellows today that throw spitters, but it doesn't make much difference—because even when the spitter was legal in my day, in both leagues you couldn't pick six good spitball pitchers. You'd take a fellow like Ed Walsh with the White Sox, the two Coveleskis, Burleigh Grimes, and the left-handed spitter in the National League, who has since lost both legs, Clarence Mitchell.

Now, Clarence was a good spitball pitcher, but Walsh was the best. He worked harder at it, had a better break, had better control of it, and he pitched in more ballgames than any pitcher in either league over a period of years.

Eddie Cicotte, he was with us in Boston, you know, he was going with a spitter for a while. He used to throw that emery ball, too, and then he developed what we call the "shine" ball. He used to have paraffin on different parts of his trousers, which was not legal, and he would just go over all the stitches with that paraffin, making the other part of the ball rougher. It was just like the emery situation, but in reverse, and an emery ball is one of the most dangerous, not like the spitter, which can be controlled. But Cicotte's main pitch was the knuckle ball, and he used that to such an extent that we called him Knuckles.

Joe Wood was with the Red Sox when I joined them, too. Now, there was a fellow who could do nearly everything well. He was a great ballplayer, not just a pitcher, he was a good outfielder, he was a good hitter, he was a good baseman, he would run like blazes, he used to work real hard before a ballgame, he was just a good all-around ballplayer and a great pitcher. And he was a fine pool player, too, and billiards. He could play any kind of a card game and well; also he was a good golfer. I think that he could have done nearly everything. If he were playing football, he'd be a good quarterback.

Joey was a natural—and talking about egotistical people, there's a guy who had terrific confidence, terrific. Without being too fresh, he was very cocky, you know. He just had "the old confidence."

I wasn't with Boston the year they won the World's Championship and Joey won those thirty-four games and then three more against the Giants, but I was at the Series and wrote a story about that final game. I saw the Snodgrass muff—he was careless, and that happens. But right after that he made a gorgeous running catch.

Earlier in that game Harry Hooper made the best catch I ever saw. I hear from Harry twice a year or so; he lives in California, and he's got plenty of the world's goods. Harry made this catch—he had his back to the ball—and from the bench it looked like he caught it backhanded, over his shoulder. After I sent my story to him, he wrote to me. "I thought it was a very good catch, too," he said, "but you were wrong in your perspective. When I ran for that ball, I ran with my back toward it and you guys with your craning necks were so excited about it, when I ran into the low fence"—you see, the bleachers came up from a low fence in Fenway—"the fence turned me around halfway to the right and I caught the ball in my bare right hand." Imagine!

In 1913 I joined the Yankees—they weren't called the Highlanders any more— and then three years later I went back to the Red Sox. Bill Carrigan, who was the Boston manager then, said, "Now that you're seasoned enough you can come back and pitch for a *big-league* team." The Yankees in those days were a terrible ballclub. In 1914 I lost sixteen games and won only seven, with an earned-run average under three. I got no runs. I would be beaten one to nothing, two to nothing, three to one, scores like that. You were never ahead of anybody. You can't win without runs. Take this fellow who's pitching for the Mets, Roger Craig, what did he lose—twenty-two, something like that? What did he win—five? One to nothing, two to nothing, terrible.

When I got to New York, Frank Chance was the manager, a great guy. He had a reputation as a really tough egg, but if you went out there and worked and hustled and showed him that you were interested in what you were doing, he would certainly be in your corner, to the extent that he would try and get you more money come contract time.

I have a watch, one of these little "wafer" watches, that Chance gave me in 1914 after I guess about the first month. I had won a couple of games for him, one of them was the opening game against the World Champion A's, and one day, just as a gesture, he said, he gave me this watch.

Frank and I were such good friends that late in 1914, when we were playing a series in Washington, after dinner, one evening he said let's take a little walk. So we went out to a park across from the hotel and sat down. "I'm going to quit," he said. "I can't stand this being manager, can't stand being the manager of this ballclub."

He said, "We're not going to get anyplace. I've got a good pitching staff"— and he did have a good pitching staff—"but you fellows are just batting your heads against the wall every time you go out there, no runs." The owners wouldn't get him any players, see, and he said, "I just can't take it—I'm going to quit."

He had already talked it over with the front office in New York, and one of

the reasons he took me out to the park was that he had told them which men he thought they should keep, and I happened to be one of three pitchers along with Slim Caldwell and Ray Fisher, and he said I know that you'll be working in vaudeville next winter and I would advise you to get yourself a two- or three-year contract, if you can, before you leave New York on your tour, which was very good advice—which advice I didn't take. I was too smart—you know how it is, very smart—so Mike Donlin and I went out on the Orpheum circuit that winter after opening at the Palace.

So Mike, before we left New York, he said, you better go over to the Yankee office and get yourself signed in before we leave for Chicago. He said, you never can tell what's going to happen. I, being very, very smart, I said, "No, I'll be worth more money to them in the spring than I am now after the publicity we will get in vaudeville this winter."

But I was wrong, because during the winter, while we were in Minneapolis at the Orpheum theater, Devery and Farrell sold the team to Ruppert and Huston. I'm quite sure I could have made a deal with Frank Farrell for a two- or three-year contract before leaving, but as I say I wasn't very smart.

When we got back east, Bill Donovan (that's Bill, not Patsy) had been appointed manager of the Yankees, and he was not in favor of anybody having a long-term contract. I didn't even last out the year with him.

It seemed every time I pitched against Washington I had Walter Johnson as an opponent, or Jim Shaw, either one. Griffith, he used to . . . I don't know . . . I had an idea he didn't pitch them against Caldwell. It seemed that every time Slim pitched, the team would get him three or four runs—though he didn't need them, he was a great pitcher.

Was Johnson as great a pitcher as they say? Let me tell you, he was *greater* than they say. He was with one of the worst ballclubs imaginable, not quite as bad as the old Yankees but almost as bad.

When I got out of the Air Service, after the War—you see, I quit baseball on the Fourth of July, I think, in 1917 and went into the Air Service—when I came out I went to work for the New York *Evening Sun*. I wrote articles, and the *Sun* used to run them every Saturday. The Wheeler Syndicate used to sell them to—wherever they could sell them, Boston, Philadelphia, Newark, anywhere they could, you know, and I used to get five, two, four, eight dollars apiece for them, and one of the stories that I wrote was about Walter Johnson.

I wrote one about Joey, too, and about Cicotte, and Mathewson, oh, so many of them. In the story about Johnson, I wondered what would have happened if he had been pitching for the Giants, who could get him five or six runs nearly every time he started, and I'm wondering if he'd *ever* lose a ballgame. I found out from Joe Vila, who was the sports editor for the Sun, that Matty didn't care very much for that.

Matty was a very good friend of Mike's, and so was McGraw, who was my sponsor into the Lambs Club. He was a Jekyll and Hyde character. Off the field he was very affable, but the minute he'd get in uniform, he was one of the toughest guys you'd ever want to know. Mike used to tell me a lot of inside information, which of course helped me when I was writing these stories.

Do you know about the movie Speaker and I made? In 1917, just before I went into the Service, we produced a motion picture of the big stars in both major leagues. We had $80,000 worth of bookings for the picture, and then they declared baseball during the War not essential, so all the bookings, were canceled. We sold the rights to the YMCA to use it in the camps all over Europe, in the ships going over and back, and in the camps here.

After the War was over I showed the film to my friend Roxy, God rest him, and he took the thing over and showed it at the Rivoli and the Rialto and down to Fifth Avenue, and then I happened to come into Wall Street to work as a stockbroker—in 1920 I started my own firm, which I still run today—and I forgot all about the film.

It was put in the morgue some place up at the Rialto or the Rivoli, and the YMCA lost their prints somewhere over in France, but I had left in the tins some cuts and out-takes of the shots of—well, Speaker, Hooper, Ruth, Wood, Matty, and Johnson and all, and I still have them. I showed the clips only about two years ago at the Pathé projection room one day and they still look pretty good.

The game's a lot different today from what it was when I played. The biggest change—and the worst one, in my opinion—is the home run. Now, let's first talk of the fellow going up to the plate. Seventy-five percent of the time he goes up there with the thought of hitting the ball out of the ballpark, and it's not too difficult to do, because they have moved the ballpark in on him. Now, in right field and center field and left field, you've got stands. They used to have a bleacher, way out, in the old days, but the only home run you'd get would be if you hit it between the fielders. "In grounds," they'd call it, a home run in grounds: if a ball got in between those fielders and if you had any speed, they wouldn't be able to throw you out. Today, if you hit a good long fly it's in one of these short stands.

In the old days they juiced up the ball some, but when they talk about the dead ball—there *never* was any dead ball that I can remember. I've got a couple of scars on my chin to prove it. I saw Joe Jackson hit a ball over the top of the Polo Grounds in right field—*over the top of it*—off one of our pitchers, and I have never seen or heard of anyone hitting it over since, and that was around 1914–15, in there.

Today's ball is livelier, no doubt of that. They are using an Australian wool now in winding the core of the ball. In the old days they used wool but not one that is as elastic as this wool. The bats are whippier, too. But the principal reason for all these homers is the concentration of the hitter on trying to hit the ball out of the park.

The fielding today? Well, any of these boys in the big leagues today could field in any league at any time. I think the better equipment has more to do with the spectacular play. You take this here third baseman up with the Yankees—Clete Boyer—he's terrific, just terrific. Larry Gardner, who played third on the Boston team with me, he was a great third baseman, and he had that "trolley-wire throw" to first, but Larry was not as agile as Boyer. I think Boyer is a little quicker. But, if you want a fellow to compare with Boyer, take Buck Weaver of that Black Sox team. He would field with Boyer any day, and throw with him, and he was a better hitter. He would be my all-time third baseman.

Players of my day, give them the good equipment, and they would be just as good or better. Now, you take a fellow like Wagner—I don't mean the Wagner we had with the Red Sox, but the Pirates' Wagner, Honus Wagner, who came to see us in Pittsburgh at the theater, and he took up the whole dressing room with that big can of his. There was one of the most awkward-looking humans you ever saw, but he made the plays, without the shovel glove. And Speaker—could a big glove have made him any better?

As an outfielder, Speaker was in a class by himself. He would play so close to the infield that he'd get in on rundown plays! Then the next man perhaps would hit a long fly into center field and he would be on his bicycle with his back to the ball—not backing away, he'd turn and run—and you'd think he had a radar or a magnet or something because just at the proper time he'd turn his head and catch the ball over his shoulder.

Those fellows, Speaker, Lewis, and Hooper, they used to practice throwing, something that you don't see anymore. Those fellows would have a cap down near the catcher and they'd see who would come closest to the cap when they'd throw from the outfield. They all had marvelous arms. Nobody would run on them, and I think that most of the people who ever saw them play would say there was no trio that could compare with them.

Mike and I, in our act, we used to do a number called, "When You're a Long, Long Way From Home." In it I used to do a recitation, and the last two lines were, "When you're on third base alone, you're still a long, long way from home." It was serious, about life being like a game of baseball. Times have changed—a boy can't peek through a knothole in a concrete fence—but that's still true.

In the year Marty McHale spoke with Ritter, a rookie named Rose broke in with the Cincinnati Reds. He played second base then—rather well, too, though he didn't *look* like a second baseman. When he moved to left field, and right field, and third base, and finally first base, he wrestled those positions to the mat as well, never stylishly but always efficiently. At the bat he conjured up no visions of DiMaggio's dignity or Williams's fluidity or Mantle's power, but he chugged along until one day he woke up to find himself within striking distance of the Everest of batting records: Ty Cobb's 4,191 hits. Pete Rose has played the game with the vigor and drive of Cobb, though without his repellent ferocity. A throwback to the values of the dead ball era, a proud anachronism, Rose has played baseball with a unique vision that has, over two decades' time, been accompanied by an engaging voice. Here, *Quotations from Chairman Pete*, or, *The Little Red Book*.

PETE ROSE

La Vie en Rose

On awards: "I have gathered together a whole heap of trophies. The only award I've never won and don't ever want to win is the Comeback of the Year Award."

On sliding headfirst: "Sliding headfirst is the safest way to get to the next base, I think. And the fastest. You don't lose your momentum. . . . And there is one more important reason that I slide headfirst. It gets my picture in the newspaper."

On being a manager: "The manager of a team is like a stagecoach. He can't move unless he has the horses."

On happiness: "Making good money and having fun doing it at the same time is almost like having a license to steal. But there is the old saying that money can't buy happiness. If it could, I would buy myself four hits every game."

On self-control: "Everyone has seen a batter strike out. This grown man throws his bat and then kicks his helmet. Why did he take it out on the helmet and the bat? He was the one who couldn't hit the ball. If you want to do something to show you are angry, go beat your own head against the wall. You are the one who struck out."

On road games: "I like to play on the road. I usually get an extra time at bat out of a road game. The visiting team always seems to hit in the ninth inning. When you are at home and are leading in the game, you lose the possible at bat in the last of the ninth."

On team loyalty: "Sparky [Anderson] used to say that you don't win any games by staying in the clubhouse. I agree with him, so I have never been late. I have never missed batting practice. I've never missed a bus. I've never missed an airplane. But I do get sick once in a while."

On tough pitchers: "When people ask me, 'Who was the toughest pitcher you ever faced?', I have to say that there has never been a pitcher who over-impressed me. That's not meant to be a bragging statement. It's just that I get up for good pitchers."

On celebrations: "I don't drink. And if you don't drink, you don't celebrate very well. The real celebration comes only when the champagne flows after you win the World Series."

On having a street named for him in Cincinnati: "They should have named an alley after me for the way I acted in high school."

On New York Mets fans: "I enjoy Shea Stadium. But the fans are something else. I look upon each game there as an experience. I get to go to a zoo and don't have to pay admission."

On emotion: "It doesn't take much to get me up for baseball. Once the National Anthem plays, I get chills; I even know the words to it now."

On Ty Cobb: "I doubt that his lifetime .367 batting average would hold up in modern-day baseball. If Ty Cobb came up in 1963 like I did, he'd have a batting average of about .320."

To Carlton Fisk, in the tenth inning of Game Six of the 1975 Series: "This is some kind of game, isn't it?"

On winning: "Somebody's gotta win and somebody's gotta lose—and I believe in letting the other guy lose."

On speed: "I'm not a great runner. I'm no Joe Morgan, but I'm not bad for a white guy."

On fame: "I always say, the only time you gotta worry about getting booed is when you're wearing a white uniform. And I've never been booed wearing a white uniform."

On his love of the game: "I'd walk through hell in a gasoline suit to keep playing baseball."

Baseball is the great repository of national myths—commonly held beliefs that may or may not be "true," in baseball or in American life: fair play (sportsmanship), the rule of law (objective arbitration of disputes), equal opportunity (each side has its innings), the brotherhood of man (bleacher demographics), and so on. Baseball also provides contests and contestants of epic scale: the oft-told tales rise to the realm of myth, from which heights they nurture life and literature. This essay was published on the *New York Times* Op-Ed page on Opening Day, 1973.

PHILIP ROTH

My Baseball Years

In one of his essays George Orwell writes that, though he was not very good at the game, he had a long hopeless love affair with cricket until he was sixteen. My relations with baseball were similar. Between the ages of nine and thirteen, I must have put in a forty-hour week during the snowless months over at the neighborhood playfield—softball, hardball, and stickball pick-up games—while simultaneously holding down a full-time job as a pupil at the local grammar school. As I remember it, news of two of the most cataclysmic public events of my childhood—the death of President Roosevelt and the bombing of Hiroshima—reached me while I was out playing ball. My performance was uniformly erratic; generally okay for those easygoing pick-up games, but invariably lacking the calm and the expertise that the naturals displayed in stiff competition. My taste, and my talent, such as it was, was for the flashy, whiz-bang catch rather than the towering fly; running and leaping I loved, all the do-or-die stuff—somehow I lost confidence waiting and waiting for the ball lofted right at me to descend. I could never make the high-school team, yet I remember that, in one of the two years I vainly (in both senses of the word) tried out, I did a good enough imitation of a baseball player's *style* to be able to fool (or amuse) the coach right down to the day he cut the last of the dreamers from the squad and gave out the uniforms.

Though my disappointment was keen, my misfortune did not necessitate a change in plans for the future. Playing baseball was not what the Jewish boys of our lower-middle-class neighborhood were expected to do in later life for a living. Had I been cut from the high school itself, *then* there would have been hell to pay in my house, and much confusion and shame in me. As it was, my family took my chagrin in stride and lost no more faith in me than I actually did in myself. They probably would have been shocked if I had made the team.

Maybe I would have been too. Surely it would have put me on a somewhat different footing with this game that I loved with all my heart, not simply for the fun of playing it (fun was secondary, really), but for the mythic and aesthetic dimension that it gave to an American boy's life—particularly to one whose grandparents could hardly speak English. For someone whose roots in America were strong but only inches deep, and who had no experience, such as a Catholic child might, of an awesome hierarchy that was real and felt, baseball was a kind of secular church that reached into every class and region of the nation and bound millions upon millions of us together in common concerns, loyalties, rituals, enthusiasms, and antagonisms. Baseball made me understand what patriotism was about, at its best.

Not that Hitler, the Bataan Death March, the battle for the Solomons, and the Normandy invasion didn't make of me and my contemporaries what may well have been the most patriotic generation of schoolchildren in American history (and the most willingly and successfully propagandized). But the war we entered when I was eight had thrust the country into what seemed to a child—and not only to a child—a struggle to the death between Good and Evil. Fraught with perilous, unthinkable possibilities, it inevitably nourished a patriotism grounded in moral virtue and bloody-minded hate, the patriotism that fixes a bayonet to a Bible. It seems to me that through baseball I was put in touch with a more humane and tender brand of patriotism, lyrical rather than martial or righteous in spirit, and without the reek of saintly zeal, a patriotism that could not so easily be sloganized, or contained in a high-sounding formula to which you had to pledge something vague but all-encompassing called your "allegiance."

To sing the National Anthem in the school auditorium every week, even during the worst of the war years, generally left me cold. The enthusiastic lady teacher waved her arms in the air and we obliged with the words: "See! Light! Proof! Night! There!" But nothing stirred within, strident as we might be—in the end, just another school exercise. It was different, however, on Sundays out at Ruppert Stadium, a green wedge of pasture miraculously walled in among the factories, warehouses, and truck depots of industrial Newark. It would, in fact, have seemed to me an emotional thrill forsaken if, before the Newark Bears took on the hated enemy from across the marshes, the Jersey City Giants, we hadn't first to rise to our feet (my father, my brother, and I—along with our inimical countrymen, the city's Germans, Italians, Irish, Poles, and, out in the Africa of the bleachers, Newark's Negroes) to celebrate the America that had given to this unharmonious mob a game so grand and beautiful.

Just as I first learned the names of the great institutions of higher learning by trafficking in football pools for a neighborhood bookmaker rather than from our high school's college adviser, so my feel for the American landscape came less from what I learned in the classroom about Lewis and Clark than from following the major-league clubs on their road trips and reading about the minor leagues in the back pages of *The Sporting News.* The size of the continent got through to you finally when you had to stay up to 10:30 P.M. in New Jersey to hear via radio "ticker-tape" Cardinal pitcher Mort Cooper throw the first strike of the night to Brooklyn shortstop Pee Wee Reese out in "steamy" Sportsman's Park in St. Louis, Missouri. And however much we might be told by teacher about the stockyards and the Haymarket riot, Chicago only began to exist for me as a real place, and to matter in American history, when I became fearful (as a Dodger fan) of the bat of Phil Cavarretta, first baseman for the Chicago Cubs.

Not until I got to college and was introduced to literature did I find anything with a comparable emotional atmosphere and aesthetic appeal. I don't mean to suggest that it was a simple exchange, one passion for another. Between first discovering the Newark Bears and the Brooklyn Dodgers at seven or eight and first looking into Conrad's *Lord Jim* at age eighteen, I had done some growing up. I am only saying that my discovery of literature, and fiction particularly, and the "love affair"—to some degree hopeless, but still earnest—that has ensued, derives in part from this childhood infatuation with baseball. Or, more accurately perhaps, baseball—with its lore and legends, its cultural power, its seasonal associations, its native authenticity, its simple rules and transparent strategies, its longueurs and thrills, its spaciousness, its suspensefulness, its heroics, its nuances, its lingo, its "characters," its peculiarly hypnotic tedium, its mythic transformation of the immediate—was the literature of my boyhood.

Baseball, as played in the big leagues, was something completely outside my own life that could nonetheless move me to ecstasy and to tears; like fiction it could excite the imagination and hold the attention as much with minutiae as with high drama. Mel Ott's cocked leg striding into the ball, Jackie Robinson's pigeon-toed shuffle as he moved out to second base, each was to be as deeply affecting over the years as that night—"inconceivable," "inscrutable," as any night Conrad's Marlow might struggle to comprehend—the night that

Dodger wild man, Rex Barney (who never lived up to "our" expectations, who should have been "our" Koufax), not only went the distance without walking in half a dozen runs, but, of all things, threw a no-hitter. A thrilling mystery, marvelously enriched by the fact that a light rain had fallen during the early evening, and Barney, figuring the game was going to be postponed, had eaten a hot dog just before being told to take the mound.

This detail was passed on to us by Red Barber, the Dodger radio sportscaster of the forties, a respectful, mild Southerner with a subtle rural tanginess to his vocabulary and a soft country-parson tone to his voice. For the adventures of "dem bums" of Brooklyn—a region then the very symbol of urban wackiness and tumult—to be narrated from Red Barber's highly alien but loving perspective constituted a genuine triumph of what my English professors would later teach me to call "point of view." James himself might have admired the implicit cultural ironies and the splendid possibilities for oblique moral and social commentary. And as for the detail about Rex Barney eating his hot dog, it was irresistible, joining as it did the spectacular to the mundane, and furnishing an adolescent boy with a glimpse of an unexpectedly ordinary, even humdrum, side to male heroism.

Of course, in time, neither the flavor and suggestiveness of Red Barber's narration nor "epiphanies" as resonant with meaning as Rex Barney's pregame hot dog could continue to satisfy a developing literary appetite; nonetheless, it was just this that helped to sustain me until I was ready to begin to respond to the great inventors of narrative detail and masters of narrative voice and perspective like James, Conrad, Dostoevsky, and Bellow.

"Baseball-American," Ring Lardner called it in his 1921 contribution to H. L. Mencken's *The American Language*. Purists then deplored the incursion of ballfield patois into the native speech, but they were way off base. How pale a thing American English would be without *bonehead, rhubarb, rain check, pinch hitter, change-up, hit-and-run, rabbit ears*, and such. William Safire's lexicographic home run was written during the baseball strike of 1981, when the players took their ball and went home. (The previous strikes alluded to in the opening words took place in 1972 and 1912; correctly, William Safire does not count the season-long rebellion of 1890, in which the players formed their own league.)

WILLIAM SAFIRE

Out of Left Field

Because baseball's third strike has so impoverished the daily reading of the nation's national-pastime junkies, here is a survey from the Hot Stove League of the effect of baseball on the American language.

When a professor of atmospheric science predicted that recent changes in the sun's activity foretold a dry spell of several years in the Northeast, another expert—Robert Harnack, a meteorologist at Rutgers—called that forecast "completely out of left field."

Where in the heavens or on earth is "left field"? How did that area on the baseball field become the metaphoric epitome of far-outedness? To come "*from* out *of* left field" is to be rooted in the ridiculous, crackbrained, farfetched; to "*be* out *in* left field" is, according to *American Speech* magazine in 1961, to be "disoriented, out of contact with reality."

When asked for the derivation, members of the Abner Doubleday Lodge of the Lexicographic Irregulars lobbed in these ideas:

"In the older, less symmetrical baseball stadia," writes Robert J. Wilson, Jr., of Riverside, Connecticut, "left field was usually 'deeper' than right, and thus coming from left field was coming in from a 'far-out' region."

Our ambassador to the European office of the United Nations, Gerald Helman, writes from Geneva: "Right field was thought of as the most difficult to play because it was the 'sun field,' and required the fielder to have a strong arm for the long throw to third. As a consequence, the good hitting, poor fielding players were put in left. . . . Because of the defensive inadequacies of left fielders, you could expect almost anything to happen when the ball was hit to them."

On the other hand: "The power of a batter in baseball or softball is to his/her 'pull,' or opposite field," posits Thomas Carter of Dayton. "Since some 90 percent of the population is right-handed, this means that many more long hits can be expected to left field. Therefore, the left fielder will usually play farther back than the other outfielders. This then leads to the linking of 'left field' to a person, thing, or idea that is far out." Could be.

"Left field is about as far as one can get from the desirable seats," suggests Morton Brodsky of Lancaster, Pennsylvania. "The home team's bench is generally, if not always, along the first-base line. This makes the preference for hometown fans (1) from home plate to first base, (2) from home plate to third base, (3) right field, (4) left field. Of course, modern stadia have seating all the way around, but I think that 'out in left field' originated in the days when there was nothing out there but a fence."

"Imagine some right-hander of yesteryear (a preponderance of pioneer pitchers were right-handed)," says Jerry Oster of New York City, "with a big sidearm delivery such that the ball, especially to a right-handed batter, seemed to come out of left field."

Since the earliest citation of the phrase appeared in *American Speech*, I queried the editor of that publication, John Algeo, who is one of the heavy hitters in the big league of linguistics today. He assumed it had at least a pseudobaseball origin and appeared early in psychiatric slang; then he tossed himself a fat pitch: "The explanation that the left field was far off from the home base overlooks the fact that the right field is equally far from the home base and the center field is even farther. Why then left field instead of right field or center field?"

Professor Algeo took a hefty cut: "My guess (and it is no more than a guess) is that the expression is a metaphor referring to a baseball field, but was never actually a baseball term. Probably it was coined by someone who watched baseball but was not a player or real aficionado.

"To be in the *outfield* is to be far out. However, the expression *out in the outfield* is uneuphonious, redundant, and too general; it doesn't make a snappy remark. *Center* and *right* both have highly positive connotations that conflict with the sense of isolation that the term was wanted for. . . . *Center* suggests all the virtues of moderation and the golden mean. *Right* suggests correctness, dexterity, and so on (we don't have to go into the political associations). *Left* is certainly the best word for associations—lefties are a minority, they are sinister (etymologically at least) and (at least by pun) they get left behind."

Mr. Algeo concurs with Irregular Carter's observation that balls hit to left field are usually hit harder, causing the fielder to play deeper: "Since the left fielder is farther removed from the center of action in the infield, his position becomes a metaphor for isolation."

In addition, consider the flakiness factor: "Center field would not be appropriate," agrees David Zinman, science editor for *Newsday*, after checking with Stan Isaacs, who used to write a sports column called "Out of Left Field," "because it is the mainstream of the outfield. 'Right' field denotes correctness. . . . On the other hand, 'left' field has overtones of radicalism in politics. Also, left-handers, particularly pitchers, are often thought of as slightly different, sometimes screwy or dizzy individuals."

Like Lucy in the comic strip "Peanuts," Mrs. Melvin Golub of Dunkirk, Maryland, disagrees with everybody; it is her experience that "one rarely hits to left field. The outfielder has little to do; hence, he is lonely. . . . When our company plays softball, my son sends me out to play left field so I can't get into too much trouble." Such an iconoclastic view flies in the face of all statistics about where most hard-hit balls go, and is truly out of left field.

Ballpark Figure

First up, we have just seen how baseball is a rich source for metaphors. How many other expressions owe their origin to the game that started as "rounders" in England, became "the New York game" in the 1840s, and was spread across the United States by the New York and New Jersey regiments during the Civil War? I don't have even a ballpark figure.

Ballpark figure, however, stems from *ball grounds* and *ball fields* in the mid-nineteenth century, to *baseball park* in the 1890s, to *in the ballpark* around 1960.

"That's the windup," says lexicographer Stuart Flexner, who intends to demolish the Abner Doubleday myth in his next book. "Now here's the pitch: Our Random House dictionary citation files show the term first started out as *in the ballpark* (1962), as when talking about figures, estimates, etc., with 'I hope that's in the ballpark.' Then, in 1968, we first recorded *ballpark figure* from *The Seattle Times*."

Evidently the ballpark was used as a microcosm: To be *in the ballpark* (even if out in left field) was to be "in this world," just as to be *out of the ballpark* meant to be "totally out of play." Thus, an estimate—or "guesstimate"—that was adjudged within the range of reasonableness was *in the ballpark*, and a number of that sort recently became a *ballpark figure*.

Baseball terms were given wide circulation by the newspaper *baseball col-*

umn (1869), a creation of *The Brooklyn Union.* "Such columns," reports Flexner, "grew into the popular *sporting column, sporting page,* and *sporting section* (created primarily for baseball fans) in the 1890s, then became known as the *sports page* or *sports section* in the 1920s."

Other baseball metaphors and their debut dates: *to keep one's eye on the ball,* 1907; *to be off base* (disrespectful, wrong), 1912, which was also the year that introduced *to have something on the ball; right off the bat,* 1916; *go to bat for* (to support or defend), 1928; *to play ball with* (cooperate), 1930; *to be in there pitching* and *to take a rain check,* also the thirties. (The first rain check Flexner has was issued in St. Louis in 1884; if you have an earlier one, send it to him. They'll never replay that game.)

We've come to the final inning. Time to head for the dugout.

This is how it was when boys' baseball was still a game, before Little League came along. The passage below is from the 1975 novel *Pride of the Bimbos*; its author is John Sayles, also a film director and screenwriter whose credits include *Return of the Secaucus Seven* and *The Brother from Another Planet*. In 1981 he wrote, "I never thought about being a writer as I grew up; a writer wasn't something to *be*. An outfielder was something to be. Most of what I know about style I learned from Roberto Clemente." The Brooklyn Bimbos of Birmingham, Alabama, are a five-man barnstorming team that plays county fairs in the South. Denzel, the prime actor here, is the nine-year-old son of player Lewis Crawford and travels with the team.

JOHN SAYLES

Pick-up Game

Denzel wandered toward them with his glove under his arm. A few were in the outfield, crowding under liners and pop-ups that a tall boy threw them. "I got it!" they called in unison, "Mine, mine!" Off to one side a dark, barrel-chested kid was playing pepper with a boy who had a bandage over his eye. The rest milled around, joking, tossing gloves and hats in the air, fighting over the remaining bat to take practice swings. They all seemed to know each other.

Denzel squatted next to a thin boy who sat on his glove at the fringe of the action, watching expectantly. He was the only one there smaller than Denzel.

"Gonna be a game?"

"Uh-huh." The thin boy looked up at him, surprised.

"They got regular teams?"

"Nope. They pick sides."

Denzel nodded.

"Hope I get to play," said the thin boy. "When the teams don't come out even I got to sit," he said, "every single time."

He waited for a word of support but Denzel just grunted and moved several feet away. Might think we come together.

The ones on what seemed to be the field hacked around a little longer until a movement to start a game began. "Let's go," someone said. "Get this show on the road."

"Somebody be captains."

"Somebody choose up."

Gradually they wandered in and formed a loose group around a piece of packing crate broken roughly in the shape of a home plate. They urged each other to get organized and shrugged their indifference over who would be the captains.

"C'mon, we don't have all day."

"Somebody just choose."

"Big kids against the little kids!" said a fat boy in glasses and they all laughed.

"Good guys against the bad guys!"

"Winners against the losers!"

"The men against the mice!"

"Okay," said the dark, barrel-chested kid, "Whynt we just have the same captains as yesterday?"

"Yeah, but not the same teams."

"Too lopsided."

"That was a slaughter."

"We got scobbed."

"Do it then," said the fat boy, "Bake and the Badger."

"Yeah, shoot for first pick."

"Let's go, choose up."

There was a sudden movement, everybody spreading in a semicircle around two of the boys, jostling not to be behind anyone, the thin boy hopping up and running to join them. Denzel got up slowly and walked to the rear of them. No sense getting all hot and bothered. No big thing. He drifted through hips and shoulders, quietly, till he stood in view of the captains.

They were shooting fingers, best four out of seven, like the World Series. The barrel-chested boy was one of the captains, the one they called the Badger, and the tall boy who had been throwing flies was the other.

Denzel slipped his glove on. It was an oversized Ted Kluszewski model his daddy had handed down to him. Each of the fingers seemed thick as his wrist and there was no web to speak of and no padding in the pocket. Orange and gunky.

The tall boy won on the last shoot and the Badger scowled.

"Alley Oop!" Bake called without even looking.

"Haw-*raaat!*" A wiry kid with arms that hung to his knees trotted out from their midst and stood by Bake. "We got it now, can't lose. Can not *lose!*"

"Purdy!" The Badger barked it like an order and a solid-looking red-haired kid marched out and took his place.

The two first picks began to whisper and nudge at their captains.

"Vernon," whispered the wiry boy, "get Vernon."

"Vernon."

Vernon came to join them, and he and Alley Oop slapped each other's backs at being together.

"Royce," whispered the big redhead. "They get Royce we've had it."

"Royce," said the Badger, and Royce was welcomed into the fold.

"Psssst!" called the fat boy with the glasses to Alley Oop and Vernon. "Have him pick me. You guys need a third sacker."

"Ernie," they said, on their toes leaning over each of Bake's shoulders, "Ernierniernie!"

"Okay, Ernie," he said, and Ernie waddled out with his glove perched on top of his head.

"Gahs looked like you needed some help," he told them. "Never fear, Ernie is here!"

The captains began to take more time in their picking. They considered and consulted and looked down the line before calling out a name. The Badger pounded quick, steady socks into the pocket of his glove while beside him Purdy slowly flapped the jaws of his first-baseman's mitt. Soon there were more that had been chosen than that hadn't. The ones who were picked frisked and giggled behind their captains while the others who hadn't were statues on display. "You," the captains said now, still weighing abilities but unenthusiastic. Finally they just pointed. The Badger walked along the straggling line of left-overs like a general reviewing troops, stood in front of his next man and jerked his thumb back over his shoulder. When there was only one spot left for even teams Denzel and the thin boy were left standing. It was the Badger's pick.

Denzel stood at ease, eyes blank. It grew quiet. He felt the others checking him over and he smelled something. Topps bubble gum, the kind that came with baseball cards. He snuck a glance at the thin boy. His eyes were wide, fixed on the Badger, pleading. He had a round little puff of a catcher's mitt that looked like a red pincushion. There was no sign of a baseball ever having landed in it, no dent of a pocket.

Denzel felt the Badger considering him for a moment, eyes dipping to the thick-fingered old-timer's glove, but then he turned and gave a slight, exasperated nod to the thin boy. "We got him."

Before Denzel could get out of the way Bake's team streamed past him onto the field.

"First base!" they cried, "Dibs on shortstop!" Trotting around him as if he were a tree, looking through the space where he stood. "Bake?" they whined, "Lemme take left huh? I always get stuck at catcher or somethin." Denzel kept his face blank and tried to work the thing back down into his throat. They all knew each other, didn't know whether he was any good or not. No big thing.

He drifted off to the side, considered going back to the van, then sat beyond the third-base line to watch. As if that was what he had come to do in the first place. Nice day to watch a ballgame. He decided he would root for Bake's side.

"Me first," said the Badger, pointing with the bat handle, "you second, you third. Purdy you clean up. Fifth, sixth, semeightnon." They had full teams so Denzel couldn't offer to be all-time catcher and dive for foul tips. You didn't get to bat but it kept you busy and you could show them you could catch. Denzel kept his glove on.

He could tell he was better than a lot of them before they even started and some of the others when the end of the orders got up. The pitching was overhand but not fast. There was a rock that stuck out of the ground for first base and some cardboard that kept blowing so they had to put sod clumps on it for second and somebody's T-shirt for third. Bake played shortstop and was good and seemed a little older than the others. The one called Purdy, the big red-headed one, fell to his knees after he struck out. Everybody had backed way up for him. Alley Oop made a nice one-handed catch in center. Whenever there was a close play at a base, Badger would run over and there would be a long argument and he would win. The thin boy had to be backed up at catcher by the batting team so it wouldn't take forever to chase the pitches that went through. The innings went a long time even when there weren't a lot of runs because the pitchers were trying tricky stuff and couldn't get it close. Denzel followed the action carefully, keeping track of the strikes and outs and runs scored, seeing who they backed up for and who they moved in for, who couldn't catch, who couldn't throw, keeping a book on them the way his daddy and Pogo had taught him he should. When fat Ernie did something funny he laughed a little along with the rest of them. Once somebody hit a grounder too far off to the left for the third baseman or left fielder to bother chasing. "Little help!" they called, and Denzel scrambled after it. He backhanded it moving away, turned and whipped it hard into the pitcher. No one seemed to notice. He sat back down and the game started up again.

The Badger's side got ahead by three and stayed there, the two teams trading one or two runs each inning. They joked and argued with each other while waiting to bat. They practiced slides and catches in stop-action slow-motion and pretended to be TV commentators, holding imaginary microphones and interviewing themselves. They kept up a baseball chatter.

"*Hum*babe!" said the team in the field, "Chuckeratinthere*iss*-gahcantit*iss*gahcatit! *Hum*babe! *Nostick*nostickchuckeratinthere—"

"*Lets*go!" said the team at bat, "*Biginninbig*inn*inwegottateamwegotta-team*bang*itonoutthere! *Letsgolets* go!"

Late in the fifth inning a mother's voice wailed over the babble from a distance.

"Jonathaaaan!"

There was a brief pause, the players looking at each other accusingly, seeing who would confess to being Jonathan.

"Jonathan Phelps you get in here!"

The thin boy with the catcher's mitt mumbled something, looking for a moment as if he were going to cry, then ran off toward the camp.

Denzel squatted and slipped his glove on again. He wore it with his two middle fingers out, not for style but so he could make it flex a little. He waited.

The tall boy, Bake, walked in a circle at shortstop with his glove on his hip, looking around. "Hey kid!"

Who me? Denzel raised his eyebrows and looked to Bake.

"You play catcher for them."

Denzel began to rise but the Badger ran out onto the field. "Whoa na! No deal. I'm not takin him. Got enough easy outs awriddy. Will play thout a catcher, you gahs just back up the plate and will have to send somuddy in to cover if there's a play there."

Denzell squatted again and looked to Bake.

"Got to have even teams," he said. "I got easy outs too. If you only got eight that means your big hitters get up more."

"I'm not takin him, that's all there is to it." The Badger never looked to Denzel. "We don't need a catcher that bad. Not gonna get stuck with some little fairy."

Bake sighed. "Okay. He'll catch for us and you can have what's his name. Hewitt."

The Badger thought a minute, scowling, then agreed. Hewitt tossed his glove off and was congratulated on being traded to the winning side.

"Okay," said Bake, "you go catch. You're up ninth."

Denzel hustled behind the plate and the game started up. There was no catcher's gear, so though it was hardball he stood and one-hopped the pitches. He didn't let anything get by him to the kid who was backing him up. He threw the ball carefully to the pitcher. There were no foul tips. Badger got on and got to third with two out. Bake called time. He sent the right fielder in to cover the play at the plate and Denzel out to right.

The one called Royce was up. Denzel had booked him as strictly a pull-hitter. He played medium depth and shaded toward center. The first baseman turned and yelled at him.

"What you doing there? Move over. Get back. This gah can cream it!"

He did what the first baseman said but began to cheat in and over with the delivery.

The second pitch was in on the fists but Royce swung and blooped a high one toward short right. Denzel froze still.

"Drop it!" they screamed.

"Choke!"

"Yiyiyiyiyi!"

"I got it!" yelled somebody close just as Denzel reached up and took it stinging smack in the pocket using both hands the way his daddy had told him and then he was crashed over from the side.

He held on to the ball. Alley Oop helped him to his feet and mumbled that he was sorry, he didn't know that he really had it. The Badger stomped down on home plate so hard it split in half.

"Look what I found!" somebody called.

"Whudja step in, kid?"

"Beginner's luck."

Denzel's team trotted in for its at bats. While they waited for the others to get in their positions Bake came up beside him.

"That mitt looks like you stole it out of a display window in the Hall of Fame," he said, and Denzel decided to smile. "Nice catch."

The first man up flied out to left and then Ernie stepped in. Ernie had made the last out of the inning before.

"Hold it! Hold it rat there!" Badger stormed in toward the plate. "Don't pull any of that stuff, who's up? Ninth man aint it? The new kid?"

"We changed the batting order," said Ernie. "You can do that when you make a substitution. The new kid bats in my spot and I bat where Hewitt was."

"Uhn-uh. No dice."

"That's the rules."

"Ernie," said Bake, stepping in and taking the bat from him, "let the kid have his ups. See what he can do."

Bake handed the bat to Denzel and the Badger stalked back into the field. It was a big, thick-handled bat, a Harmon Killebrew 34. Denzel liked the looks of the other one that was lying to the side but decided he'd stay with what he was given.

The Badger's team all moved in close to him. The center fielder was only a few yards behind second base.

"Tryn get a piece of it," said Ernie behind him, "just don't whiff, kid."

"Easyouteasyouteasyout!" came the chatter.

Denzel didn't choke up on the big bat. See what he can do.

The first four pitches were wide or too high. He let them pass.

"C'mon, let's go!"

"Wastin time."

"Swing at it."

"Let him hit," said the Badger. "Not goin anywheres."

The next one was way outside and he watched it.

"Come *awn!*" moaned the Badger, "s'rat *over!*"

"Whattaya want kid?"

"New batter, new batter!"

"Start calling strikes!"

"Egg in your beer?"

"See what he can do."

The pitcher shook his head impatiently and threw the next one high and inside. Denzel stepped back and tomahawked a shot down the line well over the left fielder's head.

"Attaboy! Go! Go!"

"Dig, baby, all the way!"

"Keep comin, bring it on!"

By the time the left fielder flagged it down and got it in Denzel was standing up with a triple.

"Way to hit! Way to hit, buddy."

"Sure you don't want him, Badger?"

"Foul ball," said the Badger. He was standing very still with his glove on his hip. "Take it over."

This time Bake and half his team ran out to argue. The Badger turned away and wouldn't listen to them.

"Get outa here," they said. "That was fair by a mile. You gotta be blind."

He wouldn't listen. "Foul ball."

"Get *off* it," they said, "you must be crazy."

Denzel sat on the base to wait it out. The third baseman sat on his glove beside him and said nice hit. The Badger began to argue, stomping around, his face turning red, finally throwing his glove down and saying he quit.

"Okay," said Bake, "have it your way."

"Nope." The Badger sulked off but not too far. "If you gonna cheat I don't want nothin to do with it."

"Don't *be* that way, Badger, dammit."

"Hell with you."

"Okay," said Bake, looking over to Denzel and shrugging for understanding, "we'll take it over."

Denzel lined the first pitch off the pitcher's knee and into right for a single. Three straight hits followed him and he crossed the plate with the tying run. The first baseman made an error and then the Badger let one through his legs and the game broke open.

Denzel sat back with the rest of the guys. They wrestled with each other and did knuckle-punches to the shoulder.

They compared talent with a professional eye.

"Royce is pretty fast."

"Not as fast as Alley Oop."

"Nobody's that fast."

"Alley Oop can *peel*."

"But Royce is a better hitter."

"Maybe for distance but not for average."

"Nobody can hit it far as Purdy."

"If he connects."

"Yeah, he always tries to kill the ball. You got to just meet it."

"But if he ever connects that thing is gonna sail."

"Kiss it goodbye."

"Going, going, *gone!*"

Denzel sat back among them without talking, but following their talk closely, putting it all in his book. Alley Oop scored and asked Bake to figure his average for him, and Bake drew the numbers in the dust with a stick till he came up with .625. That was some kind of average, everybody agreed. They batted through the order and Denzel got another single up the middle and died at second. It was getting late so they decided it would be last ups for Badger's team. The Badger was eight runs down and had given up.

Bake left Denzel in right for the last inning but nothing came his way. Purdy went down swinging for the last out and they split up. Bake and the Badger left together, laughing, but not before Bake asked Denzel his name and said see you tomorrow.

Denzel didn't tell him that he'd be gone tomorrow. That they'd have to go back to Jonathan Phelps.

Poor General Doubleday. Through no fault of his own, he is remembered chiefly today for the great game he did not start (and never professed to—all such claims were made on his behalf posthumously) and scarcely at all for the great conflict he did start (the Civil War, inasmuch as he aimed the first shot fired in defense of Fort Sumter). His ghost will find no rest in Dr. Seymour's definitive examination of our national pastime's origins. This article, contributed to the *New-York Historical Society Quarterly* in 1956, was based upon the research done for his doctoral dissertation, the first devoted to baseball. His two-volume scholarly history, *Baseball: The Early Years* and *Baseball: The Golden Age,* inspired a burst of first-rate baseball books by the academy, from Jules Tygiel, Steven Riess, and David Voigt, among others. Lest you suspect that Dr. Seymour learned his baseball in an ivory tower, let me report that he was born in Brooklyn, served as batboy for the Dodgers in 1925–27, coached semipro ballclubs, and scouted for the Red Sox.

HAROLD SEYMOUR, Ph.D.

How Baseball Began

Baseball in the United States is both a sport and a business. It is also an important social institution in our complex American society. Recognized as the "national game," it has become a symbol of America in much the same way that the Olympic Games are associated with Greece or cricket with England. Baseball even has a mythology of its own. Part of that myth enshrines its origin. Traditionally, baseball is accepted as a home-grown product; but actually it is no more indigenous to the United States than the automobile or the idea of mass production in factories. The fact that baseball, too, had its inception abroad bolsters a truth frequently overlooked or ignored—that most inventions, ideas, and institutions seldom are the work of one individual in one country.

The myth concerning the origin of baseball began to take shape in the spring of 1889 at famous Delmonico's in New York City, where some 300 people, including such public figures as Mark Twain and Chauncey M. Depew, gathered to fete the squad of professional baseball players, headed by Albert G. Spalding, just returned from their world tour. Organized baseball had just approached the end of a decade of financial success and increasing popularity in America; and Spalding, then president of the Chicago Club and also head of a thriving sporting goods business, had felt the time opportune for spreading the gospel of the American national game abroad. He therefore had headed a band of professionals, consisting of his own club and a picked group of all-stars from the rest of the National League, on a globe-circling exhibition trip that included stops at Honolulu, Australia, and the Pyramids, and a game in England with the Prince of Wales among the spectators.

At the banquet, one of the speakers, Abraham G. Mills, fourth president[1] of the National League, perhaps made overexuberant by the occasion, said he wanted it distinctly understood that "patriotism and research" had established that the game of baseball was American in origin. His audience greeted this pronouncement with enthusiastic cries of "No rounders!" Thus, according to the New York *Clipper*, the English claim that America's national game was a descendant of the English game of rounders was "forever squelched."

The "research" to which Mills referred is somewhat obscure. Perhaps he had in mind the assertions of John Montgomery Ward, a prominent player and lawyer, who had stated unequivocally the previous year that baseball did not spring from rounders but was a product of the "genius of the American Boy."

But this question as to the birthplace of the game had become a subject of controversy only recently. Prior to the decade of the eighties, rounders had been generally accepted as the ancestor of baseball. However, after the Civil War, organized teams had attained importance, and baseball evolved from a simple, primitive game into a popular show business. It had gained prestige not unmixed with American pride in having a "national game." Consequently, its devotees found it increasingly difficult to countenance the notion that their favorite sport was of foreign origin. Pride and patriotism required that the game be native, unsullied by English ancestry—even if the rounders theory could be disproved by no stronger weapons than shouting and incantation.

Nevertheless, the rounders idea somehow was not to be "forever squelched." The doctrine persisted, although without clinching evidence. The issue was unresolved for years until brought to focus in an article that appeared in *Spalding's Guide for 1903*, written by the first great baseball sportswriter, the "Father

---

[1] Mills was not the third president, as generally claimed. After the death of William A. Hulbert, the League's second president, in 1882, A. J. Soden of the Boston Club succeeded to the office for a brief interval preceding the administration of Mills. *Spalding's Official Base Ball Guide for 1883* (New York: 1883), 97. (Published annually 1877–1939 under various titles, but hereinafter referred to as *Spalding's Guide*.)

of Baseball" and the leading advocate of the rounders argument, Henry Chadwick. He had always pleaded rounders, claiming that he had played the game in England as a boy, and that early American "town ball" was very similar to it. Two conspicuous features common to both games, Chadwick pointed out, were the use of four posts for base stations and putting runners out by throwing the ball at them—"soaking" or "plugging," as it was called.

Thus challenged, Spalding, the champion of the American theory,[2] suggested settling the question once and for all. A blue-ribbon commission was appointed consisting of seven men of "high repute and undoubted knowledge of Base Ball" and including two United States senators. The committee itself supplied the window-dressing while A. G. Mills, the chairman, did what actual work was done. After collecting testimony over a period of three years, consisting of recollections but no solid documentary evidence, Mills wrote and presented a report, dated December 30, 1907, to the effect that (1) baseball originated in the United States, and (2) the first method of playing it "according to the best evidence obtainable to date" was devised by General Abner Doubleday at Cooperstown, New York, in 1839.

The remarkable part of the report was the dragooning of Doubleday and Cooperstown on the sole basis of the recollections of one Abner Graves, one-time citizen of Cooperstown. His statement was recorded in a press release issued by the commission before its final report, which was entitled "The Origin of Baseball." Graves described a game of town ball in progress between pupils of Otsego Academy and Green's Select School when

> . . . Doubleday then improved Town Ball, to limit the number of players, as many were hurt in collisions. From twenty to fifty boys took part in the game I have described. He also designed the game to be played by definite teams or sides. Doubleday called the game Base Ball, for there were four bases in it. Three were places where the runner could rest free from being put out, provided he kept his foot on the flat stone base. The pitcher stood in a six foot ring. The ball had a rubber center overwound with yarn to a size somewhat larger than the present sphere, and was covered with leather or buckskin. Anyone getting the ball was entitled to throw it at a runner between bases, and put him out by hitting him with it.[3]

[2] Significantly, Spalding contradicted his own assertions in his *Guide for 1878*, 5, where he stated that Englishmen who watched Americans playing baseball "accused them of playing rounders" and were not far out of the way since "the game unquestionably thus originated."

[3] "Statement of Abner Graves, Mining Engineer of Denver, Colorado, April 3, 1905," in the Abner Doubleday Papers, Cooperstown, New York.

Thus it was that a decision laid down by what has been called "an oecumenical council of baseball hierarchs"[4] became the basis of an American myth that persisted and continues to live down through the years. The average "fan" who knew or cared anything at all about the beginnings of the game he watched was under the impression that an inspired, spontaneous act by Abner Doubleday created it.[5]

Yet it is by no means certain that he ever was in Cooperstown. He was born in Ballston Spa, New York, and attended school at Auburn. If he did enroll at Green's Select School at Cooperstown, he certainly was not a schoolboy there in 1839, as Abner Graves claimed, since he had matriculated at West Point the previous autumn. It may well be that Doubleday had played ball with Graves and others; but if he had any significant or unusual connection with the game it is not revealed in local histories or in Doubleday's writings.[6] It

[4] Rollin L. Hartt, "The National Game," *Baseball Magazine*, II (Boston: August 1909), 42. The hand-picked commission was made up almost entirely of men who were, at one time or other, very prominent in organized baseball, including the two senators. They were Abraham G. Mills, Nicholas E. Young, Alfred J. Reach, George Wright, James E. Sullivan, Arthur P. Gorman, and Morgan G. Bulkeley.

[5] The tale found its way into print also. See for example Ralph Birdsall, *The Story of Cooperstown* (New York: 1917), 224, wherein the writer states that the "solemn form of procedure" (of the commission) "placed the matter beyond doubt." Louis C. Jones, in *Cooperstown* (New York: 1949), 60–61, equivocates, saying that recent historical evidence "appears to be uncontrovertible"; yet he continues to maintain that Graves's testimony "stands unimpaired." Writers' Program of the Iowa W.P.A., "Baseball! The Story of Iowa's Early Innings," *Annals of Iowa*, XXII (Des Moines: April 1941), 626, credited Doubleday and praised the "initiative" that later made him a business leader.

Even the *Dictionary of American Biography* (New York: 1944), V, 391, states that Doubleday "created baseball." The *Encyclopaedia Britannica* (Chicago: 1948), III, 1661, the *Encyclopedia Americana* (New York: 1948), III, 302, and *Collier's Encyclopedia* (New York: 1949), III, 214, have accepted the new evidence. *Compton's Pictured Encyclopedia* (Chicago: 1948), II, 53, takes a middle ground. More recently, Hy Turkin and S. C. Thompson, *The Official Encyclopedia of Baseball* (New York: 1951), 375, concede that most unbiased probers have been forced to acknowledge the claims of recent historical research. Nevertheless, these authors, along with baseball officials, continue to propagandize Cooperstown as a baseball "shrine"; and, since Cooperstown is irrevocably associated with Abner Doubleday, this is an indirect means of perpetuating the myth.

[6] *Chancellorsville and Gettysburg* (New York: 1882); *Gettysburg Made Plain; A Succinct Account of the Campaign and Battles, with the Aid of One Diagram and Twenty-nine Maps* (New York: 1909); *Reminiscences of Forts Sumter and Moultrie in 1860–'61* (New York: 1876). Doubleday, in recalling his boyhood, makes no mention of interest in baseball:

"You ask for some information as to how I passed my youth. I was brought up in a book store and early imbibed a taste for reading. I was fond of poetry and art and much interested in mathematical studies. In my outdoor sports I was addicted to topographical work and even as a boy amused myself by making maps of the country around my father's residence which was in Auburn Cayuga Co N.Y. [*sic*]" Abner Doubleday to Dear Sir [?], November 20, 1887, Doubleday Papers, Cooperstown, New York.

should be noted, too, that Abraham G. Mills had known Doubleday for years, dating from their association as soldiers in the Civil War; yet Mills never mentioned anything about Doubleday's alleged contribution to baseball prior to the publication of the Graves statement. For instance, why did Mills not take the obvious opportunity to proclaim Doubleday's supposed role while addressing that glittering company at Delmonico's on the origin of baseball?

The climax in the perpetuation of the Doubleday story came with the approach of 1939 when the major leagues made elaborate preparations to commemorate the "centennial" of the game. Large and impressive plans were formed for appropriate ceremonies at Cooperstown—and indeed carried out. A Baseball Hall of Fame was dedicated, a pageant portraying the historical highlights of the sport was presented, and an all-star contest between teams composed of baseball's all-time great players was played. All this was accompanied by the usual publicity build-up and fanfare.

The United States Government lent its seal of approval when the Post Office authorized a special baseball stamp marking the event. However, it did so not because of Doubleday, whose claims admittedly were "questionable," but because the date was "universally recognized in sport circles as marking the centennial"—a rather nice point. Doubleday's picture was cautiously omitted, and a sandlot scene substituted as the central motif with a house, barn, church, and school in the background.

Less fortunate, or perhaps more gullible, was a legislative committee of the State of New York charged with studying the situation. This committee held a public hearing at Cooperstown, August 7, 1937, at which representatives of the local chamber of commerce and of the local committee dealing with the problem appeared. According to the official report of the State legislature, "It was put in evidence that Cooperstown, New York, is the birthplace of baseball . . ." and the State committee recommended "that a centennial be properly celebrated at Cooperstown, New York, on the home site of the first game, the inauguration of baseball being the proud heritage of New York."

The committee went on to advocate that the event be "advertised and publicized in the pamphlets of the Conservation Department of the State of New York, and by road signs erected under its supervision. . . ." Finally, it was urged that the State of New York "appropriate . . . Ten Thousand ($10,000) . . . to be used in advertising and generally furthering the baseball . . . celebration."[7]

---

[7] *State of New York, Report of Joint Legislative Committee to Study the Situation Concerning the Inaugural Baseball Game and the Growth of the Sport.* Legislative Document 73 (Albany: 1938). Evidently the Congress of the United States, too, has fallen prey to this story. In its 1951 investigation, it concluded that baseball "is a game of American origin." "Organized Baseball; Report of the Subcommittee on the Study of Monopoly Power of the Committee on the Judiciary," *House Report,* No. 2002, p. 228, 82d Congress, 2d Session (Washington: 1952).

So it was that the Doubleday myth was crystallized and enshrined in concrete form by organized baseball. Actually, the entire edifice, which had always rested upon the flimsy foundation of an elderly man's memory of events sixty-eight years after they supposedly occurred, was constructed and sanctioned in the face of timely and unimpeachable evidence, published in the midst of centennial preparations, that Abner Doubleday had had little or nothing to do with the birth of the game; but rather, that it had sprung from rounders.[8] Adding to the difficulty, Bruce Cartwright reiterated an earlier claim that evidence in his possession showed his forebear, Alexander Cartwright, to have been the founder of baseball. Although embarrassed and chagrined, baseball officials, having already committed themselves, especially financially, to Doubleday, proceeded according to plan, while sports columnists either pointed out the discrepancy or got around it as gracefully as possible.[9]

Broadly speaking, no single person invented baseball. The game was the result of an evolutionary process over a long period of years. It is known that the ball was used from earliest civilization; and the evidence is overwhelming that it was familiar as far back as ancient Egypt and adjacent lands where the ball represented the idea of fertility.[10] And of course the Greeks were thoroughly familiar with ball play. It would be difficult to present a stronger argument for ball games than that to be found in Galen's treatise, entitled "Exercise with the Small Ball." E. Norman Gardiner, classical scholar, paraphrases this document as follows:

> The best of all exercises . . . are those which combine bodily exertion with mental recreation, such as hunting and ball-play. But ball-play has this advantage over hunting that its cheapness puts it within reach of the very poorest, while even the busiest man can find time to do it. Moreover, it can be practised with any degree of violence or moderation, at all times and in all conditions. It exercises every part of the body, legs, hands, and eyesight alike, and at the same time gives

[8] Robert W. Henderson, "Baseball and Rounders," *New York Public Library Bulletin*, XLIII (New York: April, 1939), 303–314. Aside from Henry Chadwick's protests, the first substantial debunking of the Doubleday myth was provided by Will Irwin, "Baseball: (I) Before the Professionals Came," *Collier's*, XLIII (May 8, 1909), 12.

[9] For example, the New York *Sun*, June 10, 1939, admitted the hoax, but said baseball as an American institution required a legend, so the public would therefore go ahead and take part in the "innocuous conspiracy." Fred Lieb, sportswriter, assigned to prepare a feature article on the centennial, admits he faked the story although he knew of the discrepancies in the Cooperstown myth. Frederick G. Lieb, *The Baseball Story* (New York: 1950), 15.

[10] John A. Krout, *Annals of American Sport, Pageant of America Series*, XV (New Haven: 1929), 114. Also Henderson, *Ball, Bat and Bishop*, 19. The Russians also claim that baseball originated from one of their ancient village games called lapta. *New York Times*, September 16, 1952, quoted a Soviet magazine, *Smena*: "It is well known that in Russian villages they played lapta, of which beizbol is an imitation. It was played in Russian villages when the United States was not even marked on the maps."

pleasure to the mind. In contrast with athletic exercises, which make men slow or produce one-sided development, ball-play produces strength and activity, and therefore trains all those qualities which are most valuable for a soldier. Finally, it is free from dangers. . . .[11]

To ascertain who invented baseball would be equivalent to trying to locate the discoverer of fire. But we are here concerned with what has direct bearing on the development of baseball in America, and there is sufficient evidence to indicate that various simple bat-and-ball games were indulged in by the settlers from the first. For example, the Dutch of New Netherland played "stool ball," thought to be the forerunner of cricket. Even in Puritan New England the play spirit was not as dead as commonly supposed. Ballplaying there was sufficently prominent to be forbidden by Governor Bradford of Plymouth.

Possibly the first record of an American baseball game is that mentioned in the journal of George Ewing, a Revolutionary soldier, who tells of playing a game of "base," April 7, 1778, at Valley Forge. Early familiarity with a game called baseball is understandable, for as early as 1744 John Newbery published in London *A Little Pretty Pocket-Book*, containing a rhymed description of "base-ball" along with a small picture illustrating the game.[12] Newbery, a farmer's son, accountant, patent-medicine dealer, and printer, not only was one of the first publishers of children's books, but also tried to please children as well as to improve them—a new and good idea for that time. This, like other children's books that followed it, was extremely popular and widely known—evidence that a game called baseball was familiar to English boys. The book was republished in New York in 1762, in Philadelphia in 1786, and again at Worcester, Massachusetts, in 1787. Therefore a ball game called base-ball was familiar to Americans much before 1839, the year in which Doubleday is credited with christening the game with that name.

The link between baseball and the English game of rounders is no less strong. A compilation of children's games by William Clarke called *The Boy's Own Book: A Complete Encyclopedia of All the Diversions, Athletic, Scientific and Recreative* appeared in London in 1828. A number of editions was published, but the important one is the third, which appeared in 1829. It had a description of the game of rounders.[13] That same year, 1829, the first American edition

---

[11] E. Norman Gardiner, *Greek Athletic Sports and Festivals* (London: 1910), 187–188.

[12] Much of this portion of the discussion, including the relationship between baseball and rounders, is based upon Henderson, "Baseball and Rounders," 303–314, who published his evidence after the preparations for the Cooperstown ceremonies had been inaugurated.

[13] The game was known variously in England by the names base-ball, feeder, and rounders. The latter name came to be the most commonly used. The first London edition of *The Boy's Own Book* omits rounders. A copy of the second edition has not been located. Copies of the first and third London editions are in the Cleveland Public Library.

of the volume, likewise containing the rules for rounders, was printed. From this source we learn that rounders, a favorite game of western England, was played on a field on which were placed four stones or posts from 12 to 20 yards apart in a diamond-shaped pattern. The number of contestants was not specified; those on hand merely divided into two equal groups. The "out" side scattered about the field more or less haphazardly without taking up set positions, except for the "pecker" or "feeder" (pitcher), who gently tossed the ball a short distance to the "striker" (batter) from a fixed position also marked by a stone or post. The striker, if successful in meeting the ball, ran the bases clockwise as far as he could progress, depending upon the circumstances. Outs were registered when the striker did any of the following: (1) missed three swings (three-strikes rule), (2) hit the ball behind his position (one foul out), (3) had his batted ball caught, or (4) was struck by a thrown ball while attempting to negotiate the bases. The "in" side continued until each of its members had been put out, when the side that had been in the field had its innings.

So much for the game of rounders as such. The great significance of these rules is that five years after they were published in the United States they were reprinted by a Boston company which, in a book entitled *The Book of Sports*, by Robin Carver, reproduced them practically verbatim, changing only the title from "Rounders" to "Base, or Goal Ball" because, as he said, those were "the names generally adopted in our country."[14] By means of this minor alteration English rounders became American baseball.

Again in 1835 a Providence, Rhode Island, firm published *The Boys and Girls Book of Sports*, which likewise contained the rules for rounders as they appeared in *The Boy's Own Book* of 1829, merely substituting the heading "Base, or Goal Ball." Furthermore, in 1839 yet another sporting book appeared, *The Boy's Book of Sports: A Description of the Exercises and Pastimes of Youth*, published in New Haven. Instead of merely copying previously published rules on baseball, it tried to revise and clarify those already known. In doing so, it introduced for the first time the provision that the bases, laid out to form a "diamond," be run in counterclockwise fashion.

In the late eighteenth and early nineteenth centuries many references to ball games having been played are to be found, particularly in diaries and memoirs. Some of these were written at the time, but many are memories of older men recalling boyhood days and are therefore not as reliable as the contemporary accounts. Nor is it always certain which game of ball was played. Nevertheless

---

[14] Henderson dramatized the similarity by placing the texts of the same rules from each book in parallel columns in "Baseball and Rounders," 307; Henderson, *Ball, Bat and Bishop*, 154–157.

the evidence is that simple ball games were well known and played in the settled communities along the seaboard, especially in New York and the New England States. Certainly by the first decades of the nineteenth century, ball games were a common sight on the village greens and vacant fields or pastures as well as on college campuses.

So popular was ball in Worcester in 1816 that it was prohibited in the streets; and according to Thurlow Weed, people in Rochester, New York, busy and industrious as they were, found time for recreation. There, in 1825, a baseball club of fifty members, ages eighteen to forty, met every afternoon during the ball season to play on their eight to ten acres of ground. Weed even lists the best players, among whom were some of the leading citizens. In his journal written in 1835, Cyrus Parker Bradley, born in 1818, admits he never got over his boyhood love of playing and often was told "how ridiculous it was to come from the society of antiquarians and politicians and play ball with boys of six. But it is natural to me, infected by their mood, by my early life." The mass of boys indulged in playing "goal" in Bangor, Maine, according to Albert Ware Paine in his journal of 1836, recorded when he was twenty-three years old. And in Rhode Island ball play was performed even on Sunday.

A diary entry by a Princeton student in 1786 alludes to playing "baste ball" on the campus: "A fine day, play baste ball in the campus but am beaten for I miss both catching and striking the ball." At first, however, colleges discouraged students in the practice of ball playing. At least Princeton did, passing laws in 1787 against ball games on the ground that such were "low and unbecoming gentlemen" and constituted "great danger to the health by sudden and alternate heats and colds and as it tends by accidents . . . to disfiguring and maiming those who are engaged in it. . . ." Gradually it was found that student disorder and mischief decreased when surplus energy was worked off in games. At Bowdoin in 1824, ball games were initiated by the authorities themselves as a method of reducing sickness. The recommendation was well

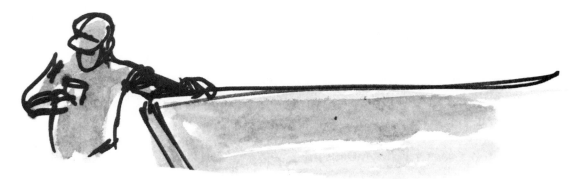

received and proved beneficial if we can take the word of Henry Wadsworth Longfellow, then a student. He wrote that ball playing

> . . . communicated such an impulse to our limbs and joints, that there is nothing now heard of, in our leisure hours, but ball, ball, ball. I cannot prophesy with any degree of accuracy concerning the continuance of this rage for play, but the effect is good, since there has been a thoroughgoing reformation from inactivity and torpitude.

Williams Latham, a student at Brown from 1823 to 1827, discussed his ball-playing experience there, explaining that sports were still unorganized; and that while ball games took place at Brown he did not enjoy them as much as he had at Bridgewater because only six or seven played on a side; hence much time was wasted running after the ball. He also complained of the pitching style because they "did throw so fair ball, They are affraid [*sic*] the fellow will hit it with his bat-stick." Likewise, at Harvard, where he finished in 1829, Oliver Wendell Holmes played ball. The same was true of George F. Hoar, who played various ball games during his boyhood in the 1830s and, after he entered Harvard in 1842, continued to engage in "the old-fashioned game of base." Hoar specified that chief among the games he played as a boy were four-old-cat, three-old-cat, two-old-cat, and base, games which, as he pointed out, were not very scientific.

These various ball games had common characteristics. They were all simple, some more so than others. All appealed to the same elementary satisfaction derived from projecting one's power by swatting and throwing an object hard and for distance, or the excitement of the race to arrive safely on the base ahead of the ball. The simplest of these early games was barn ball, limited to two players and requiring the smooth side of a building with some level ground in front of it. One boy threw the ball vigorously against the wall; the other, having taken his position about a dozen feet from the wall, struck at the rebounding ball with his bat. Upon connecting he ran to the wall and tried to return before his opponent recovered the ball and hit him with it. Naturally, they took turns, switching about after the batter was retired, so that each boy had his innings.

Apparently out of the desire to make participation of more boys possible, more advanced variations—the games of "old-cat"—were improvised. The simplest version of these, "one-old-cat," was derived from the old English game of "Tip Cat," wherein a wooden "cat," like a spindle, was placed on the ground, then tipped in the air and struck with a stick. "Old-cat" merely substituted a ball for the stick. "One-old-cat" had a batter, pitcher, and two bases. The batter hit from one base, ran to the other, and returned if possible until the ball was caught either on the fly or on one bounce. The number of lads could be increased by playing "two-, three-, or four-old-cat," which simply meant adding to the number of bases and batsmen. As the number of players increased, the opportunity and necessity for more team play presented itself.

For yet larger numbers of players, the game variously called "town-ball," "round-ball"—and later "Massachusetts ball" (to distinguish it from "the New York game")—were devised. These were the Americanized versions of English rounders and were played by large groups ranging anywhere from twelve to twenty or more on a side. Regulations varied, since there were no uniform rules; hence each community had its own particular variations—just as present-day sandlot players generally add their own touches to the official rules. One side batted around until each of its players was put out; then the other aggregation had its turn.

The frontier, however, did not nourish sport. The immediate battle to subdue the wilderness was too pressing to permit leisure for games. Labor and work, because they were essential, were glorified. The tendency, therefore, was to combine them with play whenever possible. Necessary work and needed sport frequently were synonymous. Barn-raisings or corn-huskings, required tasks, were converted into festive frolics as well. Likewise hunting and fishing were work; but the thrill of sport was not entirely absent. Such pure "sport" as was practiced on the frontier was rugged, boisterous, and even brutal, like wrestling and eye-gouging. Only when communities became more settled, enjoyed a degree of leisure, and cleared fields or village commons, did ball playing sprout and flourish; and even then sport was impeded by a lingering puritanism that frowned upon frivolity or pleasure.

In New England the belief remained that "play is folly rather than wisdom in a child; and he will soonest be an adult who puts on the adult's gravity," according to a well-known pedagogue of that section. He candidly relates how, because of his own youthful training in this belief, he made a practice, when a teacher, of cheating the pupils of as much time as possible from the fifteen minutes allotted to them at noon for sports. He continues apologetically: "I had not learned so fully as I have since done, that sports are as indispensable to the health of both the bodies and minds of children as their food, their drink, or their sleep. . . ."

Travelers noted the legal restrictions upon amusements; and one remarked upon the "hard precocity" of American youths who entered college at the age of fourteen and left at seventeen with degrees to commence business careers, with no interval to attain either gracefulness or health—"Athletic games and the bolder field sports being unknown." Enjoyment was associated with guilt—as illustrated by the Yankee who said he was "going to town, probably git [sic] good and drunk, and Lord how I'll hate it!" This attitude only slowly disappeared; as late as 1862 churchmen succeeded in having ice skating banned in Brooklyn; and of course the fight to legalize Sunday baseball took much longer.

In the South, ball playing was carried on, but not to the extent it was in the North. The pattern of Southern sport tended to be formed by the dominant planter group, whose influence far exceeded its number. The result was an inclination toward aristocratic pastimes like fox hunting. Yet ball play was not as completely foreign to that section as generally thought. A case in point is Moses Waddell's famous school in South Carolina, where students found relaxation in ball games from the stern classical curriculum.

Such simple, crude ball games as those described were played on a local, neighborhood basis and were admirably suited to the young, primarily rural America of the period. Few had great wealth or leisure. Playing sites were plentiful and convenient. Only the rudest preparation was necessary—laying "goals" or bases by driving sticks into the ground or placing flat rocks at approximate distances. Equipment requirements were minimum both in amount and cost. Any stout stick, wagon tongue, ax or rake handle made a capital bat; and a serviceable ball could be had by winding yarn around a buckshot or chunk of india rubber and then sewing on a leather cover, perhaps cut to size by the local shoemaker, to prevent unwinding. No other paraphernalia were needed. Availability of ample space, a negligible amount of inexpensive equipment, and the simple structure of the games made for popularity and wide participation. In short, the various ball games were adapted to their surroundings and in fact mirrored them.

Another feature of early nineteenth-century ball was the fact that it was overwhelmingly a participant's game. Relatively few watched; and the promoter who sold baseball games as entertainment was not to appear until a later day when American society became urbanized. This meager attendance at games and their noncommercial character are reflected in the paucity of detailed information and lack of descriptions of games in the press of the day. For example, even in 1843, an advertisement announcing the forthcoming publication of a "new and comprehensive" weekly sporting paper listed more than twenty sports it would cover, such as racing, hunting, shooting, fishing, rowing, pedestrianism, pugilism, "cricketing," skating, swimming, billiards, etc., but omitted any intent to report on ball playing.

The same applied to a leading theatrical and sports journal of the day, which contained lengthy indices of items pertaining to cricket during the 1840s, whereas baseball was disregarded. Furthermore, the absence of team play in any real or highly developed sense is to be noted; doubtless this was due to the fiercely individualistic atmosphere of a society in flux, which lacked any permanent stratification, and in which democracy was the byword. Sufficient sophistication for highly developed team play was lacking in America prior to the Civil War.

The simplicity, informality, and absence of organization in the game, plus the fact that it was not given headline attention in the contemporary press, enhanced the recreative values of ball playing, so that even the ascetic though progressive schoolteacher, William A. Alcott, confessed: "Our most common exercise was ball playing. In this, I was not very expert; but I believe I had all the healthful advantages which pertain to it, notwithstanding. It is really an excellent sport."

At the time this story was published in *The New Yorker*, 1937, Irwin Shaw was a socially conscious playwright and story writer who was fresh from his experience as a truck driver, factory worker, and semipro football player. In later years he became rich and famous as the author of such novels as *The Young Lions* and *Rich Man, Poor Man*.

IRWIN SHAW

No Jury Would Convict

"I come from Jersey City," the man in the green sweater was saying, "all the way from Jersey City, and I might of just as well stood home. You look at Brooklyn and you look at Jersey City and if you didn't look at the uniforms you'd never tell the difference."

Just then the Giants scored four runs and two men a few rows below stood up with grins on their faces and called to a friend behind us, "Johnny, Johnny! Did you see that, Johnny? You still here, Johnny? We thought you mighta left. What a team, Brooklyn!" They shook their heads in sardonic admiration, "What a team! You still here, Johnny?"

Johnny, wherever he was, didn't say anything. His two friends sat down, laughing.

The man in the green sweater took off his yellow straw hat and carefully wiped the sweatband with his handkerchief. "I been watching the Dodgers for twenty-three years," he said, "and I never seen anything like this." He put his hat on again, over his dark Greek face, the eyes deep and sad, never leaving the field where the Dodgers moved wearily in their green-trimmed uniforms. "Jersey City, Albany, and Brooklyn, that would make a good league. One helluva league. I would give Brooklyn twenty-five games headstart and let them fight it out. They would have a hard fight stayin' in the New York–Penn League. They would have to get three new pitchers. They're worse than Jersey City, I swear, worse . . ."

"Ah, now, listen," the man beside him said, "if that's the case why isn't Brooklyn in Jersey City and Jersey City in Brooklyn?"

"I don't know," the man in the green sweater said. "I honestly couldn't tell ye."

"They haven't got such a bad team."

"They ought to move them into the New York–Penn League. A major-league team . . ." He laughed sadly. "Look at that!" A man named Wilson was striking out for Brooklyn. "Look at Wilson. Why, he's pitiful. They walk two men to get at him in the International League. I bet Newark could spot them five runs and beat them every day. I'd give odds."

"You can't make a supposition like that," the man beside him protested. "They never play each other. It's not a fair supposition."

"Five runs, every day. If they didn't have those green caps they could play in a twilight league in Connecticut and nobody'd ever tell the difference, not in ten years. Look at that!" The Brooklyn shortstop fell down leaping at a grounder to his right. "No guts," the man from Jersey City said, "a major-league shortstop woulda had it and threw the man out. He fell to make a alibi."

"It was a hard-hit ball," his neighbor protested.

"Bartell woulda had it. He ain't no Bartell."

"He's got nine yards of tape on him," the man next to him said. "I saw with my own eyes in the dugout. He's a mass of cuts and bruises."

"That's Brooklyn. Always got tape all over them. They spend more money for tape than for players. Look at that."

One of the Giants hit a home run and three runs scored. The two men in front of us stood up with grins on their faces and called to their friend in back of us. "Still there, Johnny?" and sat down.

"For twenty-three years," the man in the green sweater said, "I been rootin' for this team. I'm gettin' tired of rootin' for a minor-league team in a major league. I would hate to see what would happen to those guys in Jersey City."

"I come to see them every day," his neighbor said stubbornly, "and they're a major-league team."

"Look at them," the man in the green sweater pointed his scorecard in accusation at the nine weary figures. "Take 'em one by one. Look at Wilson. Why, he's the worst ballplayer in the world. He's even worse than Smead Jolley."

He sat back triumphantly, having silenced his adversary for the moment.

He watched the play quietly for a few seconds, his Greek eyes bitter but resigned. "Why," he continued, "in Jersey City they put a catcher in to play center field instead of him. A catcher. I know Wilson."

"Wilson isn't the only one on the team," his neighbor said.

"All right. Cooney. What can Cooney do?"

"Cooney can field."

"All right, Cooney can field. But he has an air rifle for an arm. He can't reach second base in under seven bounces. Don't talk to me about Cooney."

"His arm's not so bad," the neighbor insisted.

"Not so bad? Why, Mac, if Cooney had an arm he'd be a pitcher."

"I never noticed anything wrong with his arm."

"Mac," the man in the green sweater said, "then you're the one man in the United States that don't know Cooney got a glass arm. The one man."

"How about Winsett?" his neighbor wanted to know.

Winsett was up at the plate by this time and the man in the green sweater watched him critically. "A cigar store Indian" he said finally. "Watch him swing."

"He hit sixty home runs the year before they brought him up," the Brooklyn fan said. "Cigar store Indians don't hit sixty home runs."

"I saw him," the man in the green sweater said, "when he was playin' in the International League. Do you know what he hit in the International League. . . . 250 . . . You know why? It's an outcurve league. The National League is also an outcurve league. He ought to be out somewhere playin' night baseball." At the top of his voice he called, "Come on, you cigar store Indian!"

Winsett hit a home run.

"This is a fine time to hit it," the man from Jersey City said, "they're behind seven runs and there's nobody on base and he hits a home run."

In the next inning a pitcher named Cantwell took up the bitter burden of pitching for Brooklyn. The face of the man in the green sweater lightened. "There's a pitcher," he said. "One of the best. Out in Jersey City they were goin' to give him a new automobile but he went to the Giants. Watch him!" he said as Cantwell disposed of the first two batters. "A prince of a fellow. A prince. Everybody likes him."

"He's been pitching lousy," his neighbor said, as Cantwell suddenly filled the bases.

"What do you expect?" the man from Jersey City said, anxiously watching the misery below. "He don't look like the Cantwell of Jersey City. Terry double-crossed him, he wanted to stay in Jersey City, he woulda got an automobile, but Terry took him and double-crossed him and shipped him to Brooklyn. How do you expect him to pitch? He broke his heart."

Cantwell struck out the third batter. The man in the green sweater stood up and applauded as the pitcher trudged into the dugout. "You bet your life he can pitch, the poor son of a gun, he's disgusted, the poor fella. That's it, Ben!" He sat down. "Wonderful pitcher, Ben, he's got a head."

"I never saw him strike out a man before," the Brooklyn fan said.

"There's very few of them makes a living out of strikeouts. Now if they only give Ben something to work on . . ."

Brooklyn scored three runs. Two men died on base when Wilson popped out.

"That Wilson," the man in the green sweater said, "they ought to trade him to the Salvation Army. He's the worst player in the world. Why, he's worse than Smead Jolley."

But he cheered lustily when Cantwell came through another inning unscored upon. "There's a pitcher," he said, "if I had a team, I'd buy him."

"You could buy him for the fare to Jersey City," a man in back said, "eleven cents."

"The only major leaguer on that ballclub!" the man in the green sweater said with finality. "If only those cheap bastards would buy a couple more like him, they'd have something. I'm not saying Brooklyn's bad as a town, because it's not, but they got office boys running the ballclub, office boys with snot in their ears. That cheap Grimes. I heard he used the ground keeper's truck to move his furniture in."

The Dodgers scored three more runs and the man in the green sweater was shouting triumphantly, the ancient Greek sorrow gone from his eyes for the first time in the entire afternoon. There was only one out and there was a man on third base and the Dodgers needed only one run to tie the score. Wilson was coming up to bat and the man in the green sweater groaned. "That's what happens when you have somebody like that on a team. He comes up at a time like this. That's always the way it happens. He's pitiful. In the International League they walk two batters to get at him."

But at the last moment somebody else batted for Wilson and struck out. "On low ones," the man in the green sweater said in pain, "a pinch hitter swinging at low ones."

Cantwell was to bat next.

"Let him stay up there!" the man from Jersey City shouted. "Let him win his own game." He turned to his public. "I would like to see old Ben smack one out and win the ballgame," he said, "and go right over to Terry and spit in his face."

But old Ben didn't get a chance. Grimes put a man called Spence in to bat for him and Spence popped out.

In the next inning the Brooklyn second baseman juggled a ball and another run scored. All hope fled from the dark Greek face. "Why is it," he asked, "that other teams don't do it?" He got up, preparing to leave. "A man on third and one out," he said, "and no score. They ought to shoot Grimes for that. No jury would convict. Ah," he said, moving down toward the exit gate, "I'm going to root for a winning team from now on. I've been rooting for a losing team long enough. I'm going to root for the Giants. You don't know," he said to the Brooklyn fan moving along with him, "you don't know the pleasure you get out of rooting for a winning team."

And he went back to Jersey City, leaving his heart in Brooklyn.

This article was written in September 1969, as the Mets were headed toward a miracle even greater than the Jets winning the Super Bowl and, for Met fans, at least comparable to Neil Armstrong's footprints on the moon. And yet here was Len Shecter wistfully longing for the bad old days, which he witnessed as a reporter and columnist for the New York Post. *The article grew, the following year, into a fine little book called* Once Upon the Polo Grounds.

LEONARD SHECTER

Bring Back the Real Mets!

It is not to be believed. This season, the Mets—the ever-loving New York Mets, for goodness sakes—have been involved in a pennant race. We were, none of us, ever going to be old enough to see this day. Our lot was to be forever enveloped in a cult of sweet misery, the kind enjoyed for so many years in Brooklyn when the Dodgers were "Dem Bums." The Mets played music to lose by, to love hopelessly by, to reminisce by. But there was never going to be that hot, thumping rhythm of a pennant race. Not for us. For our sons, perhaps, or their sons.

Except we had not counted on the swift pace of modern times, on the factor of dilution through additional expansion, of the knack eight years have of appearing to be a lifetime. So here we are, us Met fans, unexpectedly, shockingly, caught up in the final weeks' stampede. It is a beautiful thing, of course, and it makes tired blood surge once again. Winning has become a necessity rather than a surprise. Losing has become a disaster rather than a routine. It matters to us what the Chicago Cubs have done in the afternoon, and we get caught up in the pitching problems of the St. Louis Cardinals, and every once in a while we cast a terrified glance at the Pittsburgh Pirates.

It's exciting, exhilarating, fascinating. And yet, for some of us, a very few, there are days that will be better remembered. . . .

The kid's name was John Pappas. He was skinny, 5 foot 10 and not more than 150 pounds, and the sallow pallor of the city was on his face. He had a lot of black hair which he was wearing in a scraggly pompadour as he walked into the clubhouse of the New York Mets in St. Petersburg, Florida, that February morning in 1962, plunked down his little canvas bag with the cheap baseball shoes inside, and announced he was a pitcher and ready. The funny thing was, nobody laughed.

It couldn't happen now. A twenty-one-year-old unemployed furniture salesman from Queens who had never thrown a baseball for an organized team, he'd be seized, stuffed into a straitjacket, and whisked away to the nearest mental hospital. Then, at that time and place, however, he was handled gently. Who had ever told him, he was asked, that he could be a big leaguer? "I told myself," John Pappas said. "I'm not exactly a Herb Score, but I'm pretty fast." He stuck out his skinny, unimpressive chest.

The historical fact is that the Mets actually took a look. Johnny Murphy, then assistant to George Weiss, the club president, wasn't altogether happy about it. "He doesn't even *look* like an athlete," Murphy grumbled.

What matter? What did looks count against the kind of soaring hope that wrapped the Mets in silk and French perfume, as separate from reality as a lover's dream? For this was the springtime of a new team, the first expansion team in the National League in its first season. Oh, there was a Houston club out there someplace with the practical Paul Richards running it, who had, once the player draft to stock the teams had been completed, announced to the press: "Gentlemen, we've been had." The people around the Mets didn't feel that way. Nor the newspapermen who had pushed so hard to replace the National League Dodgers and Giants in New York. (This was so long ago there were still six newspapers in New York.) There was talk about the Mets finishing fifth, or even fourth or third. The dreams were sweet in those days.

Of course the Mets had to take a look at Pappas. Because there was always that chance that the devil had conspired to deliver Douglass (*The Year the Yankees Lost the Pennant*) Wallop's Shoeless Joe Hardy, and that the first time he threw a baseball, smoke would rise from the mitt and the catcher's hand would come out of it looking like a bag of peanuts. You don't fool around with the devil.

Murphy wouldn't let Pappas work out on the hallowed ground of the Mets' playing field. He took him down to some empty lot, and all the people covering the club went along, eyes shining, pulses pounding.

Then the skinny kid with all the hair started to warm up and it was all over.

He was no Shoeless Joe. He was no Herb Score. He couldn't even throw very hard. Indeed, he couldn't throw at all.

Too bad. But all it meant was a transference of hope to something else, to other people. It was a season for hope.

There was the hope, for example, that there really was an Elio Chacon. The Mets had shelled out $75,000 to the Cincinnati Reds for him and sent him a contract in Caracas, Venezuela, where, rumor had it, Chacon lived and played winter baseball. No reply. They sent him a letter raising their salary offer. No answer. A cable. No answer. Two more cables. Silence.

Finally, the Mets sent a cable to Sherman Jones, another of their new properties, who was playing on the same team. The cable asked Jones to get Chacon to contact the Mets.

Jones told him.

"He said O.K.," Jones was to recall. "That's all he ever said. That and yes and no, even when he talked Spanish."

In any case, the talk with Jones moved Chacon to send back his contract and ask for more money. The Mets came through, but again silence set in. Until, after training had started, this cable was received: "I AM WAITING PASSAGE. ELIO."

Murphy wasn't sure what this meant, but he arranged with an airline to deliver a ticket to Chacon's door. Acknowledgment was not forthcoming for more than a week. Then this: "I WILL REACHED MONDAY. SICK PARIENT, ELIO."

The airline told the Mets that Chacon was due at the Tampa airport at 10:57 of a Monday night, and when the time came, Lou Niss, the traveling secretary, was waiting. Chacon arrived 5 A.M. Tuesday.

"I asked him what happened to his plane," Niss said. "I still haven't been able to figure out what he said."

There was then a long press conference, the highlight of which went like this:

Q. During the World Series [between Cincinnati and the Yankees] you said you were going to get married. Did you?

A. I say only if we win the whole thing. [The Yankees won the Series.]

Q. What did you tell your girl friend?

A. I told her take it easy.

Q. Isn't she impatient?

A. No.

Q. Do you know what impatient means?

A. No.

It turned out he didn't know a lot about playing shortstop either, which is what the Mets needed him to do. Except the Mets were half a season finding out. They should have listened that spring to Jim Brosnan, the erudite Red pitcher. He was asked if Chacon could play shortstop. "Why should he?" Brosnan said. "He couldn't play second base."

The Mets always found things out too late.

It was a television commercial. The idea was that Casey Stengel, the marvelous manager of "the amazing Mets," as he had dubbed them before they owned even their first over-age ballplayer, had got into an argument with an umpire which so upset him he needed a Bromo-Seltzer to calm his stomach. It was a time when the Federal Communications Commission was attempting to crack down on people who endorsed products they really didn't use. So one of the flunkies from the advertising agency said to Stengel, "You use Bromo-Seltzer, don't you?"

"Why sure," Stengel said. "Only I never get sick, so I don't have to."

At any rate, the commercial was filmed, and most of the trouble came from Stengel overacting his bellyache. "That's a little too much," the director said.

"You mean you don't want me to die?" Stengel said. "I'm old enough."

And for the next weeks, whenever Stengel referred to the filming of the commercial, he said he did it for Alka-Seltzer.

On March 26, Jay Hook, mechanical engineer, pitcher, was kept in an exhibition ballgame against Baltimore until he had given up seventeen hits. The Mets lost, 18–8, which wasn't so bad. It was far from customary, however, to allow a young pitcher to take that kind of beating, and one can only put it down to one of Stengel's flashes of irascibility. Later, Hook was to go on to win the Mets' first league game, to stop their first long losing streak, and become the first Met pitcher to beat the Dodgers in New York. But on that March 26 he was upset enough to cry.

The situation reminded Richie Ashburn, the player who was one of the first to plug in on the sweet agony of the Met mystique, of a story. "It was in the minor leagues," he said. "I saw a team bat around three times on Warren Hacker. Now the manager goes out to take him out and he's mad. 'You can't take me out now,' Hacker says. 'I know I can get this guy out. I've got him out twice this inning.'"

Then there was Rod Kanehl. At twenty-eight, Kanehl had been in baseball eight years without playing in a major-league ballgame. Casey Stengel remembered him from a spring he'd spent with the Yankees, particularly a day in which a ball was hit over Kanehl's head and the outfield fence. Running after the ball, Kanehl went right on up and over the fence, picked it up, and climbed back onto the field. The old man was indelibly impressed, and when he saw Kanehl's name on a list of availables, he pointed a gnarled old finger and said, "I want him."

This was one of the areas in which Stengel and George Weiss were to have a running battle. One time, Stengel reported a conversation he had with Weiss about Kanehl. "Weiss says, 'I ain't seen him do anything in the field,' " Stengel rasped. "So I said, 'You're full of baloney, he can run the bases.' "

And not a great deal more, although before long he was to play every position for the Mets except pitcher and catcher, all of them with aplomb, none of them especially well. Right from the beginning, things happened to Kanehl that you put into threatening letters. The first thing he did was pull a muscle so badly that his leg took on the color of a tropical sunset and he couldn't walk for a week. The first time he got into a game—as a late-inning sub—the first ball hit to him went through his legs. And he pulled another muscle.

The next time he played—second base—he threw two double-play balls into the dirt, and when he was tried at third he was fooled on two pop fouls that dropped with sickening little thuds onto the ground behind him. (In fact, Kanehl never did learn to play second base, which he played a lot. What he couldn't do was make that flying double-play pivot. So he would plant himself on the bag and take the sliding runner's spikes in his shins. He made the DP, but he played three years with bleeding shins.)

It wasn't until late March, that first spring, that Rod Kanehl became a Met. It was against Sandy Koufax and the Dodgers. With runners on second and third in the ninth and the Mets down 3–1, Kanehl was called on to pinch-hit. This was a revolting development since Kanehl was sleeping off a terrible hangover in a corner of the dugout. When he walked out into the sun he decided that as punishment he had been struck blind.

Kanehl let the first pitch go by. "It was a good pitch," he was to say afterward, a crooked smile on his face, his dark eyes glinting with amusement. "A bummer. With hair on it. I mean it sounded like a good pitch. I didn't see it."

The next pitch was a curveball and it fooled Kanehl completely. He thought it was going to be a high fastball, started to swing, realized it was a curve as it headed down at him, and ducked away to save his life. The ball hit his bat anyway.

After that, the ball just naturally took itself down along the first-base line and Kanehl had a base hit. Two runs scored. Shocked, Koufax gave up a hit to Felix Mantilla, and the Mets won 4–3. That's how Rod Kanehl became a Met hero. Indeed, the very first Mets banner hung in the Polo Grounds, where the Mets played for their first two years, read:

WE LOVE THE METS
ROD KANEHL

When the time came that Kanehl no longer got so many lucky hits, this man who somehow represented the spirit of the team—a spirit of cheerful, willing, hilarious failure—was cut off without a backward glance. Nobody even thought to give him a job as coach. Yogi Berra got a job as coach. When you come right down to it, what the hell does Yogi Berra have to do with the Mets?

Amid all the optimistic enthusiasm that surrounded the Mets, the seventy-one-year-old Casey Stengel remained an island of sanity. Oh, he staged his little charades, picking two heavy-legged rookies named Dawes Hamilt and Bruce Fitzpatrick to trot out before visiting columnists as brilliant stars of the future. They were not, of course, and after the spring were never heard of again. But for one brief moment, Camelot. All over the country.

For the most part, though, Stengel said things like this:

"Most of our hitters are what? Putsie-downsies." He took a weak half swing, half bunt, to illustrate.

After the Mets had stirred the hearts of baseball fans all over by beating the Yankees in the ninth inning of their first spring encounter, Stengel remarked, "I'm glad we did good. It's good for the club. But we ain't so great. My pitcher didn't throw the ball over to first base so they got down and broke up two double plays. It was a good game, but we still did the same thing with men on base [not hit]. I don't know when they're going to learn."

Another time, a fan horned in on a Stengel press conference to say, "That Zimmer's the guts of your club, isn't he?"

Well, Don Zimmer was all right. He was one of those people it's supposed to be good to have around your club because he always tries so hard. Zimmer, it was true, had an intense look in his light eyes and when he walked on a baseball field he looked like a lion tamer going into the cage. In fact, though, his range around third base had become limited and his hitting soon proved illusory. Once the season started, he went 0 for 34 and was batting .080 when he was traded. Stengel must have known all the time, for what he said to the fan was, "Why, he's beyond that. He's much more. He's the perdotious quotient of the qualificatilus. He's the lower intestine."

And this one as the Mets finished spring training with a 12–15 record: "I'm mad as hell if I don't win. But I know if the other side put in their regulars I wouldna beaten them."

The day before the Mets were to play their first National League game, the lads were waiting for an elevator in the lobby of the Hotel Chase, in St. Louis, all dressed in their new team blazers which could only be described as Dodger blue. The elevator came. It was soon full. The boys in the back pushed. More got in. Altogether there were sixteen Mets in the elevator when it got stuck between floors. They were stuck for twenty minutes. "I knew it,"

Craig said in the elevator. "The first time in my life I'm going to open a season, I get stuck in an elevator. I'll probably be here for twenty-four hours."

"It wasn't so bad for the other guys," Hobie Landrith, the short catcher, said. "I'm not built high enough. I couldn't get any air down where I was."

This was taken to have been a portent of things to come with the Mets. It probably was, although it was far from the only one. A few days later, when the Mets opened at the Polo Grounds, Casey Stengel slammed the door of his newly built office. When he tried to get back into it, there was no key that fitted the lock. Workmen were summoned to disassemble the door frame.

A couple of other things happened that day. Brian Sullivan of the Metropolitan Opera and the St. Camillus Band rendered "The Star-Spangled Banner," but not together. And when the lineup was announced on the P.A. it was the wrong one, and then the Mets lost the game when Jim Marshall came off first base to take a throw he just couldn't wait to reach him and Richie Ashburn and Gus Bell let a ball drop between them in the outfield. It was also discovered after the game that Casey Stengel's undershorts were still emblazoned with the emblem of the New York Yankees.

The Mets lost their first nine games. There was no way of throwing stones at individual players. They all gave until it hurt. There was this game they lost to the Philadelphia Phillies, 11–9, for example. They lost it because Charlie Neal let two routine balls get by him at second base. They lost it because Landrith was guilty of two passed balls. They lost it because Frank ("Big Donkey") Thomas, who, it turned out, could hit home runs and was a whiz at helping stewardesses serve meals on airplanes, dropped an easy fly ball in left field. They lost it because of this kind of play:

In the second inning they were only three runs down. There were runners on first and third because Neal had let a line drive bounce off his glove. Tony Gonzales then hit a chopper back to the right side of the mound. Jim Marshall, the first baseman, came over for it. Craig Anderson, the pitcher, went after it and got it. He turned to throw it to first. Of course, no one was there. On the next play Zimmer couldn't find the handle on a little grounder and the Phillies had a five-run lead.

Stengel blamed Marshall. "Why should he go over there?" he grumbled. "He was out of place. No one knew where the hell he was."

Said Marshall: "Well, I don't know. I'm supposed to go for the ball until the pitcher calls me off. By the time he said anything, I was too far from the base to go back."

Then there was Neal. On a play like that, the second baseman ought to

come over and cover first. Neal just sort of stood there watching the play. And *that* was the Mets.

It is a distortion of history to believe, as some of the young Mets seem to now, that the old Mets were clowns who expected—even *wanted*—to lose. They lost, all right, and as Stengel once pointed out, "When you're losing, you commence to play stupid." But none of them *wanted* to lose.

This from Zimmer after the Mets had lost those first nine in a row: "It's got to get you down after a while. There ain't nobody looking to lose in this game no matter how lousy you are."

And when, after two seasons in which he had managed to lose forty six games—a record—Craig was finally traded, he sighed with great relief. "Losing," Craig said. "I never liked to lose. I never even got used to it."

It was a cold and miserable day at the Polo Grounds and the Mets were down 15–5 with two out in the ninth. A fan stood in the aisle in right field, his shoulders hunched against the cold, his hands deep in his coat pockets. He jiggled up and down for warmth and all the time he was rooting. "C'mon," he said, almost to himself. "C'mon, one more run, just one more run."

"Why one more run?" he was asked.

"That would make it six," he said. "Then you could say if they got any pitching they woulda won."

The fan turned back toward Don Zimmer, who was at the plate. "C'mon," he said. "Just one more."

Zimmer popped up to the catcher.

The fan shrugged his shoulders. "Ah well," he said. "I'll be back tomorrow. No use giving up now."

Then there was the couple who were arrested behind home plate one night for committing what, considering the location, was an act of extraordinary friendliness. "But, officer," the woman protested, "we're *married*."

One of the few rules Stengel put down for his players was that there would be no card playing. It was his belief that card playing led to gambling, gambling led to losing, and losing led to resentments. Shortly after Harry Chiti was obtained by the Mets, he went to Stengel during an airplane trip and asked for permission to start a gin-rummy game. Stengel said no. He suggested instead that if Chiti, a catcher, had nothing to do he might go over the opposition hitters. Chiti went to sleep.

The most interesting thing about Chiti is that he was obtained for "a player to be named later." When that player was finally named, it turned out to be Harry Chiti. Thus he was returned in payment for himself.

There is no other reason for his fame.

On May 9, the Mets picked up Marvelous Marv Throneberry from the Baltimore Orioles. George Weiss gleefully announced that he had managed to get Throneberry for cash, which was very hard to do. Throneberry was first called Marvelous when he was a young Yankee and it was believed, as it was about all young Yankees, that he was actually a marvelous ballplayer. He was something else.

When he came to the Mets he had a lifetime average of .238 and a reputation as a poor fielder. But as Weiss pointed out, "He has never had a chance to play regularly." The Mets gave him that chance. It revealed him.

Throneberry, twenty-nine at the time, looked much older. He was thickly built and his bald head was covered with freckles. He was from a small town in Tennessee, chewed tobacco, and had a country accent.

Although he occasionally hit the long ball, he also hit into a lot of double plays and often struck out at crucial moments. On the field he was a disaster. Very quickly, he was being booed by the generally gentle Polo Grounds fans. He had become the personification of ineptitude. His first reaction was the routine baseball-player one of savage anger. Slowly though, with the help of Richie Ashburn, whose locker was next to his in the clubhouse, he came to understand his special role. There was the rainy night, for example, after he had had one of his routinely terrible games. He sat in his underwear in front of his locker and allowed a leak in the ceiling of the decrepit old clubhouse to drip, drip, drip, directly onto his bald head.

"I deserve it," he said.

"Yes, you do," said Richie Ashburn.

Elio Chacon stopped a reporter near the batting cage in San Francisco one day. "Hey," he said, shyly. "You think we win today?"

The reporter, a gentle sort, said he was often disappointed, but he expected the Mets to win every day. Chacon nodded with satisfaction. "Well, we try every day," he said. "We try. That's muy important."

The Mets were beaten that day, twice, 11–4 and 10–3.

The Mets lost because of their pitching, hitting, fielding, and because they often had abysmal luck. They also lost because of umpires. That's what happens to bad teams. Pick a game at random in late July. The Mets were losing to St. Louis 6–4 in the ninth because they had made four errors, because of a two-out, bases-loaded, broken-bat blooper by the Cards' Ken Boyer, and because while Marvelous Marv was chasing Boyer in a rundown Stan Musial was able to score, laughing. Still, in the last of the ninth, the Mets had the tying runs on base when Choo Choo Coleman, the little catcher Stengel was trying (and failing) to build up into another Yogi Berra, was caught in a rundown between third and home. In the course of the rundown, Coleman was clearly tripped by catcher Jim Schaffer while he was not in possession of the ball. Instead of awarding Coleman home plate, umpire Mel Steiner called him out and the game was over.

When Ed Bouchee made an error on the field and then struck out with two runners on base, Marvelous Marv walked up to him, looking angry, and said, "What are you trying to do, steal my fans?"

On August 15, Al Jackson of the Mets held the Philadelphia Phillies to one run for fourteen innings. In the fifteenth, two runs scored when Tony Gonzales hit a sharp ground ball to first base. Although Marvelous Marv was there, when he put down his glove the ball just naturally jumped over it. Throneberry was not charged with an error. He had not, in fact, made an error in fifteen games.

He had a chance to make up for it all in the bottom of the fifteenth when he came up with runners on first and third. He struck out. "He ended up swinging on balls they was gonna walk him on," Stengel complained.

After the Mets had lost for the ninety-second time, Richie Ashburn said,

"They say it's easy to play on a loser. Hell it is. It's a lot easier to play on a winner. Seems to me I'm playing harder than I ever did before."

Marvelous Marv had a great September. He won several games with home runs and even started a couple of difficult and important first-to-second-to-first double plays. One day he helped beat the Dodgers with a home run and then made all three putouts in the ninth. Five kids came into the ballpark one night, each dressed in a white T-shirt with a black letter inked on. "M-A-R-V" they spelled out. The fifth wore a "!". When they climbed on top of the Mets dugout and did a dance, they were thrown out of the park. They bought their way back into the bleachers to see M-A-R-V!

Said Ashburn: "Throneberry is the people's choice. And you know why? He typifies the Mets. He's either great or terrible." He paused and turned to Throneberry. "But you better not get too good," he said. "Just drop a pop fly once in a while."

Said Throneberry: "Aw, I haven't dropped a pop fly in a week."

Throneberry did so well at the last that he received a $7,000 power boat for hitting an outfield sign more than anybody else. Ashburn received a $5,000 power boat after a vote by fans and newspapermen. Throneberry found out that since Ashburn's boat was a gift it was not taxable, but that since he had won his in a contest, his was. Said Throneberry, scratching his bald dome and looking exquisitely unhappy: "I don't understand it."

At the end of that first season, Ken McKenzie, a pitcher and the only Yale man on the club, told some of the thoughts he had about the events of the year. McKenzie: "When we started out this spring, I really thought we'd be all right, maybe even play .500 ball. I don't know what happened. *Something* happened, of course. You hear about clubs that win pennants. What happens is one guy picks up if another lets down. We've worked in reverse. We found a different way to lose every day.

"I don't think we were quite as bad as we looked. There was something this year that made every player a little worse than his potential. Our pitching, well, our pitching had a pattern. Error, base hit; error, base hit. When you're pitching good ball and there's an error behind you, you bend your back and make the pitches. This is exactly what we didn't do. We probably set a record for unearned runs. That's no alibi for the pitchers, not when he's giving up the runs after the error."

The Mets finished with a 40–120 record. They had had losing streaks of nine, eleven, thirteen, and seventeen. Said Stengel: "Strangers are hard to manage. It was like spring training all year. But I expected to win more games. I was very much shocked."

Said Throneberry: "You think the fish will come out of the water to boo me this winter?"

The Mets were not much different the next year. After the first game in 1963, Stengel stormed into his little Polo Grounds office, slammed his baseball cap down on his desk, and announced, "The attendance was robbed. We're still a fraud."

And not long after, Marvelous Marv Throneberry, playing right field, slipped and fell while chasing the first ball hit to him. He was able to hold the runner to two bases on the single and as he sat there on the wet grass, chagrin oozing from every pore, Duke Snider, now the center fielder, stood over him, hands on hips, and laughed and laughed. It was another good year.

There was never a team like the old Mets and there will never be another. It was put together by a chain of incredible coincidences: the mendacity of National League club owners who wanted to give up as few good players as possible in the expansion draft; the dogged if mistaken logic of George Weiss; the wildly improbable personality of Casey Stengel; the eccentrically shaped, decrepit, yet somehow intimate and friendly Polo Grounds, one of the last of the ballparks that made itself a factor in the playing of baseball games; the baseball-hungry fans, who could not be comfortable in the austere, cold Yankee Stadium, where triumph was cheap and tragedy nonexistent. To have been there when these coincidences collided with such shattering hilarity was to have been in a special place indeed.

Now it is all different. Casey Stengel is gone. The players, who try no harder than the old Mets, succeed more often and as a result are indistinguishable from baseball players all over. There is stuffiness in the front office. There is great concern about unimportant things. (The manager not long ago suggested to a newspaperman that he need not have blabbed in the public prints that the Mets scored their winning run on a bunt.) And, worst of all, when the Mets lose, there is nothing funny about it at all.

Do losers lose and winners win? Or are those who win, winners, and those who lose, losers? Character and destiny, chicken and egg. Riddles rampant on a field of green. Things as they are, things as they seem. Aristotle at the bat. Plato on the hill.

WILFRID SHEED

Notes on the Country Game

The 1980 World Series was supposed to feature the spoiled millionaires of Philadelphia vs. the enlightened millionaires of New York. I don't know what sort of millionaires they have in Kansas City—signals from the Sunbelt come in dimly on the Eastern Seaboard. But money and the modern ballplayer have been the talk all season, even when the lads fall to fighting over beanballs. (Nobody that rich wants to be hit in the head, goes the reasoning.)

Thus the Yankees put up with the bully-boy ravings of George Steinbrenner because they can't afford not to. New York is such a lucrative playground, in TV commercials alone, that Steinbrenner can chew out the help with impunity. Philadelphia apparently does not cast quite the same spell, so there the players chew out the manager instead. The question the World Series was *supposed* to answer was: Which is better for you, to chew or be chewed?

The Series we got did suggest that perhaps these are not baseball questions at all but messy fallout from the gossip culture. The Phillies were supposed to hate their manager so much that they might well lose four straight, or whatever it took, just to spite him. The Kansas City Royals, who, it seems, only mildly dislike their manager, should have cashed in on this quirk of brotherly love handsomely—everybody else has who's had the good luck to encounter the Phillies in October, by which time they must be a ball of seething hate.

Yet when the blather had cleared, one team had made sixty hits and the other fifty-nine; one team (a different one) had outscored the other 4.5 to 3.9 per game—which I believe comes close to the average score of all ballgames played anywhere since the beginning of time. In short, the verities triumphed over the froth of the press box. Baseball is so finely calibrated that the super teams win three out of five, and the dogs two out of five. It is not the least surprising to find two teams with exactly the same records after *160 games*. So a Series between *any* two big-league teams could be close. Yet in a World Series, these percentages fly out the window and everything is supposed to come down to character, as if ballplayers were prisoners of their nerves, like the rest of us.

The salient factor about this year's Series was that *neither* cast had been in one before. That took care of the stage-fright margin, or old Yankee edge. Maidenhood is everything in these matters. Yet while everyone else talked about money, the players themselves talked about character, as millionaires are wont to. The word must have a special meaning for them. Because as soon as a team begins to win, it *believes* it has character. Just let a couple of lucky hits fall in and the guys will say, "Yeah, we're that kind of team." The rhythm of streak and slump is so wild and unfathomable that the men riding it feel compelled to assert some kind of control over it. Contrariwise, in defeat the players "get down on themselves," search for scapegoats, question their own character. "We *proved* we had character," said the Phillies. Obviously. To win *is* to have character.

Morale also is more a function of winning than a cause of it: but it's a necessary function. It prolongs the streak from six wins to seven and picks up the junk game that could go either way, that magical third game in five.

There are some teams that sin against the Holy Ghost and reject the energy that victory brings. The Phillies were felt to be one of these, like the Red Sox. Pampered by country-club ownership, went the talk, they could not rise to the myth of team spirit, the sense that the Collective can somehow coordinate its private streaks and slumps to squeeze the extra game. Too rich, not hungry enough, injury-prone (injuries, strangely, are no excuse: character is supposed to thrive on them); teams like the Phillies are the pouting villains we need for our annual play-in-the-round.

Yet give one of them a hot hand—the Red Sox in '75, the Phillies last month—and you'll see who's pouty. Philadelphia did all the things rich brats are expressly supposed not to do. They came from behind four times in a row, counting the playoffs. Outfielder Bake McBride, the brat of brats, turned his orneriness into pure menace, treating the enemy as if they were his manager. Shortstop Larry Bowa, the team cynic, started seven double plays (a record) and cried with joy when it was all over. Pitcher Steve Carlton, who won't even talk to his friends, popped his fast ball so hard that the catcher's mitt sounded like a bat.

Perhaps the best symbol was third baseman Mike Schmidt because he seemed to personify defeat, almost to anticipate it, *without* being obnoxious, a more evolved mutant. Some dismal playoffs in the past had made him a loser in a Sartrean sense: i.e., *first* you lose, *then* you are a loser—you have defined yourself.

Yet suddenly he had his touch, and he seemed like a different man. And one realized how much one's concept of a team is a problem in perception, or propaganda. Because all the Phillies looked better in victory. For instance, the surliness in the clubhouse—was that really because they were counting their money, or was it because they just don't like reporters, the old-fashioned way? Being civilized to the press is often the only clue we have to these guys' personalities, and it isn't a bad one. But ballplayers from the outback can be unduly disturbed the first time they see themselves misquoted or laughed at in a big newspaper. A team, like an administration, is as lovable as its press corps makes it.

Baseball is pre-eminently the country game, because it takes up so much space, artificially transposed to the city where strangers boo you; the suspicious, uncommunicative rube has graced every clubhouse since Ring Lardner. In fact, you can probably find Steve Carlton himself somewhere in Lardner, right down to the hideous grimaces.

One of baseball's charming legends has Whitey Ford of New York City playing Henry Higgins to Mickey Mantle of Oklahoma and practically turning him into a boulevardier. Pete Rose struggles to perform the same task for the Phils, but it's tough work Higginsing half a squad. And of course the black styles of resentment practiced by McBride and Garry Maddox were undreamed of in Lardner, and will presumably have to be resolved outside the clubhouse.

As to those miserable objects, "today's kids," who allegedly can't stand discipline from an old-school manager—what about yesterday's kids, the Cleveland crybabies of 1940, or the Dodgers of '43, one of whom (Arky Vaughan) flung his uniform at Leo Durocher's feet? Ballplayers, rich or poor, have always been hard to handle—it is one of the few real tests of great managing—and a flinty-eyed brute like Rogers Hornsby had as little luck with it way back then as he would today.

On second thought, has anything changed as little as a major-league ballplayer, unless it be the game he plays? Babe Ruth holds a mirror to the 1920s, and the Gas House Gang might be said to reflect the Okie spirit of the 1930s.

But it's a weak reflection. You might have guessed from the hairdos in the 1960s that *something* was happening in America, but what?

You can't deduce much about an era from its ballplayers. Solitary men in a solitary game, they make their way one by one into the big leagues and out again, always slightly to the side of normal society. The team spirit they invoke so fervently is always ad hoc, always this gang this year. Their teammates, while they last, are closer than family, but they are always being ripped apart and replaced. No wonder some players are withdrawn and others full of empty good cheer. A barmaid in Lindells of Detroit told me that ballplayers were the stingiest and least friendly of all the athletes who traipsed through the place. Yet there are the Tug McGraws and Pete Roses who thrive on the change and uncertainty of the gypsy life, and who can briefly ignite the rest—as long as the rest are winning anyway.

Team spirit has little to do with the hard numbers of baseball, though it can quasi-mystically keep batting rallies going (or is it the rally itself that creates the spirit?). This Series came down to Willie Wilson's strikeouts and Willie Aikens's stone glove, and all the character in the world couldn't have done a thing about that. If Wilson never plays another Series, he will become another Mike Schmidt, a loser; if the wheel spins right, he will become Mr. October II. He will still be the same player, but he will look different. Which may be why athletes don't think much of fans.

Otherwise, chalk a small one up for the brat who chews, and file this away under "arrestingly average." Nineteen eighty was the year the percentages came back in the guise of melodrama: in other words, it was baseball at its finest.

The country game has its ugly moments, to be sure—the beanball bouts and mandatory melees that follow, or teammates duking it out in the locker room, or fans insulting/assaulting players in the parking lot. There have been on-field riots (see my own contribution to this volume), off-field tragedies (murders, suicides), and garden-variety vituperation aplenty. But nothing in recent memory has shocked and disgusted the baseball world like this explosion in the Texas Rangers' spring camp of 1977. Blackie Sherrod covered it for the *Dallas Times Herald*.

BLACKIE SHERROD

The Randle Incident

The sequence was all so incredibly swift, maybe four, five seconds at the most, and yet in afterthought, it hung there suspended in time, like slow motion or instant replay or the old newsreel films of the *Hindenburg* breaking apart reluctantly in dark Jersey skies.

There was the tableau of Frank Lucchesi and Lenny Randle talking, calmly it seemed to these witnessing eyeballs some 40 feet away—the Texas manager and his embittered player, once again debating Randle's past, present, and future with the Rangers. They stood maybe 18 inches apart, Lucchesi in his blue flowered shirt and gray slacks (he had not yet dressed for the game), Randle in his uniform, some 20 feet toward the Ranger dugout from the pregame batting cage.

There was no raising of voices, or even these jaded ears would have picked it up; no animation, no gestures, no jabbing of forefingers, no distending of neck veins. It seems to this memory that both men had their hands on hips, not belligerently but naturally as a couple guys on the street corner argue the respective talents of the Longhorns and Sooners. Three, four minutes the conversation continued while your eyewitness watched it idly, only vaguely curious at what appeared to be another review of Randle's discontent that he wasn't getting a full-scale chance at retaining his second-base job from the challenge of rookie Bump Wills.

(The debate surfaced angrily last week when Lucchesi exploded that he was "sick and tired of some punks making $80,000 moaning and groaning about their jobs." The word *punk* was the fuse.)

Lucchesi had walked on the Minnesota spring diamond, said hello to a few fans, walked away for a private chat with Jim Russo, the Baltimore superscout. (Trade talk?)

The forty-eight-year-old manager was en route back to the dugout tunnel to the locker room to get dressed when Randle approached. So the two men talked while Rangers took batting practice behind them, a cluster of players awaiting turns at the cage.

Suddenly with unbelievable quickness, Randle's right hand shot forth. No wild drawback nor windup, as a saloon brawler might use, but a straight strike from the body and here was Lucchesi falling slowly, turning to his right from the force, and there came a left with the same terrible rapidity. This was probably the blow that fractured Lucchesi's right cheekbone. Then another right and a left, all before the victim finally reached earth some 10 feet from where he was first struck. Your witness has seen the hand speed of Sugar Ray Robinson and the cobra strikes of Muhammad Ali, but the flurry of Randle's punches, all landing on the manager's face, must have broken all speed records.

After Lucchesi hit heavily on his right hip, his left arm curled above him in some helpless defense attempt, there were other Randle punches, maybe they landed, maybe not, before Bert Campaneris reacted from four strides away. He had frozen at first, probably as others stared in disbelief, but sprinted quickly to the scene, leaped astride the fallen Lucchesi and stretched his hands out, palms up, to fend off Randle. The furious player backed away, yelling, "Leave me alone!" while Jim Fregosi and others reached the dazed victim.

Then, while players carried Lucchesi to the dugout tunnel, his right eye already blue and puffing, blood trickling from his mouth, Randle preceded them to the dugout, pulled a bat from the rack and held it briefly, then dropped it and trotted to the outfield where he began to run wind sprints all alone. This was maybe the only positive move of the day, for who knows what player emotions might have followed. Ken Henderson, especially, had to be restrained when he saw Lucchesi, sitting propped against the tunnel wall while trainer Bill Zeigler tried to administer aid and judge the damage.

No witness could remember any similar baseball incident. Fights between players, surely, even spats between players and coaches, but never a player felling his manager. Eddie Robinson, the Ranger vice-president, arriving later, couldn't think of one. Sid Hudson, the veteran coach, shook his head. Burt Hawkins, the traveling secretary who watched Babe Ruth, also flunked.

So what prompted this unprecedented explosion? Randle, seemingly composed afterward, said Lucchesi had called him a "punk" again. Lucchesi, from his bed in Mercy Hospital, said this was a lie.

Was the Randle violent, savage action triggered by a remark in the apparent calm conversation? Was it a buildup of Randle emotions, of frustrations bred when he thought he was not being given enough chance to play?

A day earlier, Lenny had told Channel 4 interviewer Allan Stone, "I'm a volcano, getting ready to erupt."

"But," said Stone, "he was smiling when he said it."

If Randle's was a calculated action, would not a single punch have sufficed? What pushed him across the line into uncontrollable fury, an outburst that might end his baseball career forever? Probably no one will ever know.

In a corner of the dugout, by the bullpen telephone while Ranger players milled about in stunned aimlessness, a small white card glared from the wall. It was the lineup for Monday's game. The second line read: Randle, 2B.

Howard Ehmke was a draughthorse of a pitcher—not flashy, but dependable. At the close of the 1929 regular season, the books appeared to be closed on his career: won-lost record, 166–165. But in the World Series that year, Connie Mack gambled that the veteran had one more win left in him, and he did. Red Smith wrote this story on March 18, 1959, upon learning of Ehmke's death; so frequently did he find inspiration on the obituary page that he amassed enough elegiac columns to make for a collection of fond farewells, *To Absent Friends*. Walter W. Smith joined those friends before the book was completed; it was published with an additional farewell, by Dave Anderson.

RED SMITH

Howard Ehmke

Of all the stories Connie Mack used to tell at dinners, and he had a routine as fixed as any in vaudeville, his favorite concerned Howard Ehmke. It never varied by so much as a syllable in the telling. Late in the 1929 season, Connie would explain, it had become evident that nothing could stop the Athletics' drive to a pennant. Just before the last tour of the West, Connie called Ehmke into his tower office in Shibe Park in Philadelphia. Ehmke's days in the major leagues were ending. He sat on the bench almost all summer watching Lefty Grove, George Earnshaw, Rube Walberg, and others younger than he handling the chores on the mound. This was the scene as Connie described it:

" 'Howard,' I said, 'the time has come for us to part.'

"He looked at me. 'Mr. Mack,' he said, 'I have always wanted to pitch in a World Series.' He lifted his arm"—here Connie would raise his own thin right arm, fist clenched—" 'Mr. Mack,' he said, 'there is one great game left in this old arm.' That was what I wanted to hear. 'All right, Howard,' I told him. 'When we go west I want you to stay here. When the Cubs come in to play the Phillies, you watch them. Learn all you can about their hitters. Say nothing to anybody. You are my opening pitcher for the World Series.' "

There was a sidelight which Connie omitted from his tale, but Al Simmons supplied it. When Ehmke started to warm up for the opener with the Cubs, Simmons snorted with consternation. "Are you going to pitch *him!*" he demanded incredulously.

"Is it all right with you, Al?" Connie asked.

Simmons gulped. "Oh, well—er, well, if you say so."

Skipping that bit, Connie would go on to tell how the Cubs lunged and stabbed at Ehmke's soft stuff. He would recall the strikeouts in order—Rogers Hornsby, Hack Wilson, Kiki Cuyler, Riggs Stephenson, Gabby Hartnett, Hornsby again, then Wilson—until the total reached thirteen for an all-time World Series record.

Connie attached a lot of importance to the secrecy surrounding his plan. He made it clear that in his opinion the element of surprise was a major factor in Ehmke's success. Chances are he never knew of a conversation which Ring Lardner repeated a year later.

Lardner was writing fiction and plays by 1929, but he had many friends in baseball after his years as a sportswriter. Joe McCarthy, the Cubs' manager, was one.

"I was chatting with Joe a little before the season ended," Lardner said. " 'I'm not afraid of Grove and Earnshaw,' he told me. 'We can hit speed. But they've got one guy over there I am afraid of. He's what I call a junk pitcher—but Joe used an indelicate expression. 'His name,' he told me, 'is Howard Ehmke, and he's the sucker we're going to see in this Series.'"

So maybe the Cubs' surprise wasn't quite so great as Connie liked to believe. He did enjoy telling the story, though, and today it all comes back because the morning paper reported the death of Howard Ehmke at sixty-five.

He was a big, handsome, light-haired man, head of a successful tarpaulin and awning firm in Philadelphia, and a pretty good horse player. He used to get to Miami every year during the Hialeah meeting and it was a pleasure to encounter him there, a quiet man of warmth and charm. This season he wasn't there.

Howard lived to see his strikeout record broken by Carl Erskine, pitching for Brooklyn against the Yankees. He wasn't in the stands when it happened, though. He and Mrs. Ehmke were taking a drive in suburban Philadelphia, listening with mild interest to the radio broadcast of the game.

At first it was just another game to Howard, but as Erskine turned back one Yankee after another, it took on a special interest. When Erskine got his ninth or tenth strikeout, Howard said, "Let's park and listen to the rest of this." He pulled off the road and cut the motor.

Another Yankee struck out. Then another. Now Erskine tied Ehmke's mark but the game wasn't over. Mrs. Ehmke was watching her husband. The fourteenth Yankee went down—it could have been Don Bollweg. Howard smiled quietly.

He said nothing as the game drew to an end. The record he had held for a quarter of a century was gone. He stepped on the starter. Nothing happened. The radio had drained his battery.

No greater love hath fan than this—and as with all things in baseball, there's precedent. James Whyte Davis of the original Knickerbockers, who began play on Hoboken's Elysian Fields in 1850, penned these burial instructions in his waning years: "All relations and immediate friends are well informed that I desire to be buried in my baseball suit, and wrapped in the original flag of the old Knickerbockers of 1845, now festooned over my bureau. . . ." This, from *The Sporting News* of July 26, 1980, with a memorable last line.

THE SPORTING NEWS

Bury Me in My Old Cub Suit

Maniford (Hack) Harper of Washburn, Illinois, has lived and died with the Chicago Cubs for fifty-four years, and he's not planning to stop when he leaves this earthly vale.

Harper, sixty-five, has made a pact with a mortician to go to his grave in a Cubs uniform that he bought from his favorite team some years ago. The uniform and a bright blue cap with a red "C" on the front have been in mothballs, prepared for the day Hack is laid to rest.

"I'm going to be buried in the uniform because baseball is all I think about," said Harper. "It's my life. I don't care about cars or anything else, and I never have."

Harper's devotion to the Cubs began when he was in Shriners Hospital in Oak Park, Illinois, in 1926, at the age of eleven. Severely stricken with polio, he had been paralyzed on the right side of his body since he was seventeen months old.

He said that Cubs immortal Hack Wilson visited the hospital with some fellow players and walked up to him, tapped him on the shoulder, and said, "Stick it out, kid. Someday, you'll be able to walk."

From then on, Harper was a Cubs fan. People started calling him Hack, after the Cubs' slugger. At thirteen, he visited the tattoo parlor at a medicine show and had "CUBS" engraved on his left forearm in inch-high letters. For his high school graduation, he requested $25 to travel the 125 miles to Chicago to watch the Cubbies play for a week.

He has attended more than 1,500 games at Wrigley Field, and has collected 187 foul balls and had them autographed. He keeps them in a safe deposit box. For seven consecutive years, he traveled to Arizona to buy the first available spring-training ticket of the season—and still has the stubs to prove it.

"They're my whole life," said Harper. "Without the Cubs, I would be crazy."

Baseball analysis: Is less more? Wielding Occam's Razor, the parsimonious poet confounds the experts. From her 1971 volume, *More Poems to Solve*.

MAY SWENSON

Analysis of Baseball

It's about
the ball,
the bat,
and the mitt.
Ball hits
bat, or it
hits mitt.
Bat doesn't
hit ball, bat
meets it.
Ball bounces
off bat, flies
air, or thuds
ground (dud)
or it
fits mitt.

Bat waits
for ball

to mate.
Ball hates
to take bat's
bait. Ball
flirts, bat's
late, don't
keep the date.
Ball goes in
(thwack) to mitt,
and goes out
(thwack) back
to mitt.

Ball fits
mitt, but
not all
the time.
Sometimes
ball gets hit

(pow) when bat
meets it,
and sails
to a place
where mitt
has to quit
in disgrace.
That's about
the bases
loaded,
about 40,000
fans exploded.

It's about
the ball,
the bat,
the mitt,
the bases
and the fans.
It's done
on a diamond,
and for fun.
It's about
home, and it's
about run.

The obscure wish to be famous; the famous, to be obscure. Joe DiMaggio is a private man who plied a public trade and still does; like Garbo (and Steve Carlton), he has shielded himself from those who would use him, but this has had the paradoxical effect of making him all the more alluring to those he would repel. DiMaggio resisted the efforts of Gay Talese to interview him for *Esquire* in 1966, but the master of the profile got his man, as usual. Tom Wolfe has credited Talese with having created the "new journalism"—stylish reporting, employing the techniques of fiction—with his 1962 *Esquire* profile of another man of dignity, Joe Louis.

GAY TALESE

The Silent Season of a Hero

> *"I would like to take the great*
> *DiMaggio fishing," the old man said.*
> *"They say his father was a fisherman.*
> *Maybe he was as poor as we are and*
> *would understand."*
> —Ernest Hemingway,
> *The Old Man and the Sea*

It was not quite spring, the silent season before the search for salmon, and the old fishermen of San Francisco were either painting their boats or repairing their nets along the pier or sitting in the sun talking quietly among themselves, watching the tourists come and go, and smiling, now, as a pretty girl paused to take their picture. She was about twenty-five, healthy and blue-eyed and wearing a red turtleneck sweater, and she had long, flowing blond hair that she brushed back a few times before clicking her camera. The fishermen, looking at her, made admiring comments but she did not understand because they spoke a Sicilian dialect; nor did she notice the tall gray-haired man in a dark suit who stood watching her from behind a big bay window on the second floor of DiMaggio's Restaurant that overlooks the pier.

He watched until she left, lost in the crowd of newly arrived tourists that had just come down the hill by cable car. Then he sat down again at the table in the restaurant, finishing his tea and lighting another cigarette, his fifth in the last half hour. It was eleven-thirty in the morning. None of the other tables was occupied, and the only sounds came from the bar, where a liquor salesman was laughing at something the headwaiter had said. But then the salesman, his briefcase under his arm, headed for the door, stopping briefly to peek into the dining room and call out, "See you later, Joe." Joe DiMaggio turned and waved at the salesman. Then the room was quiet again.

At fifty-one, DiMaggio was a most distinguished-looking man, aging as gracefully as he had played on the ballfield, impeccable in his tailoring, his nails manicured, his 6-foot 2-inch body seeming as lean and capable as when he posed for the portrait that hangs in the restaurant and shows him in Yankee Stadium swinging from the heels at a pitch thrown twenty years ago. His gray hair was thinning at the crown, but just barely, and his face was lined in the right places, and his expression, once as sad and haunted as a matador's, was more in repose these days, though, as now, tension had returned and he chain-smoked and occasionally paced the floor and looked out the window at the people below. In the crowd was a man he did not wish to see.

The man had met DiMaggio in New York. This week he had come to San Francisco and had telephoned several times but none of the calls had been returned because DiMaggio suspected that the man, who had said he was doing research on some vague sociological project, really wanted to delve into DiMaggio's private life and that of DiMaggio's former wife, Marilyn Monroe. DiMaggio would never tolerate this. The memory of her death is still very painful to him, and yet, because he keeps it to himself, some people are not sensitive to it. One night in a supper club a woman who had been drinking approached his table, and when he did not ask her to join him, she snapped:

"All right, I guess I'm *not* Marilyn Monroe."

He ignored her remark, but when she repeated it, he replied, barely controlling his anger, "No—I wish you were, but you're not."

The tone of his voice softened her, and she asked, "Am I saying something wrong?"

"You already have," he said. "Now will you please leave me alone?"

His friends on the wharf, understanding him as they do, are very careful when discussing him with strangers, knowing that should they inadvertently betray a confidence he will not denounce them but rather will never speak to them again; this comes from a sense of propriety not inconsistent in the man who also, after Marilyn Monroe's death, directed that fresh flowers be placed on her grave "forever."

Some of the old fishermen who have known DiMaggio all his life remember him as a small boy who helped clean his father's boat, and as a young man who sneaked away and used a broken oar as a bat on the sandlots nearby. His father, a small mustachioed man known as Zio Pepe, would become infuriated and call him *lagnuso* (lazy) *meschino* (good-for-nothing) but in 1936 Zio Pepe was among those who cheered when Joe DiMaggio returned to San Francisco after his first season with the New York Yankees and was carried along the wharf on the shoulders of the fishermen.

The fishermen also remember how, after his retirement in 1951, DiMaggio brought his second wife, Marilyn, to live near the wharf, and sometimes they would be seen early in the morning fishing off DiMaggio's boat, the *Yankee Clipper*, now docked quietly in the marina, and in the evening they would be sitting and talking on the pier. They had arguments, too, the fishermen knew, and one night Marilyn was seen running hysterically, crying as she ran, along the road away from the pier, with Joe following. But the fishermen pretended they did not see this; it was none of their affair. They knew that Joe wanted her to stay in San Francisco and avoid the sharks in Hollywood, but she was confused and torn then—"She was a child," they said—and even today DiMaggio loathes Los Angeles and many of the people in it. He no longer speaks to his onetime friend, Frank Sinatra, who had befriended Marilyn in her final years, and he also is cool to Dean Martin and Peter Lawford and Lawford's former wife, Pat, who once gave a party at which she introduced Marilyn Monroe to Robert Kennedy, and the two of them danced often that night, Joe heard, and he did not take it well. He was very possessive of her that year, his close friends say, because Marilyn and he had planned to remarry; but before they could she was dead, and DiMaggio banned the Lawfords and Sinatra and many Hollywood people from her funeral. When Marilyn Monroe's attorney complained that DiMaggio was keeping her friends away, DiMaggio answered coldly, "If it weren't for those friends persuading her to stay in Hollywood she would still be alive."

Joe DiMaggio now spends most of the year in San Francisco, and each day tourists, noticing the name on the restaurant, ask the men on the wharf if they ever see him. Oh yes, the men say, they see him nearly every day; they have not seen him yet this morning, they add, but he should be arriving shortly. So the tourists continue to walk along the piers past the crab vendors, under the circling sea gulls, past the fish 'n' chip stands, sometimes stopping to watch a large vessel steaming toward the Golden Gate Bridge which, to their dismay, is painted red. Then they visit the Wax Museum, where there is a life-size figure of DiMaggio in uniform, and walk across the street and spend a quarter to peer through the silver telescopes focused on the island of Alcatraz, which is no longer a Federal prison. Then they return to ask the men if DiMaggio has been seen. Not yet, the men say, although they notice his blue Impala parked in the lot next to the restaurant. Sometimes tourists will walk into the restaurant and have lunch and will see him sitting calmly in a corner signing autographs and being extremely gracious with everyone. At other times, as on this particular morning when the man from New York chose to visit, DiMaggio was tense and suspicious.

When the man entered the restaurant from the side steps leading to the dining room, he saw DiMaggio standing near the window, talking with an elderly maître d' named Charles Friscia. Not wanting to walk in and risk intrusion, the man asked one of DiMaggio's nephews to inform Joe of his presence. When DiMaggio got the message he quickly turned and left Friscia and disappeared through an exit leading down to the kitchen.

Astonished and confused, the visitor stood in the hall. A moment later Friscia appeared and the man asked, "Did Joe leave?"

"Joe who?" Friscia replied.

"Joe DiMaggio!"

"Haven't seen him," Friscia said.

"You haven't *seen* him! He was standing right next to you a second ago!"

"It wasn't me," Friscia said.

"You were standing next to him. I saw you. In the dining room."

"You must be mistaken," Friscia said, softly, seriously. "It wasn't me."

"You *must* be kidding," the man said, angrily, turning and leaving the restaurant. Before he could get to his car, however, DiMaggio's nephew came running after him and said, "Joe wants to see you."

He returned expecting to see DiMaggio waiting for him. Instead he was handed a telephone. The voice was powerful and deep and so tense that the quick sentences ran together.

"You are invading my rights, I did not ask you to come, I assume you have a lawyer, you must have a lawyer, get your lawyer!"

"I came as a friend," the man interrupted.

"That's beside the point," DiMaggio said. "I have my privacy, I do not want it violated, you'd better get a lawyer. . . ." Then, pausing, DiMaggio asked, "is my nephew there?"

He was not.

"Then wait where you are."

A moment later DiMaggio appeared, tall and red-faced, erect and beautifully dressed in his dark suit and white shirt with the gray silk tie and the gleaming silver cuff links. He moved with big steps toward the man and handed him an airmail envelope, unopened, that the man had written from New York.

"Here," DiMaggio said. "This is yours."

Then DiMaggio sat down at a small table. He said nothing, just lit a cigarette and waited, legs crossed, his head held high and back so as to reveal the intricate construction of his nose, a fine sharp tip above the big nostrils and tiny bones built out from the bridge, a great nose.

"Look," DiMaggio said, more calmly. "I do not interfere with other people's live. And I do not expect them to interfere with mine. There are things about my life, personal things, that I refuse to talk about. And even if you asked my brothers they would be unable to tell you about them because they do not know. There are things about me, so many things, that they simply do not know. . . ."

"I don't want to cause trouble," the man said. "I think you're a great man, and. . . ."

"I'm not great," DiMaggio cut in. "I'm not great," he repeated, softly. "I'm just a man trying to get along."

Then DiMaggio, as if realizing that he was intruding upon his own privacy, abruptly stood up. He looked at his watch.

"I'm late," he said, very formal again. "I'm ten minutes late. *You're* making me late."

The man left the restaurant. He crossed the street and wandered over to the pier, briefly watching the fishermen hauling their nets and talking in the sun, seeming very calm and contented. Then, after he had turned and was headed back toward the parking lot, a blue Impala stopped in front of him and Joe DiMaggio leaned out the window and asked, "Do you have a car?" His voice was very gentle.

"Yes," the man said.

"Oh," DiMaggio said. "I would have given you a ride."

Joe DiMaggio was not born in San Francisco but in Martinez, a small fishing village twenty-five miles northeast of the Golden Gate. Zio Pepe had settled there after leaving Isola delle Femmine, an islet off Palermo where the DiMaggios had been fishermen for generations. But in 1915, hearing of the luckier waters off San Francisco's wharf, Zio Pepe left Martinez, packing his boat with furniture and family, including Joe who was one year old.

San Francisco was placid and picturesque when the DiMaggio's arrived, but there was a competitive undercurrent and struggle for power along the pier. At dawn the boats would sail out to where the bay meets the ocean and the sea is rough, and later the men would race back with their hauls, hoping to beat their fellow fishermen to shore and sell it while they could. Twenty or thirty boats would sometimes be trying to gain the channel shoreward at the same time, and a fisherman had to know every rock in the water, and later know every bargaining trick along the shore, because the dealers and restaurateurs would play one fisherman off against the other, keeping the prices down. Later the fishermen became wiser and organized, predetermining the maximum amount each fisherman would catch, but there were always some men who, like the fish, never learned, and so heads would sometimes be broken, nets slashed, gasoline poured onto their fish, flowers of warning placed outside their doors.

But these days were ending when Zio Pepe arrived, and he expected his five sons to succeed him as fishermen, and the first two, Tom and Michael, did; but a third, Vincent, wanted to sing. He sang with such magnificent power as a young man that he came to the attention of the great banker, A. P. Giannini, and there were plans to send him to Italy for tutoring and the opera. But there was hesitation around the DiMaggio household and Vince never went; instead he played ball with the San Francisco Seals and sportswriters misspelled his name.

It was DeMaggio until Joe, at Vince's recommendation, joined the team and became a sensation, being followed later by the youngest brother, Dominic, who was also outstanding. All three later played in the big leagues and some writers like to say that Joe was the best hitter, Dom the best fielder, Vince the best singer, and Casey Stengel once said: "Vince is the only player I ever saw who could strike out three times in one game and not be embarrassed. He'd walk into the clubhouse whistling. Everybody would be feeling sorry for him, but Vince always thought he was doing good."

After he retired from baseball Vince became a bartender, then a milkman, now a carpenter. He lives forty miles north of San Francisco in a house he partly built, has been happily married for thirty-four years, has four grand-children, has in the closet one of Joe's tailor-made suits that he has never had altered to fit, and when people ask if he envies Joe he always says, "No, maybe Joe would like to have what I have. He won't admit it, but he just might like to have what I have." The brother Vince most admired was Michael, "a big earthy man, a dreamer, a fisherman who wanted things but didn't want to take from Joe, or to work in the restaurant. He wanted a bigger boat, but wanted to earn it on his own. He never got it." In 1953, at the age of forty-four, Michael fell from his boat and drowned.

Since Zio Pepe's death at seventy-seven in 1949, Tom, at sixty-two the oldest brother—two of his four sisters are older—has become nominal head of the family and manages the restaurant that was opened in 1937 as Joe DiMaggio's Grotto. Later, Joe sold out his share, and now Tom is the co-owner of it with Dominic. Of all the brothers, Dominic, who was known as the "Little Professor" when he played with the Boston Red Sox, is the most successful in business. He lives in a fashionable Boston suburb with his wife and three children and is president of a firm that manufactures fiber-cushion materials and grossed more than $3,500,000 last year.

Joe DiMaggio lives with his widowed sister, Marie, in a tan stone house on a quiet residential street not far from Fisherman's Wharf. He bought the house almost thirty years ago for his parents, and after their death he lived there with Marilyn Monroe; now it is cared for by Marie, a slim and handsome dark-eyed woman who has an apartment on the second floor, Joe on the third. There are some baseball trophies and plaques in the small room off DiMaggio's bed-room, and on his dresser are photographs of Marilyn Monroe, and in the living room downstairs is a small painting of her that DiMaggio likes very much: it reveals only her face and shoulders and she is wearing a very wide-brimmed sun hat, and there is a soft sweet smile on her lips, an innocent curiosity about her that is the way he saw her and the way he wanted her to be seen by others—a simple girl, "a warm big-hearted girl," he once described her, "that everybody took advantage of."

The publicity photographs emphasizing her sex appeal often offended him, and a memorable moment for Billy Wilder, who directed her in *The Seven Year Itch*, occurred when he spotted DiMaggio in a large crowd of people gathered on Lexington Avenue in New York to watch a scene in which Marilyn, standing over a subway grating to cool herself, had her skirts blown high by a sudden wind below. "What the hell is going on here?" DiMaggio was overheard to have said in the crowd, and Wilder recalled, "I shall never forget the look of death on Joe's face."

He was then thirty-nine, she was twenty-seven. They had been married in January of that year, 1954, despite disharmony in temperament and time: he was tired of publicity, she was thriving on it; he was intolerant of tardiness, she was always late. During their honeymoon in Tokyo, an American general had introduced himself and asked if, as a patriotic gesture, she would visit the troops in Korea. She looked at Joe. "It's your honeymoon," he said, shrugging, "go ahead if you want to."

She appeared on ten occasions before 100,000 servicemen, and when she returned she said, "It was so wonderful, Joe. You never heard such cheering."

"Yes I have," he said.

Across from her portrait in the living room, on a coffee table in front of a sofa, is a sterling-silver humidor that was presented to him by his Yankee teammates at a time when he was the most talked-about man in America, and when Les Brown's band had recorded a hit that was heard day and night on the radio:

> . . . From Coast to Coast, that's all you hear
> Of Joe the One-Man Show
> He's glorified the horsehide sphere,

Jolting Joe DiMaggio . . .
Joe . . . Joe . . . DiMaggio . . . we want you on our side. . . .

The year was 1941, and it began for DiMaggio in the middle of May after the Yankees had lost four games in a row, seven of their last nine, and were in fourth place, five-and-a-half games behind the leading Cleveland Indians. On May 15th, DiMaggio hit only a first-inning single in a game that New York lost to Chicago, 13–1; he was barely hitting .300, and had greatly disappointed the crowds that had seen him finish with a .352 average the year before and .381 in 1939.

He got a hit in the next game, and the next, and the next. On May 24th, with the Yankees losing 6–5 to Boston, DiMaggio came up with runners on second and third and singled them home, winning the game, extending his streak to ten games. But it went largely unnoticed. Even DiMaggio was not conscious of it until it had reached twenty-nine games in mid-June. Then the newspapers began to dramatize it, the public became aroused, they sent him good-luck charms of every description, and DiMaggio kept hitting, and radio announcers would interrupt programs to announce the news, and then the song again: "Joe . . . Joe . . . DiMaggio . . . we want you on our side. . . ."

Sometimes DiMaggio would be hitless his first three times up, the tension would build, it would appear that the game would end without his getting another chance—but he always would, and then he would hit the ball against the left-field wall, or through the pitcher's legs, or between two leaping infielders. In the forty-first game, the first of a doubleheader in Washington, DiMaggio tied an American League record that George Sisler had set in 1922. But before the second game began a spectator sneaked onto the field and into the Yankees' dugout and stole DiMaggio's favorite bat. In the second game, using another of his bats, DiMaggio lined out twice and flied out. But in the seventh inning, borrowing one of his old bats that a teammate was using, he singled and broke Sisler's record, and he was only three games away from surpassing the major-league record of forty-four set in 1897 by Willie Keeler while playing for Baltimore when it was a National League franchise.

An appeal for the missing bat was made through the newspapers. A man from Newark admitted the crime and returned it with regrets. And on July 2, at Yankee Stadium, DiMaggio hit a home run into the left-field stands. The record was broken.

He also got hits in the next eleven games, but on July 17th in Cleveland, at a night game attended by 67,468, he failed against two pitchers, Al Smith and Jim Bagby, Jr., although Cleveland's hero was really its third baseman, Ken Keltner, who in the first inning lunged to his right to make a spectacular backhanded stop of a drive and, from the foul line behind third base, he threw

DiMaggio out. DiMaggio received a walk in the fourth inning. But in the seventh he again hit a hard shot at Keltner, who again stopped it and threw him out. DiMaggio hit sharply toward the shortstop in the eighth inning, the ball taking a bad hop, but Lou Boudreau speared it off his shoulder and threw to the second baseman to start a double play and DiMaggio's streak was stopped at fifty-six games. But the New York Yankees were on their way to winning the pennant by seventeen games, and the World Series too, and so in August, in a hotel suite in Washington, the players threw a surprise party for DiMaggio and toasted him with champagne and presented him with this Tiffany silver humidor that is now in San Francisco in his living room. . . .

Marie was in the kitchen making toast and tea when DiMaggio came down for breakfast; his gray hair was uncombed but, since he wears it short, it was not untidy. He said good-morning to Marie, sat down and yawned. He lit a cigarette. He wore a blue wool bathrobe over his pajamas. It was eight A.M. He had many things to do today and he seemed cheerful. He had a conference with the president of Continental Television, Inc., a large retail chain in California of which he is a partner and vice-president; later he had a golf date, and then a big banquet to attend, and, if that did not go on too long and he were not too tired afterward, he might have a date.

Picking up the morning paper, not rushing to the sports page, DiMaggio read the front-page news, the people-problems of '66: Kwame Nkrumah was overthrown in Ghana, students were burning their draft cards (DiMaggio shook his head), the flu epidemic was spreading through the whole state of California.

Then he flipped inside through the gossip columns, thankful they did not have him in there today—they had printed an item about his dating "an electrifying airline hostess" not long ago, and they also spotted him at dinner with Dori Lane, "the frantic frugger" in Whiskey à Go Go's glass cage—and then he turned to the sports page and read a story about how the injured Mickey Mantle may never regain his form.

It had all happened so quickly, the passing of Mantle, or so it seemed; he had succeeded DiMaggio as DiMaggio had succeeded Ruth, but now there was no great young power hitter coming up and the Yankee management, almost desperate, had talked Mantle out of retirement; and on September 18, 1965, they gave him a "day" in New York during which he received several thousand dollars' worth of gifts—an automobile, two quarter horses, free vacation trips to Rome, Nassau, Puerto Rico—and DiMaggio had flown to New York to make the introduction before 50,000: it had been a dramatic day, an almost holy day for the believers who had jammed the grandstands early to witness the canonization of a new stadium saint. Cardinal Spellman was on the committee, President Johnson sent a telegram, the day was officially proclaimed by the Mayor of New York, an orchestra assembled in center field in front of the trinity of monuments to Ruth, Gehrig, Huggins; and high in the grandstands, billowing in the breeze of early autumn, were white banners that read: "Don't Quit Mick," "We Love the Mick."

The banners had been held by hundreds of young boys whose dreams had been fulfilled so often by Mantle, but also seated in the grandstands were older men, paunchy and balding, in whose middle-aged minds DiMaggio was still vivid and invincible, and some of them remembered how one month before, during a pre-game exhibition at Old-timers' Day in Yankee Stadium, DiMaggio had hit a pitch into the left-field seats, and suddenly thousands of people had jumped wildly to their feet, joyously screaming—the great DiMaggio had returned, they were young again, it was yesterday.

But on this sunny September day at the Stadium, the feast day of Mickey Mantle, DiMaggio was not wearing No. 5 on his back nor a black cap to cover his graying hair; he was wearing a black suit and white shirt and blue tie, and he stood in one corner of the Yankees' dugout waiting to be introduced by Red Barber, who was standing near home plate behind a silver microphone. In the outfield Guy Lombardo's Royal Canadians were playing soothing soft music; and moving slowly back and forth over the sprawling green grass between the left-field bullpen and the infield were two carts driven by grounds keepers and containing dozens and dozens of large gifts for Mantle—a 6-foot, 100-pound Hebrew National salami, a Winchester rifle, a mink coat for Mrs. Mantle, a set of Wilson golf clubs, a Mercury 95-horse power outboard motor, a Necchi portable, a year's supply of Chunky Candy. DiMaggio smoked a cigarette, but cupped it in his hands as if not wanting to be caught in the act by teen-aged boys near enough to peek down into the dugout. Then, edging forward a step, DiMaggio poked his head out and looked up. He could see nothing above except the packed towering green grandstands that seemed a mile high and moving, and he could see no clouds or blue sky, only a sky of faces. Then the announcer called out his name—*"Joe DiMaggio!"*—and suddenly there was a blast of cheering that grew louder and louder, echoing and reechoing within the big steel canyon, and DiMaggio stomped out his cigarette and climbed up the dugout steps and onto the soft green grass, the noise resounding in his ears, he could almost feel the breeze, the breath of 50,000 lungs upon him, 100,000 eyes watching his every move and for the briefest instant as he walked he closed his eyes.

Then in his path he saw Mickey Mantle's mother, a smiling elderly woman wearing an orchid, and he gently reached out for her elbow, holding it as he led her toward the microphone next to the other dignitaries lined up on the infield. Then he stood, very erect and without expression, as the cheers softened and the Stadium settled down.

Mantle was still in the dugout, in uniform, standing with one leg on the top step, and lined on both sides of him were the other Yankees who, when the ceremony was over, would play the Detroit Tigers. Then into the dugout, smiling, came Senator Robert Kennedy, accompanied by two tall curly-haired young assistants with blue eyes, Fordham freckles. Jim Farley was the first on the field to notice the Senator, and Farley muttered, loud enough for others to hear, "Who the hell invited *him?*"

Toots Shor and some of the other committeemen standing near Farley looked into the dugout, and so did DiMaggio, his glance seeming cold, but he remaining silent. Kennedy walked up and down within the dugout shaking hands with the Yankees, but he did not walk onto the field.

"Senator," said the Yankees' manager, Johnny Keane, "why don't you sit down?" Kennedy quickly shook his head, smiled. He remained standing, and then one Yankee came over and asked about getting relatives out of Cuba, and Kennedy called over one of his aides to take down the details in a notebook.

On the infield the ceremony went on, Mantle's gifts continued to pile up— a Mobilette motor bike, a Sooner Schooner wagon barbecue, a year's supply of Chock Full O'Nuts coffee, a year's supply of Topps Chewing Gum—and the Yankee players watched, and Maris seemed glum.

"Hey, Rog," yelled a man with a tape recorder, Murray Olderman, "I want to do a thirty-second tape with you."

Maris swore angrily, shook his head.

"It'll only take a second," Olderman said.

"Why don't you ask Richardson? He's a better talker than me."

"Yes, but the fact that it comes from you . . ."

Maris swore again. But finally he went over and said in an interview that Mantle was the finest player of his era, a great competitor, a great hitter.

Fifteen minutes later, standing behind the microphone at home plate, DiMaggio was telling the crowd, "I'm proud to introduce the man who succeeded me in center field in 1951," and from every corner of the Stadium the cheering, whistling, clapping came down. Mantle stepped forward. He stood with his wife and children, posed for the photographers kneeling in front. Then he thanked the crowd in a short speech, and turning, shook hands with the dignitaries standing nearby. Among them now was Senator Kennedy, who had been spotted in the dugout five minutes before by Red Barber, and been called out and introduced. Kennedy posed with Mantle for a photographer, then shook hands with the Mantle children, and with Toots Shor and James Farley and others. DiMaggio saw him coming down the line and at the last second he backed away, casually, hardly anybody noticing it, and Kennedy seemed not to notice it either, just swept past shaking more hands. . . .

Finishing his tea, putting aside the newspaper, DiMaggio went upstairs to dress, and soon he was waving good-bye to Marie and driving toward his business appointment in downtown San Francisco with his partners in the retail television business. DiMaggio, while not a millionaire, has invested wisely and has always had, since his retirement from baseball, executive positions with big companies that have paid him well. He also was among the organizers of the Fisherman's National Bank of San Francisco last year, and, though it never came about, he demonstrated an acuteness that impressed those businessmen who had thought of him only in terms of baseball. He has had offers to manage big-league baseball teams but always has rejected them, saying, "I have enough trouble taking care of my own problems without taking on the responsibilities of twenty-five ballplayers."

So his only contact with baseball these days, excluding public appearances, is his unsalaried job as a batting coach each spring in Florida with the New York Yankees, a trip he would make once again on the following Sunday, three days away, if he could accomplish what for him is always the dreaded responsibility of packing, a task made no easier by the fact that he lately has fallen into the habit of keeping his clothes in two places—some hang in his closet at home, some hang in the back room of a saloon called Reno's.

Reno's is a dimly lit bar in the center of San Francisco. A portrait of DiMaggio swinging a bat hangs on the wall, in addition to portraits of other star athletes, and the clientele consists mainly of the sporting crowd and newspapermen, people who know DiMaggio quite well and around whom he speaks freely on a number of subjects and relaxes as he can in few other places. The owner of the bar is Reno Barsocchini, a broad-shouldered and handsome man of fifty-one with graying wavy hair who began as a fiddler in Dago Mary's tavern thirty-five years ago. He later became a bartender there and elsewhere, including DiMaggio's Restaurant, and now he is probably DiMaggio's closest friend. He was the best man at the DiMaggio-Monroe wedding in 1954, and when they separated nine months later in Los Angeles, Reno rushed down to help DiMaggio with the packing and drive him back to San Francisco. Reno will never forget the day.

Hundreds of people were gathered around the Beverly Hills home that DiMaggio and Marilyn had rented, and photographers were perched in the trees watching the windows, and others stood on the lawn and behind the rose bushes waiting to snap pictures of anybody who walked out of the house. The newspapers that day played all the puns—"Joe Fanned on Jealousy"; "Marilyn and Joe—Out at Home"—and the Hollywood columnists, to whom DiMaggio was never an idol, never a gracious host, recounted instances of incompatibility, and Oscar Levant said it all proved that no man could be a success in two national pastimes. When Reno Barsocchini arrived he had to push his way through the mob, then bang on the door for several minutes before being admitted. Marilyn Monroe was upstairs in bed, Joe DiMaggio was downstairs with his suitcases, tense and pale, his eyes bloodshot.

Reno took the suitcases and golf clubs out to DiMaggio's car, and then DiMaggio came out of the house, the reporters moving toward him, the lights flashing.

"Where are you going?" they yelled. "I'm driving to San Francisco," he said, walking quickly.

"Is that going to be your home?"

"That *is* my home and always has been."

"Are you coming back?"

DiMaggio turned for a moment, looking up at the house.

"No," he said, "I'll never be back."

Reno Barsocchini, except for a brief falling out over something he will not discuss, has been DiMaggio's trusted companion ever since, joining him whenever he can on the golf course or on the town, otherwise waiting for him in the bar with other middle-aged men. They may wait for hours sometimes, waiting and knowing that when he arrives he may wish to be alone; but it does not seem to matter, they are endlessly awed by him, moved by the mystique, he is a kind of male Garbo. They know that he can be warm and loyal if they are sensitive to his wishes, but they must never be late for an appointment to meet him. One man, unable to find a parking place, arrived a half-hour late once and DiMaggio did not talk to him again for three months. They know, too, when dining at night with DiMaggio, that he generally prefers male companions and occasionally one or two young women, but never wives; wives gossip, wives complain, wives are trouble, and men wishing to remain close to DiMaggio must keep their wives at home.

When DiMaggio strolls into Reno's bar the men wave and call out his name, and Reno Barsocchini smiles and announces, "Here's the Clipper!", the "Yankee Clipper" being a nickname from his baseball days.

"Hey, Clipper, Clipper," Reno had said two nights before, "where you been, Clipper? . . . Clipper, how 'bout a belt?"

DiMaggio refused the offer of a drink, ordering instead a pot of tea, which he prefers to all other beverages except before a date, when he will switch to vodka.

"Hey, Joe," a sportswriter asked, a man researching a magazine piece on golf, "why is it that a golfer, when he starts getting older, loses his putting touch first? Like Snead and Hogan, they can still hit a ball well off the tee, but on the greens they lose the strokes. . . ."

"It's the pressure of age," DiMaggio said, turning around on his bar stool. "With age you get jittery. It's true of golfers, it's true of any man when he gets into his fifties. He doesn't take chances like he used to. The younger golfer, on the greens, he'll stroke his putts better. The old man, he becomes hesitant. A little uncertain. Shaky. When it comes to taking chances the younger man, even when driving a car, will take chances that the older man won't."

"Speaking of chances," another man said, one of the group that had gathered around DiMaggio, "did you see that guy on crutches in here last night?"

"Yeah, had his leg in a cast," a third said. "Skiing."

"I would never ski," DiMaggio said. "Men who ski must be doing it to impress a broad. You see these men, some of them forty, fifty, getting onto skis. And later you see them all bandaged up, broken legs. . . ."

"But skiing's a very sexy sport, Joe. All the clothes, the tight pants, the fireplace in the ski lodge, the bear rug—Christ, nobody goes to ski. They just go out there to get it cold so they can warm it up. . . ."

"Maybe you're right," DiMaggio said. "I might be persuaded."

"Want a belt, Clipper?" Reno asked.

DiMaggio thought for a second, then said, "All right—first belt tonight."

Now it was noon, a warm sunny day. DiMaggio's business meeting with the television retailers had gone well; he had made a strong appeal to George Shahood, president of Continental Television, Inc., which has eight retail outlets in Northern California, to cut prices on color television sets and increase the sales volume, and Shahood had conceded it was worth a try. Then DiMaggio called Reno's bar to see if there were any messages, and now he was in Lefty O'Doul's car being driven along Fisherman's Wharf toward the Golden Gate

Bridge en route to a golf course thirty miles upstate. Lefty O'Doul was one of the great hitters in the National League in the early thirties, and later he managed the San Francisco Seals when DiMaggio was the shining star. Though O'Doul is now sixty-nine, eighteen years older than DiMaggio, he nevertheless possesses great energy and spirit, is a hard-drinking, boisterous man with a big belly and roving eye; and when DiMaggio, as they drove along the highway toward the golf club, noticed a lovely blond at the wheel of a car nearby and exclaimed, "Look at *that* tomato!" O'Doul's head suddenly spun around, he took his eyes off the road, and yelled, "Where, *where?*" O'Doul's golf game is less than what it was—he used to have a two-handicap—but he still shoots in the 80s, as does DiMaggio.

DiMaggio's drives range between 250 and 280 yards when he doesn't sky them, and his putting is good, but he is distracted by a bad back that both pains him and hinders the fullness of his swing. On the first hole, waiting to tee off, DiMaggio sat back watching a foursome of college boys ahead swinging with such freedom. "Oh," he said with a sigh, "to have *their* backs."

DiMaggio and O'Doul were accompanied around the golf course by Ernie Nevers, the former football star, and two brothers who are in the hotel and movie-distribution business. They moved quickly up and down the green hills in electric golf carts, and DiMaggio's game was exceptionally good for the first nine holes. But then he seemed distracted, perhaps tired, perhaps even reacting to a conversation of a few minutes before. One of the movie men was praising the film *Boeing, Boeing,* starring Tony Curtis and Jerry Lewis, and the man asked DiMaggio if he had seen it.

"No," DiMaggio said. Then he added, swiftly, "I haven't seen a film in eight years."

DiMaggio hooked a few shots, was in the woods. He took a No. 9 iron and tried to chip out. But O'Doul interrupted DiMaggio's concentration to remind him to keep the face of the club closed. DiMaggio hit the ball. It caromed off the side of his club, went skipping like a rabbit through the high grass down toward a pond. DiMaggio rarely displays any emotion on a golf course, but now, without saying a word, he took his No. 9 iron and flung it into the air. The club landed in a tree and stayed up there.

"Well," O'Doul said, casually, "there goes *that* set of clubs."

DiMaggio walked to the tree. Fortunately the club had slipped to the lower branch and DiMaggio could stretch up on the cart and get it back.

"Every time I get advice," DiMaggio muttered to himself, shaking his head slowly and walking toward the pond, "I shank it."

Later, showered and dressed, DiMaggio and the others drove to a banquet about ten miles from the golf course. Somebody had said it was going to be an elegant dinner, but when they arrived they could see it was more like a county fair; farmers were gathered outside a big barnlike building, a candidate for sheriff was distributing leaflets at the front door, and a chorus of homely ladies were inside singing *You Are My Sunshine.*

"How did we get sucked into this?" DiMaggio asked, talking out of the side of his mouth, as they approached the building.

"O'Doul," one of the men said. "It's his fault. Damned O'Doul can't turn *anything* down."

"Go to hell," O'Doul said.

Soon DiMaggio and O'Doul and Ernie Nevers were surrounded by the crowd, and the woman who had been leading the chorus came rushing over and said, "Oh, Mr. DiMaggio, it certainly is a pleasure having you."

"It's a pleasure being here, ma'am," he said, forcing a smile.

"It's too bad you didn't arrive a moment sooner, you'd have heard our singing."

"Oh, I heard it," he said, "and I enjoyed it very much."

"Good, good," she said. "And how are your brothers Dom and Vic?"

"Fine. Dom lives near Boston. Vince is in Pittsburgh."

"Why, *hello* there, Joe," interrupted a man with wine on his breath, patting DiMaggio on the back, feeling his arm. "Who's gonna take it this year, Joe?"

"Well, I have no idea," DiMaggio said.

"What about the Giants?"

"Your guess is as good as mine."

"Well, you can't count the Dodgers out," the man said.

"You sure can't," DiMaggio said.

"Not with all that pitching."

"Pitching is certainly important," DiMaggio said.

Everywhere he goes the questions seem the same, as if he has some special vision into the future of new heroes, and everywhere he goes, too, older men grab his hand and feel his arm and predict that he could still go out there and hit one, and the smile on DiMaggio's face is genuine. He tries hard to remain as he was—he diets, he takes steam baths, he is careful; and flabby men in the locker rooms of golf clubs sometimes steal peeks at him when he steps out of the shower, observing the tight muscles across his chest, the flat stomach, the long sinewy legs. He has a young man's body, very pale and little hair; his face is dark and lined, however, parched by the sun of several seasons. Still he is always an impressive figure at banquets such as this—an *immortal,* sportswriters called him, and that is how they have written about him and others like him, rarely suggesting that such heroes might ever be prone to the ills of mortal men, carousing, drinking, scheming; to suggest this would destroy the myth, would disillusion small boys, would infuriate rich men who own ballclubs and to whom baseball is a business dedicated to profit and in pursuit of which they trade mediocre players' flesh as casually as boys trade players' pictures on bubble-gum cards. And so the baseball hero must always act the part, must preserve the myth, and none does it better than DiMaggio, none is more patient when drunken old men grab an arm and ask, "Who's gonna take it this year, Joe?"

Two hours later, dinner and the speeches over, DiMaggio is slumped in O'Doul's car headed back to San Francisco. He edged himself up, however, when O'Doul pulled into a gas station in which a pretty red-haired girl sat on a stool, legs crossed, filing her fingernails. She was about twenty-two, wore a tight black skirt and tighter white blouse.

"Look at *that*," DiMaggio said.

"Yeah," O'Doul said.

O'Doul turned away when a young man approached, opened the gas tank, began wiping the windshield. The young man wore a greasy white uniform on the front of which was printed the name "Burt." DiMaggio kept looking at the girl, but she was not distracted from her fingernails. Then he looked at Burt, who did not recognize him. When the tank was full, O'Doul paid and drove off. Burt returned to his girl; DiMaggio slumped down in the front seat and did not open his eyes again until they'd arrived in San Francisco.

"Let's go see Reno," DiMaggio said.

"No, I gotta go see my old lady," O'Doul said. So he dropped DiMaggio off in front of the bar, and a moment later Reno's voice was announcing in the smoky room, "Hey, here's the Clipper!" The men waved and offered to buy him a drink. DiMaggio ordered a vodka and sat for an hour at the bar talking to a half dozen men around him. Then a blond girl who had been with friends at the other end of the bar came over, and somebody introduced her to DiMaggio. He bought her a drink, offered her a cigarette. Then he struck a match and held it. His hand was unsteady.

"Is that me that's shaking?" he asked.

"It must be," said the blond. "I'm calm."

Two nights later, having collected his clothes out of Reno's back room, DiMaggio boarded a jet; he slept crossways on three seats, then came down the steps as the sun began to rise in Miami. He claimed his luggage and golf clubs, put them into the trunk of a waiting automobile, and less than an hour later he was being driven into Fort Lauderdale, past palm-lined streets, toward the Yankee Clipper Hotel.

"All my life it seems I've been on the road traveling," he said, squinting through the windshield into the sun. "I never get a sense of being in any one place."

Arriving at the Yankee Clipper Hotel, DiMaggio checked into the largest suite. People rushed through the lobby to shake hands with him, to ask for his autograph, to say, "Joe, you look great." And early the next morning, and for the next thirty mornings, DiMaggio arrived punctually at the baseball park and wore his uniform with the famous No. 5, and the tourists seated in the sunny grandstands clapped when he first appeared on the field each time, and then they watched with nostalgia as he picked up a bat and played "pepper" with the younger Yankees, some of whom were not even born when, twenty-five years ago this summer, he hit in fifty-six straight games and became the most celebrated man in America.

But the younger spectators in the Fort Lauderdale park, and the sportswriters, too, were more interested in Mantle and Maris, and nearly every day there were news dispatches reporting how Mantle and Maris felt, what they did, what they said, even though they said and did very little except walk around the field frowning when photographers asked for another picture and when sportswriters asked how they felt.

After seven days of this, the big day arrived—Mantle and Maris would swing a bat—and a dozen sportswriters were gathered around the big batting cage that was situated beyond the left-field fence; it was completely enclosed in wire, meaning that no baseball could travel more than thirty or forty feet before being trapped in rope; still Mantle and Maris would be swinging, and this, in spring, makes news.

Mantle stepped in first. He wore black gloves to help prevent blisters. He hit right-handed against the pitching of a coach named Vern Benson, and soon Mantle was swinging hard, smashing line drives against the nets, going *ahhh ahhh* as he followed through with his mouth open.

Then Mantle, not wanting to overdo it on his first day, dropped his bat in the dirt and walked out of the batting cage. Roger Maris stepped in. He picked up Mantle's bat.

"This damn thing must be thirty-eight ounces," Maris said. He threw the bat down into the dirt, left the cage and walked toward the dugout on the other side of the field to get a lighter bat.

DiMaggio stood among the sportswriters behind the cage, then turned when Vern Benson, inside the cage, yelled, "Joe, wanna hit some?"

"No chance," DiMaggio said.

"Com'on, Joe," Benson said.

The reporters waited silently. Then DiMaggio walked slowly into the cage and picked up Mantle's bat. He took his position at the plate but obviously it was not the classic DiMaggio stance; he was holding the bat about two inches from the knob, his feet were not so far apart, and, when DiMaggio took a cut at Benson's first pitch, fouling it, there was none of that ferocious follow through, the blurred bat did not come whipping all the way around, the No. 5 was not stretched full across his broad back.

DiMaggio fouled Benson's second pitch, then he connected solidly with the third, the fourth, the fifth. He was just meeting the ball easily, however, not smashing it, and Benson called out, "I didn't know you were a choke hitter, Joe."

"I am now," DiMaggio said, getting ready for another pitch.

He hit three more squarely enough, and then he swung again and there was a hollow sound.

"Ohhh," DiMaggio yelled, dropping his bat, his fingers stung, "I was waiting for that one." He left the batting cage rubbing his hands together. The reporters watched him. Nobody said anything. Then DiMaggio said to one of them, not in anger nor in sadness, but merely as a simply stated fact, "There was a time when you couldn't get me out of there."

It is the anthologist's prerogative, I am told, to include one of his own best bits. Of all my baseball writing, this opening chapter of *Baseball's Ten Greatest Games*, published in 1981, may not be the best—others must answer to that—but it is my favorite. Come along now: the Tigers of Cobb and Crawford are about to do battle with the Athletics of Plank and Waddell, and the lines at the ticket booths are long.

JOHN THORN

September 30, 1907: You Are There

Game time is two o'clock, sixty minutes from now, but the 18,000 seats in Philadelphia's Columbia Park were filled hours ago and the gates have just been closed. You and I were fortunate to squeeze into the standing-room section roped off here on the center-field grass. A seat in the grandstand or bleachers would have been nicer, I know, but we mustn't complain: at least we gained admission, unlike the swarms of disgruntled fans milling outside the fences, and the thousands who risk their necks on the rooftops of houses which overlook this rickety wooden stadium.

Who would have imagined that a Monday date with the Detroit Tigers, perennial also-rans, could produce such a crush of humanity? Two years back, when the A's fought the Giants in the World Series, they didn't come close to filling up the park. But this summer the City of the Quakers has gone baseball mad as four teams—Chicago, Cleveland, Detroit, and Philadelphia—have played leapfrog with first place in the hottest pennant race of the young century. Now, though, with only one week left in the regular season, two of the teams have dropped off the chase—the White Sox, the "hitless wonders" who swept last year's World Series; and the Cleveland "Naps," as they are called in tribute to their star player-manager, Napoleon Lajoie.

Last Friday, when Connie Mack's Athletics took the field behind their Chippewa curveballer, Chief Bender, they were one-half game in front of the Tigers, who countered with their ace, Wild Bill Donovan. Though the A's cuffed him for thirteen hits, Donovan held on for a 5–4 victory. Rain washed out Saturday's contest, which was rescheduled for today as the second game of a doubleheader. What about yesterday, you ask? Sunday ball will not be legal in the state of Pennsylvania till 1934.

So it has come down to this: If the Tigers can take both ends of the twin bill, they will almost certainly capture the pennant. Even if they only get a split, they will still leave town in first place and will enjoy a scheduling edge over the A's: Detroit's last seven matches will be with the Washington Senators and St. Louis Browns, two weaklings, while the A's will have to contend with Mr. Lajoie's formidable Naps, in addition to the Senators.

The players are out on the field now, loosening up for the game. Warming up in foul territory for the A's is Jimmy Dygert, a chunky right-hander whose spitball has baffled the league this season. Do you recognize that tall, muscular guy over in left field, joking with the fans? He's Rube Waddell, the A's left-handed flamethrower, who leads the league in strikeouts every year. But don't expect to see him pitch today. He's been having a running feud with several of his teammates. Tired of Rube's antics off the field and lack of dedication on it, they have given him halfhearted support in recent outings. This bad blood may have cost the A's three or four games they ought to have won; today, Mack knows, is no time for less than all-out effort.

While we're on the subject of running feuds, look over there in the right-field corner, where young Ty Cobb is exercising by himself. Only twenty years old, he's on his way to the first of twelve batting titles, yet half the Tigers won't speak to him and several have fought him with their fists. Despite his slashing bat and his savage abandon on the base paths, young Tyrus came within a hairbreadth of being traded this spring. New manager Hughie Jennings, fed up with all the bickering on his team, arranged a deal with the New York Highlanders (later known as the Yankees) whereby Detroit would swap the greatest hitter of all time for a nondescript pitcher named Buffalo Bill Hogg. Only a last-minute hesitance kept Cobb from one day playing in the same outfield with Babe Ruth!

But enough talk of what might have been. It is nearly time to play ball. Hey, what's that commotion in the grandstand? The frustrated fans who were locked outside the park at one o'clock are now pouring over the right-field fence. The Keystone Cops rush toward the disturbance, but they don't have a chance. One gate-crasher they could nab, or ten, but not the hundreds who are scaling the wall. And look behind you—now they are cascading over the entire length of the outfield fence, thousands of them! The already crowded standing-room section begins to resemble a New York City subway car at rush hour.

As I was about to say before the ruckus started, Detroit will go with Donovan again. He's had two days' rest, all he really needs (a few weeks ago this workhorse beat Cleveland twice in two days). And besides, Philly is Bill's hometown. His family and friends are in the park, and Jennings wants to give him a chance to show off.

Donovan has been remarkable all year long. After closing the books on 1906 with 9–15 mark, his worst ever, the thirty-year-old hurler decided he didn't want to pitch anymore; he figured he was a pretty good hitter, and declared that from now on he'd play first base. Jennings knew better than to believe him. He let Donovan play a little first base in spring camp, but held him out of action once the season began. April passed and so did much of May with Donovan on the bench, begging to return to the mound. But Ee-Yah Hughie (a nickname he earned by his bloodcurdling shouts of "Ee-Yah!" to urge on his team) let Bill cool his heels on the sidelines until May 24, when he was finally permitted to pitch. His pent-up energies burst forth on the American League to the tune of twenty-five victories against only four defeats—and he might easily have gone 29–0, because his four losses came by scores of 1–0, 4–3, 4–2, and 4–1.

A roar rises from the crowd as Dygert strolls to the mound and the other A's take their positions: Ossie Schreck behind the plate, Home Run Harry Davis at first, Danny Murphy at second, Simon Nicholls at short, Hall-of-Famer Jimmy Collins at the hot corner; and an outfield of, left to right, Topsy Hartsel, Rube Oldring, and Socks Seybold. Defensively the A's are steady but not sensational. Except for Oldring and Nicholls, who are first-year starters, the other six fielders are "graybeards" over thirty, and three of them are on the steep part of their downhill slide—Collins, thirty-seven; Seybold, thirty-six; and Davis, thirty-four.

The avalanche of fence-vaulters continues even as Dygert sends his first pitch in to Davy Jones, Detroit's slap-hitting left-fielder. But as the Tigers go down in the first without a hit, the procession slows to a trickle and finally ends. There simply isn't a square inch of space left in which to put one more rooter.

Now the Tigers take their turn in the field. The battery is Donovan and Boss Schmidt, an ex-boxer whose fist shattered Cobb's nose last year; the inner ring consists of Claude Rossman at first, Germany Schaefer at the second sack, Charley O'Leary at short, and Rowdy Bill Coughlin at third; the outer circle shows Jones in left and Hall-of-Famers Sam Crawford and Cobb in center and right. Both offensively and defensively, the strength of this young club—not

a starter over thirty—resides in the outfield, though Rossman, too, is first-rate.

There is a buzz of anticipation in the air as Topsy Hartsel steps to the plate. And what's more, there are two brass bands, cowbells, cymbals, gongs, sirens, bugles, frying pans—all banging and clattering together to unnerve the Detroit fielders. Hartsel, a 5-foot 5-inch mighty mite, is an ideal leadoff man whose specialty is drawing the base on balls and letting the heavy hitters bring him around. This time, however, Hartsel rips a Donovan fastball for a single, and on the first pitch to Nicholls, he steals second. Connie Mack has identified the weak link in the Detroit defense—catcher Schmidt's erratic arm—and has exploited it immediately. Nicholls lays down a sacrifice bunt and Hartsel takes third. It's only the first frame, but the A's are playing for one run. Clearly Mack doesn't think he'll be getting many more off Wild Bill.

Now the managerial wheels are really spinning. Jennings moves his infield in, unwilling to concede the run on a hard-hit grounder; but Donovan spoils the strategy by walking Seybold. Now the shortstop and second baseman must pull back for a possible double-play ball. And Harry Davis complies, smacking one to the shortstop's left—but the ball kicks off O'Leary to second-baseman Schaefer, who picks it up and throws . . . too late. It's a hit. The run is in, Athletics occupy first and second, and there is still only one man down.

Danny Murphy follows with a bunt toward first which he beats out, loading the bases. Donovan has not exactly been bludgeoned, but he is being nibbled to death. Jimmy Collins lifts a fly to left, deep enough to score Seybold. Two down, but the A's will not let go of the Tiger tail yet. Oldring wallops a ball into the overflow crowd here in center field, a ground-rule double, and Davis comes home to make the count 3–0. The fans are giving a razzing to Donovan now, and his partisans, seated in the third-base deck, look awfully glum. At last Schreck is retired, and the A's take the field to an ovation.

Claude Rossman opens the Tiger second with a single to center. Coughlin then raps one to the mound but Dygert, in his haste to start the double play in motion, throws the ball into the dirt and both men are safe. Here's Schmidt, brandishing his big war club as he steps into the batter's box. He squares to bunt, and delicately lays one down to advance the runners. Just between you and me, I think Schmidt ought to have swung away. With the eighth- and ninth-place hitters to follow, and his team down 3–0, this was no time for Jennings to give up an out. Yes, second-guessing the manager is a bit unfair, but who can resist?

O'Leary, a little fellow with a very light stick, also knocks one back to Dygert, who once again sets sights on Rossman, now hung up between third and home. Back and forth Claude dances, trying to give O'Leary time to reach second base. Back and forth, back and forth in the rundown—until Dygert fires one to Schreck at close range that bounces off his chest protector. Rossman rushes past him to score. 3–1. Now Dygert's errant tosses in the field take their effect on the mound. He sends four wide ones to Donovan, loading the bases. Mr. Mack invites the rattled youngster to soothe his nerves with an early shower and in comes—Rube Waddell!

Connie Mack is a hunch player, and he's playing a big one now: First of all, that Waddell woke up sober this morning, and second, that his teammates would not throw away a pennant just to deny the Rube a win. As it turns out, Rube does not put his fielders to the test. Coming in with the bases loaded, he fans Davy Jones and Germany Schaefer with a combination of rising fastballs and explosive curves, then struts around the mound as the fans go wild. In later years Branch Rickey is to say that "when Waddell had control—and some sleep—he was unbeatable." Rube must have had a very tranquil Sunday night, for he fans Cobb and Rossman in the third and Schmidt and O'Leary in the fourth, making it six strikeout victims of the eight men he's faced.

While Waddell is making tabby cats of the Bengals, the A's resume their assault on Donovan. Socks Seybold opens the third with a double to right and chugs home on Davis's two-bagger to left. Murphy's bunt single then advances Davis to third, from where he scores on Oldring's force-out.

The 5–1 lead looks like money in the bank, and the A's even widen their margin in the fifth. Home Run Harry Davis, the league's four-base champ the last three years, leads off with his specialty, a booming drive over the scoreboard in right. Murphy is put down, but Jimmy Collins drives one against the scoreboard and into the crowd for an automatic double. Umpire Silk O'Loughlin jogs out to request return of the ball, as is the custom of the times, and the gentleman in the bowler hat who caught it assents.

Jennings has still given no sign to his bullpen—either he doesn't wish to embarrass Wild Bill in front of his folks; or he has given up on the contest and, with another game yet to play today, doesn't want to deplete his small staff. Whichever is the case, the A's are pleased to continue the shellacking. Oldring whacks a drive toward the corner in left. Davy Jones drifts back on the ball until he senses the crowd behind him, then, as is his habit, shies off; the catchable ball drops into the first row of standees for a run-scoring double.

The fifth inning ends without further ado as Donovan whiffs Schreck and Waddell. Loping toward the bench, Jones is intercepted at third base by a bunch of angry teammates; they threaten him with all sorts of mayhem if the game is lost, as now seems certain. Davy's faintheartedness has cost his team a run; however, one run doesn't look so very large when you're trailing 7–1.

But the complexion of the game changes radically in the top of the seventh, as shabby Philadelphia fielding enables the Tigers to tally four times on only one hit. Oldring muffs Donovan's lazy fly to open the door, and then Waddell experiences his first lapse of control, walking Jones. Schaefer follows with a perfect double-play grounder to Nicholls, but the kid kicks it.

Now the bases are loaded for Sam Crawford, the left-handed slugger who played alongside Waddell in the old Western League in 1899 and who, like the Rube, will be honored with a plaque in Cooperstown. So far today, Crawford has had no luck with Waddell; but this time Rube gets a pitch up in the strike zone where Sam likes it, and the ball goes sailing over Seybold's head for two bases and two runs.

Cobb, up next, has gone out weakly in his previous trips to the plate and does so once more; but Schaefer scores as Ty is thrown out at first. Crawford, who advanced to third on the play, himself comes in to score as Murphy scoops up Rossman's ground shot in the hole and fires to first in time. Coughlin, too, is put out, but the Tigers are now in striking distance at 7–5.

The A's get one back on their half of the inning on a single by Murphy, sacrifice by Collins, single by Oldring, and groundout by Schreck. Staggering through seven innings, Donovan has been walloped for fourteen hits, but Jennings will not take him out unless he asks out. And Wild Bill won't ask.

Fred Payne, who replaced Boss Schmidt behind the plate a few innings back, is retired to lead off the eighth. But O'Leary doubles and daringly steals third with Donovan at the bat. Wild Bill cannot bring him home, but Davy Jones does, with a single that cancels out the run he gave the A's in the fifth inning.

Well, here we are in the top of the ninth with the A's still up by a score of 8–6. Waddell has shown signs of weakening, but Mack will stick with him as the left-handed heart of the Tiger batting order—Crawford, Cobb, and Ross-man—comes up. (In 1907 there are not yet any relief specialists on the lines of a Bruce Sutter or Rich Gossage; and with pitching staffs that comprise five or at most six men, managers cannot play Captain Hook, yanking hurlers as they please.)

When Crawford loops a single over second base, the boisterous crowd falls into a moment's eerie silence—but erupts again as Cobb stands in for his turn. The Georgia Peach stirs up silent admiration for his skills and vocal hostility for his attacking, almost driven style of play. In a series with the Highlanders earlier this month he scored from first base on Rossman's sacrifice bunt! Like a man possessed, he circled the bases at full tilt while the stunned New Yorkers fumbled the ball around. Cobb doesn't play just to beat you; he wants to destroy you, and the A's rooters have taken particular delight in his futility at the plate today.

Waddell starts Cobb off with a fastball up and in, a tough pitch for Ty, who leans over the plate. He nonchalantly watches it go by. Waddell figures Cobb is looking for a ball out over the plate, perhaps one he can punch to the opposite field. So, Rube will say in later years, "I throws another for the inside corner and the second the ball leaves my hand I know I made a bum guess. This Cobb, who didn't seem to notice the first one, steps back like he had the catcher's sign, takes a toehold, and swings. I guess the ball's goin' yet."

Out it soars, over the right fielder, over the roped-in fans, and over the fence, coming to earth in the middle of 29th Street. A tie game! Connie Mack is so stunned he falls off the end of the A's bench, landing on a pile of bats. Cobb is not a home-run hitter—no one really is in this decade, not even Home Run Harry Davis, who will top the league with eight. And besides, the ball Cobb hit had been in play since the fifth inning and must have been pretty beat up. How could he have sent it so far? And did he steal the sign as Waddell suspected?

How he managed to wallop it so far no one can explain, but Cobb did know that he would get another fastball up and in. By casually letting the first pitch go by, he duped Waddell into thinking he was looking for a pitch away. Ty figured that Rube would try to cross him up and fire another in the identical spot. He was so confident he had pegged Rube's thoughts that as Waddell uncorked the pitch he jumped back off the plate and swung with everything he had in him.

Mack, scrambling to his feet, waves his scorecard frantically toward the bullpen. The great Eddie Plank, whom Mack had intended to hold out for the second game, comes running in as Waddell trudges slowly to the clubhouse. Mack's gamble on the Rube has proved a bust. Plank tosses in a few warm-up throws to Mike Powers, who has replaced Schreck, then sets down Rossman, Coughlin, and Payne in order.

Donovan blanks Philly in the ninth and tenth, and in the eleventh takes the mound to defend a lead. In the top of the inning Cobb had hit another long drive to right, this one landing in the overflow crowd, and Rossman had followed with a single to put Detroit up 9–8. But in the A's half, Nicholls doubles, Wild Bill wild-pitches him to third, and the run comes in on Davis's long fly.

The Tigers threaten in the twelfth, loading the bases with two outs, but Hartsel catches up with Crawford's drive down the left-field line. The A's also fail to score.

This game is nearly three hours old, a common enough duration today but quite uncommon at the turn of the century, when games were usually completed in ninety minutes or less. If someone doesn't win pretty soon, there won't be enough daylight to play the second game. With each passing moment, victory becomes more and more urgent for the A's. If the second game is not played today, no makeup will be scheduled.

Donovan and Plank breeze through the thirteenth. Though he must be weary from all the pitches he's thrown, Wild Bill is getting better as the contest wears on. In the early part of the game he seemed to have been throwing his "drop ball" (or sinker, as we know it) too hard, not giving it a chance to rotate and dip. Coming in straight as a string, it proved very hittable. But now as he tires, his arm-swing slows and he gets more "action" on the ball.

In the bottom of the fourteenth, Bill serves up a fastball to Harry Davis that the powerful first-sacker drives to deep center. Here comes Crawford racing back to the rope . . . he is leaning against the crowd to brace for the catch. But now a policeman runs in front of him, obscuring Sam's view with that comical high bobby's hat. The ball lands at Crawford's feet and bounds into the crowd!

Davis is perched at second base, believing he's hit a ground-rule double. But Jones and Cobb are racing out to center field to confront umpire O'Loughlin; they and Crawford believe interference should be called and the batter ruled out. The stadium is in an uproar. O'Loughlin, whose call it properly is, wavers and wavers, infuriating both the Tigers and the A's. At last he decides there *was* interference, and calls Davis out. But Silk's colleague, Tommy Connolly, who was behind the plate (only two umps work a game at this time), now offers *his* opinion—namely, that there was no interference and Davis should hold second base. Back and forth the players race between the umpires as the dispute rages. Even Connie Mack, known as a mild-mannered man for all his sixty-six years in baseball, uncharacteristically leaves the bench and harangues O'Loughlin long and loud.

Utter pandemonium erupts. The A's clear their bench and come galloping out to center field, followed in no time by the entire Tiger team. Nearly a thousand fans join them on the outfield grass, as do the police. Monte Cross, a fifteen-year veteran closing out his career as the A's backup shortstop, rushes into the mob with his fists doubled. He is promptly decked by Charley O'Leary.

Cross then dusts himself off and sets upon Claude Rossman, who gives back what he got and more. As Cross is being pummeled, to the rescue comes Waddell, freshly showered and in street clothes. Donovan grabs Waddell and tries to restrain him, but Rube will not be denied his fun, and tears loose. Donovan, however, is arrested by a cop who sees a chance to serve his hometown as never before.

Now Germany Schaefer approaches the policeman and sweetly points out to him, "My good man, you can't arrest Donovan. Why, the stands are filled with his Irish relatives. Pinch him, and they'll tear us apart."

"Perhaps I acted hastily," the cop concedes, releasing Donovan and collaring Rossman.

At last the warring factions are untangled and Rossman, too, is released. Seeking to reestablish their authority, the umpires declare Davis out because of the policeman's interference; they also banish both Rossman and Cross. Pitcher Ed Killian is recruited to replace Rossman at first base, and play resumes. The fans, who have slowly subsided in their anger, flare up anew as Danny Murphy singles. They know full well that Davis would have come in with the winning run on that hit.

As the autumn sky dims, the game winds on. It is plain now that there will be no second contest, and that the A's must win this one to regain first place. But they are unable to mount another threat; that wild fourteenth inning seems to have done them in. Plank continues to pitch masterfully; though he allows Cobb to reach third in the top of the seventeenth, he strands him there.

In the home half, young Eddie Collins pinch-hits for Oldring and singles, but does not score either. With the players scarcely able to see the ball and, by Cobb's description, "guess-hitting," at ten minutes to six the umpires call the game. It goes down in the record books as a tie.

But in fact the Tigers are the winners, for they retain their hold on first place. They go on to Washington, where in the opener they will come from behind to defeat a raw-boned rookie named Walter Johnson. While Detroit is sweeping the four-game set with the Senators, the A's will drop one to the Naps. Despite the final-week heroics of Jimmy Dygert, who will hurl three shutouts in four days, the Mackmen are dead.

Who were the heroes of this remarkable game? Cobb, certainly; his homer—one of only eleven the Tigers hit *all season long*—kept the game alive in the ninth and provided him with what he would always call his greatest day. For the A's, old Harry Davis, who drove in four runs, and young Rube Oldring, who drove in three. And Rube Waddell, who deserved a better fate.

And most of all, Bill Donovan, who allowed eight runs and fourteen hits through seven innings, and only one run and six hits over the next ten. Wild Bill threw well over two hundred pitches for the game in a display of stamina and heart the likes of which we will surely not see again.

John Updike is a jack of all literary trades—novelist, essayist, story writer, critic, poet—and, uniquely, their master as well. Baseball fans will remember his classic account of Ted Williams's final game, "Hub Fans Bid Kid Adieu," published in *The New Yorker* in 1960 and reprinted extensively since. Figuring that you've read that piece (if you haven't, you owe yourself), I turned to this lesser-known but beautiful effort—written when he was twenty-four—from Updike's first book, *The Carpentered Hen and Other Tame Creatures.*

JOHN UPDIKE

Tao in the Yankee Stadium Bleachers

Distance brings proportion. From here
the populated tiers
as much as players seem part of the show:
a constructed stage beast, three folds of Dante's rose,
or a Chinese military hat
cunningly chased with bodies.
"Falling from his chariot, a drunk man is unhurt
because his soul is intact. Not knowing his fall,
he is unastonished, he is invulnerable."
So, too, the "pure man"—"pure"
in the sense of undisturbed water.

"It is not necessary to seek out
a wasteland, swamp, or thicket."
The old men who saw Hans Wagner
scoop them up in lobster hands,
the opposing pitcher's pertinent hesitations,
the sky, this meadow, Mantle's thick baked neck,
the old men who in the changing rosters see

a personal mutability,
green slats, wet stone are all to me
as when an emperor commands
a performance with a gesture of his eyes.

"No king on his throne has the joy of the dead,"
the skull told Chuang-tzu.
The thought of death is peppermint to you
when games begin with patriotic song
and a democratic sun beats broadly down.
The Inner Journey seems unjudgeably long
when small boys purchase cups of ice
and, distant as a paradise,
experts, passionate and deft,
wait while Berra flies to left.

The Year the Yankees Lost the Pennant has suffered the sad fate of being swallowed up by *Damn Yankees*, the estimable Broadway musical and film which, of course, was based on the book. And Douglass Wallop's witty update of the Faust legend reads as well now as it did when it was new, in 1954. The setting for this excerpt: the 1958 pennant race is in its final day. The chronically awful Washington Senators—"first in war, first in peace, last in the American League," in Charlie Dryden's quip—are tied with the Yankees. They have soared from the nether regions of the standings since July, when Joe Hardy, the ultimate phenom, materialized out of thin air. Joe Hardy is in fact a middle-aged Senator fan named Joe Boyd who has sold his soul to the Devil, a Mr. Applegate. On this day Joe is waiting for something dreadful to happen because he now knows, as any sensible being would have recognized long ago, that the Devil is a Yankee fan.

DOUGLASS WALLOP

The Devil's Due

September 29, 1958, was a bright crisp day in the nation's capital. The wind had shifted during the night, and all over the city the flags were standing out to the southeast against a deep blue sky.

The flags were what Joe noticed first that morning when he rose and looked from the window of his hotel room. The flags: and then the taste of the autumnal air, a taste to stir the memory. For years it had been such weather as this that he had awaited through the long, humid Washington summers. In the past on such a day he would have stepped whistling from the house, grateful that the worst had finally ended, happy in his job.

It was ironic that such weather had been chosen for what surely would be the most miserable day of his life. Miserable not alone for his own sake, but for the misery he knew would come to an entire city; to an entire country, or surely that part of it lying west of the Hudson River.

Standing by the window, looking down at the street, seeing the people stream forth from the trolleys, walk briskly to their jobs, he winced with guilt. On the lips of these people, and those like them all over the city, there could be no conceivable topic but the game; in their hearts nothing less than confidence of victory. For why else would a team be lifted from the abyss and led so far if not intended for victory? Anything less would be cruelly incomprehensible. And it was he, Joe Hardy, the greedy and the gullible, who had led them within sight of the vision and who must stand helplessly by now while the vision was snatched away.

Team of destiny . . .

"Joe," said his waitress at breakfast, "I got ten dollars bet on you with my cousin in The Bronx, and I'm already counting the money."

Looking up from his eggs, he smiled, unable to reply.

After breakfast, he walked, and on every side he could feel the drama. It spoke from the newspaper headlines, from the makeshift scoreboards erected in shop windows; from the television sets assigned this day to the use of sidewalk viewers; and it spoke from the faces of the people themselves, from their greetings and snatches of conversation.

"It's Ransom gonna pitch."

"Ransom's only had two days' rest."

"It's still gonna be Ransom. That's what van Buren said."

There is a quality in the human soul, perverseness perhaps, that keeps hoping even when the cards are stacked, even when there is no hope. And for fleeting moments, feeling the drama, the excitement, Joe forgot Applegate; for fleeting moments he let himself feel the hope these people were feeling.

At other times, as he walked the familiar blocks near the hotel, blocks now transformed by the holiday atmosphere, he told himself that at least he had been able to give them this much. Today they were part of a setting, part of a drama, which all the world watched. He had given them pride of team; he had given them admiration for the fantastic feat the team had accomplished since July. He had given them . . .

But these thoughts gave him no comfort. They were specious, just as hope was self-torture.

He was dressing for the game, surrounded by guys alive with excitement, guys exchanging determined promises, guys with whom he would not be playing after today.

After today . . .

Hearing them was pain. And there was pain in watching Benny van Buren's attempt to maintain a crusty, taciturn, managerial air, when it was apparent that inside he was fluttering. For Mr. van Buren, like the fans, could not believe that a team so singled out by destiny could be left hanging in second place.

Now Mr. van Buren was opening a telegram, tacking it with others on the dressing-room bulletin board. Telegrams from well-wishers all over the globe, one from a fan in the Fiji Islands.

Mr. van Buren cleared his throat to speak. Standing near him was Mr. Welch, bundled now in his heavy winter overcoat since the change in weather, his eyes shining.

"Fellows," Mr. van Buren was saying, "first of all I wanna announce that it'll be Ransom going for us today, and we couldn't put the ball in better hands. . . ."

Sammy Ransom. Sammy of the gaunt, impassive visage . . . Sammy who would be pitching with only two days' rest . . . who, in the late innings, would lose the snap from his fireball and then would try to get by on heart alone . . . Sammy who had no way of knowing that heart stood for nothing with a slob named Applegate.

"And I also wanna say this," Mr. van Buren continued. "I hope we win today. I'm expecting to win. But whether we win or lose, I want to tell you guys that you've given me joy that seldom comes to a manager. You guys have played the greatest baseball I've ever seen in my life. . . ."

And when Mr. van Buren concluded, up jumped Rocky Pratt, a regenerated character by now, a man of team spirit, a man who never complained of headaches from excessive TV viewing. "Listen, Ben," he shouted, "all that stuff sounds fine, but there's just one thing wrong with it. We're not gonna lose. We're gonna win. Hey, you guys, who's thinking about losing?"

"Nobody," was the answering chorus.

"Then let's go out there and *win*," Pratt thundered.

An ovation rocked the park as the team took the field. It was a park this day jammed to the aisles. Even to its far reaches, there was not an empty seat . . . except . . .

Trotting out to his right-field post, Joe looked, and after the National Anthem was played, looked again. Two empty seats there were. Neither Applegate nor Lola was in the seat to which their season tickets entitled them. Applegate, so confident of the outcome that he disdained even to be a witness. And Lola . . . perhaps absent from heartbreak. But who could say about Lola?

The plate umpire signaled to play ball. Ransom peered in for his signal, wound up, let fire, and thus began a game that would live forever in the minds of men.

Pitching for the Yankees that day was Bix Kilgallen, a right-hander who already had twenty-three victories to his credit, and who, like Ransom, was a fireballer. But Kilgallen was not right that day; if Applegate was determined to exact the quintessence in cruelty, he could not be managing it more expertly, Joe thought. Even to the last he was dangling the bait.

For after the Yankees went out in order in the first, Joe came up in the Senators' half and rifled the second pitch on a line to deepest center. With his great speed, he beat the relay for an inside-the-park home run, and the score was 1–0. The ball park rocked with sound. The Yankees, although they still conducted themselves with the mien of champions, now looked not so tall in their uniforms, nor so lethal at bat.

And in the fourth, Joe, up again, lashed a towering drive over the scoreboard in right center. Although Joe's two homers were the only hits Kilgallen had yielded, he was yanked then in favor of Buttons Avery, the Yankees' venerable relief artist, famed for his control and his poise in the clutch.

Meanwhile Ransom, his fastball kicking like a live thing, was mowing down the champions with the precision of a machine-gunner. A single to left in the second, a scratch hit in the fifth, were all the Yankees could muster. In the sixth, his control momentarily gone, he walked the first two batters but steadied and came out of the frame unscathed.

And Joe, first man up in the seventh, doubled sharply to right center. A bunt and a long fly brought him around, and the score was 3–0.

Although the ballpark was still rocking, it was with sadness that Joe returned to the bench and sat watching while Sammy Ransom stroked the rabbit's foot Rocky Pratt had supplied for the occasion, the rabbit's foot he had been stroking between innings all through the game. How pitiably impotent was a rabbit's foot compared with what the Yankees had going for them today.

And yet, where was Applegate?

As Joe took the field for the eighth, it occurred to him there was nothing to prevent Applegate from occupying a seat in some other part of the stadium. A ruse of that sort would be completely in character, and he scanned the upper decks, looking for a flash of bright yellow sports shirt. There were these in plenty but no wearer, at least at such a distance, did he recognize as Applegate.

Nor did Applegate appear in the Senators' half of the eighth.

The ninth began, and although it was against his better judgment, Joe dared to hope.

The stands were hushed now, as tensely silent as they had been that day in Philadelphia before he had spoiled poor Bobby Schantz's no-hitter.

Only three outs away. Joe leaned forward as Ransom faced the first Yankee batter; Ransom, who had performed so gallantly. Three quick outs . . .

"Joe Hardy stinks out loud."

The rasping voice left no doubt. There sat Applegate in his accustomed seat.

"You stink, Hardy," he shouted.

Applegate, on his feet, brandishing a rolled score card, and holding his nose.

And then Joe could look no more because the first Yankee lined a ball over his head which he turned and chased to the base of the right-field wall, taking the carom neatly and whipping it into the infield in time to hold the hit to a double.

Applegate was fluttering his handkerchief in Joe's direction.

And Joe knew this was it.

The next batter singled sharply to center. The run scored, and it was now 3–1.

"How d'ya like that, Hardy?" Applegate was shouting. The partisan crowd was telling him to shut up and sit down but he took no notice. "That's the first one, Hardy," he bellowed. "And you ain't seen nothing yet."

And it was true. In quick succession, the next two Yankee batters pumped singles to left and center, scoring another run and putting men on first and third. It was now 3–2, and the gallant Ransom had had it. With slumped shoulders, he stood near the mound while a relief pitcher was called in from the bullpen.

"You lousy four-flusher, Hardy," Applegate was yelling.

The relief man was Bill Gregson, who had saved many a game for the team that summer. Van Buren could have made no better choice. Working craftily, Gregson got the first batter he faced on a long fly to left. That was out number one, but it also scored the runner from third, and the score now was tied at 3–3, with a man still on first. Shaving the corners too closely, Gregson walked the next man, but the one following went out on a pop-up behind second.

"Okay, Hardy," Applegate yelled. "This is it right here. This is the ballgame, old pal."

Not doubting it, Joe leaned forward. The runners led off. Gregson wound up, delivered. Ball one. Then strike one, and then . . .

The hit was a humpback, arching softly over the second baseman's head toward short right field and sinking fast. The Yankee runners were streaking down the base paths. And Joe Hardy was digging straight ahead, digging for the last notch of speed, diving with outstretched glove, and picking the ball off the grass tops, then falling hard to the ground, rolling over and over, but with his bare hand holding the ball aloft to prove it had been caught, and the roar that surged through the park was as much a roar of amazement as applause.

Picking himself up, Joe glanced at Applegate, who sat glumly back in his seat, and Joe realized that not even Applegate had expected him to catch that ball, realized it had been meant to fall safely, and that other hits would have followed, breaking the game wide open in favor of the Yankees, putting it beyond reach, and giving the Yankees their tenth consecutive pennant.

And as he trotted back to the bench, doffing his cap to the roar of the crowd, he realized something else. There was an acute pain in his right shoulder where he had hit the ground. And he felt suddenly winded, very tired. He, who had felt neither physical pain nor fatigue since the night of July 21st.

All's fair in love and war, Applegate had said. Applegate had not expected him to make that catch. Applegate was capable of playing it as dirty as the occasion demanded. . . .

He felt his stomach. It was still flat and hard.

The bench was silent, except for Mr. van Buren, who kept muttering over and over, as a man in a trance, "You saved it for us, Joe. That catch saved it for us. Can you win it for us now, Joe?"

Third up, Joe walked slowly over and selected a bat, then stooped at the edge of the dugout and watched while the first batter flied out to left.

One away. He advanced to the on-deck circle. *No, Ben, I don't think I can do it this time.* He looked up at the clear, blue sky beyond the left-field grandstand. *I've done it for you all season, but not this time. There's a guy sitting out there along the right-field line. I'm afraid he's too much for us, Ben.*

Two away.

Joe strode to the plate, and the sound that rose on the afternoon air was an appeal, a concerted plea from 30,000 fans, who seemed to sense that if the Senators didn't win it here and now with Hardy, the Yankees would wrap it up in the tenth, and second place would be a bitter reality.

Joe stepped in, set his spikes. *Even if I can't hit the one we need,* he thought, *it would be the greatest pleasure in the world to hit a hard one foul into the right-field boxes, maybe catch Applegate off guard.*

But that was trivial now.

He faced the pitcher.

The ball zipped in. Joe didn't offer. He was reminded of that first day in Detroit when he had faced Rocky Pratt. He had frozen then, and the feeling was the same now.

Strike two, and again he hadn't offered.

You've got no guts. And Applegate wins everything. He's made a monkey of you at every turn.

But his shoulder ached, and he felt very tired.

The Yankee pitcher curved one wide of the plate, tempting him. And it was now strike two, ball one.

The windup, and it was coming in, letter-high, near the outside corner, and with all his strength Joe swung, saw the ball start out on a line toward deep center field; and he was streaking for first, saw the ball clear the center fielder's head; and he was moving for second and the ball was rolling all the way to the center-field wall, the center fielder in pursuit; and he was digging for third and ahead of him he saw the third-base coach, flailing his arms, signaling him to go all the way.

And when it happened it was like a medicine ball, hard in the stomach. Joe faltered; then, clenching his fists, came on again, rounded third and headed for home, but now his temples pounded and his stomach quivered out ahead of him and his breath was coming in short, dry, harsh sobs, and the uniform was too tight, and his legs felt like wood. But he lumbered on down the third-base line, a third-base line that seemed unfamiliar now, and the figure of the Yankee catcher was like a giant in armor, standing there, blocking the plate. And Joe slid, reaching with his toe for a corner of the plate. And the ground came up hard to meet him, jolting his whole body. And the ball was jabbed hard against his thigh, like a hammer blow. He heard the umpire yell, "Safe!" and then he was rolling over and over, away from the plate, reaching for his cap, jamming it tight over his head, keeping his face to the ground, because he knew now that he was a middle-aged real-estate salesman named Joe Boyd.

He saw the Yankee catcher turn with a bellow of rage to confront the umpire; saw the whole Yankee infield and then the outfield, and then the bench rush for the umpire, bellowing as they came; and then the Senators were rushing up from their own bench. And keeping low to the ground, dodging among the swarming players, and moving at times animal-like on all fours, he reached the now-empty dugout and, still bent low, descended the steps leading to the dressing room. At the bottom he paused, and, mounting one step, peered cautiously over the coping.

The melee was furious. The Yankee catcher angrily dashed his cap to the ground. Yankee players confronted the umpire chest to chest, and then, running in from right field, came Applegate.

Snatching up the catcher's cap from the ground, he jammed it onto his own head and advanced menacingly on the beleaguered plate umpire. Jaw outthrust, he began to bark insults about the umpire's judgment, eyesight, ancestry, and sense of direction.

The umpire stood firm, arms folded, head held high, face inscrutable. For a few seconds he endured the tirade, then turned his back, but Applegate circled with him, jaw thrust even closer now, banging fist into palm.

Mr. van Buren stood aside from the fray, smiling, and as Joe watched he was joined by Mr. Welch, also smiling. Mr. van Buren draped an arm over the old man's shoulder, then bent slightly so that Mr. Welch could do likewise, and they stood, smiling, the manager and the owner of a pennant winner.

For the umpire, with a final nervous flick at the plate with his whiskbroom, was turning and heading off the field, still nagged by Applegate and the Yankees, but still imperiously adamant.

As they advanced, Joe ducked and fled into the dressing room; and although he knew his misery would be compounded now; although he knew he would be subjected to the rigors of hell without even the saving grace of youth and athletic prowess, even so the victory had been won, and he could not resist a glow of triumph. For this moment, at least, what did it matter that his personal punishment would be fearsome? Applegate, for once, had been foiled. The Senators had copped the pennant. The Yankees were finally a second-place team.

Nor could he resist a faint smile at the memory of Applegate's enraged countenance as he confronted the umpire. For the afternoon had proved an axiom long known to baseball men, and known now even to Applegate.

And this was that not even the devil could force an umpire to change his decision.

Philip Roth wrote earlier of how his baseball years prepared him for literature; here George Will reveals the roots of his conservatism: a misplaced trust. This piece, written in 1974, was collected in *The Pursuit of Happiness and Other Sobering Thoughts*. The Cubs' pursuit of a pennant since 1945 has driven more souls to drink than to temperance. Maybe by the time you read this the Cubs will have made it to the World Series and will have made a liberal of Mr. Will.

GEORGE F. WILL

The Chicago Cubs, Overdue

A reader demands to know how I contracted the infectious conservatism for which he plans to horsewhip me. So if you have tears, gentle reader, prepare to shed them now as I reveal how my gloomy temperament received its conservative warp from early and prolonged exposure to the Chicago Cubs.

The differences between conservatives and liberals are as much a matter of temperament as ideas. Liberals are temperamentally inclined to see the world as a harmonious carnival of sweetness and light, where goodwill prevails, good intentions are rewarded, the race is to the swift, and a benevolent Nature arranges a favorable balance of pleasure over pain. Conservatives (and Cub fans) know better.

Conservatives know the world is a dark and forbidding place where most new knowledge is false, most improvements are for the worse, the battle is not to the strong, nor riches to men of understanding, and an unscrupulous Providence consigns innocents to suffering. I learned this early.

Out in central Illinois, where men are men and I am native, in 1948, at age seven, I made a mad, fateful blunder. I fell ankle over elbows in love with the Cubs. Barely advanced beyond the bib-and-cradle stage, I plighted my troth to a baseball team destined to dash the cup of life's joy from my lips.

Spring, earth's renewal, a season of hope for the rest of mankind, became for me an experience comparable to being slapped around the mouth with a damp carp. Summer was like being bashed across the bridge of the nose with a crowbar—ninety times. My youth was like a long rainy Monday in Bayonne, New Jersey.

Each year the Cubs charged onto the field to challenge anew the theory that there are limits to the changes one can ring on pure incompetence. By mid-April, when other kids' teams were girding for Homeric battles at the top of the league, my heroes had wilted like salted slugs and begun their gadarene descent to the bottom. By September they had set a mark for ineptness at which others—but not next year's Cubs—would shoot in vain.

Every litter must have its runt, but my Cubs were almost all runts. Topps baseball bubble-gum cards always struggled to say something nice about each player. All they could say about the Cubs' infielder Eddie Miksis was that in 1951 he was tenth in the league in stolen bases, with eleven.

Like the boy who stood on the burning deck whence all but he had fled, I was loyal. And the downward trajectory of my life was set. An eight-year-old could not face these fires without being singed, unless he had the crust of an armadillo, and how many eight-year-olds do?

Of the sixteen teams that existed in 1949, all have since won league championships—all but the Cubs. And which of the old National League teams was first to finish in tenth place behind even the expansion teams? Don't ask. Since 1948 the Cubs have played more than 6,000 hours of losing baseball. My cruel addiction continued. In 1964 I chose to do three years of graduate study at Princeton because Princeton is midway between Philadelphia and New York—two National League cities. All I remember about my wedding day in 1967 is that the Cubs dropped a doubleheader.

Only a team named after baby bears would have a shortstop named Smalley—a right-handed hitter, if that is the word for a man who in his best year (1953) hit .249. From Roy Smalley I learned the truth about the word "overdue." A portrait of this columnist as a tad would show him with an ear pressed against a radio, listening to an announcer say, "The Cubs have the bases loaded. If Smalley gets on, the tying run will be on deck. And Smalley is overdue for a hit."

It was the most consoling word in the language, "overdue." It meant: in the long run, everything is going to be all right. No one is really a .222 hitter. We are all good hitters, all winners. It is just that some of us are, well, "overdue" for a hit, or whatever.

Unfortunately, my father is a right-handed logician who knows more than it is nice to know about the theory of probability. With a lot of help from Smalley, he convinced me that Smalley was not "overdue." Stan Musial batting

.249 was overdue for a hot streak. Smalley batting .249 was doing his best.

Smalley retired after eleven seasons with a lifetime average of .227. He was still overdue.

Now once again my trained senses tell me: spring is near. For most of the world hope, given up for dead, stirs in its winding linen. But I, like Figaro, laugh that I may not weep. Baseball season approaches. The weeds are about to reclaim the trellis of my life. For most fans, the saddest words of tongue or pen are: "Wait 'til next year." For us Cub fans, the saddest words are: "This is next year."

The heart has its reasons that the mind cannot refute, so I say:

Do not go gently into this season, Cub fans, rage, rage against the blasting of our hopes. Had I but world enough, and time, this slowness, Cubs, would be no crime. But I am almost halfway through my allotted three-score-and-ten and you, sirs, are overdue.

That's Mohandas Gandhi, not Jesse Gonder, and references in this piece to "the Mahatma" have nothing to do with Branch Rickey. A funny, funny sketch. By the way, when Gandhi is introduced to Babe Ruth, the Sultan of Swat, he wonders where that sultanate is. He should know. There is an Indian state of Swat, now a part of Pakistan, that once had a Sultan, or Akhond, whose death in 1878 was reported by the *Times of India* (Bombay) under the headline "The Akhond of Swat Is Dead." This report prompted Edward Lear to write a poem, "The Akond of Swat," which was surely some sportswriter's inspiration for Ruth's "title." (Lear's ditty began like this: "Who, or why, or which, or *what*, / Is the Akond of SWAT? / Is he tall or short, or dark or fair? / Does he sit on a stool or a sofa or chair, / Or SQUAT, / The Akond of Swat?")

CHET WILLIAMSON

Gandhi at the Bat

History books and available newspaper files hold no record of the visit to America in 1933 made by Mohandas K. Gandhi. For reasons of a sensitive political nature that have not yet come to light, all contemporary accounts of the visit were suppressed at the request of President Roosevelt. Although Gandhi repeatedly appeared in public during his three-month stay, the cloak of journalistic silence was seamless, and all that remains of the great man's celebrated tour is this long-secreted glimpse of one of the Mahatma's unexpected nonpolitical appearances, written by an anonymous press-box denizen of the day.

Yankee Stadium is used to roaring crowds. But never did a crowd roar louder than on yesterday afternoon, when a little brown man in a loincloth and wire-rimmed specs put some wood on a Lefty Grove fastball and completely bamboozled Connie Mack's A's.

It all started when Mayor John P. O'Brien invited M. K. ("Mahatma") Gandhi to see the Yanks play Philadelphia up at "The House That Ruth Built." Gandhi, whose ballplaying experience was limited to a few wallops with a cricket bat, jumped at the chance, and 12 noon saw the Mayor's party in the Yankee locker room, where the Mahatma met the Bronx Bombers. A zippy exchange occurred when the Mayor introduced the Lord of the Loincloth to the Bambino. "Mr. Gandhi," Hizzoner said, "I want you to meet Babe Ruth, the Sultan of Swat."

Gandhi's eyes sparkled behind his Moxie-bottle lenses, and he chuckled. "Swat," quoth he, "is a sultanate of which I am not aware. Is it by any chance near Maharashtra?"

"Say," laughed the Babe, laying a meaty hand on the frail brown shoulder, "you're all right, kiddo. I'll hit one out of the park for you today."

"No hitting, please," the Mahatma quipped.

In the Mayor's front-row private box, the little Indian turned down the offer of a hot dog and requested a box of Cracker Jack instead. The prize inside was a tin whistle, which he blew gleefully whenever the Bambino waddled up to bat.

The grinning guru enjoyed the game immensely—far more than the A's, who were down 3–1 by the fifth. Ruth, as promised, did smash a homer in the seventh, to Gandhi's delight. "Hey, Gunga Din!" Ruth cried jovially on his way to the Yankee dugout. "Know why my battin' reminds folks of India? 'Cause I can really Bangalore!"

"That is a very good one, Mr. Ruth!" cried the economy-size Asian.

By the top of the ninth, the Yanks had scored two more runs. After Mickey Cochrane whiffed on a Red Ruffing fastball, Gandhi remarked how difficult it must be to hit such a swiftly thrown missile and said, "I should like to try it very much."

"Are you serious?" Mayor O'Brien asked.

"If it would not be too much trouble. Perhaps after the exhibition is over," his visitor suggested.

There was no time to lose. O'Brien, displaying a panache that would have done credit to his predecessor, Jimmy Walker, leaped up and shouted to the umpire, who called a time-out. Managers McCarthy and Mack were beckoned to the Mayor's side, along with Bill Dinneen, the home-plate umpire, and soon all of Yankee Stadium heard an unprecedented announcement: "Ladies and gentlemen, regardless of the score, the Yankees will come to bat to finish the ninth inning."

The excited crowd soon learned that the reason for such a breach of tradition was a little brown pinch hitter shorter than his bat. When the pinstriped Bronx Bombers returned to their dugout after the last Philadelphia batter had been retired in the ninth, the Nabob of Nonviolence received a hasty batting lesson from Babe Ruth under the stands.

Lazzeri led off the bottom of the stanza, hitting a short chop to Bishop, who rifled to Foxx for the out. Then, after Crosetti fouled out to Cochrane, the stadium became hushed as the announcer intoned, "Pinch-hitting for Ruffing, Mohandas K. Gandhi."

The crowd erupted as the white-robed holy man, a fungo bat propped jauntily on his shoulder, strode to the plate, where he remarked to the crouching Mickey Cochrane, "It is a very big field, and a very small ball."

"C'mon, Moe!" Ruth called loudly to the dead-game bantam batter. "Show 'em the old pepper!"

"I will try, Mr. Baby!" Gandhi called back, and went into a batting stance unique in the annals of the great game—his sheet-draped posterior facing the catcher, and his bat held high over his head, as if to clobber the ball into submission. While Joe McCarthy called time, the Babe trotted out and politely corrected the little Indian's position in the box.

The time-out over, Grove threw a screaming fastball right over the plate. The bat stayed on Gandhi's shoulder. "Oh, my," he said as he turned and observed the ball firmly ensconced in Cochrane's glove. "That *was* speedy."

The second pitch was another dead-center fastball. The Mahatma swung, but found that the ball had been in the Mick's glove for a good three seconds before his swipe was completed. "Steerike two!" Dinneen barked.

The next pitch was high and outside, and the ump called it a ball before the petite pundit made a tentative swing at it. "Must I sit down now?" he asked.

"Nah, it's a ball," Dinneen replied. "I called it before you took your cut."

"Yes. I *know* that is a ball, and I did swing at it and did miss."

"No, no, a ball. Like a free pitch."

"Oh, I see."

"Wasn't in the strike zone."

"Yes, I see."

"So you get another swing."

"Yes."

"And if you miss you sit down."

"I just *did* miss."

"Play ball, Mister."

The next pitch was in the dirt. Gandhi did not swing. "Ball," Dinneen called.

"Yes, it is," the Mahatma agreed.

"Two and two."

"That is four."

"Two balls, two strikes."

"Is there not but one ball?"

"Two balls."

"Yes, I see."

"And two strikes."

"And if I miss I sit down."

Ruth's voice came booming from the Yankee dugout: "Swing early, Gandy baby!"

"When is early?"

"When I tell ya! I'll shout '*Now!*' "

Grove started his windup. Just as his leg kicked up, the Bambino's cry of "*Now!*" filled the park.

The timing was perfect. Gandhi's molasses-in-January swing met the Grove fastball right over the plate. The ball shot downward, hit the turf, and arced gracefully into the air toward Grove. "*Run,* Peewee, *run!*" yelled Ruth, as the crowd went wild.

"Yes, yes!" cried Gandhi, who started down the first-base line in what can only be described as a dancing skip, using his bat as a walking stick. An astonished Grove booted the high bouncer, then scooped up the ball and flung it to Jimmie Foxx at first.

But Foxx, mesmerized by the sight of a sixty-three-year-old Indian in white robes advancing merrily before him and blowing mightily on a tin whistle, failed to descry the stitched orb, which struck the bill of his cap, knocking it off his head, and, slowed by its deed of déshabillé, rolled to a stop by the fence.

Gandhi paused only long enough to touch first and to pick up Jimmy's cap and return it to him. By the time the still gawking Foxx had perched it once more on his head, the vital vegetarian was halfway to second.

Right-fielder Coleman retrieved Foxx's missed ball and now relayed it to Max Bishop at second, but too late. The instant Bishop tossed the ball back to the embarrassed Grove, Gandhi was off again. Grove, panicking, overthrew third base, and by the time left-fielder Bob Johnson picked up the ball, deep in foul territory, the Tiny Terror of Tealand had rounded the hot corner and was scooting for home. Johnson hurled the ball on a true course to a stunned Cochrane. The ball hit the pocket of Cochrane's mitt and popped out like a muffin from a toaster.

Gandhi jumped on home plate with both sandaled feet, and the crowd exploded as Joe McCarthy, the entire Yankee squad, and even a beaming Connie Mack surged onto the field.

"I ran home," giggled Gandhi. "Does that mean that I hit a run home?"

"A home run, Gandy," said Ruth. "Ya sure did."

"Well, technically," said Umpire Dinneen, "it was a single and an overthrow and then—"

"*Shaddup,*" growled a dozen voices at once.

"Looked like a homer to me, too," the ump corrected, but few heard him, for by that time the crowd was on the field, lifting to their shoulders a joyous Gandhi, whose tin whistle provided a thrilling trilling over the mob's acclaim.

Inside the locker room, Manager McCarthy offered Gandhi a permanent position on the team, but the Mahatma graciously refused, stating that he could only consider a diamond career with a different junior-circuit club.

"Which club would that be, kid?" said the puzzled Bambino.

"The Cleveland Indians, of course," twinkled the Mahatma.

An offer from the Cleveland front office arrived the next day, but India's top pinch hitter was already on a train headed for points west—and the history books.

George Brunet is not the only man to pitch in Organized Baseball in his late forties, but no other graybeard has ever hurled so many innings. In the majors, not Satchel Paige, Phil Niekro, Hoyt Wilhelm, or Jack Quinn. In the minors, not even Lefty George, who pitched over 100 innings at age fifty-seven, or Earl Caldwell, who at age forty-eight—with his son as his catcher—led his league in ERA. How to explain Brunet, the man with the golden arm? Must be something in the water.

STEVE WULF

Béisbol Is in His Blood

On the day he became eligible to collect his major-league pension, George Brunet of Aguila de Veracruz pitched a three-hitter to defeat León 3–0. Brunet's manager, a fellow by the name of Willie Davis, gave him a forty-fifth-birthday present by doubling in the first run and scoring the second. After the game the ballclub threw a surprise party for *El Viejo*, the Old Man. Brunet, genuinely surprised, blew out the candles and, with a tear in his eye, said to his friends, *"Muchas gracias. Nadie nunca a hecho esto para mi."* Nobody had ever done that for him. After twenty-eight years in professional baseball, thirty different uniforms and 4,719 innings, George Brunet was finally given a day, June 8, in Veracruz, Mexico.

Brunet's odyssey, surely the most arduous in the history of baseball, began in 1953 when he was a seventeen-year-old kid in Ahmeek, Michigan. Brunet was signed by Schoolboy Rowe and Muddy Ruel of the Detroit Tigers. If those names don't date him, just consider that Carl Yastrzemski, the present-day patriarch of the majors, was in the ninth grade. "They gave me $500," Brunet recalls. "I bought a dining-room set for my parents, a coat for my mother and a night on the town."

Brunet first reported to Shelby, North Carolina, in the Class D Tar Heel

League, but he had to pass through Alexandria, Virginia, Seminole, Oklahoma, Hot Springs, Arkansas, Seminole again, Abilene, Kansas, Crowley, Louisiana, and Columbia, Missouri, before reaching Kansas City and the big leagues in 1956.

"I remember my debut," he says. "We were ahead 4–2 in the fourth, but the Red Sox had the bases loaded. Bobby Shantz would normally come in, but for some reason George Susce, the pitching coach, told me to go. I remember riding out of the bullpen in a brand-new pink Lincoln Continental. I had no idea who was up, and now that I think about it, Hal Smith, the catcher, knew better than to tell me. The guy swings at my first fastball and misses, then fouls off another one, and I'm ahead 0–2 when it dawns on me that I'm pitching to Ted Williams. This is my idol. My legs start shaking. Somehow I get the ball up to the plate, and he hits a sharp grounder that Vic Power at first base turns into a double play. When I got back to the dugout and sat down, I literally cried out of relief. The next day Williams comes over to me before the game and says, 'Kid, if you keep that fastball down, you've got a long career ahead of you.' "

There are two points to that story: 1) Guys that George Brunet once played with are now worth big money in vintage bubble-gum cards, and 2) Ted Williams knew what he was talking about.

In the next eight seasons the well-traveled Brunet went down to Little Rock, back up to Kansas City, down to Buffalo, down to Little Rock again, out to Portland, Oregon, up to the Athletics once more, down to Louisville, up to Milwaukee, down to Vancouver, across to Hawaii, over to Oklahoma City, up to Houston, down to Oklahoma City again, up to Baltimore, down to Rochester, back to Oklahoma City, and finally, in 1964, up to Los Angeles.

From 1965 through 1968, Brunet was one of the leading left-handed pitchers in the league, averaging 226 innings a year with an ERA of 3.03. He began to bounce around again in 1969, when he was traded to the Seattle Pilots. In 1970 he pitched for the Washington Senators, managed by Ted Williams, and the Pittsburgh Pirates. In 1971 the St. Louis Cardinals used him for only nine innings. He went back to Hawaii for the rest of 1971 and all of 1972. While in Hawaii, he got an offer to pitch in Japan, but held out, waiting for a call from the Minnesota Twins. The call hasn't come, and Brunet never made it back to the big time. He left with a career won-lost record of 69–93 and a 3.62 ERA. His pension time, according to Brunet, comes to "thirteen years, three months and twenty days."

In his peripatetic career Brunet has pitched for a lot of peripatetic teams. He belonged to the Philadelphia Athletics for a short time before they moved to Kansas City, and later to Oakland. He pitched for the Milwaukee Braves before they were shifted to Atlanta, the Houston Colt 45s before they became the

Astros, the Los Angeles Angels before they adopted California, the Pilots before they turned into the Milwaukee Brewers, and the Senators before they were transformed into the Texas Rangers. Not only did these teams have identity crises, but they were also bad.

Brunet has survived because he has a great left arm. It is such a medical marvel, in fact, that he has had arm trouble just once. "That was back in 1958, a blood clot in my throwing arm," he says. "Kept me out for two weeks." Other pitchers have labored as long as Brunet, but almost all of them were relievers. Brunet has been a starter almost exclusively all this time. Performing in the Mexican League in the summer and the Mexican Pacific League in the winter, Brunet throws about 400 innings a year, although his statistics in the winter league aren't included in his official record. And he has made no concession to age. He is still a fastball and curveball pitcher, and he still challenges hitters, which is rare in the Mexican League, where nobody over 6 feet gets to see a fastball. When he pitched the three-hitter on his birthday, Brunet struck out Ivan Murrell, a former San Diego Padre and the Mexican League home run leader, three times. "He still goes after you," says Murrell. "He's better than a lot of guys in the majors right now."

Before a strike cut short the season by two months, Brunet had eight shutouts, which is only two short of the league record. But even if the strike forestalled Brunet's pursuit of the record, it didn't stop him from pitching. He merely joined Coatzacoalcos, one of the six teams that stayed together to play a new schedule.

Over the course of his career, Brunet has struck out 3,631 batters, which easily surpasses Walter Johnson's major-league lifetime record of 3,508. Even more amazing, Brunet has pitched all this time with nothing on under his uniform pants, which certainly makes him the greatest pitcher in baseball history never to wear a jockstrap and cup. "I just always felt more comfortable that way," he says. "Of course, getting out of the way of ground balls up the middle has cost me a few singles over the years."

His independent streak has always gotten Brunet in trouble. Perhaps the best measure of his arm is that it has persuaded so many teams to overlook the rest of him. "I was never a guy to hang around and kiss anyone's butt," he says. "I didn't have the right kind of personality for managers. If I didn't pitch as well as I did, I wouldn't have had any career at all."

Brunet mentions the spring of 1959, when he was going north with the A's as the fifth starter. A couple of nights before the A's broke camp, he and some of the boys were painting West Palm Beach, Florida, red. About 2 A.M. Brunet found himself directing traffic in front of the team's hotel. One of the cars he stopped contained Parke Carroll, the A's G.M., and Harry Craft, the manager. After Brunet showed up late for a team meeting the next day, George Selkirk, the farm director, called him in for a little chat. "George told me I really screwed up," Brunet recalls. "He said they were going to have to make an example of me and send me down." The A's did more than just send him down. Early the next season they traded him to the Braves.

In Milwaukee, Brunet found his role model, pitcher Bob Buhl. "One time we were pulling into a city," he says, "and Charlie Dressen [the manager] gets up in the front of the bus and says that anybody not in their room by midnight will be fined $500. Well, Buhl marches right up to Dressen, peels $500 off his bankroll, hands it to him, and walks off the bus. Now that's class."

Brunet even antagonized the one manager who gave him a chance, Bill Rigney. "I lost a lot of one-run games with the Angels," he says, "and Rigney used to say to me, 'I owe you a game,' every time he took me out. But one time I really got angry when he took me out, and we had words in the dugout. He knew enough to stop, but I just had to keep going. Finally, Rigney starts counting, '$100, $200, $300.' I didn't stop until he hit $700. Then I went in and tore the clubhouse apart. The next day I came in and wrote out a check for $700 to the Fred Hutchinson Cancer Fund."

Brunet was never much for running, either, which annoyed his pitching coaches and helped build his considerable girth. Nowadays Brunet looks a little like Yastrzemski gone to seed. In 1973 Hawaii manager Rocky Bridges gave him his walking papers because, he said, Brunet was out of shape. After a brief stop in Eugene, Oregon, Brunet was out of baseball. "I spent part of the year coaching some kids in a senior division league in Anaheim," he says. "We weren't far from the Angels' ballpark, so I could see the lights every night. One night I just looked at those lights and said, 'What the hell am I doing here?'"

So Brunet headed for Mexico, Poza Rica to be exact. He became one of the best pitchers in the league (62–55, 2.55 ERA) on one of the worst teams. In 1977—this should come as a chuckle to his former managers—Brunet even took over as the manager of Poza Rica. "It wasn't bad, but it got embarrassing losing every night," he says, explaining why he went back to pitching. On June 20 of that year, at the age of forty-two, he threw a no-hitter. He pitched in Poza Rica again in 1978, striking out 208 batters in 246 innings, and last year he was traded twice—to the expansion team in Coatzacoalcos and then to Mexico City. Overall, he won fourteen games and had a 3.13 ERA. Before the start of this season he was again traded, this time to a new team in Veracruz. Before the strike began on July 2, he was 11–10 with a 2.61 ERA.

Brunet says he's devoted to his three children back home in Anaheim, but he only gives them the three or four weeks between seasons. He is sensitive to the hardships of the Mexican ballplayer, who earns as little as $400 a month, yet as soon as the strike (over the formation of a players' association) was called, he found himself another team.

Brunet has adapted well to Mexican life. Most ballplayers from the States don't last more than a year or two, but Brunet is now in his eighth season. Each established club is allowed only three imports, while expansion teams get four, and former major leaguers like George Scott, Mike Kekich, Clarence Gaston, Mike Paul, and Bart Johnson have found their way south of the border. The Mexican League is Class AAA in designation, but it seems closer to Double A in performance. An American can make good money—Brunet earns about $3,500 a month—and it's a way to keep a career alive. That is, if you call this living.

For one thing, there's the travel. A short bus trip is six hours. Gaston recalls going from León to Tabasco in twenty-one hours—approximately the time it takes to travel from Philadelphia to Miami. Players can pass the hours by counting the crosses at the side of the road on hairpin turns. If the buses don't get to the players, Montezuma's revenge will. Almost nobody escapes. And sometimes the illness can be much worse. One Veracruz relief pitcher went on the disabled list this year with food poisoning.

Playing in the league can also be a frightening experience. The local police sometimes like to hang out in the dugout, wielding M-16s as if they were Louisville Sluggers. Brunet says he's had a gun pulled on him five or six times. "No big deal," he says. Sometimes the local fauna can be just as scary. Ballplayers say there is nothing quite like the sight of fans pelting each other and the field with live snakes.

The high emotional pitch also takes some getting used to. "If it weren't against the law, they really would kill the umpire," says Brunet. In a game between Veracruz and León, an argument with the umpire not only brought the León manager to home plate, but also coaches, players, a dwarf bat boy known as Spider, reporters, photographers, radio announcers and interested spectators. As usually occurs in the States, too, the umpire prevailed.

As for life outside the ballpark, well, sitting in front of an air conditioner is a major form of recreation. Mexico is, in the word of Veracruz centerfielder Victor M. Felix, "ccchhhottt." Last year Felix played for Tabasco, which didn't have a sauce named after it for nothing. Another favorite pastime among Mexican Leaguers is lighting up the local brand of smoke. Outfield grass refers to what the players have during batting practice, not what lies beyond the infield. Brunet prefers the more traditional methods of intoxication. He's slowed down some since his days in the majors, though. His pet Chihuahua, Nurci, keeps him in line. "She won't come near me when I'm drunk," he says.

There are times when Brunet finds himself caught between two worlds. "I'm still an outsider down here. But it's not easy going back to the States, either," he says. "When I do go back, I don't know what they're talking about. It's like I just heard about the Lindbergh baby." But Brunet's position has made him a sort of unofficial ambassador in the Mexican League. Americans are always coming to him for advice, and he's always willing to tell them what not to eat, where to have a good time, and whom to watch out for. "You've got to watch your glove at all times," he warns. "Even on the bench. You can never catch these kids. They just walk in, walk out, and the glove is gone."

Some of the children may be thieves, but they are also a big part of what's special about Mexican baseball. They hang over the dugouts and even sit on the benches. They've especially taken to Davis, whom they call "Wee-lee," as in "Wee-lee, *pelota*, Wee-lee, *pelota*." Davis doesn't know Spanish, and the children don't know English, but they communicate. As one Veracruz coach says, "*Béisbol* universal." Veracruz even has its own verison of the San Diego Chicken, the Aguila, a plump old man swathed in red-cotton feathers.

Veracruz is Mexico's largest port and oldest city, a working town that relies more on shipping than on tourism. Veracruz also has a baseball history: Josh Gibson, Monte Irvin, and Cool Papa Bell have played there. Several years ago the ballclub was sold and moved to Aguascalientes, but this year the team returned with Bobby Avila as the principal owner. Avila, the 1954 American League batting champion with Cleveland, is the former mayor of Veracruz. The club had been averaging 4,000 fans per game before the strike, thanks in no small part to Brunet and Davis.

In their four months together, Brunet and the forty-year-old Davis made quite a team. Davis's philosophy of running a ballclub can best be summed up by his belief that "if you step on people in this life, you're going to come back as a cockroach." Needless to say, he runs a loose ship, which suits Brunet just fine.

Davis brings special skills to the job. Twice during Brunet's birthday shutout he somehow conjured up double plays. He is so mesmerizing that he even has Brunet believing in reincarnation. George believes he can come back as a major-league reliever. Very soon.

"I know I can pitch two or three innings at a time up there," he says. "I know I can pitch better than what's his name, Burgermeyer [Tom Burgmeier, who, unbeknownst to Brunet, is having a fine season]. But somebody would have to ask me, and those days are gone. People up there must think I'm a fat old man who can barely get the ball up to the plate. Guys come down here and say, 'George, is that you? I thought that was your son pitching down here.'

"Maybe I'll go home in September and ask Jim Fregosi if I can work out with the Angels. All I ask is for someone to give me thirty pitches on the side and I'll show them what I can do. If I can't do it, fine. They can say, 'What is this piece of dog doo doing out here?' "

But Brunet hasn't been toiling all this time just for another shot in the major leagues. "To be honest with you, it's the only thing I know," he says. "Nobody's going to take a forty-five-year-old man and train him for a new career. Besides,

I can't think of anything that has made me happier than pitching. Still, I wish I had a dollar for every batter I ever faced." That, George, would come to more than $20,000.

If and when Brunet gives it up, he has a standing offer to be a fishing guide from Jerry Crider, a former White Sox pitcher who runs a hunting and fishing lodge on the coast of Mexico. Brunet would especially like that, because of what happened thirty years ago when the whole thing started.

"It was on my fifteenth birthday," he recalls. "I was going fishing when it began to rain, so I headed back. I wandered over to one of the games they played in Ahmeek. They needed a pitcher, so they asked me. Most of those guys were a lot older than I was, and I had on my fishing boots with the hobs on them. But damn if I didn't go out there and throw a no-hitter. Hell, this is easy, I thought. Little did I know."

Baseball is a backward-looking game. We believe the good old days—when we, along with our idols, were the boys of summer—to have been played in the Garden of Eden. Change can only be for the worse. As Lardner mourned the passing of the dead-ball style of play, succeeding generations waxed nostalgic over their departed sluggers. But as Jonathan Yardley notes in this passage from his 1977 biography, *Ring*, Lardner's disillusionment with baseball proceeded from more than the jackrabbit ball; the snake had entered the garden in the form of Arnold Rothstein, and such favorites as Eddie Cicotte and Joe Jackson had been among the eight who fell.

JONATHAN YARDLEY

Frank Chance's Diamond

They were in many respects really just big overgrown boys, and Ring loved the ones who were natural, without pretense, hard players on the field and genial companions off it. Utterly without pretensions himself, he naturally gravitated to those players who shared his unaffected ease. The longer he covered baseball regularly, the more he concentrated on the game itself, and the more he tended to focus his attention—and his admiration—on those men who played it as he believed it should be played.

In that regard, it is important to emphasize that although the form of the game and its rules have changed remarkably little over the years, baseball before the introduction in 1920 of what Ring called "Br'er Rabbit Ball" was markedly different in style and execution. A couple of statistics make the point plainly enough: In 1911 home runs were hit at an average of .41 per game for *both* teams; a half-century later, in 1961, the figure was 1.90, an increase of more than four and a half times. By the same token, in 1911 triples were hit at a rate of 1.07 per game; in 1961 the figure was .53, a decrease of almost exactly one half.

The home run is the hallmark of the power game, the triple of the speed game. The home run symbolizes a game dominated by brute force, one in which victory can be won by the proverbial "single swing of the bat." The triple, by contrast, is emblematic of a game in which more complex skills dominate: the skill of the batter in placing hits and his speed in covering the bases, as well as the skill of the fielder in holding the runner to as few bases as possible. Objective students of baseball would say that both the power game and the speed game have their merits, and that the balance between the two that has evolved since 1961—the biggest home-run year in baseball history, and one of the least interesting seasons artistically—has produced a "better" game than ever before. But Ring in this respect was no objective student at all. He had been brought up on "dead-ball" baseball, and he simply would not accept any other kind as a legitimate form of the game. By the same token, the standards of excellence he came to believe in were shaped by the dead-ball game, and they remained his standards despite the ways in which baseball changed.

Though it would be three more years before he would express his understanding of baseball excellence with absolute clarity, Ring gave a strong indication of the direction in which he was moving in a piece written for the Chicago *Examiner* in August 1912. He was discussing the White Sox, who were having an indifferent year, and he went to some lengths to single out a player who had gotten little attention:

Morris Rath, Jimmy Callahan's second baseman, appears to be doomed to go through his baseball career without recognition as a star, and this despite the fact that he is one of the steadiest ball players in the American League.

Rath is referred to by his mates as the brains of the White Sox infield. This title was given him by Matty McIntyre in a spirit of kidding, and yet it is anything but undeserved. Morris is probably no smarter than either of the Sox third basemen, Lord and Zeider, and he is usually so quiet that his headwork goes unnoticed. He seldom is guilty of a foolish play, and his "noodle" is so well thought of by the manager that he is often entrusted with the job of signing for waste pitches, and throws with runners on.

In the International League last season Rath hit well over .300. In fact, his figure was closer to .400. His extra base clouts were few and far between and his record of stolen bases was nothing to boast of. At present, he is a few points below .300, but he has the happy habit of reaching first base oftener than any one else on the team. He is a hard man to pitch to, a man who seldom swings at bad balls.

Rath is shy of bodily strength and ability to steal his way around the paths. Otherwise, he is a mighty good ball player and a man who can be depended on to hold up his end, offensively and defensively.

Everything Ring most admired, and not just in ballplayers, is suggested there. It happens that Rath turned out to be not the ballplayer Ring thought him to be—he played only three more seasons, and those with mixed results—but he helped Ring locate the essence of what he admired. That was: reliability, hard work, "brains," self-improvement, fulfillment of one's abilities whatever their limits, selflessness. Three years later Ring elaborated on the point in four baseball articles he wrote for *American Magazine*. In effect, he used the four articles to identify his own baseball heroes and to explain why they were heroic. The pieces are written in a strained effort at idiomatic language that is now difficult to read without wincing, but it is worth the effort to gain an understanding of what Ring was saying.

The first piece was a tribute to the Boston Braves of 1914, the "Miracle Braves" who had been led by their manager, George Stallings, from last place in late July to the National League championship and then a shocking World Series victory over the redoubtable Philadelphia Athletics. Ring had sentimental reasons for admiring the Braves—he had covered them for the Boston *American* in 1911 (the year he and Ellis married), when they were hopeless losers known as the Rustlers—but there was no sentimentalism in his assessment of their success. They won, he made clear, because Stallings had goaded them to play at or above their best, and the players were willing to make the effort:

> I say the Braves won by hustlin' and fightin' rather than because they was a aggregation o' world-beaters. . . . A club that cops in spite of a few weaknesses has did more than a club that cops because they's no other club in their class. . . . The kind o' men that can do their best in a pinch is the kind that's most valuable in baseball or anywhere else. They're worth more than the guys that's got all the ability in the world but can't find it when they want it.

Ring, who knew better than anyone else that his own talents were limited, held in the highest respect those people "that can do their best."

The second article was called "Some Team" and was Ring's "line o' dope," his personal all-star team. Its members were: Nap Rucker of Brooklyn and Willie Mitchell of Cleveland, left-handed pitchers; Walter Johnson of Washington, Grover Cleveland Alexander of the Philadelphia Phillies, Christy Mathewson of the New York Giants, and Eddie Cicotte of the White Sox, right-handed pitchers; Jimmy Archer of the Cubs and Ray Schalk of the White Sox, catchers; Jake Daubert of Brooklyn, first base; Eddie Collins of the Philadelphia Athletics, second base; Rabbit Maranville of the Boston Braves, shortstop; Frank Baker of the Athletics, third base; Ty Cobb of Detroit, Tris Speaker of the Boston Red Sox, and Joe Jackson of the White Sox, outfielders. As Ring acknowledged, a few of the selections were surprising, notably that of Nap Rucker, but his reasons for choosing Rucker were revealing: ". . . I'm choosin' him because he ain't no flash in the pan, as they say. He's been pitchin' long enough to show that he ain't no accident, and he ain't nowheres near through. . . . Rucker knows what he's out there for. He ain't like a lot o' these pitchers that leaves their brains on the bench." To the reliability for which he had cited Morris Rath, Ring wrote: "They ain't a smarter pitcher in baseball and they's nobody that's a better all-round ballplayer, no pitcher, I mean." Still another requirement, then, was added: versatility, the ability to contribute to one's team in more than one way.*

The last two pieces were about Ty Cobb and Christy Mathewson, the individual players Ring most admired. That these were the two he chose was vivid testimony to his refusal to let a player's personality color his evaluation of his performance. Cobb probably was the most hated man ever to play major-league baseball. He was a racist, a bully, and a psychopath. He drew no distinction between teammates and opponents; he fought them all, and all of them detested him. Mathewson, on the other hand, was such an upright, kind, and selfless individual that some skeptics wondered if he was for real. He was a graduate of Bucknell, he looked like a combination of Dink Stover and Frank Merriwell, and according to Hugh Fullerton, he "specializes in chess and when on the circuit spends his evenings at chess clubs playing the local champions."

All of which made absolutely no difference to Ring. He did make a half-hearted effort to portray Cobb as a decent fellow, but what really mattered to him was Cobb the ballplayer. When Cobb came into the league in 1905, Ring wrote, "he runs bases like a fool" and "he couldn't hit a left-hander very good." Despite these lapses he was a fine, indeed an extraordinary, player, but that wasn't good enough for him:

> That was when he first come up here. But Ty ain't the guy that's goin' to stay fooled all the time. When he wises up that somebody's got somethin' on him, he don't sleep nor do nothin' till he figures out a way to get even. . . . He seen he couldn't hit the curve when it was breakin', so he stood way back in the box and waited till it'd broke. Then he nailed it. . . .

Cobb was widely accused by jealous fellow players of being "lucky" (as if he had any control over that), but Ring felt that "he makes his own luck" by heady play. Cobb could do his best in a pinch, and so could Mathewson:

> They's a flock o' pitchers that knows a batter's weakness and works accordin'. But they ain't nobody else in the world that can stick a ball as near where they want to stick it as he can. . . . I s'pose when he broke in he didn't have no more

---

* There is a sad footnote to "Some Team." One of the men Ring considered but did not select was Ray Chapman, the young shortstop for the Indians. "Chapman at Cleveland's goin' to be good," Ring wrote, "if he don't have no more accidents." Five years later Chapman was killed by a beanball.

control than the rest o' these here collegers. But the diff'rence between they and him was that he seen what a good thing it was to have, and went out and got it.

One thing Matty had little of, however, was luck. For all his brilliance, for all his 367 victories and his stunning 2.13 lifetime earned-run average, he lost some of the most heartbreaking games in some of the most brutal circumstances. Worst of them all was the final game of the 1912 World Series, when his Giant teammate, Fred Snodgrass, made the famous error that led to two unearned Red Sox runs and a crushing loss. Ring was there, and he filed this report:

BOSTON, MASS., Oct. 16—Just after Steve Yerkes had crossed the plate with the run that gave Boston's Red Sox the world's championship in the tenth inning of the deciding game of the greatest series ever played for the big title, while the thousands, made temporarily crazy by a triumph entirely unexpected, yelled, screamed, stamped their feet, smashed hats and hugged one another, there was seen one of the saddest sights in the history of a sport that is a strange and wonderful mixture of joy and gloom. It was the spectacle of a man, old as baseball players are reckoned, walking from the middle of the field to the New York players' bench with bowed head and drooping shoulders, with tears streaming from his eyes, a man on whom his team's fortune had been staked and lost, and a man who would have proven his clear title to the trust reposed in him if his mates had stood by him in the supreme test. The man was Christy Mathewson.
  Beaten, 3 to 2, by a club he would have conquered if he had been given the

support deserved by his wonderful pitching, Matty tonight is greater in the eyes of New York's public than ever before. Even the joy-mad population of Boston confesses that his should have been the victory and his the praise.

No, Ring didn't let his admiration for Mathewson influence his appreciation for the pitcher's courage, or vice versa, but he did have a special feeling for this great man who had such bad luck. In the fall of 1925 Mathewson died of tuberculosis—the same disease that contributed to Ring's death eight years later—and Ring, despite his normal dislike for such assignments, agreed to be publicity chairman of the Christy Mathewson Memorial Foundation, which was raising funds for a gymnasium and memorial rotunda at Bucknell, and a cross at Saranac Lake, where he died.

Ring may have been thinking about Matty when he wrote, in a 1930 piece on "Br'er Rabbit Ball," that "I have always been a fellow who liked to see efficiency rewarded. If a pitcher pitched a swell game, I wanted to see him win it. So it kind of sickens me to watch a typical pastime of today in which a good pitcher, after an hour and fifty minutes of deserved mastery of his opponents, can suddenly be made to look like a bum by four or five great sluggers who couldn't have held a job as bat boy on the Niles High School scrubs." From the day of its introduction, the lively ball preyed on Ring's mind: it had ruined *his* game. Once, in the late twenties, he dropped into the press box at the Polo Grounds and watched a few innings. When he got up to leave, a reporter pointed to the batter, Chuck Klein, and said, "There's a fellow can hit 'em." Ring replied, "Swings good, but how far do you think he'd hit 'em with the old ball?" In the summer of 1932, when illness forced John McGraw to retire, Ring wrote him a nostalgic letter:

> . . . Baseball hasn't meant much to me since the introduction of the TNT ball that robbed the game of the features I used to like best—features that gave you and Bill Carrigan and Fielder Jones and other really intelligent managers a deserved advantage, and smart ball players like Cobb and Jim Sheckard a chance to do things.
>
> You and Bill Gleason and Eddie Collins were among the few men left who personified what I enjoyed in "the national pastime."

What must be stressed, however, because so often exactly the opposite is claimed, is that Ring had not given up on baseball per se. He made his changed attitude quite clear in a column written in 1921: "I got a letter the other day asking why didn't I write about baseball no more and I usen't to write about nothing else, you might say. Well friends, may as well admit that I have kind of lose interest in the old game, or rather it ain't the old game which I have lose interest in it, but it is the game which the magnates has fixed up to please the public with their usual good judgment."

Ring wanted baseball to be what it had been—or what he remembered it as being—when he was young. The game he remembered was clean, honorable, ordered, subtle, intricate, beautiful, somehow *natural*. The game he saw for the last dozen years of his life was, he thought, corrupt, obvious, tainted, graceless, *unnatural* because it did not always appropriately reward the diligent and the lazy. In some measure he was right, in some measure he was merely nostalgic and even sentimental. Yet it is not pure coincidence that the Black Sox Scandal occurred in 1919, that the jackrabbit ball was introduced in 1920. Baseball was not the only American institution that was corrupted in the wake of world war and the beginning of that disastrous experiment in institution-alized morality, Prohibition. It's just that of the institutions that were cor-rupted, this was the one Ring knew best. It had been too large a part of his life for him to part with it without grief.